THE
ROMANCE
OF
ARTHUR

THE ROMANCE OF ARTHUR

edited by

James J. Wilhelm
and
Laila Zamuelis Gross

GARLAND PUBLISHING, INC. • NEW YORK & LONDON
1984

Library of Congress Cataloging in Publication Data
Main entry under title:

The Romance of Arthur.

Bibliography: p.
Includes index.
1. Arthurian romances. I. Wilhelm, James J. II. Gross,
Laila Zamuelis. III. Title.
PN6071.A84R6 1984   808.8′0351   83-48252
ISBN 0-8240-9098-5 (alk. paper)
ISBN 0-8240-9099-3 (pbk. : alk. paper)

Design by Laurence Walczak

Frontispiece: Detail from tapestry. Nicolas Bataille: "Christian Heroes: King Arthur."
Metropolitan Museum of Art. The Cloisters Collection. Munsey Fund, 1932.

Printed on acid-free, 250-year-life paper
Manufactured in the United States of America

CONTENTS

PREFACE

This anthology was devised in order to bring under one cover some of the richly diverse materials related to the romantic lore of King Arthur. It begins with history and pseudo-history, touches on Celtic folklore, where Arthur's legendary roots are discernible, and then enters the broad stream of imaginative literature, where the fantastic clearly takes precedence over the factual. The time span covered is the millennium from 450 to 1485, when the romance of Arthur took root and flowered.

Selections from Latin chronicles and early Welsh literature were deemed indispensable from the start. It was also obvious that Geoffrey of Monmouth's pseudo-historical work, which exerted a profound influence on later artists, had to be included, but from there it was difficult to make selections. In order to facilitate the process, the editors polled a number of scholars in England and America for assistance. It was clear from the many replies that the three essential works, at least for an English-speaking reader (for whom the work is aimed), were the *Lancelot* of Chrétien de Troyes, the anonymous *Sir Gawain and the Green Knight*, and *Le Morte Darthur* of Sir Thomas Malory. It was decided to include the first two in their entireties, with a selection of the major passages from Malory. The *Alliterative Morte Arthure* was added as a bridge between Geoffrey of Monmouth and Malory.

From the start the editors decided to commission everything freshly, since the antiquated translation of *Lancelot* by W. W. Comfort is a major hindrance to its appreciation. The *Alliterative Morte Arthure* was available in a recently published translation, and Malory's work, it was finally decided, should retain its original syntax, with only the spelling modernized and a few other minor changes.

Of course, it was difficult to omit many of the beautiful Arthurian works that one would have liked to have here. But length was a strong deterrent against including such important works as Gottfried von Strassburg's *Tristan* or Wolfram von Eschenbach's *Parzival* or Wace's *Roman de Brut*, and it was felt that none of these works would admit abridgment in the way that Malory's work does, since *Le Morte Darthur* is actually composed of many separate units.

A number of people were extremely helpful in putting this book together. Aside from those who answered the questionnaire, the editors would like to thank Andrew Welsh for his painstaking reading of *Sir Gawain* and William Harper for designing the map. The first chapter could not have been written without the careful suggestions and admonitions of Geoffrey Ashe. Gary Kuris of Garland provided the enthusiasm needed during every step of production.

The editors hope that these new, modern translations will make the perennially renewable world of Arthur even more accessible than it has been in the past.

Laila Zamuelis Gross
James J. Wilhelm

New York City
May 15, 1983

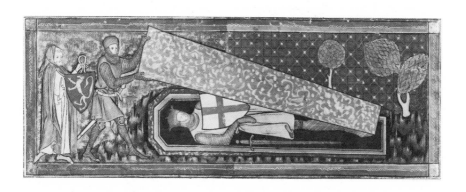

"The Opening of the Graves." From the Lancelot Manuscript, French, fourteenth century. Pierpont Morgan Library.

THE ROMANCE OF ARTHUR

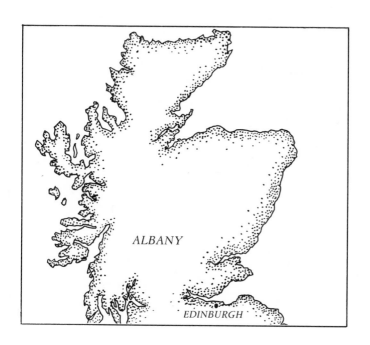

ALBANY

EDINBURGH

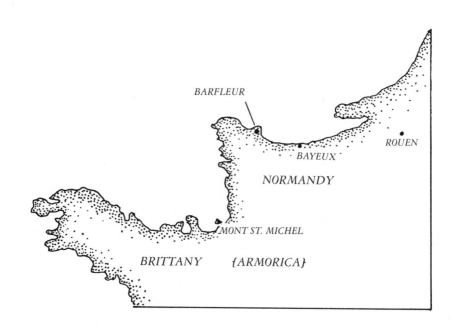

BARFLEUR

ROUEN

BAYEUX

NORMANDY

MONT ST. MICHEL

BRITTANY   {ARMORICA}

chapter I

ARTHUR IN
THE LATIN CHRONICLES

James J. Wilhelm

The romantic legend of King Arthur and his knights of the Round Table seems more and more to have had some foundation in history. A man named Artorius in Latin or Arthur in Welsh and English is mentioned in the Latin histories that describe the collapse of the christianized Roman Empire in Great Britain and the invasions of the Angles, Saxons, and Jutes from the lowlands of northern Germany.

After the Romans' conquest of Britain, begun in A.D. 43, they extended their advanced culture into the faraway Celtic island and later promoted the spread of Christianity there. Eventually the Roman Empire was weakened in the west by barbarian invasions. Denuded of troops, Britain passed from imperial control in 410, and the Britons were thrown back on their own resources. They still preserved something of Roman civilization, regarding themselves as Roman citizens who were superior to their insular barbaric enemies, the Irish, Scots, and the Picts from the never-Romanized northern region, and to the Germanic peoples of Holland, Germany, and Scandinavia, who were often marauding.

The first important writer to speak of these events was Gildas, a monk who around the year 547 composed his polemical treatise *On the Downfall and Conquest of Britain (De excidio et conquestu Britanniae)*. In Chapter 23 he tells how a "proud tyrant," whom we usually associate with the British chieftain Vortigern, and his counselors asked "the most ferocious Saxons of cursed name" to come over from Germany to help them fight against their insular enemies. This was a most impolitic move. Seeing that the island was relatively defenseless, the Saxons probably inflicted some losses on the British enemies, but then turned on their hosts themselves. They drove the Britons into the hills of Wales and Cornwall, where their descendants live even today, speaking the Celtic tongues of Welsh (or Cymric) and Cornish. Gildas speaks of these dispersed people in this way:

Chapter 25. And so many of the miserable survivors, who were trapped in the mountains, were slain in droves. Others, driven by hunger, stretched their hands to the enemy, offering themselves into endless servitude—if they were not cut down at once in an act that was kinder. Others ran off to overseas regions with loud wailings of grief. . . . Still others trusted their lives to the mountainous highlands, the menacing cliffs and crags, the dense forests, and the rugged sea caves, remaining, however timorously, in their homelands.

Then some time passed, and the cruel invaders retreated to their home bases. . . . The survivors collected their strength under the leadership of Ambrosius Aurelianus, a most temperate [*modestus*] man, who by chance was the only person of Roman parentage to have come through the catastrophe in which his parents, who had once worn the royal purple toga, had been killed, and whose present-day descendants have far degenerated from their former virtue. He and his men challenged their previous conquerors to battle, and by the grace of God, victory was theirs.

Chapter 26. From that time, now the native citizens and now the enemy have triumphed . . . up to the year of the siege of Mount Badon [*Badonici montis*], when the last but certainly not the least slaughter of these lowly scoundrels occurred, which, I know, makes forty-four years and one month, and which was also the time of my birth. [Text in Chambers, *Arthur*, pp. 236–237]

Gildas seems to offer us many details, but his language is overdramatized and ambiguous, especially with reference to "forty-four years." Is that the span of time from the arrival of the Saxons or from the leadership of Ambrosius? Also, we do not know the date of Gildas's birth; his death is listed as 572 in the highly suspect *Annals of Cambria*, below. And who was Ambrosius Aurelianus? He is also mentioned by the other important chronicler, Nennius, and William of Malmesbury links him with Arthur, whom Gildas ignores. Yet despite his omissions and ambiguities, Gildas clearly establishes the milieu from which the legend springs: a downtrodden people finds salvation in a great military leader who is connected with the civilization of Rome and the Holy Church. As for the intriguing Mount Badon, it has been identified as Bath, Badbury, and Baddington, although many authorities today connect it with Liddington Castle near Swindon.

The next Latin writer, the Venerable Bede (673?–735), tends largely to repeat Gildas in his *Ecclesiastical History of the English Nation* (731):

Book 1, Chapter 15. In the year of Our Lord 449. . . . At that time the races of the Angles or the Saxons were invited by the previously mentioned king [Vortigern] to come to Britain in three long ships. . . . After the enemy had killed or dispersed the natives of the island, they went home, and the natives gradually recollected their strength and courage, and they came out of their hiding places and collectively called on heaven for help to avoid a general disaster. At that time they had as their leader Ambrosius Aurelianus, a temperate man, who by chance was the only person to have come out of the previously mentioned catastrophe in which his parents, who had a famous royal name, had been killed. With him in command the Britons gathered their strength and challenged their previous conquerors to battle. With the help of God they won the victory. And from that time, now the native citizens and now the enemy have triumphed, up to the year of the siege of Mount Badon, when the Britons inflicted great losses on their enemies, approximately forty-four years after their arrival in Britain. [Text in Chambers, pp. 237–238]

The span of forty-four years is clarified, and since the arrival time is dated the year for the battle is put at 493. This date is not totally unlikely, although Bede's indebtedness to Gildas does not inspire much confidence in his presentation.

The first Latin chronicle to mention the name "Arthur" is *The History of the Britons* (*Historia Brittonum*), which is believed to have been compiled about 800 by a Welshman named Nennius. (See Chapter II for an earlier reference in Welsh.) This work was written in Latin, but many scholars feel that Nennius based his details about the Twelve Battles of Arthur upon native Welsh sources. We should remember that the modern Welsh people are the direct survivors of the ancient Britons. The passage has always led many to believe that there must be something historically real behind it, despite the sacramental nature of the number "twelve" and the shadowy geography, yet only the Caledonian Forest of Scotland and the City of the Legion (almost certainly the Welsh Caerleon) can be identified:

> *Chapter 56.* At that time the Saxons were thriving and increasing in multitudes in Britain. With [their leader] Hengist dead, his son Octha crossed over from the left side of Britain to the realm of the Kentishmen, and from him are descended the kings of Kent.
>
> Then Arthur fought against these people along with the kings of the Britons, and he was the leader in their battles. His first battle was at the mouth of the River Glein. The second to the fifth took place above the River Dubglas [Douglas or Dark Water], in the region of Linnuis. The sixth battle occurred at the River Bassas. The seventh was a battle in the Forest of Celidon, that is: the Battle of the Caledonian Forest. The eighth was at Castle Guinnion, in which Arthur carried an image of St. Mary, the Perpetual Virgin, on his shoulders, and the pagans were put to flight on that day, and there was a great massacre of them through the power of Our Lord Jesus Christ and his mother Mary. The ninth battle was in the City of the Legion. The tenth was fought on the banks of the River Tribruit. The eleventh occurred on Mount Agned. The twelfth was the Battle of Mount Badon, in which nine hundred and sixty men fell from a single attack of Arthur, and nobody put them down except him alone, and in every one of the battles he emerged as victor. But although the others were overcome in the battles, they sent for help from Germany, and their forces were ceaselessly reinforced. The Saxons brought over leaders from Germany to rule the Britons up to the reign of Ida, son of Eobba, the first king of Beornica. [Text in Chambers, pp. 238–239]

Later in his history, Nennius includes the following passage, which shows that the legend of Arthur was already becoming a popular myth:

> *Chapter 73.* There is another wonder in the region known as Buelt—a heap of stones piled up with the footprint of a dog upon it. While hunting the boar Troynt, Cabal, the hunting dog of Arthur the soldier, stepped on a stone, and Arthur later collected a pile beneath this and called it Carn Cabal. Men come to carry away the stone in their hands for a day and a night, yet the next day the imprinted stone is back on the pile.
>
> There is another wonder in the region called Ercing. It is a tomb near a brook that is called the Mound of Anir, for Anir is the man buried there. He was the son of Arthur the soldier, who killed and buried him there. Men come to measure the mound, which is sometimes six feet long, sometimes nine or twelve or fifteen. However you measure it again and again, you will never get the same figure— and I have tried this myself.

The Carn Cabal has been identified as existing in Breconshire in southern Wales, while Ercing has been placed in Herefordshire. The hunting of the boar figures prominently in the Welsh *Tale of Culhwch and Olwen* in Chapter III.

The next document is called *The Annals of Cambria*, another name for Wales, which the Welsh themselves call Cymru. It dates from the 900s, and offers these dates, which nowadays seem to be a bit late:

> 518 A.D. The Battle of Badon, in which Arthur carried the cross of Our Lord Jesus Christ for three days and three nights on his shoulders, and the Britons were victors. . . .

> 539 A.D. The Battle of Camlann, in which Arthur and Medraut both fell; and there was widespread death in Britain and in Ireland. . . .

> 572 A.D. Gildas died. . . .

This source, suspect as it is, nevertheless supplies us with a mention of a final catastrophic battle in which Arthur will go down, along with a man whose name evolves into Modred or Mordred. Although this figure will eventually become an adversary, he could here be one of Arthur's allies.

The next source is *The Legend of St. Goeznovius*, a Latin account of the life of the Breton St. Goeuznou. The work bears the date of 1019. That has been dismissed by J. S. P. Tatlock as too early, but Léon Fleuriot has since defended it as correct. In any case, an important article in *Speculum* by the Arthurian authority Geoffrey Ashe has shown that the legend must be examined closely. It is important because it establishes a continental base of operation for Arthur, which figures in the work of Geoffrey of Monmouth and later writers. It establishes, in short, a historical link between Britain and Brittany, which we know existed in literature for the transmission of such tales as those of Tristan and Parsifal. The pertinent section runs as follows:

> After the passage of time the usurping King Vortigern, in order to guarantee support for himself for the defense of the realm of insular Britain, which he was ruling unjustly, invited some warlike men from the region of Saxony and made them his allies in his kingdom. Since these were heathenish and devilish men, who from their natures lusted to make human blood flow, they called down many evils upon the British.
> Shortly afterward their arrogance was checked for a time by the great Arthur, King of the Britons, who forced them for the most part from the island or into servitude. But after this same Arthur had brilliantly won many victories in Britain and Gaul, he was finally called from human life, and the way once again lay open to the Saxons to return to the island to oppress the British, to overthrow churches, and to persecute saints. [Text in Chambers, p. 242]

Before this the anonymous author had described how a Briton had emigrated to Gallic Armorica and founded many colonies, thereby linking the insular and continental Britons and Bretons.

The next important chronicler is the Englishman William of Malmesbury, who wrote *The Deeds of the English Kings* (*De rebus gestis regum Anglorum*) in about the year 1125. In one passage from Book 1, Section 8, he verifies the earlier writings and notes that the Bretons (or Britons or both) now treat the deeds of the heroic Arthur (*bellicosi Arturis*) as if he were an Earthly Messiah:

> But with Vortimer [Guortimer, son of Vortigern] dead, the vigor of the Britons flagged, and their hopes diminished and flowed away, and indeed would have vanished entirely if Ambrosius, the lone survivor of the Romans who ruled after Vortigern, had not checked the unruly barbarians with the exemplary assistance of the heroic Arthur. This is that Arthur who is raved about even today in the trifles of the Bretons (Britons)—a man who is surely worthy of being described in true histories rather than dreamed about in fallacious myths—for he truly sustained his sinking homeland for a long time and aroused the drooping spirits of his fellow citizens to battle. Finally at the siege of Mt. Badon, relying on the image of the Lord's mother, which he had sewn on his armor, looming up alone, he dashed down nine hundred of the enemy in an incredible massacre. [Text in Chambers, pp. 249-250]

Then in Book 3, Section 287, William adds more of the kind of information that tends toward the creation of a myth linking a hero to the land around him:

> At that time [1066-87] in the province of Wales known as Ros was found the tomb of Walwen [Gawain], who was the by no means degenerate nephew of Arthur through his sister. He ruled in that part of Britain which is still called Walweitha and was a warrior most famous for his courage; but he was driven from his rule by the brother and the nephew of Hengist, though he made them pay dearly for his exile. He shared deservedly in his uncle's praise, because for several years he postponed the collapse of his tottering homeland.
>
> However, the tomb of Arthur is nowhere to be found—that man whose second coming has been hymned in the dirges of old. Yet the sepulcher of Walwen . . . is fourteen feet long. It is said by some that Walwen's body was cast up from a shipwreck after he had been wounded by his enemies, while others say that he was murdered by his fellow citizens at a public feast. And so the truth lies in doubt, though neither story would lessen the assertion of his fame. [Text in Chambers, p. 250]

The passage also marks the entry of the name Walwen (Gawain) into Latin literature, showing that the future paragon of courtly excellence had already developed a legend of his own by 1125.

The next important writer is Geoffrey of Monmouth, whose *History of the Kings of Britain* combines history with legend in a highly imaginative form. The Arthurian segment of his work is given at length in Chapter IV. This section will close with a writer later than Geoffrey, the Norman-Welsh Giraldus Cambrensis, who lived from about 1146 to 1223 and was patronized by King Henry II of England. In his *On the Instruction of Princes* (*De instructione principum*), written in the 1190s, Giraldus gives a fascinating description of Arthur's grave and also mentions Queen Guinevere and the magician Morgan the Fay, who plays an important role in *Sir Gawain and the Green Knight*:

> Then Arthur's body, which legends have fancifully treated as being phantomlike at its end and carried away by spirits to a faroff place where it is immune to death,

was discovered in these days of ours, buried deep in the earth in a hollowed-out oaktree located between two stone pyramids that had been set up a long time ago in a holy burial ground at Glastonbury. The body was revealed by strange and almost miraculous signs and was transported to a church with great honor and fittingly housed in a marble tomb that bore a lead cross with a stone placed under it. . . . I myself have seen this, and I have traced the letters engraved on the cross, which do not project forward but rather inwardly toward the stone: "Here lies buried the famous King Arthur with Guinevere [Wenneveria] his second wife on the Island of Avalon."

There are several things to note here, for he did indeed have two wives, of whom the last was buried with him, and her bones were found at the same time with her husband's, but set apart in this way: two-thirds of the tomb toward the head contained the bones of the man, while the other third held the woman's remains. A golden handful of woman's hair was found there, retaining its fresh wholeness and radiance, but when a certain monk greedily reached out and grabbed it the hair dissolved into dust.

Now although there had been certain indications in writings that the body would be found there . . . and visions and revelations were made to many virtuous and holy men, King Henry II of England revealed everything to the monks, just as he had heard it recited to him by a Welsh bard who sang of ancient deeds: that they would find the body sixteen feet deep in the earth in a hollow oak, not in a marble tomb. It had been buried this deeply so that the Saxons, who took over the island after Arthur's death, and whom he had vigorously beaten back while alive and had almost totally destroyed, could not find it; and that is why the inscription was turned inwardly toward the stone. . . .

The burial place is now known as Glastonbury, and in ancient times it was called the Island of Avalon. It is indeed almost an island, being surrounded by marshes; and so in the British language it was called Inis Avallon or Apple Island, since apples grow there in abundance. Then too Morgan, the noble matron and lady-ruler of those parts, who was closely related by blood to King Arthur, transported Arthur after the Battle of Kemelen [Camlan] to this island, now called Glaston, to heal his wounds. In the British language it was once called Inis Gutrin (that is, Glass Island), and for that reason the Saxons dubbed it Glastonbury, since *glas* means "glass" in their tongue, and *bury* is "city" or "camp."

You should also know that Arthur's bones were huge. . . . His shinbone, when placed on the ground by a monk next to that of the tallest man there, reached three fingers beyond the man's knee. And his skull was so broad and long as to be a wonder or marvel, and the space between his brows and eyes was the breadth of a full palm. There appeared on him also ten wounds or more, largely scarred over, except for one, which was larger than the rest and showed a big cut, which seemed to have been lethal. [Text in Chambers, pp. 269–271]

These are the most important Latin writings for the question of Arthur's actual existence. Work done in the 1980s by Geoffrey Ashe and others has shown that behind the puzzling traditions we may glimpse the figure of a known British leader who took an army to Gaul in the final confusions surrounding the collapse of the Western Roman Empire. This man is documented overseas as "Riothamus," a name that latinizes a Celtic title meaning "Supreme King"; and it could have been used as the official epithet of a chieftain whose actual name was something else—Arthur, for instance. Hints in *The Legend of St. Goeznovius* do in fact suggest that its author is referring to the same person when he indicates that Arthur went over to Gaul, and several other medieval writers give Arthur much the same dating as this "Supreme King." If the identification or semi-identification is correct, there is an even broader base for assuming Arthur's true historical presence.

Similarly, work has been done to try to identify Camelot and other places of Arthurian interest. Leslie Alcock has made a good case for placing the otherwise mythical Camelot in Cadbury. There are also possible or probable locations for numerous other sites. Tintagel Castle has long been known to have existed in Cornwall, while Mt. Badon has been identified most convincingly as Liddington Castle near Swindon, and the Isle of Avalon probably was, as the chronicles themselves say, Glastonbury.

But for many readers of Arthurian tales the historical side, while fascinating, is the least important part of a broad vehicle of legend and myth that has replenished the European imagination for centuries, from Chrétien de Troyes to T. H. White. The true father of this mythic material is the pseudo-historian Geoffrey of Monmouth, whose work appears in Chapter IV. Meanwhile, aside from the chronicles, which were written by men of the church who were often Germanic rather than Celtic in their sympathies, the myth of Arthur grew where he properly belonged: among the common people who had been displaced in Wales and Cornwall and who were looking desperately for a messianic figure of salvation. Their literature appears in Chapters II and III.

Bibliographic note: All historical citations are taken from E. K. Chambers's *Arthur of Britain*, which, although published in 1927 (reprinted by Barnes and Noble in 1964), remains a standard source. For Tatlock's discussion of *Goeznovius* see *Speculum*, 14 (1939), 361–365; for Fleuriot's see *Les Origines de la Bretagne* (1980), p. 277. Ashe's consideration of "Riothamus" appears in *Speculum*, 56 (1981), 301–323. See also Some General Books in English for Further Reading at the end of this work.

chapter II

ARTHUR IN
THE EARLY WELSH TRADITION

John K. Bollard

The texts in this chapter include most of the Welsh references to Arthur that are earlier than Geoffrey of Monmouth's *History of the Kings of Britain*, and they give evidence that stories of Arthur and his men were well integrated into the body of Welsh tradition before the twelfth century. These tales and poems do not portray an abstract and elegant world where Arthur is surrounded by his knights and where questions of courtly conduct predominate. The poetry here gives us a glimpse of a society in which the realities of war were ever present. The most persistent images are those of blood, death, and grief. Surely these poems, whether evoking figures of history or of legend, served in some measure to help both poet and audience to understand and to cope with those same fierce images as they occurred and reoccurred in their own war-torn lives.

Medieval Welsh verse is not narrative, and it tends to be more allusive than informative. It does, however, make frequent references to characters, events, and stories that the original audience must have recognized. Some of these references are familiar to us today because the names or tales have survived in some other source. But because narrative traditions develop and change over a period of time, we can rarely be absolutely certain that the tale known to us is the same one that was intended in the earlier poetry. The very words of a language also undergo changes over time, and, especially when dealing with the earliest records of a culture quite different from our own, we cannot always be sure that a word had the same range of meaning in some past century that it has for us today. Faced with a similar problem, thirteenth- and fourteenth-century scribes may have imperfectly understood the older manuscripts they were copying, thus generating new errors that are left for us to puzzle over. For all of these reasons there is much that is tentative in these translations of early Welsh texts. Even though there are many obscurities, however, it seems preferable to give a single version of each, rather than to intersperse the translations with alternative readings or append lengthy discussions.

Sometime around the year 600 Mynyddog the Wealthy, a ruler of the Gododdin,* in what is now southern Scotland, assembled a company of warriors from all over Britain. For a year they feasted at his expense before attacking and suffering a disastrous defeat from a much larger English force at Catraeth, which is probably the modern Catterick in Yorkshire. All but one of the three hundred warriors were killed. The survivor may have been the poet Aneirin, who is mentioned, as Neirin, in Chapter 62 of the chronicle attributed to Nennius. Whether or not he was actually present at the battle, the poet was contemporary with the fallen heroes, and he composed a long series of elegiac stanzas eulogizing them. From the surviving thirteenth-century copy of this poem, called *The Gododdin*, we can piece together the outline of the events of this expedition. The poem was undoubtedly passed on orally for many years; its language changed with the development of Welsh, and additional stanzas and references were added to the original composition. The extant poem, therefore, presents a complex puzzle that we cannot completely solve. The standard edition of the poem is *Canu Aneirin*, edited with Welsh notes and introduction by Ifor Williams (University of Wales, 1938); it has been translated and discussed in some detail by Kenneth Jackson in *The Gododdin* (Edinburgh University, 1969).

In the following stanza praising a certain Gwawrddur there is nothing that would exclude it from being part of the original composition of Aneirin. The reference to Arthur, therefore, may well be the earliest surviving mention of him, and the poet himself may have been born during Arthur's lifetime. Within a generation or two after his death Arthur has become an ideal warrior to whom others are compared, and we can see here the beginnings of the long-lasting tradition by which other heroes were glorified and their tales enhanced simply by coupling them with the name of Arthur:

> He pierced over three hundred of the finest.
> He struck at both the center and the flank.
> He was worthy in the front of a most generous army.
> He gave out gifts from his drove of steeds in the winter.
> He fed black ravens [killed many of the enemy] on the wall
>   of the fortress, though he was not Arthur.
> He gave support in battle.
> In the van, an alder shield-wall was Gwawrddur.

Curiously enough, the name of Gwawrddur is again coupled with that of Arthur in a fragmentary and obscure poem in the late thirteenth-century manuscript known as *The Book of Taliesin* (edited by J. G. Evans, Llanbedrog,

---

Note on the pronunciation of Welsh names: Pronounce *a* as in father, *ai*, *au*, and *ei* as in aisle, *aw* as in now, *c* as in cat, *ch* as in Scottish loch, *dd* as in then, *e* as in bed, *f* as in of, *ff* as in effect, *g* as in go, *i* as in bid, *th* as in think, *u* as in busy or bead, *w* as in with or as the vowel in tooth, *y* as in myth or city in a single or final syllable and as in alive or glove in other syllables. Pronounce *ll* with the tongue in the same position as for *l* by gently blowing air, without voice, past the side of the tongue (the *l* in English clean is very similar). The stressed syllable in Welsh is almost always the next-to-last syllable.

1910). This poem, which is manifestly some centuries older than the manuscript, praises the horses of traditional heroes. The names in the following
two lines were chosen partly on the basis of rhyme, and the poet may have
even taken the name of Gwawrddur from his knowledge of *The Gododdin*:

> And the horse of Gwythur and the horse of Gwawrddur
> and the horse of Arthur, fearless in causing pain.

The following poem is included in this collection because it is a contemporary elegy written in praise of Owain, a sixth-century lord of Rheged
in northern Britain, who was drawn into and achieved some prominence in
the Arthurian cycle. Owain son of Urien appears frequently in later
Arthurian tales, especially as the hero of a romance that gained widespread
popularity in Europe. He is the hero of *Yvain*, by Chrétien de Troyes, and
appears in the Middle English *Ywain and Gawain*.

The present poem is found in *The Book of Taliesin* and has been edited by
Ifor Williams and J. E. Caerwyn Williams in *The Poems of Taliesin* (Dublin
Institute for Advanced Studies, 1968). It was composed by the sixth-
century poet Taliesin, who is mentioned in the Nennian chronicle. Taliesin's
elegy reveals the poet's personal sense of the loss of his lord, patron, and
friend:

Elegy for Owain son of Urien

> The soul of Owain son of Urien,
> may the Lord consider its need.
> The lord of Rheged whom the heavy greensward covers,
> it was not shallow to praise him.
> The grave of a man renowned in song, of great fame.
> His whetted spears were like the dawn's rays,
> since no equal is found
> to the resplendent lord of Llwyfenydd,
> reaper of enemies, captor,
> with the nature of his father and his forebears.
> When Owain killed Fflamddwyn,
> it was no harder than sleeping.
> The broad host of Lloegr sleep
> with the light in their eyes.
> And those who did not retreat
> were bolder than necessary.
> Owain punished them severely,
> like a pack of wolves attacking sheep.
> A worthy man above his many-colored arms,
> who gave horses to suitors;
> though he hoarded them as a miser,
> they were shared for the sake of his soul.
> The soul of Owain son of Urien,
> may the Lord consider its need.

As the Anglo-Saxons gained sway over what is now England, many of
the displaced British traditions were relocated in Wales. Considerable evidence for this can be seen in a series of seventy-five stanzas known as "The
Stanzas of the Graves," composed during the ninth or tenth century. These

verses list the traditional Welsh gravesites of legendary heroes, a number of whom are known to have been rulers or warriors from other parts of Britain. The earliest version of this poem is found in the thirteenth-century manuscript known as *The Black Book of Carmarthen*, which has been edited, annotated, and translated in full by Thomas Jones in *Proceedings of the British Academy* (1967).

A few of the names in "The Stanzas of the Graves" figure in Arthurian tradition. Gwalchmai is the Welsh name of the character better known to us in English as Gawain; Bedwyr, whose name is frequently coupled with that of Cei (Sir Kay) in early Welsh Arthurian tradition, appears in French and English as Bedivere; March is the King Mark of the Tristan legend. However, most important for Arthurian studies is a much-debated line naming Arthur: *anoeth bit bet y Arthur*. The troublesome word in this line is *anoeth*; it has been variously interpreted, but other instances of the word suggest that a likely sense in this context is "thing difficult to find or obtain; a wonder." A tradition that Arthur's grave was unknown may reflect (or may even have given rise to) a belief that Arthur was not dead and that he would return as a deliverer. Such a belief was certainly current among the Bretons by the early twelfth century. William of Malmesbury's comments, quoted in Chapter I, on the grave of Walwen and on the unknown site of Arthur's grave strongly suggest that William had a knowledge of Welsh traditions about the graves of heroes similar to what is found in this poem:

From *"The Stanzas of the Graves"*

The grave of Gwalchmai in Peryddon
as a reproach to men;
in Llanbadarn the grave of Cynon.

The grave of the son of Osfran at Camlan
after many a slaughter;
the grave of Bedwyr on Tryfan hill.

The grave of Owain son of Urien in a square grave
under the earth of Llanforfael;
in Abererch, Rhydderch the Generous.

A grave for March, a grave for Gwythur,
a grave for Gwgawn Red-sword;
hard to find in the world, a grave for Arthur.

Another character originally independent of any connection with Arthur is Geraint son of Erbin. Like Owain, he too became the hero of a widely known Arthurian romance, though in the French version by Chrétien de Troyes, *Erec and Enide*, the hero is given a Breton name, Erec. Early genealogical evidence points to a late sixth-century date for Geraint, and his name is frequently connected with southwestern Britain and south Wales. Geraint son of Erbin may possibly be the Geraint referred to in *The Gododdin* in the line "Geraint before the South, the battle-cry was given," a line that seems to be faintly echoed in the poem given below.

This tenth- or eleventh-century poem in praise of Geraint is found in several manuscripts, though only the verses found in the earliest version from *The Black Book of Carmarthen* are translated here. It has been edited in Welsh by Brynley F. Roberts in *Astudiaethau ar yr Hengerdd: Studies in Early Welsh Poetry* (University of Wales, 1978). This poem is a series of three-line stanzas or *englynion* (singular *englyn*), and its effect is achieved through the use of repetition with some variation in each englyn. One stanza mentions Arthur as taking some part in the battle of Llongborth, perhaps the modern Langport in Somerset. This is a significant reference for two reasons. It shows that at a fairly early date Geraint, a hero from the southwest of Britain, was being brought into the penumbra of Arthur's fame, as were other heroes from the north. This is also the first known instance of the title "emperor" being applied to Arthur, a title that is regularly used in later Arthurian tales and romances in Welsh. Thus this poem provides further evidence of the early growth of Arthurian legend, and it illustrates a step in the gradual transfiguration of early historical leaders into the traditional knights of Arthur's court:

Geraint filius Erbin

Before Geraint, afflictor of the enemy,
I saw white steeds with fetlocks bloodstained,
and after the battle-cry—grievous death.

Before Geraint, disinheritor of the enemy,
I saw steeds with fetlocks bloodstained from battle,
and after the battle-cry—grievous reflection.

Before Geraint, oppressor of the enemy,
I saw steeds, white their skin,
and after the battle-cry—grievous silence.

At Llongborth I saw wrath
and biers more than many
and men blood-red before the rush of Geraint.

At Llongborth I saw hewing,
men in battle with heads bloodied
before great Geraint, son of his father.

At Llongborth I saw spurs
and men who would not retreat before spears
and drinking wine from bright glass.

At Llongborth I saw the weapons
of men and blood flowing,
and after the battle-cry—grievous burial.

At Llongborth I saw Arthur
(brave men hewed with iron),
emperor, ruler of battle-toil.

At Llongborth were killed Geraint's
brave men from the Devon lowlands,
but before they were killed, they killed.

Swiftly there ran under Geraint's thigh
long-legged horses, fed on wheat,
red, with the rush of speckled eagles.

Swiftly there ran under Geraint's thigh
long-legged horses, grain was theirs,
red, with the rush of black eagles.

Swiftly there ran under Geraint's thigh
long-legged horses, grain scattering,
red, with the rush of red eagles.

Swiftly there ran under Geraint's thigh
long-legged horses, grain-consuming,
red, with the rush of white eagles.

Swiftly there ran under Geraint's thigh
long-legged horses, with the leap of a stag,
with the roar of a blaze on a mountain waste.

Swiftly there ran under Geraint's thigh
long-legged horses, grain-greedy,
grey-tipped their hair like silver.

Swiftly there ran under Geraint's thigh
long-legged horses, deserving grain,
red, with the rush of blue eagles.

Swiftly there ran under Geraint's thigh
long-legged horses, grain their food,
red, with the rush of grey eagles.

When Geraint was born, open were
the gates of Heaven; Christ gave what was asked—
a noble form, Britain's glory.

One of the most interesting, if perplexing and tantalizing, early Arthurian sources is a tenth- or eleventh-century poem, also in *The Black Book of Carmarthen*, which begins as a dialogue between Arthur himself and the porter Glewlwyd Mighty-grip. The poem is largely a catalog of names in which Arthur praises his warriors. The place-name "Tryfrwyd" of line 48 is undoubtedly a reference to the battle listed in the Nennian chronicle, with its earlier orthography, as having been "fought on the banks of the River Tribruit."

However, in this poem we have moved away from the more or less historical milieu of the earlier poetry into the realm of legend, mythology, and folktale. Some of the names in the poem come not from early historical tradition but from Celtic mythology. Mabon son of Modron and Manawydan son of Llŷr, for instance, are names that can be traced back to the names of early Celtic deities. An important place in this poem is given to Cei (pronounced "Ky" like "sky"). In later tradition he becomes the obstreperous Sir Kay, but here he is, or has become, more than simply a renowned warrior; he appears in this poem as a slayer of witches and monsters. Unfortunately

the manuscript is defective, and the poem breaks off at the end of a page
before we learn how Cei fared against the Clawing Cat (Welsh *cath palug*):

[Arthur:]   What man is the porter?

[Glewlwyd:]   Glewlwyd Mighty-grip.
             Who asks it?

[Arthur:]   Arthur and Cei the Fair.

[Glewlwyd:]   Who comes with you?

[Arthur:]   The best men in the world.

[Glewlwyd:]:   To my house you will not come
             unless you deliver them.

[Arthur:]   I shall deliver them
             and you will see them.
             Wythnaint, Elei,
             and Sywyon, these three;
             Mabon son of Modron,
             servant of Uther Pendragon,
             Cystaint son of Banon,
             and Gwyn Godybrion;
             harsh were my servants
             in defending their rights.
             Manawydan son of Llŷr,
             profound was his counsel.
             Manawyd carried off
             shields pierced and battle-stained.
             And Mabon son of Mellt
             stained the grass with blood.
             And Anwas the Winged
             and Lluch of the Striking Hand,
             they were defending
             on the borders of Eidyn.
             A lord would protect them;
             my nephew would give them recompense.
             Cei would entreat them
             as he struck them by threes.
             When the grove was lost
             cruelty was suffered.
             Cei would entreat them
             while he cut them down.

[Cei (?):]   Though Arthur was but playing,
             blood was flowing
             in the hall of Afarnach
             fighting with a hag.
             He pierced the cudgel-head
             in the halls of Dissethach.
             On the mount of Eidyn
             they fought with Dog-heads;
             by the hundred they fell.

[Arthur:]   They fell by the hundred
            before Bedwyr the Fine-sinewed
            on the strand of Tryfrwyd.
            Fighting with Garwlwyd,
            fierce was his nature
            with sword and shield.
            Vain was an army
            compared to Cei in battle.
            He was a sword in battle;
            he pledged with his hand.
            He was a resolute chieftain
            of a host for the country's good.
            Bedwyr and Bridlaw,
            nine hundred to listen,
            six hundred to disperse
            would his attack be worth.
            The servants that I had,
            it was better when they were alive.
            Before the lords of Emrys
            I saw Cei in haste;
            prince of plunder,
            the tall man was hostile.
            His revenge was heavy;
            his anger was sharp.
            When he drank from the buffalo horn
            he would drink for four;
            when he came into battle
            he would strike like a hundred.
            Unless it were God who did it,
            Cei's death could not be achieved.
            Cei the Fair and Llachau,
            they made slaughter
            before the pain of the blue-tipped spears.
            In the uplands of Ystafngwn
            Cei pierced nine witches.
            Cei the Fair went to Anglesey
            to destroy lions;
            his shield was small
            against the Clawing Cat.
            When people ask
            who pierced the Clawing Cat
            (nine score warriors would fall for its food,
            nine score champions
            and. . . .

The name of Llachau, which is coupled with that of Cei above, also occurs in another tenth- or eleventh-century poem from *The Black Book of Carmarthen* in a series of englynion lamenting the deaths of traditional Welsh heroes. Though little is known about Llachau, he was clearly a figure of some importance in early Arthurian tradition, for in addition to these early references his name is invoked no less than eight times by the twelfth- and thirteenth-century Welsh bards. The englyn in which he is named below is of particular interest because it names Arthur as his father:

I have been where Llachau was slain,
son of Arthur, marvelous in songs,
when ravens croaked over blood.

Firmly ensconced in mythological tradition is an important Arthurian poem in *The Book of Taliesin*, to which a later hand has added the title *Preiddeu Annwfn*, "The Spoils of Annwn." The historical poet Taliesin had gradually become a figure of legend and folklore himself, and various poems with mythological content were attributed to him. "The Spoils of Annwn" is obscure both in its language and in its allusions, and no satisfactorily complete edition or translation has been published since R. S. Loomis's work; see *Wales and the Arthurian Legend* (University of Wales, 1956). The following translation is speculative, and ellipses have been used where the text defies translation.

The general outline is clear. Annwn is the Celtic otherworld. At times it would appear that Annwn is coextensive with the world in which we live, though it may not be discernible. In some sources, such as this poem, it seems to be an island. In the first part of the medieval Welsh prose masterpiece known as *The Four Branches of the Mabinogi* the story is related how Pwyll, a ruler of Dyfed in southwest Wales, repaid a debt of honor to Arawn, the king of Annwn, by remaining for a year in Annwn in Arawn's form and by defeating one of Arawn's enemies in single combat. Upon his return to his own land Pwyll became known as Pwyll, Head of Annwn. The latter half of the story tells of the strange circumstances surrounding the birth and rearing of Pwyll's son, Pryderi. The second branch of *The Mabinogi* tells, among other things, of a magical cauldron that could restore the dead to life. In a battle in Ireland in which this cauldron was eventually destroyed the entire population of Ireland was killed except for five pregnant women, and all of the Welsh army was slain except for seven survivors, among whom were Pryderi and Taliesin.

It is clear that "The Spoils of Annwn" reflects much of this same mythological material in an Arthurian context. The poem alludes to a journey to Annwn in Arthur's ship Prydwen. The purpose of this journey was apparently to rescue Gwair, known elsewhere as a renowned prisoner, and perhaps to bring back among the spoils of war the cauldron of the Head of Annwn. This magical cauldron also bears some affinity to that of Diwrnach the Giant in the story of *Culhwch and Olwen*.

The latter part of the poem remains obscure, though the poet seems to be discontented with the lowly men and cowardly monks around him, in contrast to the warriors whom he accompanied on Arthur's disastrous expedition to Annwn. Thus, like much early Welsh verse, "The Spoils of Annwn" is an expression of loss and grief, reflected most poignantly in the refrain "except for seven, none returned":

The Spoils of Annwn

I will praise the Lord, the Sovereign, the King of the land,
who has extended his rule over the strand of the world.

Well equipped was the prison of Gwair in Caer Siddi [Fairy Fortress],
according to the story of Pwyll and Pryderi.
None before him went to it,
to the heavy blue chain; it was a faithful servant whom it restrained,
and before the spoils of Annwn sadly he sang.
And until Judgment Day our bardic song will last.
Three shiploads of Prydwen we went to it;
except for seven, none returned from Caer Siddi.

I am honored in praise, song is heard.
In Caer Pedryfan [Four-cornered (?) Fort], four-sided,
my eulogy, from the cauldron it was spoken.
By the breath of nine maidens it was kindled.
The cauldron of the Head of Annwn, what is its custom,
dark about its edge with pearl?
It does not boil a coward's food; it had not been so destined.
The sword of Lluch Lleawg was raised to it,
and in the hand of Lleminawg it was left.
And before the door of the gate of hell, lanterns burned.
And when we went with Arthur, renowned conflict,
except for seven, none returned from Caer Feddwid [Fort of Carousal].

I am honored in praise, song will be heard.
In Caer Pedryfan, island of the strong door,
noon and jet-black are mixed.
Bright wine their drink before their warband.
Three shiploads of Prydwen we went on the sea;
except for seven, none returned from Caer Rigor.

I, lord of learning, do not deserve lowly men.
Beyond Caer Wydr [Glass Fort] they had not seen Arthur's valor.
Three score hundred men stood on the wall;
it was difficult to speak with their watchman.
Three shiploads of Prydwen we went with Arthur;
except for seven, none returned from Caer Goludd.

I do not deserve lowly men, slack their defense.
They do not know what day . . . ,
what hour of the midday God was born,
who. . . .
They do not know the Speckled Ox, thick his headring,
seven score links in his collar.
And when we went with Arthur, disastrous visit,
except for seven, none returned from Caer Fanddwy.

I do not deserve lowly men, slack their attack.
They do not know what day . . . ,
what hour of the midday the lord was born,
what animal they keep, silver its head.
When we went with Arthur, disastrous strife,
except for seven, none returned from Caer Ochren.

Monks crowd together like a choir of whelps
from the battle of lords who will be known.

Is the wind of the same path? Is the sea of the same water?
Is the fire, irresistible tumult, of the same spark?

Monks crowd together like a pack of wolves
from the battle of lords who will be known.
They do not know when darkness and dawn separate,
or the wind, what is its path, what does it divide,
what does it destroy, what land does it strike?
The lost grave of a saint and earth.

I will praise the Lord, the Great Prince.
May I not be sad; Christ will endow me.

From the earliest times the Celtic peoples have used triple groupings as a means of classifying, remembering, and passing on a wide range of information and lore. Laws, genealogical and geographical information, rules of poetic composition, and much else besides have come down to us arranged in triplets. One such body of lore has survived in various collections known as *The Triads of the Isle of Britain*, which preserve the names of the traditional heroes of Welsh legend, along with summaries of or references to stories about many of them. Poets and storytellers who memorized or copied them down could then draw upon these lists for names, details, and stories as they needed them. The earliest and most important versions of these triads are found in thirteenth-, fourteenth-, and fifteenth-century manuscripts, but the information they contain is demonstrably much older. The standard edition and discussion is *Trioedd Ynys Prydein: The Welsh Triads*, edited by Rachel Bromwich (University of Wales, 1961; rev. 1978)—itself an invaluable store of information about the development of Arthurian legend. The number of each triad in Bromwich's edition is given below in brackets.

Of the ninety-six triads in this collection those translated below mention Arthur or other characters well known in Arthurian literature, thus giving us a glimpse of the scope of Arthurian lore in Wales before the publication of Geoffrey of Monmouth's *History of the Kings of Britain*. It should perhaps be made explicit here that the triads are written in prose, not verse, with the exception of the englyn recited by Arthur himself in Triad 18W. Other verse, such as the englyn he recites in *Culhwch and Olwen*, has also been attributed to Arthur, and these poems account for his inclusion among the Three Frivolous Bards of Triad 12. Many of the names in these triads have been encountered in the poetry above; other names are readily recognizable. A few names are better known in their French or English forms. Bishop Bidwini (Triad 1) also turns up in the catalog in *Culhwch and Olwen* and he is probably the original of the Bishop Bawdewyn (Baudwin or Baldwin) who sits next to Ywain son of Urien in line 112 of *Sir Gawain and the Green Knight*. Medrawd (54) is the Medraut of *The Annals of Cambria* and the Modred or Mordred of Malory and others. Gwenhwyfar (54, 56, 80, 84) is Guinevere.

From *The Triads of the Isle of Britain*

Three Tribal Thrones of the Isle of Britain: Arthur as Chief Ruler in Mynyw, and David as Chief Bishop, and Maelgwn Gwynedd as Chief Elder; Arthur as

Chief Ruler in Celli Wig in Cornwall, and Bishop Bidwini as Chief Bishop, and Caradog Strong-arm as Chief Elder; Arthur as Chief Ruler in Pen Rhionydd in the North, and Gerthmwl Wledig as Chief Elder, and Cyndeyrn Garthwys as Chief Bishop. [1]

Three Men of Substance of the Isle of Britain: Gwalchmai son of Gwyar, and Llachau son of Arthur, and Rhiwallawn Broom-hair. [4]

Three Chieftains of Arthur's Court: Gobrwy son of Echel Mighty-thigh, Cadriaith son of Porthawr Gadw, and Ffleudur Fflam. [9]

Three Frivolous Bards of the Isle of Britain: Arthur, and Cadwallawn son of Cadfan, and Rahawd son of Morgant. [12]

Three Favorites of Arthur's Court, and Three Battle-horsemen; and they never sought a captain over them. And Arthur composed an englyn:
These are my Three Battle-horsemen:
Menedd, and Lludd of the Breastplate,
and the Pillar of the Welsh, Caradog. [18W]

Three Red-reapers of the Isle of Britain: Rhun son of Beli, and Lleu Skillful-hand, and Morgant the Wealthy. But one was more of a Red-reaper than the three; Arthur was his name. For a year neither grass nor plants would come up where one of the three walked, but for seven years none would come up where Arthur walked. [20W]

Three Diademed Men of the Isle of Britain: Drystan son of Tallwch, and Hueil son of Caw, and Cei son of Cenyr the Fine-bearded. But one was diademed above the three of them; that was Bedwyr son of Bedrawg. [21]

Three Unbridled Ravagings of the Isle of Britain: The first of them, when Medrawd came to Arthur's court in Celli Wig in Cornwall; he left neither food nor drink in the court he did not consume, and he also pulled Gwenhwyfar out of her chair of state, and then he struck a blow upon her. And the second Unbridled Ravaging, when Arthur came to Medrawd's court; he left neither food nor drink in either the court or the cantref [district]. And the third Unbridled Ravaging, when Aeddan the Treacherous came as far as Dumbarton to the court of Rhydderch the Generous, and he left neither food nor drink nor animal alive. [54]

Three Great Queens of Arthur: Gwenhwyfar daughter of Cywryd Gwent, and Gwenhwyfar daughter of Gwythyr son of Greidiawl, and Gwenhwyfar daughter of Gogfran the Giant. [56]

And these were his Three Mistresses: Indeg daughter of Garwy the Tall, and Garwen daughter of Henin the Old, and Gŵyl daughter of Gendawd. [57]

Three Unfortunate Counsels of the Isle of Britain: Giving to Julius Caesar and the men of Rome a place for the forefeet of their horses on the land, in payment for the horse Meinlas. And the second, allowing Horsa and Hengist and Ronnwen into this isle. And the third, Arthur dividing his men thrice with Medrawd at Camlan. [59]

Three Men of the Isle of Britain most courteous to guests and strangers: Gwalchmai son of Gwyar, and Cadwy son of Geraint, and Cadriaith son of Saidi. [75]

Three Faithless Wives of the Isle of Britain; Three daughters of Culfanwyd of Britain: Essyllt [Isolde] Fair-hair, mistress of Trystan, and Penarwan, wife of Owain son of Urien, and Bun, wife of Fflamddwyn; and one was more faithless than those three: Gwenhwyfar, wife of Arthur, since she shamed a better man than any of them. [80]

Three Futile Battles of the Isle of Britain: One of them was the Battle of Goddau; it was brought about because of a bitch together with a roebuck and a lapwing. The second was the Battle of Arfderydd, which was brought about because of a lark's nest. And the third was the worst; that was Camlan. And that was brought about by the quarrel between Gwenhwyfar and Gwenhwyfach. This is the reason those were called Futile: because they were brought about by such a fruitless cause as that. [84]

chapter III

THE TALE
OF CULHWCH AND OLWEN

Richard M. Loomis

Like Geoffrey of Monmouth, the unknown author of *Culhwch and Olwen* was a storyteller who worked with abundant resources: stories from ancient Celtic myth, popular international folktales, traditional lore of the island of Britain, and some materials from the currents of classical and continental literature. Calchas, the Trojan soothsayer, for example, makes an unexpected appearance in *Culhwch* as one of the innumerable sons of the northern hero and progenitor Caw of Pictland (Scotland). But whereas Geoffrey, writing in Latin for a European audience, imitates what he knew of the Roman historians, the author of *Culhwch* engages his Welsh audience by drawing the whole world into the compass of a Celtic vision.

To make that Celtic vision more familiar I have translated or identified many names in *Culhwch*. For Welsh titles and epithets I give equivalents in English, and for place-names, modern forms or bracketed locations; for names built from Welsh words I give English translations, sometimes in brackets after the Welsh, often in English alone. Only thus, I believe, can an English reader taste some of the pleasure of the author's rapid, punning sport with language.

Welsh scholars have estimated the date of the composition of *Culhwch* as the late eleventh century, and it may have been set down in its surviving form about 1100. The period following the Norman Conquest was a time of heightened national consciousness and self-expression among the Welsh, who regarded the Normans as possible allies against the English. *Culhwch* has features of subject and technique that resemble Irish saga, perhaps reflecting Irish influences associated with the Welsh leader Gruffudd ap Cynan, who after a period of exile in Dublin landed with a military force near St. David's in 1081, an event similar to a stage of the hunt of Twrch Trwyth in *Culhwch and Olwen*. (See the note on Welsh pronunciation in the introduction to Chapter II.)

The inventiveness of the author of *Culhwch* is shown in the playful triads he introduces into his tale. As Rachel Bromwich notes, none of his triads are the traditional ones. All suggest a burlesque of the form, or at least an adaptation of the form to this storyteller's purposes. He tells of a young Welsh lord, Culhwch, who declines to marry his stepmother's daughter and is therefore visited with a curse or destiny (Irish, *geis*) pronounced by the stepmother: that he shall marry no one but Olwen, the daughter of the giant Ysbaddaden Pencawr (Chief Giant). The tale shows us how, with the help of Arthur and Arthur's followers, Culhwch does win Olwen. The form of the tale resembles Celtic manuscript illumination: a single initial letter elaborated with interwoven strands, abstract curving mazes, and multiple implanted figures of humans, animals, and grotesques that can engage our attention for their separate charms yet are fashioned to a lavish harmonic texture, like a monarch's robe. The monarch for whom *Culhwch and Olwen* is a robe of state is Arthur, who is shown, as in Geoffrey of Monmouth, to be a lord of many lands and prodigious powers, capable of fierce fighting yet courteous and affectionate toward such a hero as Culhwch.

The story demonstrates that it is a form of heroism to seek help—help from men and women, help from animals, help from those with supernatural powers. A related theme developed in *Culhwch and Olwen* is the fruitfulness of fear: the emotions induced by fearful things can generate heroic response. Culhwch's birth provides the first image of that. He was born in a pig-run. His mother had wandered there in a state of madness from which she was delivered, only to be provoked by fear of the pigs into giving birth to her son. Later Culhwch's stepmother seeks to dominate him by marriage to her daughter; when he declines that relationship, she lays on him the hazardous destiny of courting the giant's daughter. Instead of collapsing in terror he thrills with love for the Olwen whom he has not yet seen.

Culhwch's father sends him for help to his kinsman Arthur, and at Arthur's castle the young man demands admittance and rides into the hall. Later Olwen advises Culhwch to promise her father whatever he asks as a condition for winning her in marriage. "If he doubts you, you will fail," she tells him. In the ensuing exchange between Culhwch and Ysbaddaden it is demonstrated again that Culhwch can show daring resolve. In the heroic tradition that is a step toward victory, though boasting without fulfillment by deeds is empty. Culhwch's confidence is saved from rashness and vanity by his trust in Arthur's help. As the dialogue with Ysbaddaden concludes, it becomes clear that Culhwch's adventure will not be solely a quest for a partner in marriage but a confrontation with a formidable oppressor. The shepherd Custennin has lost all but one son to the giant Ysbaddaden, and the giant asserts that Arthur himself is his vassal (though Arthur tells Culhwch he has never heard of Olwen's parents). To win Olwen requires killing her giant-father; Goreu son of Custennin and all whom the giant has oppressed would also find liberation thereby. The rare and difficult things (*anoetheu*) that must be obtained for the winning of Olwen emerge as implements for contending with the giant, as well as tests to prepare for mortal confrontation with him.

Another pig dominates the conclusion of the tale, the great wild boar named Twrch Trwyth. *Twrch* means "boar"; *trwyth* means "steeping, soaking" (the name may possibly derive from the Irish word *triath* "king;

boar"). In *Culhwch* Twrch Trwyth gets dunked in the Severn; a proficient swimmer, he is last seen plunging off the coast of Cornwall into the ocean! The wild pig with supernatural attributes is a motif of the earliest Celtic art. Other godlike figures from Celtic paganism survive in *Culhwch and Olwen*: Mabon son of Modron is believed to be derived from the Romano-British deity Apollo Maponos; and his mother, Modron, from the Celtic goddess Matrona. Gwyn son of Nudd appears elsewhere in Welsh literature as a leader of the Welsh fairy-troop. In *Culhwch* Gwyn son of Nudd is said to be filled with demons so that the earth might be spared; yet he is a follower of Arthur's, and Arthur both consults him and holds him in check.

Proven and equipped, Arthur's heroes come at last to trim the giant for his daughter's marriage. Trimming hair was a mark of homage by which a vassal entered a lord's service, or a kinship relationship was acknowledged, or—with reverse significance, as in the insult of plucking the beard—an enemy was subdued. Thus Arthur honorably trims Culhwch's hair and then invites him to name what he desires as a gift (*cyfarws*, a reward bestowed by a lord upon one who serves or follows him). Ysbaddaden, on the other hand, is shaved to the bone by Caw and then beheaded by Goreu. Caw's name is modified in an earlier episode to *Cadw*, meaning "to keep": he is a faithful custodian. *Goreu* means "best." The Best One and the Faithful One free all whom Ysbaddaden has oppressed in his tyranny; and Culhwch can marry the beautiful and faithful Olwen. What was originally pronounced against him as a curse has become for Culhwch his fulfilling happiness.

Though that is a happy ending for Culhwch, the tale is not sentimental in its depiction of the triumph of good over evil. Indeed, the mounting, almost endless difficulties and the need for every sort of assistance in meeting them present a cumulative image for the obstacles that impede the generous of heart. And notes of sadness and tragedy are struck. There is the melancholy figure of Culhwch's mother, who would care for her son beyond her death. Even Ysbaddaden is depicted as almost pathetic in his rage, almost tragic in his acceptance of his doom. The warrior family of Bwlch, Cyfwlch, and Sefwlch may strike us as comic when we first meet them in the long list of Arthur's companions (they have grandchildren named Oh, Cry, and Shriek). But when that same family is named by Ysbaddaden as one of the resources to be commandeered by Culhwch in his pursuit of Twrch Trwyth, the names suggest rather the violence and terror of battle. The grandchildren are now called "witches." The shift in tone is heightened by our ironic knowledge that these are already members of Arthur's entourage. The giant's naming of them foreshadows his own death.

But more significantly, this tale of triumph for Culhwch through the help of Arthur contains reminders of Arthur's tragedy—his death at Camlan against rebel forces. One moment is singularly poignant: Cei or Kei (the name I use, as the medieval manuscripts do, for readier identification as the Welsh character from whom the later, different Kay of the continental and English romances develops) has plucked the beard of Dillus and brought it to Arthur. We have previously learned that Kei has both warmth and coldness of nature. Arthur responds with a jesting insult: if Dillus were alive, he'd be your death! Kei takes offense, and in words of significance in this tale of helping and being helped, the narrator tells us that Kei would never help Arthur again. Arthur, unaware of that future defection, gallantly utters once more his generous question, "Which is best of the rare and difficult things to seek now?"

Bibliographic note: There is no critical edition of *Culhwch and Olwen*; one must use diplomatic editions of the two manuscripts in which the tale is extant, the *White Book of Rhydderch* (dated about 1350) and the *Red Book of Hergest* (1385–1410). Since the nineteenth century it has been included with ten other tales in a group known by the rather enigmatic name of the *Mabinogion.* Some of the major editions are: J. Gwenogvryn Evans and Sir John Rhys, *The Text of the Mabinogion and Other Welsh Tales from the Red Book of Hergest* (Oxford, 1887), with *Culhwch and Olwen* on pp. 100–143; and J. Gwenogvryn Evans, *The White Book Mabinogion* (Pwllheli, 1907); this has been reprinted with an introduction by R. M. Jones, under the Welsh title *Llyfr Gwyn Rhydderch* (University of Wales, 1973), with the text of *Culhwch and Olwen* on pp. 226–254, the incomplete White Book text being supplemented by the Red Book text (pp. 245–254).

I have consulted the translations of Lady Charlotte Guest (first published in 1849) in *The Mabinogion* (Everyman's Library, 1906), pp. 95–135; Gwyn Jones and Thomas Jones, *The Mabinogion* (Everyman's Library, 1949), pp. 95–136; Jeffrey Gantz, *The Mabinogion* (Penguin, 1976), pp. 134–176; and Patrick K. Ford, *The Mabinogi and Other Medieval Welsh Tales* (University of California, 1977), pp. 119–157. The reader of *Culhwch and Olwen* (as of Geoffrey of Monmouth) should also have at hand Rachel Bromwich's *Trioedd Ynys Prydein* (University of Wales, 1961; 2nd edition, 1978), for an exact and sensitive commentary on characters and motifs of early Welsh literary tradition. Patrick Ford's introduction to *The Mabinogi* has a valuable discussion of mythic themes in *Culhwch* and the other tales he translates. For literary relationships, particularly the Irish affinities, see Idris Foster on *Culhwch and Olwen* in R. S. Loomis, ed., *Arthurian Literature in the Middle Ages* (Oxford, 1959), pp. 31–39. A recent critical study of *Culhwch and Olwen* is that of Brynley Roberts in A. O. H. Jarman and G. R. Hughes, eds., *A Guide to Welsh Literature* (Christopher Davies, 1976), I, pp. 214–220.

Culhwch and Olwen

Cilydd son of Lord Celyddon wanted a wife as noble as himself. The wife he chose was Goleuddydd daughter of Lord Anlawdd.* After he lodged with her, the country went to prayers that they might have an heir. And through the prayers of the country, they had a son. And from the hour

---

*See the note on Welsh pronunciation in the introduction to Chapter II.

that she became pregnant, she went mad and would not approach any dwelling-place. When her time came, her right mind came to her. It came in a place where a swineherd was keeping a herd of pigs. And from fear of the pigs the queen gave birth. And the swineherd took the boy and came to the court. And the boy was baptized, and the name Culhwch was given him, because he was born in a pig-run. But the boy was noble; he was a first cousin to Arthur; and he was entrusted to the care of foster parents.

And after that the boy's mother, Goleuddydd daughter of Lord Anlawdd, became sick. She called her husband to her and said, "I shall die of this sickness, and you will want another wife. Nowadays wives are the bestowers of gifts. But it is bad for you to deprive your son. So I beg you not to choose a wife until you see a briar with two heads upon my grave."

He promised her that. She summoned her counselor to her and asked him to strip the grave every year so that nothing would grow on it. The queen died. Then the king sent a servant every morning to see whether anything was growing on the grave. After seven years the counselor forgot to do what he had promised the queen. One day while hunting the king came to the cemetery; he wanted to see the grave that might permit him to marry. And he saw the briar.

When he saw it, the king went to be advised where he could find a wife. One of his advisers said, "I know a woman well suited for you to marry. She is the wife of King Doged." They agreed to go seek her. And they killed the king and carried his wife home with them, and an only daughter she had with her. And they conquered that king's land.

One day the good woman went out for a walk and came to the house of an old hag in the town who had no teeth in her head. The queen said, "Old woman, tell me what I shall ask you, for God's sake. Where are the children of the man who took possession of me by violence?" The hag answered, "He has no children." The queen said, "A sad thing for me, to come to a childless man." The hag said, "There is no need to be sad. It is prophesied he will have an heir, and by you, since he has not had one by another woman. Besides, do not be sorrowful, he has one son."

The good woman went home happy. And she asked her husband, "What reason did you have to hide your children from me?" The king said, "I will not hide him." They sent messengers for the boy, and he came to the court. His stepmother said to him, "It would be good for you to marry, son, and I have a daughter fit for any nobleman in the world." The boy responded, "I am not yet old enough to marry." She said, "I shall lay a destiny on you: that your side will not strike a woman until you win Olwen daughter of Ysbaddaden Chief Giant."

The boy blushed, and love of the girl entered all his limbs, though he had not yet seen her. His father said to him, "Ho, my son, why are you reddening? What's the matter with you?"

"My stepmother has sworn that I shall not have a wife until I take Olwen daughter of Ysbaddaden Chief Giant."

"It's easy for you to do that, son," said his father to him. "Arthur is your first cousin. Go to Arthur so that he can trim your hair, and ask that of him as a gift for you."

The boy went off on a steed with a dapple-grey head. It was four winters old, firm-jointed and shell-hoofed, with a bridle of tubular gold in its mouth.

A costly gold saddle was under the boy, and two sharpened silver spears in his hand. A battle-ax was in his hand, from ridge to edge as long as a grown man's forearm. It would draw blood from the wind; it would be swifter than the swiftest dew from the stalk to the ground, when the dew is heaviest in June. A sword with a golden hilt was on his thigh, and its blade was gold. And on him a shield of braided gold having the color of the lightning of heaven in it and an ivory boss. And two greyhounds white of breast, dappled, were in front of him, with a collar of red gold about the neck of each one, from the swell of the shoulder to the ear. The one that was on the left side would be on the right, and the one that was on the right side would be on the left, like two sea-swallows playing around him. The four hooves of the steed cut four divots, like four swallows in the air over him, now above him, now under him. A four-cornered purple mantle was on him, with an apple of red gold at each corner; each apple was worth a hundred cattle. There was precious gold worth three hundred cattle in his footgear of shoes and stirrups, from the top of his thigh to the end of his toe. Not a strand of hair on him out of place, so light was the steed's pace under him, heading for the gate of Arthur's court.

The youth said, "Is there a gatekeeper?"

"There is. And you, you may lose your head because you ask. I am gatekeeper for Arthur every first day of January. But my deputies for the rest of the year are none other than Huandaw and Gogigwr and Llaesgymyn and Penpingion, who goes on his head to spare his feet, neither heavenward nor earthward, but like a rolling stone on the floor of the court."

"Open the gate."

"I will not."

"Why won't you open it?"

"Knife has gone into meat and drink into the drinking horn, and there is a thronging in Arthur's hall. No one may enter but the son of a king of legitimate rule or a craftsman who brings his craft. There is mash for your dogs and grain for your horse and hot hearty chops for you, with wine overflowing and delightful songs before you. Food for fifty men awaits you in the guest house; men from afar eat there, and the sons of foreign lands who offer no craft in Arthur's court. It will not be worse for you there than with Arthur in his court. A woman to sleep with you and delightful songs before your two knees. Tomorrow at midmorning, when the gate is opened for the throng that came here today, the gate will be opened for you first, and you will sit in Arthur's hall wherever you choose, from its upper to its lower end."

The youth said, "I will do none of that. If you open the door, it is well. If you do not open it, I will bring shame on your lord and slander on you. And I shall raise three shouts at the door of this gate that will be as loud at the top of Pengwaedd in Cornwall as in the depths of Dinsol in the North and in Esgeir Oerfel in Ireland. And every pregnant woman in this court will miscarry, and for those who are not pregnant, their wombs will become an affliction so that they will never be pregnant from this day on."

Glewlwyd Mighty-grip answered, "Whatever you may shout regarding the laws of Arthur's court, you will not be let in till I go speak to Arthur first."

And Glewlwyd came into the hall. Arthur said to him, "Have you news from the gate?"

"I do. Two-thirds of my life are past, and two-thirds of yours. I was once in Fort Se and Asse, in Sach and Salach, in Lotor and Ffotor. I was once in India the Great and India the Less. I was once in the battle of the two Ynyrs, when the twelve hostages were brought from Llychlyn. And I was once in Europe. I was in Africa, and in the islands of Corsica, and Fort Brythwch and Brythach and Nerthach. I was there when you slew the band of Gleis son of Merin, when you slew Black Mil son of Dugum. I was there when you conquered Greece in the East. I was once in Fort Oeth and Anoeth and Fort Nefenhyr. Nine fair generous rulers we saw there. But I never saw a man so handsome as the one who is now at the door of the gate."

Arthur said, "If you came in walking, go out running. And whoever looks at the light and shuts his eyes, an injunction on him. Let some serve with golden drinking horns and some with hot hearty chops, till there be enough food and drink for him. It's a disgrace to leave in wind and rain such a man as you speak of."

Kei [Cei, Kay] said, "By the hand of my friend, if my counsel were taken, the laws of the court would not be broken for him."

"Not so, good Kei. We are noblemen so long as we are sought after. The greater the reward we give, the greater will be our nobility and our praise and our glory."

And Glewlwyd came to the gate and opened the gate to Culhwch. And Culhwch did not dismount at the gate on the mounting block, as everyone did, but came inside on his steed. Culhwch said, "Hail, chief prince of this island! Greetings to the lower end of this house no less than to the upper! Greetings equally to your lords and your men and your warriors. May none be without a share of the greeting I give you. May your grace be as full as my greeting, and your faith, and your glory in this island!"

"By God's truth, so be it, chieftain! Greetings to you as well! Sit between two of the warriors, with delightful song before you, and the privilege of an heir upon you, a successor to a kingdom, as long as you are here. And when I distribute my goods to guests and men from afar, it shall be with your hand that I shall begin in this court."

The youth said, "I did not come here to seek food and drink. But if I get my gift, I shall give recompense for it and praise it. If I do not get it, I shall deprive you of your renown as far as your fame has reached to the four quarters of the world."

Arthur said, "Though you do not dwell here, chieftain, you shall have the gift your mouth and tongue may name, as far as the wind dries, as far as the rain wets, as far as the sun runs, as far as the sea spreads, as far as there is earth—except for my ship and my mantle, and Caledfwlch [Hard Breach] my sword, and Rhongomyniad [Lance Hewer] my spear, and Wynebgwrthucher [Face of Evening] my shield, and Carnwennan [Bright Hilt] my knife, and Gwenhwyfar [Guinevere] my wife."

"God's truth on that?"

"You shall have it gladly. Name what you will."

"I will. I want my hair trimmed."

"You shall have that." Arthur took a golden comb and scissors with silver handles, and he combed his hair. And he asked who he was; Arthur said, "My heart grows tender towards you. I know you come of my blood. Say who you are."

"I shall: Culhwch son of Cilydd son of Lord Celyddon, by Goleuddydd daughter of Lord Anlawdd, my mother."

Arthur said, "It is true: you are a first cousin to me. Name what you will, and you shall have it, whatever your mouth and tongue may name."

"God's truth to me on that? And the truth of your kingdom?"

"You shall have it gladly."

"I ask you to get me Olwen daughter of Ysbaddaden Chief Giant. And I call upon your warriors to confirm this."

The Catalog of Arthur's Companions

To confirm that gift from Arthur he called upon Kei, and Bedwyr [Bedivere], and Greidawl Gallddofydd, and Gwythyr son of Greidawl, and Greid son of Eri, and Cynddylig the Guide, and Tathal Open-deceit, and Maelwys son of Baeddan, and Cnychwr son of Nes [Conchobar mac Nesa], and Cubert son of Daere, and Fercos son of Poch [Fergus mac Róich], and Lluber Beutach, and Corfil Berfach [Conall Cernach], and Gwyn son of Esni, and Gwyn son of Nwyfre [Firmament], and Gwyn son of Nudd, and Edern son of Nudd, and Cadwy son of Geraint, and Fflewdwr the Flame-lord, and Rhuawn the Strong son of Dorath, and Bradwen son of Prince Moren, and Prince Moren himself, and Dalldaf son of Cimin Cof, and the son of Alun of Dyfed, and the son of Saidi, and the son of Gwryon, and Uchdryd Protector in Battle, and Cynwas Cwryfagyl, and Gwrhyr Rich-in-Cattle, and Isberyr Cat-claw, and Gallgoid Gofynynad, and Duach and Brathach and Nerthach, sons of Gwawrddur Cyrfach [Steel-king the Hunch-back]—from the uplands of Hell did these men come. And Cilydd Hundred-holds, and Hundred-holds Hundred-hands, and Bog Hundred-claws, and Esgeir Gulhwch the Reed-cutter, and Door Iron-fist, and Glewlwyd Mighty-grip, and Llwch Stormy-hand, and Restless the Winged, and Sinnoch son of Seventh, and Wadu son of Seventh, and Naw son of Seventh, and Gwen-wynwyn son of Naw son of Seventh, and Bedyw son of Seventh, and Gobrwy son of Echel Mighty-thigh, and Echel Mighty-thigh himself. And Prince son of Roycol, and Dadweir the Blind-headed, and Garwyli son of Gwythawg Gwyr, and Gwythawg Gwyr himself. And Excess son of Ricca, and Menw son of Teirgwaedd [Little Son of Three Cries], and Enough son of Too-much, and Selyf [Solomon] son of Sinoid, and Gwsg son of Lineage, and Strength son of Strong, and Brave-lad son of Tryffin, and Boar son of Perif, and Boar son of Restless, and Iona, King of France, and Watch son of Watch-dog. And Teregud son of Iaen, and Sulien son of Iaen, and Bradwen son of Iaen, and Moren son of Iaen, and Siawn son of Iaen, and Cradawg son of Iaen—men of Fort Dathal, kin of Arthur's on his father's side.

Scorn son of Caw, and Iustig son of Caw, and Honor son of Caw, and Angawdd son of Caw, and Smith son of Caw, and Holly son of Caw, and Stalk son of Caw, and Patron-saint son of Caw, and Gwyngad son of Caw, and Path son of Caw, and Red son of Caw, and Meilyg son of Caw, and Cynwal son of Caw, and Protector son of Caw, and Striker son of Caw, and

Someone son of Caw, and Gildas son of Caw, and Calcas son of Caw, and Huail son of Caw—he never begged at a lord's hand.

And Samson Dry-lip, and Taliesin Chief of Bards, and Manawydan son of Llŷr, and Llary son of Lord Casnar, and Sberin son of Fflergant king of Brittany, and Saranhon son of Short-couch, and Ground son of Acre, and Anynnawg son of Menw son of Teirgwaedd, and Gwyn son of Nwyfre [Firmament], and Flame son of Firmament, and Geraint son of Erbin, and Ermid son of Erbin, and Dywel son of Erbin, and Gwyn son of Ermid, and Cyndrwyn son of Ermid, and Arrogant One-cloak, and Eiddon the Magnanimous, and Rheiddwn Arwy, and Excess son of Ricca—a brother to Arthur on his mother's side, his father being the chief elder of Cornwall. And Llawnrodded the Bearded, and Nodawl Cut-beard, and Berth son of Cado, and Rheiddwn son of Beli, and Isgofan the Generous, and Isgawyn son of Banon. And Morfran son of Tegid; no man put his weapon into him at Camlan, he was so ugly; everyone supposed he was a devil assisting; he had hair on him like a stag's hair. And Sandde Angel-face; no man put his spear in him at Camlan, he was so fair; everyone supposed he was an angel assisting. And Saint Cynwyl, one of the three men who escaped from Camlan; he parted last from Arthur, on his horse Hengroen [Old-skin].

And Uchdryd son of Erim, and Eus son of Erim. And Winged Henwas [Old Servant] son of Erim, and Henbeddestyr [Old Walker] son of Erim, and Sgilti Lightfoot son of Erim. Three features had these three men: Henbeddestyr never found a man who ran as fast as he did, on horseback or on foot; Henwas the Winged, no four-footed creature could ever travel alongside him the length of an acre, let alone a distance farther than that; Sgilti Lightfoot, when the impulse was on him to go on his lord's errand, he never took a road, provided he knew where he was going, but if there were trees, he would go on the tops of the trees, and if there was a mountain, he would go on the tips of the reeds, and all his life, not a stalk bent under his feet, much less broke, he was so light.

Teithi Hen [Old Right] son of Gwynnan, whose land the sea overran and who himself just barely escaped and came to Arthur; his knife had this feature, that from the time he came here, the hilt never stayed on it, and because of that, a sickness developed in him and a weakness as long as he lived, and he died of that. And Carneddwr son of Gofynion the Old, and Gwenwynwyn son of Naf, Arthur's first warrior, and Llygadrudd Emys [Red-eye the Stallion], and Gwrfoddw the Old (they were Arthur's uncles, his mother's brothers). Culfanawyd son of Gwryon, and Llenlleawg the Irishman from the headland of Gamon, and Dyfnwal the Bald, and Dunarth the King of the North. Terynon Twryf Liant, and Tegfan the Lame, and Tegyr Talgellawg. Gwrddywal son of Efrei, and Morgant the Generous. Gwystyl son of Nwython, and Rhun son of Nwython, and Llwydeu son of Nwython, and Gwydre son of Llwydeu by Gwenabwy daughter of Caw, his mother (Huail his uncle stabbed him, and for that there was hatred between Arthur and Huail, because of the wound).

Drem son of Dremidydd [Sight son of Vision] who saw from Celliwig in Cornwall as far as Pen Blathaon in Scotland when a fly would rise in the morning with the sun. And Eidoel son of Nêr, and Glwyddyn the Steward, who built Ehangwen [Spacious-fair], Arthur's hall. Cynyr Fair-beard; Kei was said to be son to him, who said to his wife, "If there is something of me in your son, girl, his heart will always be cold, and there will be no warmth in his hands; another feature will he have if he is my son, he will be stubborn; another feature will he have, when he carries a load, great or small, it will never be seen either from in front or from behind; another feature will he have, no one will stand water and fire as well as he; another feature will he have, there will not be a servant or officer like him."

Henwas [Old Lad] and Hen Wyneb [Old Face] and Hen Gedymddeith [Old Companion]. Gallgoig, another one; whatever town he came to, though there were three hundred homesteads there, if he needed anything, he never allowed sleep on a man's eye while he was there. Berwyn son of Cyrenyr, and Paris, King of France (for whom the citadel is called Paris). Osla Big-knife, who carried Bronllafn Ferllydan [Sloping Blade, Short and Wide]; when Arthur and his armies came to the edge of a river, a narrow place was found on the water, and his knife in its sheath was placed across the river, and it would be enough of a bridge for the armies of the Three Realms of Britain [England, Wales, and Scotland] and its Three Adjacent Islands [Wight, Man, and Anglesey] and their booty.

Gwyddawg son of Menestyr, who killed Kei (and Arthur killed him and his brothers to avenge Kei). Garanwyn son of Kei, and Amren son of Bedwyr [Bedivere]. And Eli, and Myr, and Rheu Rhwydd Dyrys [Rheu the Generous and Wild], and Rhun Rhuddwern [Red-alder], and Eli, and Trachmyr, Arthur's chief huntsman. And Llwydeu son of Cel Coed, and Huabwy son of Gwryon, and Gwyn Godyfron, and Gweir Dathar the Attendant, and Gweir son of Cadellin the Pay-master. And Gweir Treacherous-valor, and Gweir Bright-shaft (uncles of Arthur, his mother's brothers).

The sons of Llwch Stormy-hand from beyond the violent sea. Llenlleawg the Irishman, and Ardderchawg [the Excellent One] of Britain. Cas [Enmity] son of Saidi, Gwrfan Rough-hair, Gwilenhin the King of France, Gwitard son of Aedd the King of Ireland, Garselid the Irishman, Panawr the Chief of the Host, Atlendor son of Naf, Gwyn Hywar the overseer of Cornwall and Devon, one of the nine who plotted the battle of Camlan. Celi, and Cuel, and Gilla Stag-leg (he would leap three hundred acres in one bound, the chief leaper of Ireland).

Sol, and Gwadyn Osol, and Gwadyn Oddeith [Blazing Sole]. Sol could stand all day on one foot. If Gwadyn Osol stood on top of the greatest mountain in the world, it would become a level plain under his foot. When something hard met Gwadyn Oddeith, the bright fire of his soles was like the hot metal when it is drawn from the forge; he cleared the way for Arthur in battle.

Tall Erwm and Tall Atrwm. The day they came to a feast, they would seize three districts for themselves, feasting till noon and drinking till night. When they went to sleep, they would consume the heads of insects from hunger, as if they had not eaten food before. When they went to a feast, they left neither fat nor lean, neither hot nor cold, neither sour nor sweet, neither fresh nor salt, neither boiled nor raw.

Huarwar son of Halwn, who, as his reward, asked Arthur for his fill. He was one of the three great plagues of Cornwall and Devon when they got him his fill. Not a faint smile was found on him except when he was full.

Gwarae Golden-hair. The two whelps of the bitch Rhymhi. Gwyddrud, and Gwydden the Obscure. Sugyn son of Sugnedydd [Suck son of Sucker], who would suck up the sea on which there were three hundred ships till there was nothing but dry beach; he had red breast-fever. Cacamwri, Arthur's servant; let him be shown a barn, though the harvest of thirty plows were in it, he would strike it with an iron flail till it was no better for the planks and the cross-beams and the side-beams than for the small oats in the bin on the floor of the barn.

Llwng [Damp], and Dygyflwng, and Anoeth the Bold. And Tall Eiddyl and Tall Amren (they were two servants of Arthur). And Gwefyl son of Gwastad [Lip son of Constant]; the day he was sad, he would let one of his lips down to his navel and the other would be a hood upon his head.

Uchdryd Cross-beard, who would cast his projecting red beard across fifty rafters in Arthur's hall. Elidyr the Guide. Ysgyrdaf and Ysgudydd; they were servants of Gwenhwyfar [Guinevere]; on their errand, their feet were as swift as their thoughts. Brys [Haste] son of Brysethach, from the Hill of the Black Fernbrake in Britain. And Gruddlwyn Gor [Cheek-bush the Dwarf].

Bwlch [Breach] and Cyfwlch [Perfect] and Sefwlch, sons of Cleddyf Cyfwlch [Perfect Sword], grandsons of Cleddyf Difwlch [Unbroken Sword]. Their three shields were three brilliant gleams; their three spears were three pointed thrusts; their three swords were three sharp carvers. Glas [Blue], Glesig, Gleisad, their three dogs. Call [Prudent], Cuall [Foolish], Cafall [Steed], their three horses. Hwyrddyddwg [Late-bearer] and Drwg-ddyddwg [Ill-bearer] and Llwyrddyddwg [Full-bearer], their three wives. Och [Oh] and Garym [Cry] and Diasbad [Shriek], their three grandchildren. Lluched [Plague] and Neued [Want] and Eisywed [Need], their three daughters. Drwg [Bad] and Gwaeth [Worse] and Gwaethaf Oll [Worst of All], their three maidservants.

Eheubryd daughter of Cyfwlch, Gorasgwrn daughter of Nerth [Big-bone daughter of Strength], Gwaeddan daughter of Cynfelyn Ceudod, the Half-wit.

Dwn the High-spirited Chieftain. Eiladar son of Pen Llarcan, Cynedyr the Wild son of Hetwn the Pay-master. Sawyl the Overlord, Gwalchmai [Gawain] son of Gwyar, Gwalhafed son of Gwyar. Gwrhyr the Interpreter of Languages, who knew all languages. And Cethtrwm the Priest.

Clust son of Clustfeinad [Ear son of Hearer]; if he were buried seven fathoms in the earth, he would hear an ant fifty miles away when it rose from its couch in the morning. Medyr son of Medredydd [Skill son of Hitter], who from Celliwig would hit a wren on Esgeir Oerfel in Ireland precisely through its two legs. Gwiawn Cat-eye, who would cut a corner [of a lid] on the eye of a gnat without harm to the eye. Ol son of Olwydd [Track son of Tracker]; seven years before he was born, his father's pigs were stolen, and when he grew to be a man, he tracked the pigs and came home with them in seven herds. Bidwini [Baudwin] the Bishop, who blessed Arthur's food and drink.

The gentle, gold-torqued maidens of this island. Besides Gwenhwyfar [Guinevere], the first lady of this island, and her sister, Gwenhwyach, and Rathtyen, the only daughter of Clememyl, Celemon daughter of Kei, and Tangwen daughter of Gweir Dathar, the Attendant. Gwen Alarch [White Swan] daughter of Cynwal Hundred-pigs, Eurneid daughter of Clydno Eidin, Eneuawg daughter of Bedwyr [Bedivere]. Enrhydreg daughter of Tuduathar, Gwenwledyr daughter of Gwaredur the Hunchback, Erdudfyl daughter of Tryffin, Eurolwyn daughter of Gwyddolwyn the Dwarf. Teleri daughter of Peul, Indeg daughter of Garwy the Tall. Morfudd daughter of Urien of Rheged. Beautiful Gwenlliant the Great-hearted Maiden. Creiddylad daughter of Lludd Silver-hand, the girl of most grandeur who ever lived in the three realms of Britain and its three adjacent islands; and for her Gwythyr son of Greidawl and Gwyn son of Nudd fight every May Day till Doomsday. Ellylw daughter of Neol Cyncrog (she lived for three generations). Essyllt [Isolde] Fair-neck and Essyllt Slender-neck.

In the name of all these did Culhwch son of Cilydd implore his gift.

The Quest for Olwen

Arthur said, "Ah, chieftain, I have never heard of the maiden you speak of, nor of her parents. I shall gladly send messengers to find her. Give me time to find her." The youth said, "Gladly. From this night till the same night next year."

And then Arthur sent messengers to every land in his domain to find the maiden. From that night till the same night a year later the messengers went wandering. By the end of the year Arthur's messengers had found nothing. And then Culhwch said, "Everyone has received his gift, but I am still without one. I shall leave and take your honor with me."

Kei said, "Ah, chieftain, you scorn Arthur too much. Come with us; till you say she is nowhere in the world or till we find her, we shall not part from you." Then Kei stood up. Kei had this feature, that for nine nights and nine days he would hold his breath under water. For nine nights and nine days he would go without sleep. A sword stroke of Kei's no physician could heal. Well endowed was Kei: he would be as tall as the highest tree in the wood when it pleased him. Another feature he had: his natural heat was so great that when it rained hardest, whatever was in his hand would be dry a handsbreadth above and below his hand. And when it was coldest for his companions, that heat would be kindling for them to light a fire.

Arthur called on Bedwyr [Bedivere], who never feared a quest on which Kei would go. It was true of Bedwyr that no one in this island was as handsome as he, except Arthur and Drych son of Cibddar [Mirror son of Cup-lord]. And this too, that though he were one-handed, three warriors would not draw blood faster than he in the same field with him. Another feature he had, that there would be one thrust of his spear to nine counter-thrusts.

Arthur called on Cynddylig the Guide, "Go on this quest for me with the chieftain." He was no less able a guide in a land he had never seen than in his own land. He called Gwrhyr, Interpreter of Languages, who knew all languages. He called Gwalchmai [Gawain] the son of Gwyar, because he never came home without the quest he had gone seeking. He was the best on foot and the best on horseback. He was Arthur's nephew, his sister's son, and his first cousin. Arthur called on Menw son of Teirgwaedd, because if they came to a heathen land, he could cast a spell on them so that no one would see them, but they would see everybody.

They went off till they came to a great open plain. There they saw a fort that was the greatest fort in the world. They walked that day. When they thought they were near to the fort, they were no nearer than before. And the second and the third day they walked. And they barely came there. But when they came to the same field as the fort, they saw a great flock of sheep there without limit or end to it, and a shepherd on top of a mound tending the sheep. He had a cloak of skins on him and at his side a furry mastiff larger than a stallion of nine winters. It was his custom that he never lost a lamb, much less a grown animal. No company had ever gone past him that he had not done them injury or death. His breath would burn every dead tree and bush on the field right to the ground.

Kei said, "Gwrhyr, Interpreter of Languages, go talk to that man there."

"Kei, I promised to go only as far as you would go too."

"Let us go together."

Menw the son of Teirgwaedd said, "Do not be afraid to go there. I will cast a spell on the dog so that he will not hurt anyone."

They came to where the shepherd was. And they said to him, "You are well off, shepherd."

"May it never be better for you than for me."

"By God, yes, for you are a chief!"

"There is no harm can damage me but for my wife."

"Whose are the sheep you are tending, and who owns the fort there?"

"Slow-witted men that you are. It is known throughout the world that it is the fort of Ysbaddaden Chief Giant."

"And you, who are you?"

"Custennin son of Mynwyedig am I. And because of my wife, my brother Ysbaddaden Chief Giant did me damage. And you, who are you?"

"Messengers of Arthur are here, seeking Olwen."

"Ah, men! God help you! For all the world, do not do it! No one has come seeking that who went away with his life."

The shepherd stood up; and as he got up, Culhwch gave him a golden ring. The shepherd tried to wear the ring, but it would not go on him. And he put it on the finger of his glove and went home and gave the glove to his wife. She took the ring from the glove. "From where did this ring come to you, husband?" she said. "It is not often that you have treasure."

"I went to the sea to find sea-food, and look! I saw a dead body coming in with the waves. I never saw a dead body as beautiful as that. And on its finger I found this ring."

"Alas, husband, the sea does not leave the dead in it beautiful. Show me that body."

"Wife, he whose body it is you will soon see here!"

"Who is he?" said his wife.

"Culhwch son of Cilydd son of Lord Celyddon, by Goleuddydd daughter of Lord Anlawdd, his mother; he has come to seek Olwen."

Two feelings were hers: joy that her nephew, her sister's son, was coming to her; and sorrow because she had never seen anyone go away with his life who had come on that quest.

They came to the gate of the court of the shepherd Custennin. She heard the sound of their coming. She ran to meet them joyfully. Kei took a log from the woodpile. And she came to meet them, to try to put her hands around their necks. Kei put the stake between her two hands. She squeezed the stake till it became a twisted twig. Kei said, "Woman, if you had squeezed me like that, no one else would ever need to love me. That's a bad love!"

They came to the house, and they were attended. After a while, when they all went thronging, the woman opened a stone chest that was in front of the chimney, and a lad with curly yellow hair rose from it. Gwrhyr said, "It would be a pity to hide a lad like this. I know it is for no fault of his that he is punished."

The woman said, "He is the remnant. Ysbaddaden Chief Giant has slain twenty-three of my sons, and I have no more hope of this one than of the others."

Kei said, "Let him keep company with me, and we shall not be slain except together."

They ate. The woman said, "What have you come here for?"

"We come to seek Olwen."

"For God's sake, since no one from the fort has seen you yet, turn back!"

"God knows we shall not turn back till we see the girl. Will she come where she may be seen?"

"She comes here every Saturday to wash her head. And in the basin where she washes, she leaves all her rings, and neither she nor her messenger ever comes for them."

"Will she come here if she is sent for?"

"God knows I will not kill my own dear soul! I will not trap one who trusts me. But if you pledge to do her no injury, I will send for her."

"We give our word," they said.

She was sent for. And she came, with a robe of flame-red silk about her; and a torque of red gold around the girl's neck, and precious pearls on it and red gems. Her hair was yellower than the flowers of the broom. Her flesh was whiter than the foam of the wave. Her palms and her fingers were whiter than buds of sweet clover amid the fine gravel of a welling spring. Not the eye of the mewed hawk, not the eye of the thrice-mewed falcon, not any eye was lovelier than hers was. Her two breasts were whiter than the breast of the white swan; redder were her two cheeks than the reddest foxgloves. Whoever saw her would be filled with love for her. Four white clovers would grow up behind her wherever she went. And because of that, she was called Olwen [White-track].

She entered the house and sat beside Culhwch on the front bench, and as soon as he saw her, he recognized her. Culhwch said to her, "Ah, girl, it is you that I have loved. Come with me."

"I cannot do that, for sin would be charged to you and to me. My father has asked me to pledge not to leave without his counsel, because there is life for him only until I go off with a husband. But I'll give you advice, if you will take it. Go ask my father for me. And however much he may ask of you, promise to get it. And you shall win me. But if he doubts a thing, you will not win me, and it will be well for you if you escape with your life."

"I promise all that, and I shall get it."

She went to her chamber. They got up to follow her to the fort. And they killed nine gatekeepers who were at nine gates, without a man crying out, and nine mastiffs without one of them squealing. And they went on to the hall. They said, "Greetings to you, Ysbaddaden Chief Giant, from God and man!"

"And you, where are you going?"

"We come to seek your daughter Olwen for Culhwch son of Cilydd."

"Where are my worthless servants and my louts?" he said. "Raise the forks under my two eyelids so that I can see my intended son-in-law." That was done. "Come here tomorrow. I will give you some answer."

They arose, and Ysbaddaden Chief Giant seized one of the three poisoned stone spears that were at his hand and threw it after them. And Bedwyr caught it and threw it back and pierced Ysbaddaden Chief Giant squarely through the kneecap. Said the giant, "Cursed savage son-in-law! I shall walk the worse on a slope. The poisoned iron has hurt me like a gadfly's sting. Cursed be the smith who made it and the anvil he made it on, it is so sore!"

They lodged that night in the house of Custennin. On the next day they came to the hall with majesty and with fine combs fixed in their hair. They said, "Ysbaddaden Chief Giant, give us your daughter in exchange for her dowry and her marriage fee to you and her two kinswomen. And unless you give her, you will meet your death because of her."

"She and her four great-grandmothers and her four great-grandfathers are still alive. I have to confer with them."

"You will do that," they said. "Let us go to our food." As they got up, he took the second stone spear that was at his hand and threw it after them. And Menw the son of Teirgwaedd caught it and threw it back and pierced him in the middle of the breast, so that it came out in the small of the back.

"Cursed savage son-in-law! The hard iron has hurt me like the bite of a many-mouthed leech. Cursed be the forge where it was heated. When I go up a hill, there will be tightness in the chest for me and stomachache and frequent queasiness."

They went to their food. And on the third day they came to the court. They said, "Ysbaddaden Chief Giant, do not shoot at us any more. Do not seek harm for yourself and mortal injury and death."

"Where are my servants? Raise the forks—my eyelids have fallen over the balls of my eyes—so that I can look at my intended son-in-law."

They got up. And as they got up, he took the third poisoned stone spear and threw it after them. And Culhwch caught it. And he threw it back just as he wanted to and pierced him through the eyeball so that it came out at the nape of the neck.

"Cursed savage son-in-law! So long as I am left alive, the sight of my eyes will be the worse. When I go against the wind, they will water. There will be headache and dizziness for me at every new moon. Cursed be the forge where it was heated! The poisoned iron has pierced me like the bite of a mad dog."

They went to their food. The next day they came to the court. They said, "Do not shoot at us, nor seek the deadly injury and harm and martyrdom that are upon you—and what might be worse, if you keep after it. Give us your daughter."

"Where is he who is said to be seeking my daughter?"

"It is I who seek her, Culhwch son of Cilydd."

"Come here where I may see you." A chair was placed under him, facing him. Ysbaddaden Chief Giant said, "Is it you who seek my daughter?"

"It is I who seek her."

"I want your pledge that you will not do me less than justice."

"You have my pledge."

"When I have got what I shall name to you, you will get my daughter."

"Name what you will."

"I will. Do you see that great brushwood there?"

"I do."

"I want it uprooted from the earth and burnt on the ground so that the char and its ashes will be fertilizer for it. And I want it plowed and sown so that by morning when the dew dries, it will be ripe, and from it, food and drink may be made for your wedding guests and the girl's. And I want all this done in one day."

"It's easy for me to manage that, though you think it's not easy."

"Though you manage that, there's something you won't get: a farmer to farm that land. And no one can do it but Amaethon son of Dôn. He won't come with you freely, and you can't force him."

"It's easy for me to manage that, though you think it's not easy."

"Though you manage that, there's something you won't get: Gofannon son of Dôn to come to the top of the field to tend the iron blades. He won't work freely except for a legitimate king; you can't force him."

"It's easy for me to manage that, though you think it's not easy."

"Though you manage that, there's something you won't get: the two oxen of Gwlwlydd Wineu, yoked together to plow that hard land well. He won't give them freely, and you can't force him."

"It's easy for me to manage that, though you think it's not easy."

"Though you manage that, there's something you won't get: I want the Yellow-white and the Speckled Ox yoked together."

"It's easy for me to manage that, though you think it's not easy."

"Though you manage that, there's something you won't get: the two horned oxen, one from the farther side of Mynydd Bannawg [the Horned Mountain], and the other from this side; and to drive them together after the same plow. They are Nyniaw and Peibiaw, whom God turned into oxen for their sins."

"It's easy for me to manage that, though you think it's not easy."

"Though you manage that, there's something you won't get: do you see that red tilled ground there?"

"Yes."

"When I first met the girl's mother, nine hestors [eighteen bushels] of flaxseed were sown there; neither black nor white has come from it yet. And I still have that measure. I want it sown in the new ground, so that it may become a white linen veil for my daughter's head at your wedding-feast."

"It's easy for me to manage that, though you think it's not easy."

"Though you manage that, there's something you won't get: honey nine times sweeter than the honey of the first swarm, without drone or bees, to make bragget for the feast."

"It's easy for me to manage that, though you think it's not easy."

"Though you manage that, there's something you won't get: the cup of Llwyr son of Llwyrion, that has the best drinks in it. For there's no vessel in the world except it that can hold that strong drink. You won't get it from him freely, and you can't force him."

"It's easy for me to manage that, though you think it's not easy."

"Though you manage that, there's something you won't get: the basket of Gwyddneu Garanhir. If the world, three times nine men at a time, came around it, everyone would get from it the food he wanted, as he liked it. I'd like to eat from it the night my daughter sleeps with you. He won't give it freely to anyone, and you can't force him."

"It's easy for me to manage that, though you think it's not easy."

"Though you manage that, there's something you won't get: the drinking horn of Gwlgawd Gododdin, for pouring for us that night. He won't give it freely, and you can't force him."

"It's easy for me to manage that, though you think it's not easy."

"Though you manage that, there's something you won't get: the harp of Teirtu to entertain me that night. When a man pleases, it plays itself; when wished, it is silent. He will not give it freely, and you can't force him."

"It's easy for me to manage that, though you think it's not easy."

"Though you manage that, there's something you won't get: the birds of Rhiannon, that waken the dead and put the living to sleep; these I would have entertain me that night."

"It's easy for me to manage that, though you think it's not easy."

"Though you manage that, there's something you won't get: the cauldron of Diwrnach the Irishman, the Steward of Odgar son of Aedd, King of Ireland, to boil the meat for your wedding guests."

"It's easy for me to manage that, though you think it's not easy."

"Though you manage that, there's something you won't get: I have to wash my head and shave my beard. I want the tusk of Ysgithyrwyn Chief Boar for shaving me. It won't do me any good unless it's pulled from his head alive."

"It's easy for me to manage that, though you think it's not easy."

"Though you manage that, there's something you won't get: no one in the world can pull it from his head but Odgar son of Aedd, King of Ireland."

"It's easy for me to manage that, though you think it's not easy."

"Though you manage that, there's something you won't get: I don't trust anyone to keep the tusk but Cadw [Caw] of Scotland. The sixty districts of Scotland are subject to him. He won't come freely from his kingdom, and he can't be forced."

"It's easy for me to manage that, though you think it's not easy."

"Though you manage that, there's something you won't get: I have to stretch out my hairs to shave myself. I'll never stretch them out unless we get the blood of the Dark Black Witch, daughter of the Pale White Witch, from the head of the Valley of Sorrow in the uplands of Hell."

"It's easy for me to manage that, though you think it's not easy."

"Though you manage that, there's something you won't get: I can't benefit from the blood unless we get it warm. There's no vessel in the world that keeps the warmth of a liquid put inside it except the bottles of Gwyddolwyn the Dwarf that keep the warmth in them from when liquid is put inside them in the east till they are carried to the west. He won't give them freely, and you can't force him."

"It's easy for me to manage that, though you think it's not easy."

"Though you manage that, there's something you won't get: some may desire milk. There's no way to get milk for everybody till we get the bottles of Rhynnon Rough-beard. No liquid ever goes sour in them. He won't give them freely to anyone, and he can't be forced."

"It's easy for me to manage that, though you think it's not easy."

"Though you manage that, there's something you won't get: no comb and scissors are in the world by which to dress my hair, it's so rough, except the comb and scissors that are between the two ears of the boar Twrch Trwyth son of Lord Taredd. He won't give them freely, and he can't be forced."

"It's easy for me to manage that, though you think it's not easy."

"Though you manage that, there's something you won't get: Twrch Trwyth can't be hunted till you catch Drudwyn the young dog of Greid son of Eri."

"It's easy for me to manage that, though you think it's not easy."

"Though you manage that, there's something you won't get: there's no leash in the world that will hold him except the leash of Bog Hundred-claws."

"It's easy for me to manage that, though you think it's not easy."

"Though you manage that, there's something you won't get: there's no collar in the world that will hold the leash except the collar of Hundred-holds Hundred-hands."

"It's easy for me to manage that, though you think it's not easy."

"Though you manage that, there's something you won't get: the chain of Cilydd Hundred-holds to hold the collar and the leash together."

"It's easy for me to manage that, though you think it's not easy."

"Though you manage that, there's something you won't get: no huntsman in the world is capable of hunting with that dog except Mabon son of Modron, who was taken from his mother when he was three nights old. It's not known where he is, nor in what condition, whether alive or dead."

"It's easy for me to manage that, though you think it's not easy."

"Though you manage that, there's something you won't get: White Dun-mane, the horse of Gweddw, swift as a wave is he, to be under Mabon for hunting Twrch Trwyth. He won't give him freely, and you can't force him."

"It's easy for me to manage that, though you think it's not easy."

"Though you manage that, there's something you won't get: Mabon will never be found nor will it be known where he is until you find Eidoel son of Aer, his foremost kinsman, for he will be unrelenting in searching for him. He is his first cousin."

"It's easy for me to manage that, though you think it's not easy."

"Though you manage that, there's something you won't get: Garselid the Irishman. He is the chief huntsman of Ireland. Twrch Trwyth will never be hunted without him."

"It's easy for me to manage that, though you think it's not easy."

"Though you manage that, there's something you won't get: a leash from the beard of Dillus the Bearded, because there's nothing else that can hold those two young dogs [the two whelps of the bitch Rhymhi; an omitted request?]. And you can't use it unless it's pulled from his beard while he's alive and plucked with wooden tweezers. He won't let anyone do that to him while he's alive, and it's useless dead, because it'll be brittle."

"It's easy for me to manage that, though you think it's not easy."

"Though you manage that, there's something you won't get: no huntsman in the world can hold those two young dogs except Cynedyr the Wild, son of Hetwn the Leper. He's nine times wilder than the wildest wild animal on the mountain. You'll never get him, and you'll never get my daughter."

"It's easy for me to manage that, though you think it's not easy."

"Though you manage that, there's something you won't get: you won't hunt Twrch Trwyth until you get Gwyn son of Nudd, in whom God has put the spirit of the demons of Annwn [the Welsh Otherworld], lest this world be ruined. They won't get along without him there."

"It's easy for me to manage that, though you think it's not easy."

"Though you manage that, there's something you won't get: no horse will be of use to Gwyn to hunt Twrch Trwyth except Black, the horse of Moro Oerfeddawg."

"It's easy for me to manage that, though you think it's not easy."

"Though you manage that, there's something you won't get: until Gwilenhin, the King of France, comes, Twrch Trwyth will not be hunted without him. It displeases him to leave his kingdom, and he will never come here."

"It's easy for me to manage that, though you think it's not easy."

"Though you manage that, there's something you won't get: Twrch Trwyth will never be hunted without getting the son of Alun of Dyfed. He's a good one for unleashing the dogs."

"It's easy for me to manage that, though you think it's not easy."

"Though you manage that, there's something you won't get: Twrch Trwyth will never be hunted till you get Aned and Aethlem. They would be swift as a gust of wind. They were never unleashed on a beast that they did not kill."

"It's easy for me to manage that, though you think it's not easy."

"Though you manage that, there's something you won't get: Arthur and his huntsmen to hunt Twrch Trwyth. He is a powerful man, but he will not come with you. The reason is that he is subject to my authority."

"It's easy for me to manage that, though you think it's not easy."

"Though you manage that, there's something you won't get: Twrch Trwyth can never be hunted until you get Bwlch and Cyfwlch and Sefwlch, sons of Cilydd Cyfwlch, grandsons of Cleddyf Difwlch. Their three shields are three brilliant gleams. Their three spears are three pointed thrusts. Their three swords are three sharp carvers. Their three dogs are Glas, Glesig, and Gleisad. Their three horses are Call, Cuall, and Cafall. Their three wives are Hwyrddyddwg and Drwgddyddwg and Llwyrddyddwg. Their three witches are Oh and Cry and Shriek. Their three daughters are Plague and Want and Need. Their three maidservants are Bad and Worse and Worst of All. The three men will sound their battle-horns, and all the others will come to make battle-cry, until no one would be concerned if the sky fell to the earth."

"It's easy for me to manage that, though you think it's not easy."

"Though you manage that, there's something you won't get: the sword of Wrnach the Giant. Twrch Trwyth can never be slain except with that. He will not give it to anyone, neither for a price nor as a favor, and you can't force him."

"It's easy for me to manage that, though you think it's not easy."

"Though you manage that, there's something you won't get. You will get sleeplessness at night seeking these things. But you will not get them, and you will not get my daughter."

"I shall have horses and horsemen, and my lord and kinsman Arthur shall get me all those things. And I shall win your daughter. And you will lose your life."

"Go now. You are not responsible for food or clothing for my daughter. Seek those things, and when they are won, you shall win my daughter, too."

The Expeditions of Arthur's Men: Wrnach's Sword

That day they went forth until evening, till there appeared a fort of stone and mortar, the greatest fort in the world. With amazement they saw a dark man coming from the fort who was larger than three of this world's men. They said to him, "Where is it you come from, man?"

"From the fort that you see there."

"Who owns the fort?"

"Slow-witted men that you are, there's no one in the world who doesn't know who owns this fort. Wrnach the Giant owns it."

"What courtesy is there for a guest and a man from afar stopping at this fort?"

"Ah, chieftain, God help you! No guest has ever come out of there with his life. No one gets in there except one who brings his craft."

They went to the gate. Gwrhyr, the Interpreter of Languages, said, "Is there a gatekeeper?"

"There is. And you, you may lose your head because you ask."

"Open the gate."

"I will not."

"Why won't you open it?"

"Knife has gone into meat and drink into the drinking horn, and there is a thronging in Wrnach's hall. Except for a craftsman who brings his craft, the gate is not opened."

Kei said, "Gatekeeper, I have a craft."

"What craft do you have?"

"I am the best burnisher of swords in the world."

"I will go tell that to Wrnach the Giant and bring an answer to you."

The gatekeeper came inside. Wrnach the Giant said, "Have you news from the gate?"

"I do. There is a company at the door of the gate who want to come in."

"And have you asked whether they have a craft?"

"Yes. And one of them said that he can burnish swords."

"That one I have needed. For some time I've been looking for someone to polish my sword, and I haven't found him. Let that one in, since he has a craft."

The gatekeeper came and opened the gate, and Kei came inside alone. And he greeted Wrnach the Giant. A chair was set under him. Wrnach the Giant said, "Is it true what is said of you, that you can burnish swords?"

"I can." The sword was brought to him. Kei took a mottled whetstone from under his arm. "Which do you prefer on it, a white hilt or a dark hilt?"

"Whatever you would prefer if it were your own that you were working on."

He polished one half of the blade for him and put it in his hand. "Does that suit you?"

"More than anything in my land, I wish all of it were like this. It's unfortunate that a man as good as you has no companion."

"Very well, sir, I have a companion, though he doesn't follow this craft."

"Who is he?"

"Let the gatekeeper go out, and I'll tell his special features. The head of his spear will leave its shaft and draw blood from the wind and come down again on the shaft." The gate was opened, and Bedwyr came in. Kei said, "Bedwyr is proficient, though he can't practice this craft."

And there was great talk among the men outside, of Kei and Bedwyr coming inside. And a young lad came inside with them, the only son of Custennin the Shepherd. What he and his companions with him did, as if it were nothing for them, was to go across the three courtyards till they came inside the fort. His companions said to the son of Custennin, "You did it! You're the best man!" From then on, he was called Goreu [Best] son of Custennin. They went separately to their lodgings, to manage to kill their lodgekeepers without the giant knowing.

The polishing of the sword was finished, and Kei put it in the hand of Wrnach the Giant, as if to inspect whether the work satisfied him. The giant said, "The work is good, and I am satisfied." Kei said, "Your sheath has spoiled your sword. Give it to me to remove the wooden side-pieces from it, and I can make new ones for it." And he took the sheath, with the sword in his other hand. He came above the giant as if to put the sword in its sheath. He drove it into the giant's head, and the blow cut his head off. They laid waste to the fort and made off with what treasures they wanted. On that very day a year later they came to Arthur's court, with the sword of Wrnach the Giant.

The Oldest Animals and the Freeing of Mabon

They told Arthur what had happened to them. Arthur said, "What's best of those rare and difficult things for us to seek first?"

They said, "It's best to search for Mabon son of Modron, but we can't find him till we first find Eidoel son of Aer, his kinsman."

Arthur rose up, and the warriors of the Island of Britain with him, to go to seek Eidoel. And they came to the outer fortress of Glini, where Eidoel was in prison. Glini stood on the rampart of the fort and said, "Arthur, what do you want of me, that you do not leave me alone on this rocky hill? I have no wealth here and nothing pleasant, neither wheat nor oats do I have, even if you were not trying to do me damage."

Arthur said, "I have not come here to harm you, but to seek a prisoner of yours."

"I shall give you the prisoner, though I hadn't planned to give him to anyone. And with that, you shall have my strength and my support."

The men said to Arthur, "Lord, go home. You cannot go with your army to seek things as slight as these."

Arthur said, "Gwrhyr, Interpreter of Languages, it is right for you to go on this quest. You have all languages, and you share language with some of the birds and animals. Eidoel, it is right for you to go searching with my men—he is your first cousin. Kei and Bedwyr, I hope you will achieve the quest on which you go. Go on this quest for me."

They went till they came to the Blackbird of Cilgwri. Gwrhyr asked her, "In God's name, do you know anything of Mabon son of Modron, who was taken when three nights old from between his mother and the wall?"

The Blackbird said, "When I first came here, a smith's anvil was here, and I was a young bird. No work has been done on it except when my beak was at it every evening. Today there is no more of it than the size of a nut that is not worn away. God's revenge on me if I have heard anything about the man you ask for. But what is right and fitting for me to do for Arthur's messengers, I shall do. There is a species of animal that God made before me; I shall go as your guide there."

They came to where the Stag of Rhedynfre was. "Stag of Rhedynfre, we have come to you here as Arthur's messengers, because we know no animal older than you. Tell us whatever you may know about Mabon son of Modron, who was taken from his mother when three nights old."

The Stag said, "When I came here first, there was only one antler on either side of my head, and there were no trees here except one oak sapling. And that grew into an oak with a hundred branches, and afterward the oak fell, and today there is nothing but a red stump of it. From then till today I have been here, and I have heard nothing of the person you ask for. But since you are Arthur's messengers, I will be your guide to where there is an animal God made before me."

They came to where the Owl of Cwm Cawlwyd was. "Owl of Cwm Cawlwyd, here are messengers of Arthur. Do you know anything about Mabon son of Modron, who was taken from his mother when three nights old?"

"If I knew anything, I'd tell it. When I first came here, the great valley you see was a wooded glen. And a race of men came to it, and it was laid waste, and a second wood grew there. And this is the third wood. And as for me, my wings are mere stumps. From then till today I haven't heard anything about the man you ask for. But I will be a guide for Arthur's messengers, till you come to where there is the oldest animal in this world and the most traveled, the Eagle of Gwernabwy."

Gwrhyr said, "Eagle of Gwernabwy, we have come as messengers of Arthur to you, to ask you whether you know anything about Mabon son of Modron, who was taken from his mother when three nights old."

The Eagle said, "I came here a long time ago, and when I first came here I had a stone, and from its top I could peck at the stars every night. Now it is only a fist high. From then till today I have been here, and I have not heard anything about the man you ask for. But on one expedition I went looking for my food to Llyn Llyw. And when I came there, I dug my claws into a salmon, supposing he would be my food for a long time. And he pulled me into the depths till it was hard for me to get free of him. What I and all my family did was to go and attack him, and try to destroy him. He sent messengers to come to terms with me. And he himself came to me, to have fifty harpoons removed from his back. Unless he knows something of what you are after, I know of none who may. But I will be your guide to where he is."

They came to where he was. The Eagle said, "Salmon of Llyn Llyw, I have come to you with Arthur's messengers, to ask whether you know anything about Mabon son of Modron, who was taken from his mother when three nights old."

"I'll tell as much as I know. With every tide I go up along the river till I come beside the wall of Caer Loyw [Gloucester]. And there I found such grief as I never found before. In order that you may believe it, one of you should come on my two shoulders here."

And it was Kei and Gwrhyr, Interpreter of Languages, who went on the two shoulders of the Salmon. And they advanced till they came to the wall where the prisoner was. There was wailing and grieving that they could hear on the other side of the wall. Gwrhyr said, "What man mourns in this stone house?"

"Ah, man, there is cause for the one here to be sad. Mabon son of Modron is here in prison. And no man was so painfully imprisoned in such a prison as I, not the prison of Lludd Silver-hand nor that of Greid son of Eri."

"Have you hope of getting free, either for gold or silver or worldly wealth, or by battle or by fighting?"

"Whatever is had of me will be won by fighting."

They returned from there and came to where Arthur was. They told where Mabon son of Modron was in prison. Arthur summoned the warriors of this island and went to Caer Loyw, where Mabon was in prison. Kei and Bedwyr went on the two shoulders of the fish. While Arthur's warriors attacked the fort, Kei broke open the wall and took the prisoner on his back, fighting on with the men as before. And Arthur came home and Mabon came with him, free.

Dillus the Bearded and Other Quests

Arthur said, "Now what's best of the rare and difficult things for us to seek first?"

"The best is to seek the two young dogs of the Bitch of Rhymhi."

Arthur said, "Is it known where she is?"

One said, "She is at Aber Deu Gleddyf [the estuary at Milford Haven]."

Arthur came to the house of Tringad at Aber Cleddyf, and he asked, "Have you heard of her here? What does she look like?"

He said, "She looks like a she-wolf. And she goes about with her two young dogs. She has often killed my livestock. And she's down in Aber Cleddyf in a cave."

Arthur put to sea in his ship Prydwen, and the others went on land to hunt the bitch, and so they surrounded her and her two young dogs. And for Arthur's sake, God transformed them back to their own shape. Arthur's army dispersed one by one, two by two.

And while Gwythyr son of Greidawl was walking one day over a mountain, he heard crying and sad groaning, and it was a fearful sound to hear. And he hurried in that direction. And when he came there, he drew his sword and cut down an anthill to the ground and thus saved the ants from fire. And they said to him, "Take God's blessing and ours with you. What no man can ever recover, we will come to recover for you." Afterward they came with the eighteen bushels of flaxseed that Ysbaddaden Chief Giant had named to Culhwch, in full measure, without anything missing from it, except one flaxseed. And the lame ant brought that one before night.

When Kei and Bedwyr were sitting atop Mount Pumlumon, on Carn Gwylathyr, in the greatest wind in the world, they looked around them and saw a great smoke to the south, far away from them, not crossing over with the wind. And then Kei said, "By the hand of my friend, look there, the fire of a hero!" They hurried toward the smoke and came near and watched from a distance as Dillus the Bearded singed a wild boar. Yet he was the greatest hero who ever kept free of Arthur. Bedwyr said to Kei, "Do you know him?"

"I know him," said Kei. "That's Dillus the Bearded. There's no leash in the world that can hold Drudwyn, the young dog of Greid son of Eri, except a leash from the beard of the fellow you see there. And it's no good unless it's pulled live from his beard with wooden tweezers, because it will be brittle if it's dead."

"What's our plan for that?" said Bedwyr.

Kei said, "We'll let him eat his fill of meat, and after that, he'll go to sleep." While Dillus did that, they made wooden tweezers. When Kei knew for sure that he was alseep, he dug beneath his feet the biggest pit in the world. He hit him a blow too big to measure and forced him down into the pit till they completely plucked out his beard with the wooden tweezers. And after that they killed him altogether.

And from there the two of them went to Celliwig in Cornwall with a leash from the beard of Dillus the Bearded, and Kei put it in Arthur's hand. And then Arthur sang this *englyn* [traditional Welsh stanza]:

> Kei made a leash
> From the beard of Dillus son of Eurei.
> If he were well, he'd be your death!

And because of that, Kei sulked, so that the warriors of this island barely made peace between Kei and Arthur. And still, neither when Arthur lacked resources nor his men were slaughtered would Kei go with him in his need from that time on.

And then Arthur said, "Which is best of the rare and difficult things to seek now?"

"It is best to seek Drudwyn, the young dog of Greid son of Eri."

A little before this Creiddylad daughter of Lludd Silver-hand went with Gwythyr son of Greidawl. And before he slept with her Gwyn son of Nudd came and took her away by force. Gwythyr son of Greidawl gathered an army and came to fight with Gwyn son of Nudd. And Gwyn was the victor, and he imprisoned Greid son of Eri, and Glinneu son of Taran, and Gwrgwst the Half-naked, and Dyfnarth his son. And he imprisoned Oben son of Nethawg and Nwython and Cyledyr the Wild, his son. And he killed Nwython and took out his heart. And he forced Cyledyr to eat his father's heart, and for that reason Cyledyr went mad. Arthur heard of this and came to the north and summoned Gwyn son of Nudd to him, and released his noblemen from Gwyn's prison. And he made peace between Gwyn son of Nudd and Gwythyr son of Greidawl. This is the peace that was made: to keep the maiden in her father's house, undisturbed by either side. And every May Day from that day till Doomsday, there should be fighting between Gwyn and Gwythyr. And whichever of them won on Doomsday would take the girl. And when these noblemen were reconciled thus, Arthur got Dun-mane the horse of Gweddw, and the leash of Bog Hundred-claws.

After that Arthur went to Brittany, with Mabon son of Mellt and Gware Golden-hair, to seek the two dogs of Glythfyr the Breton. And after getting them, Arthur went to the west of Ireland for Gwrgi Seferi and also Odgar son of Aedd, King of Ireland. From there Arthur went to the north and captured Cyledyr the Wild. Then he went after Ysgithyrwyn Chief Boar. And Mabon son of Mellt went with the two dogs of Glythfyr the Breton in his hand, and Drudwyn, the young dog of Greid son of Eri. And Arthur himself went on the hunt, with his dog Cafall in his hand. And Caw of Scotland mounted Llamrei, Arthur's mare, and joined the encounter. He took a hatchet as weapon and fiercely and brilliantly went after the boar and split its head in two and took the tusk. It was not the dogs that Ysbaddaden had named to Culhwch that killed the boar, but Cafall, Arthur's own dog.

The Hunting of Twrch Trwyth

And after the slaying of Ysgithyrwyn Chief Boar, Arthur and his followers went to Celliwig in Cornwall. From there he sent Menw son of Teirgwaedd to see whether the treasures were between the two ears of Twrch Trwyth. For it would be base to go fight with him if he did not have the treasures. But *he* was there, certainly; he had already devastated a third of Ireland. Menw went seeking the treasures, and the place where he saw them was at Esgeir Oerfel in Ireland. Menw changed himself into a bird and alighted above Twrch's lair. He tried to pluck one of the treasures from him. But he didn't get a thing except one of his bristles. The boar got up very fiercely and shook himself so that some of his poison got onto him; from then on, Menw was never without a sore.

After that Arthur sent a messenger to Odgar son of Aedd, King of Ireland, to ask for the cauldron of Diwrnach of Ireland, his Steward. Odgar asked him for it. Diwrnach said, "God knows, though he should be better for getting one glimpse of it, he won't have it." And Arthur's messenger came back from Ireland with a "no." Arthur set out with a light force with him and boarded Prydwen his ship and went to Ireland. They went to the house of Diwrnach the Irishman. The troops of Odgar saw their number. After they ate and drank their portion, Arthur asked for the cauldron. Diwrnach answered that if he were to give it to anyone, he would give it at the word of Odgar, King of Ireland. After he said no to them, Bedwyr got up and took hold of the cauldron and put it on the back of Hygwydd, Arthur's servant. He was brother by the same mother to Cacamwri, Arthur's servant, and his regular function was to carry Arthur's cauldron and to start a fire under it.

Llenlleawg the Irishman seized Caledfwlch [Arthur's sword] and swung
it in a circle and killed Diwrnach the Irishman and all his band. The hosts of
Ireland came and fought with them. And when the hosts fled utterly, Arthur
and his men went in their presence into his ship, and with them was the
cauldron full of the treasure of Ireland. And they disembarked at the house
of Llwydeu son of Cel Coed at Porth Cerddin in Dyfed. And [a place called]
"Cauldron's Measure" is there.

And then Arthur assembled the soldiers to be found in the Three Realms
of Britain and its Three Adjacent Islands, and those in France and Brittany
and the Land of Summer; and the available choice hounds and celebrated
horses. And he went with all these forces to Ireland. And there was great
fear and trembling in Ireland because of him. And after Arthur landed, the
saints of Ireland came to him to ask his protection. And he gave them
protection, and they in turn gave him their blessing. The men of Ireland
came to Arthur and gave him a tribute of food.

Arthur came to Esgeir Oerfel in Ireland, to the place where Twrch
Trwyth was, and his seven young pigs with him. Dogs were unleashed at
him on every side. That day till evening, the Irish fought with Twrch
Trwyth. Despite that, one-fifth of Ireland was laid waste.

The next day Arthur's warband fought with Twrch Trwyth; apart from
what they got of evil from him, they got nothing good. The third day
Arthur himself fought with him—for nine nights and nine days. He killed
only one youngling of his pigs. The men asked Arthur what was the explan-
ation for that pig [Twrch Trwyth]. He answered, "He was a king, and for
his sins God turned him into a pig."

Arthur sent Gwrhyr, Interpreter of Languages, to try to talk to him.
Gwrhyr went in the form of a bird and alighted above the lair of him and his
seven young pigs. And Gwrhyr, the Interpreter of Languages, asked him,
"For His sake who made you in this shape, if you can speak, I implore one
of you to come and talk with Arthur."

Grugyn Silver-bristle gave a response. Like wings of silver were all his
bristles; the path he took through wood and meadow could be seen by how
his bristles shone. This is the answer Grugyn gave: "By Him who made us
in this shape, we will not do it, and we will say nothing to Arthur. It was
enough evil that God did to us, who made us in this shape, without you,
too, coming to fight with us."

"I tell you that Arthur will fight for the comb and the razor and the
scissors that are between the two ears of Twrch Trwyth."

Grugyn said, "Until his life is first taken, those treasures will not be
taken. And tomorrow morning we shall set out from here and go to
Arthur's land and do the greatest damage there that we can."

They set out by sea for Wales. And Arthur came with his armies and his
horses and his dogs aboard Prydwen. And a sharp eye they kept on them.
Twrch Trwyth landed at Porth Clais in Dyfed [to the south of St. David's].
That night Arthur came as far as Mynyw [St. David's]. The next day Arthur
was told they had gone by. And he overtook Twrch Trwyth killing the
cattle of Cynwas Cwryfagyl, after killing the men and beasts that were
in Deu Gleddyf [the region about the estuary at Milford Haven] before
Arthur's coming.

From the time Arthur came Twrch Trwyth headed from there toward Presseleu [the Preseli mountain range in north Pembrokeshire]. Arthur came there with the world's armies. He sent his men to the hunt: Eli and Trachmyr and Drudwyn, the young dog of Greid son of Eri, in his own hand; and Gwarthegydd son of Caw on another flank, with the two dogs of Glythfyr the Breton in his hand; and Bedwyr with Cafall, Arthur's dog, in his hand. And he grouped all the soldiers on either side of the Nyfer [a stream in north Pembrokeshire]. The three sons of Cleddyf Difwlch came, men who had won great fame at the killing of Ysgithyrwyn Chief Boar.

And then Twrch Trwyth set out from Glyn Nyfer and came to Cwm Cerwyn, and there he stood at bay. And he killed four of Arthur's champions: Gwarthegydd son of Caw, and Tarawg of Allt Clwyd, and Rheiddwn son of Eli Adfer, and Isgofan the Generous. After killing these men he again stood at bay against them. And he killed Gwydre son of Arthur, and Garselid the Irishman, and Glew son of Ysgawd, and Isgawyn son of Banon. And then he himself was wounded.

The next morning at break of day some of the men overtook him. And he killed Huandaw, Gogigwr, and Penpingion, three servants of Glewlwyd Mighty-grip, so that God knows there was no servant of his in the world but Llaesgymyn, a man who improved no one's situation. And along with these he killed many men of the land, and Gwlyddyn the Builder, Arthur's Chief Builder. And then Arthur overtook him at Pelumiawg, and he slew Madawg son of Teithion, Gwyn son of Tringad son of Nefedd, and Eiriawn Penlloran. From there he went to Abertywi and made a stand against them. He killed Cynlas son of Cynan and Gwilenhin, King of France. He went from there to Glyn Ystu, and then the men and dogs lost him.

Arthur summoned Gwyn son of Nudd to him, and asked him if he knew anything of Twrch Trwyth. He said that he did not. Thereupon all the huntsmen went hunting the pig, to the Vale of Llychwr. And Grugyn Silver-hair and Llwydawg the Pursuer descended upon them and slew the huntsmen so that none of them escaped alive except one man. In response Arthur came with his armies to where Grugyn and Llwydawg were and unleashed against them all the appointed dogs. And as soon as Grugyn and Llwydawg stood at bay, Twrch Trwyth came to protect them. Since they crossed the Irish Sea, he had not seen them till then. The men and dogs fell upon him. He broke into flight to Mount Amanw. Then one of his young pigs was slain, and they went at it life for life. Twrch Llawin was killed and another of his pigs named Gwys. They moved on to Amanw Vale, and there Banw and Benwig were killed. From that place, none of his pigs accompanied him alive except Grugyn Silver-hair and Llwydawg the Pursuer.

They proceeded to Lake Ewin, where Arthur overtook him. Twrch made a stand and killed Echel Mighty-thigh and Arwyli son of Gwyddawg Gwyr and many other men and dogs. From there he went to Lake Tawy. Then Grugyn Silver-bristle separated from them and went to Fort Tywi and on to Ceredigion. After him went Eli and Trachmyr and a great throng. He came as far as Garth Gregyn, and there he was killed.

Llwydawg the Pursuer was in the vicinity and killed Rhuddfyw Rhys and many besides. Then Llwydawg went as far as Ystrad Yw. There the men of Brittany encountered him. He killed Tall Peisawg, the King of Brittany, and Red-eye the Stallion, and Gwrfoddw, Arthur's uncles, his mother's brothers. Then Llwydawg himself was slain.

Twrch Trwyth then made his way between the Tawy and Ewyas [a region in southeastern Wales]. Arthur summoned the men of Cornwall and Devon to stop him at the mouth of the Severn. Arthur said to the warriors of the island: "Twrch Trwyth has slain many of my subjects. By men's valor, so long as I live, he shall not go to Cornwall! I will not chase after him any more, but will go at him life for life! You do what you will."

What happened is that by his counsel an army of knights, and dogs of the island with them, was sent to Ewyas; from there they came back to the Severn and ambushed Twrch Trwyth with whatever tested fighters were in the island. They drove him battling into the Severn. And Mabon son of Modron went with him into the Severn River on White Dun-mane, Gweddw's steed, and Goreu son of Custennin, and Menw son of Teirgwaedd, between Llyn Lliwan and the estuary of the River Wye. And Arthur fell on him, and the champions of Britain with him. Osla Big-knife closed in, and Manawydan son of Llŷr, and Cacamwri, Arthur's servant, and Gwyngelli surrounded him. First they grabbed him by the feet and dunked him in the Severn till it flooded over him. On one side Mabon son of Modron spurred his horse and got the razor from him; and on the other side, Cyledyr the Wild on another horse plunged with him into the Severn and took the scissors from him. Before they could remove the comb, Twrch found land with his feet, and from the time he reached land, no dog nor man nor horse could keep up with him till he got to Cornwall.

Whatever trouble they had had trying to get those treasures, they had worse trouble trying to rescue the two men from drowning. As Cacamwri was pulled up, two millstones pulled him back to the depths. As Osla Big-knife was running after Twrch, his knife fell from its sheath, and he lost it; then his sheath got filled with water, and when he was pulled up his sheath dragged him down to the depths.

Arthur went on with his armies till he reached Twrch Trwyth in Cornwall. Whatever trouble he had had before was play compared with what he now had seeking the comb. Yet through trouble upon trouble the comb was won from him. Then Twrch Trwyth was harried out of Cornwall and driven straight into the sea. Afterward it was never known where he went, and Aned and Aethlem with him. And Arthur went from there to Celliwig in Cornwall to bathe and cast off his weariness.

The Witch's Blood

Arthur said, "Are there now any of the rare and difficult things that we do not have?"

One of the men said, "There is. The blood of the Dark Black Witch, daughter of the Pale White Witch, from the head of the Valley of Sorrow in the uplands of Hell."

Arthur set out for the north and came to where the hag's cave was. And it was the advice of Gwyn son of Nudd and Gwythyr son of Greidawl to send Cacamwri and his brother Hygwydd to fight the witch. But when they came inside the cave, the witch attacked them and seized Hygwydd by the hair of his head and threw him to the ground under her. And Cacamwri grabbed her by the hair of her head and pulled her off Hygwydd to the ground. But she turned on Cacamwri and beat them both down and disarmed them and drove them out whooping and howling.

Arthur was infuriated to see his two servants almost killed, and he attempted an assault on the cave. And then Gwyn and Gwythyr said to him, "It's not decent or pleasing for us to see you wrestling with a witch. Send Tall Amren and Tall Eiddil into the cave."

And they went in. And if there was a bad time for the first two, there was a worse time for these two, till God knows whether any of the four of them could have got out of the place if they hadn't all four been placed on Arthur's mare, Llamrei.

Then Arthur occupied the entrance to the cave and overcame the hag with his knife Carnwennan and cut her in half, so that she became two tubs of blood. Caw of Scotland took the witch's blood and kept it with him.

The Winning of Olwen

And then Culhwch set out, and with him Goreu the son of Custennin and those who wished ill to Ysbaddaden Chief Giant, taking the rare and difficult things with them and heading for his court. And Caw of Scotland came and shaved the giant's beard—the flesh and skin to the bone, and the two ears completely. And Culhwch said, "Have you been shaved, man?"

"I have," he said.

"And is your daughter mine now?"

"She is," he said, "but you don't have to thank me for that. Instead thank Arthur, the man who made it happen for you. If I had my way, you would never win her. But it is past the time to take away my life."

And then Goreu son of Custennin seized him by the hair of his head and dragged him after him to the refuse mound and cut off his head and put it on the post of the castle yard. And he took possession of the fort and his territory.

And that night Culhwch slept with Olwen. And she was his only wife as long as she lived. And the armies of Arthur dispersed, each to his own country.

And thus did Culhwch win Olwen daughter of Ysbaddaden Chief Giant.

chapter IV

ARTHUR IN
GEOFFREY OF MONMOUTH

Richard M. Loomis

In the early twelfth century Geoffrey of Monmouth fashioned a work of fiction in the guise of history that first made Arthur known to the wide world of Europe as a king with a remarkable chivalric career. The territory and the town of Monmouth by which Geoffrey is identified is in southeastern Wales, west of Gloucester and northeast of Cardiff (map on pages 2–3). It is here and in nearby regions that Geoffrey locates the principal events of Arthur's life: his birth and death in Cornwall, his cosmopolitan court at Caerleon, his victory over the Saxons on a hill in Bath (Geoffrey's identification of the Mount Badon named by Gildas as the site of a British victory over the Saxons). Most of Arthur's activity is military, but while his battles range from one end of Britain to another and include rapid (and undocumented) conquests of Ireland, Iceland, and Scandinavia, his great continental campaigns are fought in France. The prominence that Geoffrey gives to Brittany in these campaigns may derive from his being of Breton ancestry. He certainly knows and exploits the historic bonds between the ancient British and the Bretons and reveals in his work the cultural kinship of Wales and Brittany that was still alive in the twelfth century. Geoffrey was intimately acquainted with a circle of clerical scholars at Oxford and probably resided there for more than two decades. In 1151, near the end of his life, he was elected Bishop of St. Asaph's in north Wales.

The book that contains his account of Arthur appeared about 1136–38. It is a Latin history titled *Historia regum Britanniae* (*The History of the Kings of Britain*). By "Britain" he means the island realm that was conquered by Rome and then achieved independent eminence before being conquered by the Saxons. What he chronicles is, therefore, the Fall of Britain, the same subject (though from a different perspective) as that of the sixth-century castigator of the vices of the British, the monk Gildas (cited in Chapter I). Within this tragic frame Geoffrey has glorious tales to tell, and he introduces obscure but hopeful Welsh prophecies of a restored Britain. His line of

British rulers begins with the legendary figure of Brutus, grandson of Aeneas, who migrated to Britain (accordingly named for him) and who, like Aeneas in Italy, founded a race and a civilization. The last British ruler in Geoffrey's history is Cadwallader, who died, he tells us, in 689, in religious retirement at Rome, when the overthrow of his kingdom was being secured by the well-disciplined Saxons. The Saxon conquerors were conquered themselves in the eleventh century, and Geoffrey was witness to the energies and achievements of the new Norman lords of England. He had patrons among those lords, such as Robert, Earl of Gloucester, the "noble duke" to whom he will not confide the scandalous details of the adulterous union of Modred and Guinevere; and Alexander, Bishop of Lincoln, whose large diocese, created by the Normans, included Oxford and was an intellectual capital of the age.

Geoffrey's Arthur, the British ruler whose imperial armies could challenge Rome, is like no British ruler known to history (though some Roman emperors, including Constantine the Great, had campaigned and lived in Britain). But Arthur has an unmistakable likeness to the Norman rulers of Geoffrey's own world, whose domains included as much of Britain as they could subdue and also lands on the continent, where Geoffrey's Arthur triumphs. This Arthur provided the Normans with an image of valorous non-Saxon control of Britain, which it was in their interest to promote. Not accidentally, a grandson of Henry II, Arthur of Brittany, was named for Geoffrey's hero; and in the fifteenth century the elder brother of King Henry VIII would be named Arthur from a similar wedding of legend and dynastic ambition.

The popularity enjoyed by Geoffrey's history is not accounted for solely by its providing material for political propaganda. It is literary entertainment of abiding interest, its genre being the historical romance. It is, more precisely, romantic history, an effort to recount the past that draws on some authentic records and much oral tradition, folktale, conjecture, and above all, the intelligence and imagination of an author seeking to make dramatic sense of the fragments of his nation's past. His achievement is measured by the ores extracted from his work and richly developed by later poets—the Lear story, Sabrina, and Arthur among others.

Geoffrey claims to be translating into Latin from the British language (i.e., Welsh or Breton), his source being a book given him by his learned friend Walter, Archdeacon of Oxford. Walter's book has not been found—may be itself a fiction—yet Geoffrey of Monmouth did use such written sources as the Latin historical works of Gildas, Bede, and Nennius, and Welsh and Breton genealogies, heroic poems, and tales. The name "Merlin," for example, is his invention, but the character is compounded by him from a character in Nennius, a warrior-poet of Welsh tradition named Myrddin, and the living Welsh institution of the inspired political prophet.

Geoffrey orders his materials with architectonic mastery. Like the Romanesque cathedrals of his age, his account of Arthur aspires to the grandeur of Rome. It has largeness, symmetry, rhythmic repetitions, contrived effects of contrast, and vigorously chiseled details. It mingles barbaric images with classical and Christian motifs, and it has pathos and irony. The foreground action is military combat and political maneuver, but the actors are human. Adultery brackets the life of Arthur: his mother's unwittingly adulterous union with Uther Pendragon and his wife's union with Modred, which leads to Arthur's death. Arthur himself is brave and steadfast—but the wars he wages, like all wars, are grim. The broken people of the north beg Arthur, through their religious leaders, not to exterminate them. He relents, to his credit, though we are chilled that extermination should have been his first intention. When he grants a similar relief to the Saxons, they betray his trust and return to ravage the Britons. Yet Geoffrey can show us those Saxons in a later moment of human tenderness: the brother-chieftains Baldulf and Colgrin, embracing in joyful reunion within the besieged city of York.

Each moment, each life, is given a setting that compels the reader to a recognition of the changing contours of reality and the larger forces that may move beyond the grasp of individual control or comprehension. Arthur's triumphs are balanced by his defeats. Just as he is celebrating imperial victories amid the splendors of a Caerleon that rivals Rome, envoys from Rome arrive to denounce him and to demand a humiliating tribute, thereby provoking new global conflict. When Arthur is subsequently about to advance against the city of Rome, he learns of Modred's betrayal and must return to the place of his birth and there die. Geoffrey concludes with the Arthur of Welsh and Breton myth: after being slain in battle against Modred, he is taken to the Isle of Avalon for the healing of his wounds. Having become a hero of world literature, Arthur has lived his charmed life ever since.

Bibliographic note: The translation that follows is based on the edition of Acton Griscom (Longmans, Green, 1929). I have consulted the translations of J. A. Giles (1848); Sebastian Evans, as revised by Charles W. Dunn (Dutton, 1958); and Lewis Thorpe (Penguin, 1966). The passages I translate are those relating to Arthur; I indicate their location in Geoffrey's work by the conventional book and chapter divisions. Where possible I have given modern and familiar forms to the names. Thorpe's translation offers an index that correlates all of Geoffrey's names. J. S. P. Tatlock gives detailed findings on Geoffrey's names, sources, subjects, and techniques in *The Legendary History of Britain* (University of California, 1950). A judicious assessment of Geoffrey's life and work is given by John Jay Parry and Robert A. Caldwell as Chapter 8 of *Arthurian Literature in the Middle Ages*, ed. R. S. Loomis (Oxford, 1959).

There are inconsistencies in Geoffrey. He speaks, for instance, of the forty islands in Loch Lomond, but later implies that their number is sixty. I have left such oversights uncorrected and unannotated; the reader who notices them may often infer a suitable correction or may consult the references I have named for commentary.

The History of the Kings of Britain

[Geoffrey's account of Arthur is preceded by his treatment of the reign of the virtuous Aurelius Ambrosius—a figure from history eulogized by Gildas—who struggled to preserve British civilization only to be treacherously poisoned at the instigation of one of his own countrymen, Paschent, in league with the Saxon enemy—a treachery that anticipates Modred's. It is the death of this king at Winchester that occasions the first portent of the coming reign of Arthur.]

Book 8, the conclusion of chapter 14 through chapter 17:

While this was happening at Winchester, a star appeared of amazing size and brightness, having a single ray. This ray ended in a fiery ball spread out in the shape of a dragon, and from its mouth there issued two beams, one of which seemed to reach beyond the area of Gaul, while the other bent toward the Irish Sea, in seven smaller rays.

When this star appeared three times, all who saw it were overcome with fear and astonishment. The king's brother, Uther, who was pursuing the enemy in Wales, was no less overcome with dread, and he summoned wise men to tell him what the star meant. Among others he ordered Merlin called, who had accompanied the army so that the fighting might be managed with his counsel. Standing before the commander, he was told to explain the meaning of the star. He burst into tears, invoked his prophetic spirit, and said: "O irreparable loss! O bereaved people of Britain! O the passing of a most noble king! The glorious king of the Britons is dead, Aurelius Ambrosius, by whose death we shall all die, unless God brings help. Hurry, noble commander! Hurry, Uther, and do not put off fighting the enemy! Victory will be yours, and you shall be king of all Britain. For that star signifies you, as does the fiery dragon under the star. But the beam that is extended to the region of Gaul is the sign of a future son of yours who will be supremely powerful and whose might will control all the kingdoms that this beam covers. The other beam represents a daughter whose sons and grandsons in succession will have the kingship of Britain."

Although wondering whether Merlin had proclaimed the truth, Uther nonetheless advanced against the enemy as before. He had come so near St. David's that a half-day's march remained. When his approach was reported to Gillomanius and Paschent and the Saxons who were there, they went out against him to engage in battle. Once these caught sight of each other, they drew up their battle lines on either side, advanced face to face, and fought. In the fighting soldiers died on both sides, as happens in such encounters. When much of the day had passed, Uther finally prevailed and, with the slaying of Gillomanius and Paschent, achieved victory. The barbarians retreated therefore and sped to their ships but were cut down in flight by native citizens, who pursued them. Through Christ's favor victory fell to the commander, who after that great effort, made his way to Winchester as quickly as possible. For messengers had come who reported the king's death and that he was to be buried by the bishops of the land near the monastery of Ambrius, inside the Giant's Circle, which Aurelius, when alive, had ordered to be made. At the word of his death the bishops and abbots and all the clergy of the province assembled in Winchester, and they arranged for a funeral that was fitting for so great a king. Since he had decreed while alive that he should be buried in the cemetery he had made, they carried him there and laid him in the earth with royal rites.

His brother, Uther, took possession of the crown of the island after a convocation of the clergy and the people of the kingdom, and with the consent of all he was elevated to be king. Remembering the interpretation Merlin had given to the previously mentioned star, he ordered that two dragons be made of gold, like the dragon he had seen at the end of the star's ray. When these were completed with wonderful craftsmanship, he presented one to the cathedral church of Winchester and kept the other for himself, to carry into battle. From that time, therefore, he was called Uther *Pendragon*, which means in the British tongue "dragon's head."

Book 8, *most of chapter 19 through chapter 20:*

The following Easter Uther commanded the lords of the realm to meet in London so that he might wear the crown and celebrate so great a day with ceremony. They all made their preparations accordingly and from their various cities came together at the time of the feast. The king celebrated the occasion as he had planned and with his lords enjoyed himself. They were all happy, because he had welcomed them with a glad heart. So many nobles had gathered, with their wives and daughters, as were worthy of the joyful banquet. Among them was Gorlois, the Duke of Cornwall, with his wife, Igerna, whose beauty surpassed that of all the other women in Britain. When the king noticed her amid the rest, he grew warm with sudden love for her, so that, neglecting the others, he gave all his attention to her. To her alone he continually sent dishes; to her he sent wine-cups of gold by his personal messengers. He smiled at her several times and exchanged playful words. When her husband perceived this, he was immediately outraged and left the court without permission. No one there was able to summon him back, because he dreaded the loss of the one thing he loved most.

Angry at this, Uther ordered him to return to the court, to get satisfaction from him for the offense. When Gorlois failed to obey him, the king was enraged and swore to lay waste to his territory unless he promptly made satisfaction. Without delay, since the bitterness between them persisted, the king collected a great army, advanced on Cornwall and set fire to the towns and fortified settlements. But Gorlois, since his troops were fewer, dared not confront him and consequently chose to fortify his castles until he could win help from Ireland. Since he was more troubled about his wife than himself, he placed her in the castle of Tintagel, beside the sea, which he regarded as a more secure retreat. He himself withdrew to the citadel of Dimilioc, lest they both be in danger together if misfortune overtook them. When that was made known to the king, he went to the fort where Gorlois was and besieged it and closed off every approach to it.

Finally, after a week had passed, being mindful of his love for Igerna, the king summoned Ulfin of Ridcaradoch, a friend and soldier of his, and told him what he felt in these words: "I burn with love for Igerna, and I do not think I can avoid danger to my health unless I win her. Tell me how I can satisfy my desire, or I shall die from torment." Ulfin answered: "And who can tell you what to do, when no power exists by which we might get to her in the castle of Tintagel? For it stands on the sea and is enclosed by the sea on all sides, and there is no other access to it than that which a narrow causeway of rock affords. Three armed soldiers can block the way, even if you were to make a stand there with the whole kingdom of Britain. But if Merlin the prophet were to give help, I think you could get what you want by his direction." The king put faith in this and had Merlin summoned, since he had also come to the siege.

Called at once, Merlin, when he stood in the king's presence, was ordered to propose how the king might satisfy his longing for Igerna. Upon discovering the anguish the king was suffering because of her, Merlin marveled at his great love and said, "To gain what you wish, you must use new arts unheard of in your day. I know by my drugs how to give you the appearance of Gorlois, so that you will resemble him in everything. If you follow my instructions, I will make you look exactly like him, and I will make Ulfin like Jordan of Tintagel, his servant. I shall be the third, disguised as yet another, and you will be able to go to the castle for Igerna and gain admittance."

The king approved and paid close heed. After having entrusted the siege to his subordinates, he submitted to Merlin's drugs and was transformed into the likeness of Gorlois. Ulfin was also changed into Jordan, and Merlin into Britaelis, so that it was evident to no one what their appearance had been before. Then they set out for Tintagel and came to the castle at dusk. After they hurriedly told the gatekeeper that the duke had arrived, the doors were opened and the men were admitted. For who could suspect anything, since Gorlois himself was thought to be present? The king then spent the night with Igerna and satisfied himself with the lovemaking he had longed for, for he had deceived her by the disguise he had assumed. He had deceived her, too, with false words that he artfully contrived. He said he had come in secret from the besieged fort so that he might take care of the one he so loved and of his castle. Believing him, therefore, she denied nothing that he asked. This night also she conceived that most renowned of men, Arthur, who afterward won fame by his extraordinary valor.

In the meantime, when it was learned at the siege that the king was not there, the army, acting on its own, tried to assault the walls and to provoke the besieged duke to battle. He, behaving as rashly as they, came forth with his soldiers, thinking that with his little band he might resist so many men in arms. As they fought on all sides, Gorlois was among the first to be slain, and his followers were scattered. The besieged fort was captured, and the riches stored there were divided in unequal portions. For as luck and boldness served them, each one snatched with an open claw.

When the savagery of this action was at last finished, messengers came to Igerna reporting both the death of the duke and the end of the siege. But when they saw the king sitting beside her in the likeness of the duke, they blushed and marveled that he whom they had left for dead at the siege should have arrived thus before them unharmed. For they were ignorant of the drugs Merlin had compounded. So the king laughed at such reports and embraced the duchess, saying, "I am certainly not dead, but as you see yourself, I am alive. Yet I mourn the destruction of my fortress and the slaughter of my comrades. Now we have to fear lest the king show up and take us captive in this castle. I will therefore go first to meet him and be reconciled with him, so that nothing worse will befall us." He went out and sought his army and, after the appearance of Gorlois was removed, he reappeared as Uther Pendragon. When he learned all that had happened, he mourned the death of Gorlois but rejoiced that Igerna was freed from the bond of marriage. Therefore he went back to Tintagel Castle, took it, and took Igerna, and had his wish. They dwelt together thereafter as equals, bound by a great love, and had a son and a daughter. The son's name was Arthur and the daughter's, Anna.

Books 9, 10, and the first two chapters of Book 11:

After the death of Uther Pendragon the leaders of the Britons assembled from the various provinces in the city of Silchester and proposed to Dubricius, Archbishop of Caerleon, that he consecrate the king's son, Arthur, as king. Necessity drove them, for the Saxons, upon hearing of the death of King Uther, had invited their countrymen from Germany and under the leadership of Colgrin were trying to exterminate the Britons. Already they had subdued all that portion of the island that extends from the Humber to the Sea of Caithness. Distressed for the plight of his country and joined by the bishops, Dubricius therefore invested Arthur with the crown of the kingdom. Arthur was a youth of fifteen years, of remarkable valor and generosity, whose natural goodness displayed such grace that he was loved by virtually all the people. After receiving the royal insignia, he observed the custom of generously bestowing gifts to all. So many soldiers thronged to him that he ran out of resources for giving. But while a naturally generous and spirited man may thus temporarily lack means, he will not remain poor. Arthur, accordingly, in whom courage was combined with generosity, decided to harry the Saxons, so that he could bestow their wealth on the retainers who served him. Justice recommended this course as well, since Arthur had a hereditary claim to the kingship of the entire island. He gathered the youths subject to him and set out for York.

As soon as this was revealed to Colgrin, he assembled Saxons, Scots, and Picts, and came to meet Arthur with a great multitude near the River Douglas. When they joined battle there, the greater part of both armies was in mortal danger. But Arthur prevailed. He chased the fleeing Colgrin and laid siege to him at York, where he had gone. When Baldulf heard of his brother's flight, he advanced to the siege with six thousand men to set Colgrin free. At the time when his brother had been fighting Arthur, Baldulf was on the coast awaiting the arrival of Duke Cheldric, who was expected to bring them help from Germany. When he was ten miles from the city, Baldulf decided to travel by night and make a clandestine attack. Once Arthur learned of this, he ordered Duke Cador of Cornwall to meet Baldulf that night with six hundred knights and three thousand foot-soldiers. Cador discovered the route the enemy was taking, made a surprise attack, and, after rending and killing the Saxons, forced the survivors to flee.

Baldulf was greatly distressed that he could not bring help to his brother and debated how he might manage to confer with him. For he thought he could work out some rescue by joint counsel, if he could get to him. Since he could not approach in any other way, he shaved off his hair and beard and took on the guise of a harp-player. Strolling outside the British camp, he performed like a harper with melodies that he composed on the instrument.

Because no one suspected him, he gradually drew near the city walls, maintaining his disguise. As soon as those inside the city recognized him, he was hoisted up by ropes to the other side of the wall and brought to his brother. Upon seeing his own brother, he was revived by wished-for kisses and embraces, as if he had been raised from death. They conferred at great length. Finally, just when they had given up hope of escaping, envoys returned from Germany. Led by Duke Cheldric, they had gathered six hundred ships filled with brave soldiers.

At this news Arthur's advisers persuaded him not to maintain the siege any longer, to avoid committing themselves to hazardous conflict if so many enemy troops should arrive. Arthur took the counsel of his attendants and withdrew to London. There he convened the clergy and sought the advice of the leaders of his whole domain as to what would be the best or safest way to resist the pagans' invasion. At length a consensus was reached, and envoys were sent to Brittany to King Hoel to report to him the crisis in Britain. Hoel was the son of Arthur's sister, his father being Budicius, the King of the Armoricans. When he heard of the distress being inflicted upon his uncle, Hoel ordered his fleet readied. After assembling fifteen thousand armed men, he took the next fair wind and landed at Southampton. Arthur received him with due honor and they embraced again and again. A few days later they made for Kaerluideoit, which was under siege by the pagans I have spoken of. This city is in the province of Lindsey, located on a hill between two rivers, and is also called Lincoln. When they arrived there with all their forces to do battle with the Saxons, they inflicted unheard-of slaughter. That day, six thousand Saxons fell, some of whom died by drowning in the rivers, some by the sword. The rest abandoned the siege in terror and fled.

Arthur pursued them without pause till they came to the Wood of Caledon. There from all sides the Saxons converged in their flight and tried to resist Arthur. Defending themselves vigorously, they massacred the Britons. For they managed to avoid the weapons of the British by availing themselves of the protection of the trees. When he saw this, Arthur commanded the trees in that part of the forest to be cut down and the trunks set in a ring so that escape would be denied the Saxons. He was determined to besiege them, shut in thus, for so long that they would die of hunger. After enclosing them, he ordered his squadrons to surround the forest, and he remained there three days. When the Saxons ran out of food, they petitioned for release, for fear they might die of sudden starvation. It was agreed that in exchange for leaving behind all their gold and silver, they would be permitted to return to Germany with only their ships. They promised in addition that they would give Arthur tribute from Germany and would send hostages from there. After conferring with his advisers, Arthur granted their petition. He retained their treasure and hostages for the tribute to be paid and only allowed them to depart.

On their return home, as they put to sea, the Saxons regretted their agreement and turned their sails about, headed for Britain, and came ashore at Totnes. They seized the land and depopulated the country as far as the Severn Sea, assailing the inhabitants with mortal wounds. Then they made a march toward the district of Bath and laid siege to the town. When this was reported to the king, he was outraged at their betrayal and ordered that justice be done to their hostages, who were to be hanged at once. Postponing the campaign he had launched against the Scots and Picts, he sped to relieve the siege of Bath, though troubled by the greatest of anxieties, since he was leaving in the city of Alclud his nephew Hoel, who was seriously ill. After he entered the province of Somerset and neared the siege, he spoke these words: "Because the Saxons, who are known for being ungodly and hateful, have scorned to keep faith with me, I, who remain faithful to my God, will strive to be avenged on them today for the blood of my countrymen. Arm yourselves, men! Arm, and manfully attack those we shall surely conquer, with the help of Christ!"

While Arthur was saying this, holy Dubricius, Archbishop of Caerleon, climbed to the top of a hill and cried out in a loud voice: "Men marked with Christian faith, let your devotion to your countrymen and your country be constant. If your countrymen are slain by the treachery of the pagans, it will be a lasting reproach to you, unless you press on to defend them. Fight for your country, and if death comes, suffer death willingly for your country. For that is a victory and health for the soul. Whoever undergoes death for his brothers gives himself a living sacrifice to God and swerves not from following Christ, who consented to lay down His life for His brothers. Should then any of you suffer death in this war, may that death be a penance and purification for him, if he does not shrink from accepting it thus."

Gladdened by the holy man's benediction, each of them soon hurried to arm and obey his precepts. Arthur himself, dressed in a leather corselet appropriate for so great a king, placed on his head a helmet of gold engraved with the figure of a dragon. A circular shield on his shoulders, called Pridwen, on which was painted the image of holy Mary, the Mother of God, kept him always mindful of her. He was girded with the best of swords, Caliburn, which had been made on the Isle of Avalon. And a spear called Ron graced his right hand. This was a hard, broad spear apt for giving wounds.

After the companies were drawn up, Arthur boldly invaded the Saxon lines, which were drawn up in their usual wedge formations. The Saxons fought back courageously all day, repelling the Britons everywhere. As the sun set, the Saxons took a nearby hill, planning to hold it as their camp. Trusting in the great number of their comrades, the mountain alone seemed to be all they needed. But when the next sun restored the day, Arthur climbed to the top with his army, even though in the ascent he lost many of his men. For the Saxons rushing forward from the summit struck blows more easily, since men marching downward could wound with more speed than those marching upward. But the Britons, who had taken the summit with great force, grappled arm to arm with the enemy. Fronting them with their breasts, the Saxons strained every muscle to resist. When most of the day passed in this fashion, Arthur was indignant that the Saxons were succeeding and that victory was not yet his. Consequently he drew his sword Caliburn, proclaimed the name of St. Mary, and cast himself with a swift rush into the dense lines of the enemy. Invoking God's name, he slew with a single blow every man he struck. Nor did he cease his assault until he killed four hundred and seventy men with only his sword Caliburn. At sight of this the Britons came after him in close-packed squadrons, killing on all sides. Colgrin fell in that place and Baldulf his brother, and many thousands of others. Cheldric, however, seeing the peril of his allies, at once turned to flee with the survivors.

The king, having therefore achieved victory, ordered Cador, the Duke of Cornwall, to pursue the enemy, while Arthur himself hastened toward Albany [Scotland]. For he had been informed that the Scots and the Picts had besieged his nephew Hoel in the town of Alclud, where Arthur, as I said before, had left him seriously ill. For this reason Arthur hurried to his aid, lest he be captured by the barbarians. The Duke of Cornwall, accompanied by ten thousand men, decided not to chase the fleeing Saxons yet, but instead advanced toward their ships to prevent their boarding them. As soon as he gained possession of these, he fortified them with superior soldiers who were to deny entrance to the pagans if they ran toward them. Then he hastened after the enemy, ready to execute the command of Arthur to massacre pitilessly all those whom he found. The Saxons, who just before had thundered with instinctive savagery, now fled with quaking heart; some sought the recesses of the woods; some, the mountains and the mountain caves, to win some chance for life. Since nothing afforded them protection, they afterward came to the island of Thanet with their battle-line in pieces. The Duke of Cornwall followed them there, slaughtering as he was accustomed to do. He did not rest till, after Cheldric was captured, he forced them all to surrender, and hostages were taken.

Once peace was established, he went on to Alclud, which Arthur had already liberated from the pagans' control. Then he led his army to Moray, where the Scots and Picts were under siege, fighting for the third time against the king and his nephew. Having been overcome by Arthur, they had retreated to that region, and, when they came to Loch Lomond, they occupied the islands there, in search of a secure refuge. This lake has forty islands and is fed by sixty streams, and only one river flows from it to the sea. Sixty cliffs are visible in the islands, supporting the same number of eagles' nests; the eagles gather each year and, with a high-pitched cry that they give in unison, proclaim anything extraordinary that is about to happen in the kingdom. The enemy I spoke of fled to these islands to use the lake as a defense, but it was little help to them. For Arthur assembled a fleet and made a circuit of the rivers and by besieging the enemy for fifteen days crushed them with such famine that they died by the thousands.

While Arthur was subduing them thus, Gillmaurus, the King of Ireland, joined by an enormous number of barbarians, arrived with his fleet to bring help to those under siege. Arthur broke off the siege, began to turn on the Irish, and forced them, assailed without pity, to return home. Having won immediate victory, he was again free to destroy the race of the Scots and Picts, which he did with inflexible severity. Since he spared none of them the moment each was taken, all the bishops of that poor land, with all the clergy under their authority, advanced together barefoot, carrying relics of the saints and holy treasures of the church, to implore the king's mercy for the deliverance of their people. As soon as they were admitted to his presence, they begged him on their knees to have pity on a nation broken in spirit. He had brought peril enough and had no need to exterminate to the last one the handful who survived. He should grant a small portion of the land to them, who were consenting to bear forever the yoke of subjection. Since they appealed to the king in this way, pity moved him to tears, and, yielding to the prayers of the holy men, he granted them mercy.

After this Hoel explored the site of the lake I have mentioned and marveled that there should be so many streams, islands, cliffs, and eagles' nests, and all in the same number. Since that impressed him, Arthur approached and told him there was another pool in the same district even more remarkable. It was not far from there and had a width of twenty feet and the same length, and a depth of five feet. Whether it had been made square by human art or by nature, it breeds four kinds of fish in its four corners, and the fish of one part are not found in another. He added that there was another lake in Wales near the Severn, which the natives call Llyn Lliawn. When the tide flows into it, the sea is received as by a whirlpool, and while the pool sucks in the surge, it never gets so filled that seawater tops its banks. And when the sea ebbs, the lake spews out the swallowed waters as high as a mountain and eventually covers and splashes its banks. Meanwhile, if the people of all that area stand nearby facing the lake and their clothes get sprinkled with the waves, they can scarcely, or not at all, avoid being sucked into the lake. But if their backs are turned, they need not fear being sprinkled, even when they stand on the shore.

Having granted mercy to the Scots, the king made for York, to celebrate the feast of the approaching Nativity of the Lord. When he entered the city, he mourned to see the desolation of the sacred churches. For after blessed Archbishop Samson was expelled with other men of devout faith, the half-burned temples ceased to be used for the worship of God—so thoroughly had been the effect of the pagans' rage. Arthur convened the clergy and people and appointed his chaplain, Piramus, to the metropolitan see. He restored the churches that had been leveled to the ground and endowed them with religious communities of men and women. He restored to their hereditary privileges the nobles who had been driven away by the disruption of the Saxons.

There were three brothers in that place descended from the royal line: namely, Loth, Urian, and Auguselus, who had exercised command in those parts before the Saxons came to power. Wishing therefore to bestow their native right upon them as he had done for the other nobles, Arthur gave back to Auguselus the royal power of the Scots, and to his brother Urian, the scepter of Moray. Loth he restored to the dukedom of Lothian. In the time of Aurelius Ambrosius Loth had married Arthur's sister, who bore him Gawain and Modred. When he had finally brought the state of the whole country to its original dignity, Arthur married a woman named Guinevere, who was descended from a noble family of Romans and reared in the household of Duke Cador. She was the loveliest woman in all the island.

At the start of the following summer he readied his fleet and went to the island of Ireland, which he wished to subject to himself. At his landing King Gillmaurus, whom I have already spoken of, came to fight against him with a throng beyond counting. When battle broke out, Gillmaurus's naked and unarmed people were pitifully cut down on the spot and ran to wherever some place of refuge lay open to them. Gillmaurus was captured immediately and forced to surrender. The other princes of the land surrendered in consequence, stunned at what had happened to the king.

With all of Ireland conquered Arthur directed his fleet toward Iceland and took possession of it after defeating the inhabitants. When word spread through the other islands that no nation could resist him, Doldavius, the King of Gotland, and Gunhpuar, the King of the Orkneys, came on their own, pledged tribute, and made their submission. When winter had passed, Arthur returned to Britain, settled the realm in secure peace, and remained there for twelve years.

Then he summoned all who were most distinguished from kingdoms far and wide and began to enlarge his household and to have such elegance in his court that he stirred emulation in people living far away. The result was that whoever had a noble spirit counted himself nothing unless in dress or arms he bore himself like Arthur's knights. As his magnanimity and valor became celebrated throughout the world, extreme dread filled the rulers of kingdoms overseas that, if they were crushed by an invasion of Arthur's, they might lose the nations they governed. Troubled with gnawing concern, then, they rebuilt their towns and the ramparts of their cities and constructed fortifications in strategic places, so that if Arthur should be provoked to move against them, they would have a refuge in case of need. And when this was told to Arthur, he felt exalted that he was a source of dread to everyone, and he longed to win all of Europe for himself.

Arthur had ships prepared and went first to Norway, in order to honor his sister's husband, Loth, with that country's crown. But Loth was the nephew of Sichelm, the King of the Norwegians, who had just then died and willed his kingdom to Loth. The Norwegians were opposed to accepting Loth and promoted a certain Riculf to the royal power. They fortified their cities and thought themselves able to resist Arthur. Loth had a son, Gawain, who was twelve years old at the time; he had been entrusted by his uncle to the service of Pope Sulpicius, who had knighted him. When therefore, as I started to say, Arthur landed on the coast of Norway, King Riculf met him with all the people of the country and began to fight. Ater much blood had been shed on both sides, the Britons finally won and with an assault killed Riculf and many others. After this victory mounting flames swept the cities. The natives were scattered, and the Britons did not refrain from violence until they subdued to Arthur's rule all of Norway and Denmark as well.

Upon the surrender of these lands, after promoting Loth to be king of Norway, Arthur sailed to Gaul. He organized divisions and began to ravage the country on every side. Gaul was then a province of Rome, charged to the Tribune Frollo, who governed it on behalf of Emperor Leo. When Frollo learned of Arthur's approach, he led all the armed soldiery obedient to his power to do battle with Arthur, but he could not stand against him. For the youth of the islands that he had just conquered joined Arthur, so that he was known to have such a powerful army that it was hard for any other to overpower it. The better members of the armed forces of Gaul, indebted to Arthur by his largess, also entered his service. When he saw that he was heading toward the worst of the battle, Frollo forsook his camp at once and raced to Paris with a few companions. There he regrouped his scattered people, garrisoned the city, and once more ventured to fight Arthur. But just as Frollo was negotiating to strengthen his army with help from his neighbors, Arthur unexpectedly arrived and laid siege to him in the city. After a month passed, Frollo grieved that his people were dying of hunger, and he proposed to Arthur that they two alone should enter upon a duel, and the one to whom victory fell would gain the other's kingdom; for Frollo was great in stature and daring and courage. These qualities made him excessively sure of himself, and he offered this proposal so that he might by this means have a chance for deliverance. When it was communicated to Arthur, Frollo's proposal pleased him enormously, and he sent word back that he would be ready to abide by these terms. A pledge was therefore given on both sides, and the two met on an island outside the city, while the people awaited what was to come of their encounter.

They were both appropriately armed and mounted on horses of wonderful speed, and it was not obvious who might win. Standing on opposite sides with lances raised, they suddenly spurred their horses and struck at one another with mighty blows. But by managing his lance more surely Arthur hit Frollo in the upper chest and, keeping clear of Frollo's weapon, with all his strength knocked him to the ground. Arthur unsheathed his sword, too, and was hurrying to kill him, when Frollo stood up quickly and, with his lance held straight before him, ran at Arthur. He sank a mortal wound into the breast of Arthur's horse and forced them both to fall. When the Britons saw the king prostrate, they feared that he was slain. Scarcely could they be kept from violating their pledge and attacking the Gauls as one body. But just as they were considering breaching the pact, Arthur swiftly got to his feet, holding his shield in front of him, and with a rapid dash attacked the menacing Frollo. Now face to face they redoubled their matching blows, each intent on the death of the other. Frollo finally found an opening and hit Arthur on the brow. If he had not blunted his sword's edge by striking Arthur's helmet, Frollo might have dealt a mortal wound. Blood was flowing, and when Arthur saw that his corselet and shield were red, he was inflamed with a more burning anger. Using all his strength, he hoisted Caliburn and drove it through the helmet and into the head of Frollo, dividing it in two. With this wound Frollo fell, his heels beating the earth, and he loosed his spirit to the winds. As soon as that became known to the army, the inhabitants of the city ran in a body, opened the gates, and handed the city over to Arthur.

This victory achieved, he divided his army in two. One part he entrusted to Duke Hoel and commanded him to go fight Guitard, Duke of the men of Poitou. With the other part of the army Arthur would devote himself to subduing the remaining provinces that resisted him. Hoel entered Aquitaine, invaded the cities of that land, and forced Guitard, harried by much fighting, to surrender; and he depopulated Gascony with sword and flame and subjugated their princes. When nine years had passed and Arthur had brought all of Gaul under his control, he returned to Paris. There he held court, convened the clergy and people, and established the affairs of the kingdom in peace and law. Then he granted Neustria, which is now called Normandy, to his Cupbearer, Bedivere. To his Seneschal, Kay, he granted the province of Anjou. And he bestowed many other provinces on noblemen who had been in his service. When all the cities and peoples were at peace, he went back to Britain at the beginning of the spring.

When the feast of Pentecost drew near, Arthur, whose heart was full of happiness after such a triumph, desired to hold his court then. He would place the crown of the kingdom on his head and call to the feast the kings and dukes subject to him, so that he might celebrate the feast with reverence and renew lasting peace among his princes. Having told his attendants what he desired, he accepted their advice that he carry out his plan in Caerleon. For it was located in a delightful spot in Glamorgan, on the River Usk, not far from the Severn Sea. Abounding in wealth more than other cities, it was suited for such a ceremony. For the noble river I have named flows along it on one side, upon which the kings and princes who would be coming from overseas could be carried by ship. But on the other side, protected by meadows and woods, it was remarkable for royal palaces, so that it imitated Rome in the golden roofs of its buildings. It was distinguished by two churches, one of which, built in honor of the martyr Julius, was beautifully graced with a virgin choir of nuns dedicated to God. The other was founded in the name of blessed Aaron, the friend of Julius, with an attached convent of canons, and was the third metropolitan see of Britain. Moreover, the city had a college of two hundred philosophers, learned in astronomy and other arts, who diligently observed the courses of the stars and with sound interpretations foretold to King Arthur wonders to come in that time. Famous for so many pleasant features, Caerleon was made ready for the announced feast.

Messengers were sent to various kingdoms, and those who deserved to attend the court were invited, from the parts of Gaul as well as from the neighboring islands of the ocean. Consequently there came Auguselus, the King of Albany, now called Scotland; Urian, the King of the men of Moray; Cadwallo Long-Arm, the King of the Venedotians, who are now called the North Welsh; Stater, the King of the Demetians, that is, the South Welsh; Cador, the King of Cornwall; the archbishops of the three metropolitan sees, that is, London and York, as well as Dubricius of Caerleon. Dubricius was the Primate of Britain and Legate of the Apostolic See, so renowned for religion that by his prayers he could cure anyone who was gravely ill.

Noble lords of noble cities came: Morvid, Earl of Gloucester; Mauron of Worcester; Anarauth of Salisbury; Artgualchar of Guerensis, now called Warwick; Jugein from Leicester; Cursalem from Caistor; Kynniarc, Duke of Durobernia; Urbgennius from Bath; Jonathal of Dorchester; and Boso of Rydychen, that is, Oxford. In addition to these lords heroes of equal honor came: Donaut map Papo, Cheneus map Coil, Peredur map Eridur, Grifud map Nogord, Regin map Claut, Eddelivi map Oledauc, Kynar map Bangan, Kynmaroc, Gorbonian map Goit, Worloit, Run map Neton, Kymbelin, Edelnauth map Trunat, Cathleus map Kathel, Kynlit map Tieton, and many others whose names it is tiring to enumerate. From the neighboring islands came Gillmaurus, King of Ireland; Malvasius, King of Iceland; Doldavius, King of Gotland; Gunvasius, King of the Orkneys; Loth, King of Norway; Aschil, King of the Danes. From nations overseas came Holdin, Duke of Flanders; Leodegarius, Earl of Boulogne; Bedivere the Cupbearer, Duke of Normandy; Borellus of Maine; Kay the Seneschal, Duke of Anjou; Guitard of Poitou; the Twelve Peers of the parts of Gaul, led by Gerin of Chartres; Hoel, Duke of the Armorican Britons, with the nobles subject to him. They marched with such an array of trappings, mules, and horses that it is difficult to record. Besides these there remained no prince of any worth on this side of Spain who did not come at that call. No wonder—Arthur's generosity, famous throughout the world, had attracted everyone by his love.

When they had finally all gathered in the city, the feast being now at hand, the archbishops were led to the palace to crown the king with the royal diadem. Since the court was convening in his diocese, Dubricius, vested for mass, undertook responsibility for the ceremony. After the king was crowned, he was led in procession to the church of the metropolitan see. The two archbishops, one on the right and one on the left, escorted him. But four kings, that is, of Albany and Cornwall, Demetia and Venedotia, whose privilege it was, went before him bearing four golden swords. A choir of many religious orders performed with marvelous melodies. From another quarter the archbishops and bishops led the queen, crowned with her regalia, to the church of the nuns. Four queens of the kings named above carried four white doves in front of her, as was the custom. All the women followed her there with great joy. Afterward, when the procession was completed, so many organs were played, so many songs performed in each church, that from the surpassing sweetness the knights in attendance did not know which church they should visit first. Hence they rushed in crowds now to this one, now to that one, and if the whole day had been given to this celebration, it would not have wearied them.

After the masses were sung in both churches, the king and queen laid aside their crowns and put on lighter adornments. He went to dine at his palace with the men, she to another palace with the women, for the Britons kept the ancient custom of Troy by which the men celebrated feasts separately with men, the women with women. When they had been seated as the dignity of each demanded, Kay the Seneschal, decked in ermine, was accompanied by a thousand nobles, all wearing ermine, who served the dishes with him. On the other side just as many diversely gowned followed Bedivere the Cupbearer, who was wearing miniver, and with him distributed many different kinds of drinks. In the palace of the queen, also, countless servants decked in various ornaments presented their service according to custom. If I should describe all of them, I would make too prolix an account. For Britain was then restored to such a state of distinction that it excelled other kingdoms in the burgeoning of wealth, the lavishness of ornaments, the elegance of its inhabitants. Every knight in Britain who was noted for valor had clothing and arms identical in color, and the women had exquisitely matching garments. They deigned to love no man till he was three times proven in military combat. Thus the women were made more chaste, and the knights more valiant because of their love of them.

Having feasted, they all went to fields outside the city, different ones to play different games. Soon knights who had knowledge of tournaments arranged a mock-battle. Women looking on from stations on the walls playfully roused them to mad flames of love. After the tournament they passed the remaining time in contests, some with bows and arrows, some with spears, some by hurling heavy rocks, some with stones, some with dice, and in a variety of other pleasant games. Whoever achieved victory in his game was rewarded by Arthur with generous gifts. The first three days were spent thus, and when the fourth day came, all were summoned who had done him service, to receive recognition, and each was endowed with possessions, that is, cities and castles, archbishoprics, episcopacies, and other rewards.

Then blessed Dubricius, desiring to live as a hermit, resigned from the archiepiscopal see. In his place was consecrated David, the king's uncle, whose life was a model of all goodness for those whom he had taught. To succeed the Archbishop of York, Saint Samson of Dol, Tebaus was chosen, a well-known priest of Llandaff, endorsed by Hoel, King of the Armorican Britons, who was impressed by the man's life and virtue. The see of Silchester went to Maugannius, and Winchester to Diuvanius. Eledenius was chosen bishop of Alclud.

While Arthur was distributing these honors among them, unexpectedly there entered, with measured steps, twelve men of mature age and dignified countenance, carrying olive branches in their right hands as the sign of a diplomatic mission. After saluting the king, they presented a letter to him on behalf of Lucius Hiberius, which read: "Lucius, Procurator of the Republic, to Arthur, King of Britain, the greetings he has deserved. With great amazement I marvel at the insolence of your tyranny. I marvel, I say, remembering the injury you have done to Rome, and I am outraged that you have transgressed and avoid acknowledging the fact. Nor are you in haste to recognize what it is to have offended criminally the Senate, which you know the entire world should obey. For the tribute of Britain, which the Senate commanded you to pay—since Gaius Julius Caesar and other men of Roman rank received it many times—you have presumed to withhold, neglecting the command of so great an authority. You have also seized Gaul from Rome, you have taken the province of Burgundy, you have seized all the islands of the ocean, whose kings, while Roman power held sway there, paid tax to my ancestors. Since, therefore, the Senate has voted to have redress for your accumulated offenses, I order you to come to Rome by mid-August of the coming year, so that, giving satisfaction to your masters, you may accept the sentence that their justice will pronounce. Otherwise I myself will go to your lands, and whatever your madness has wrested from the Republic, I will venture to restore to Rome by the sword."

Once those words were spoken before the kings and lords, Arthur accompanied them to a gigantic tower that was at the gatehouse, to debate what should be done to counter these commands. But as they started to climb the steps, Duke Cador of Cornwall, who had a jovial disposition, broke into a laugh with these words in the king's presence: "Till now, I have feared that the quiet rest the Britons have known through a long peace might make them cowardly and deprive them of fame for warfare, in which they are thought to excel other races. Indeed, where there is no practice of arms but the enticements of dice and women and other amusements, it is no wonder that cowardice should stain what once there was of virtue, honor, courage, and fame. For it has been almost five years since we have indulged in those pleasures and have not been exercised in war. It is to free us from this sloth that God has stirred the Romans to such a mood, that they might restore our valor to its original state." These and like remarks he made to the others as they went to the benches.

Once they had all gathered there, Arthur spoke: "Comrades in good fortune and bad," he said, "whose valiant spirits I have before now tested, both in giving counsel and in waging war, now put your minds together and prudently decide what you think we should do about these commands. For whatever is carefully foreseen by a wise man is more easily borne when it comes time for realization. We shall more easily bear the assault of Lucius if with common zeal we plan in advance how we can withstand it. I do not think that we should fear him greatly, since he demands on unreasonable grounds the tribute he wants from Britain. For he says that it should be given to him because it was paid to Julius Caesar and his successors, who were induced by civil dissension among our ancestors to make an armed attack on them and subdue them to Roman power by force and violence, as our country was then reeling from domestic troubles. Since they conquered the land thus, they taxed it unjustly. For nothing acquired by force and violence is justly possessed by anyone. Because the Romans used violence, he makes an unreasonable claim, thinking us to be tributaries to him by right. And since he presumes to exact from us what is not due him, let us by parallel reasoning seek from him the tribute of Rome, and whoever emerges the stronger, let him make off with what he wishes to possess! For if he concludes that a tax should be paid him because Julius Caesar and other Roman leaders once conquered Britain, I believe on the same grounds that Rome ought to pay you tribute, since my ancestors conquered it in ancient times. For Belinus, the most fortunate King of the Britons, with the help of his brother, Brennius, Duke of Burgundy, after hanging twenty of the higher-ranking Romans in the middle of the Forum, took the city and, after taking it, held it for a long time. And Constantine, the son of Helena, and Maximian, each of them a blood relative of mine, who succeeded one another in wearing the crown of Britain, gained the throne of Roman rule. Do you not therefore think that a tax should be sought from the Romans? As to Gaul, however, or the nearby islands of the sea, no answer is to be given, since Rome avoided defending them when we were subduing them to our power."

After Arthur spoke thus, Hoel, the King of the Armorican Britons, who was ordered to speak before the others, responded with these words: "Even if we could each summon to mind and profoundly review all things, I do not think that anyone could find advice better than what the good sense of your keen foresight yields. For your deliberation, touched with Ciceronian eloquence, has met our need. Therefore we should staunchly praise the plan of a constant man like you, the act of a wise soul, and the performance of superior counsel. For if by the argument just expressed, you choose to go to Rome, I do not doubt that we shall have the victory while we defend our liberty, while we justly exact from our enemies what they tried to take from us. For whoever tries to steal another's possessions deserves to lose his own possessions to the very one whom he attacks. Since, then, the Romans want to take our possessions from us, we should surely take theirs from them, if we have an opportunity to do battle. This is a battle deeply desired by all the Britons! Consider the Sibylline prophecies, which testify in verses that three times there will be one born of British stock who will obtain the rule of Rome! Two times the oracles have already been fulfilled, since it is clear, as you have said, that the famous princes Belinus and Constantine have worn the regalia of the Roman Empire. But now we have you as the third to whom the summit of this great honor is promised. Hasten, therefore, to take what God wishes to grant! Hasten to subdue that which itself wishes to be subdued! Hasten to exalt us all! We will not flee from being wounded or losing life so that you may be raised on high. In order that you may accomplish this, I shall join you with ten thousand armed men!"

When Hoel had finished speaking, Auguselus, the King of Albany, offered to make known what he felt about it: "From realizing that my lord desires the things he has spoken of, a joy has fallen on my soul that I cannot express before him. It seems that we have accomplished nothing in the conquests we have inflicted on so many and such great kings, so long as the Romans and the Germans remain unhurt, and we do not manfully avenge on them the injuries that they once did to our countrymen. Now, since liberty to do battle is promised us, I rejoice exceedingly, and I burn with desire for the day we shall meet. I thirst for their blood as I would for a spring, if for three days I had been kept from drinking. Ah, shall I ever see that day? How sweet will be the wounds I shall receive or give, when we engage hand to hand! And that death will be sweet which I face in avenging our fathers, in defending our liberty, in exalting our king. Let us advance on those half-men, and in our advance let us be steadfast, so that once they are defeated, we may possess their honors with a happy victory. I shall augment our army with two thousand armed knights, and infantry as well."

After the others had said what yet remained to be said, each of them promised Arthur as many men as they owed in their feudal service, so that in addition to those the Duke of Armorica had pledged, there were added from the island of Britain alone sixty thousand armed men. But the kings of the other islands, since they were not accustomed to have cavalry, pledged infantry as each one was obliged, so that from the six islands—Ireland, Iceland, Gotland, the Orkneys, Norway, and Denmark—one hundred and twenty thousand were enrolled. From the duchies of Gaul—Flanders, Ponthieu, Normandy, Maine, Anjou, Poitou—eighty thousand. From the twelve districts of those who went with Gerin of Chartres, twelve hundred. The total number of the army was therefore one hundred and eighty-three thousand, three hundred, besides foot soldiers, who were not easily counted.

King Arthur received them all, ready and united, into his service, and he ordered them to go home again quickly and organize the promised army, and at the beginning of August to speed to the port of Barfleur, so that with him, on the border of the territory of Burgundy, they might confront the Romans. He instructed the emperors through their envoys that he was by no means going to pay them tribute, nor would he go to Rome to submit to their sentence regarding that. Instead he wanted from them that which they had decreed by judicial sentence as a claim from him. The envoys therefore departed, the kings departed, the chieftains departed, and they did not put off executing what they had been commanded to do.

Once the import of this reply was known, at the command of the Senate Lucius Hiberius issued a proclamation to the Kings of the East to raise an army to go with him to conquer Britain. Swiftly there assembled Epistrofus, the King of the Greeks; Mustensar, the King of the Africans; Ali Fatima, the King of Spain; Hirtacius, the King of the Parthians; Boccus of the Medes; Sertorius of Libya; Serses, the King of the Itureans; Pandrasus, the King of Egypt; Micipsa, the King of Babylon; Politetes, the Duke of Bithynia; Teucer, the Duke of Phrygia; Evander of Syria; Echion of Boeotia; Hippolytus of Crete, with dukes and nobles subject to him. And from the

Senate, in order, came Lucius Catellus, Marius Lepidus, Gaius Metellus Cocta, Quintus Milvius Catullus, Quintus Carucius, and more, to a total count of four hundred thousand, one hundred and sixty. All things necessary being arranged, they made for Britain at the start of August.

When Arthur learned of their approach, he entrusted the security of Britain to his nephew Modred and Queen Guinevere. He led his army to the port of Southampton, where he put to sea with a strong wind blowing. But as with joy he divided the deep sea, surrounded by countless ships on a prosperous course, a profound sleep overtook him about midnight. In his sleep he saw in a dream a bear flying through the sky, at whose roar all the coasts trembled. And a terrible dragon flew from the west, which lit up the land with the splendor of its eyes. They met and engaged in an awesome fight. With fiery breath the dragon burned the bear as it rushed forward again and again and hurled it burnt to the earth. Awakened by that, Arthur told those standing near what he had dreamed. They interpreted it, saying that the dragon represented him, but the bear represented some giant he was going to encounter. Their fight was the sign of a battle that would be between them, and the dragon's victory was the victory that would come to Arthur. But Arthur interpreted it otherwise, believing that the vision was rather about himself and the emperor. After night passed and dawn reddened at last, they landed at the port of Barfleur. Promptly they set up their tents and then waited for the kings of the islands and the dukes of the adjoining provinces to arrive.

While they waited, Arthur was told that a giant of extraordinary size had come from Spain and had seized Helena, the niece of Duke Hoel, from her guardians and fled with her to the summit of the mountain now called Mont St. Michel. The soldiers of that land went in pursuit but could do nothing against the giant. Whether they attacked him by sea or by land, he either sank their ships with huge stones or killed them with many kinds of spears. And he caught several of them and devoured them half-alive.

The next night, therefore, at two in the morning, taking Kay the Seneschal and Bedivere the Cupbearer, Arthur left his tent, unknown to the rest, and made his way to the mountain. Endowed as he was with great strength, he scorned to lead an army against such monsters, and he hoped to give inspiration to his men by showing that he alone was enough to destroy them. As they neared the mountain, they saw a fire burning atop it. Another fire was on a smaller mountain, toward which, on the king's orders, Bedivere the Cupbearer sailed. He could not reach it otherwise, since it stood in the sea. Just as he had begun his ascent to the top, Bedivere heard a woman's wail. His first response was to shudder, not knowing whether the monster was there. Quickly recovering courage, he drew his sword, but when he got to the top, he found only the fire he had seen and a newly made grave, and beside it an old woman sobbing and wailing. When she caught sight of him, she checked her tears at once and broke out: "Unhappy man, what calamity brings you here? Unspeakable are the pains of death you are about to suffer! I pity you, since a loathsome monster will consume the flower of your youth tonight. For there will come a depraved giant of hated name, who carried to this mountain the duke's niece, whom I have just buried here, and me, her nurse. By a kind of death never heard of—and swiftly—the giant will do away with you! Ah, how sad your fate, bright child. . . . With fear in her tender breast while that abomination embraced her, she ended her life, which was worthy of a longer duration. Because he burned with hateful lust and could not disfigure her with his shameful intercourse—she was another soul for me, another life, another sweetness in joy—he used force and violence on me, unwilling, I swear to God and by all my years! Flee, my friend! Flee, lest he come (for it is his habit) to have intercourse with me and so find you and tear you to pieces in pitiful slaughter!"

Moved as much as human nature can be, Bedivere calmed her with friendly words. He promised the comfort of quick relief and returned to Arthur to tell him all that he had discovered. Arthur mourned the girl's death and told them he would permit only himself to attack the giant, but if necessity demanded, they should come to help and advance like men to his side. So they directed their steps from there to the greater mountain, left their horses with the squires, and, with Arthur leading, climbed the mountain.

The beast was there at the fire, his lips stained with the gore of half-eaten swine. He had consumed some and was roasting others impaled on spits, with live coals underneath. As soon as he saw them, having expected nothing of the sort, he hurried to grab his club, which two young men could hardly lift off the ground. In response the king drew his sword and, with shield extended, lunged as fast as he could to reach him before he got his club. But the giant, accustomed to evil calculation, had already seized it. He struck the king upon the raised shield, with such force as to fill the entire coast with the sound of the blow and deafen Arthur's ears. But Arthur, who burned with bitter anger, hoisted his sword and gave such a wound to the giant's brow that, though not mortal, the blood flowing from it over his face and eyes blinded them from clear seeing. The giant had deflected the blow with his club and so spared his forehead a deadly wound. Yet, blinded by the flowing blood, he got up more enraged and, like a wild boar passing the spear of a hunter, he rushed past the sword toward the king. Grabbing Arthur around the waist, he forced him to bend his knees to the ground. Arthur soon summoned his strength and got free. With speed—now here, now there—he thrashed the beast with his sword and did not rest till a death-wound was struck. He drove the whole blade against the skull-cover that protected the brain. Then the detestable one cried out and, like an oak uprooted by the force of winds, collapsed with a great crash.

The king burst into a laugh. He ordered Bedivere to cut off the giant's head and give it to one of the squires to carry to the camp, to be a spectacle for gazers. Arthur declared that he had never found another of equal strength since the time he had killed huge Retho of Mount Arvaius, who had invited him to fight. From the beards of kings that he had slain, Retho had made a cloak for himself; he ordered Arthur to cut his beard neatly and send the detached part to him. As Arthur surpassed the other kings, so, in his honor, Retho would fasten his beard above the other beards. If he would not oblige, Retho pressed him to fight. The one who emerged stronger would carry off the cloak as well as the loser's beard. Thus the contest began. Arthur was the victor, and he got Retho's beard and his cloak. Afterward he used to say he had never met anyone as strong as Retho.

Having gained the victory, as I said, when the ensuing night gave place to dawn, they returned to their tents with the head. Crowds ran to marvel at it, giving praise to him who had freed the country from such voraciousness.

Hoel, however, grief-stricken for the death of his niece, had a church built on her grave, upon the mount where she lay. Taking its name from the girl's grave, it is called to this day "Helena's Tomb."

When all those whom Arthur had been awaiting finally assembled, he advanced from there to Autun, where he believed the emperor was. But as soon as he reached the River Aube, he was informed that the emperor had pitched his camp not far from there and was marching forward with an army so great that, they said, Arthur could not oppose it. Not in the least frightened on that account, Arthur chose not to give up what he had started, but pitched his own camp on the bank of the river, from where he would be free to lead his army out, and where, in case of need, he could retreat. He dispatched two leaders, Boso of Oxford and Gerin of Chartres, together with his nephew Gawain, to Lucius Hiberius, to tell him that he should withdraw from Gallic territory or the next day come to test which of them had the greater right to Gaul. The youths of the court were consequently moved to great high spirits and began urging Gawain to start something in the emperor's camp, to give them an occasion to engage with the Romans.

The envoys went to Lucius accordingly and ordered him to leave Gaul, or the next day to come to fight. When Lucius answered them that he had an obligation not to withdraw but rather to move ahead and take command of Gaul, his nephew Gaius Quintillianus was present and said that the Britons excelled more in boasting and threats than they did in bravery or valor. Gawain was immediately infuriated. He unsheathed the sword that he was wearing and lunged at Gaius, cut off his head, and then started back to the horses with his comrades. The Romans followed in pursuit, some on foot, some on horseback, straining to avenge their fellow citizen upon the rapidly fleeing envoys. But Gerin of Chartres, when one of the Romans began to strike at him, turned around without warning, aimed his lance, and with all his strength threw the man to the ground, pierced straight through his armor and mid-body. Boso of Oxford envied the man of Chartres for showing such courage, and, turning his own horse about, thrust his lance into the throat of the first man he met, forcing him to fall mortally wounded from the horse on which he had been chasing him. Meanwhile Marcellus Mutius, longing with all his heart to avenge Quintillianus, was already threatening Gawain from behind and was just on the point of capturing him when Gawain turned around suddenly and, with the sword he was carrying, hacked through his helmet and head clear to the chest. He commanded him to report in Hell to Quintillianus—whom Gawain had slain in the Roman camp—that this was the way the Britons excelled in threats and boasting. He rejoined his comrades then and urged each to return blow for blow and strive to put down his opponent. They agreed and went back to the fight, and each of them unhorsed his man. The Romans pursuing them could not, whether they struck with swords or lances, capture them or unhorse them.

But it is said that, as they pursued near a certain wood, some six thousand Britons suddenly marched out. Upon learning of the flight of their leaders, they had hidden there to give them aid. As they emerged, they spurred their horses and, filling the air with shouts and holding their shields before their breasts, they attacked the Romans without warning and put them to instant flight. Chasing them as one man, they knocked some from their horses with their lances, took some captive, and some they killed. When news of that came to the Senator Petreius, he made haste to join his fellow soldiers with a company of ten thousand men, and he forced the Britons to race back to the wood from which they had sallied—not without loss for the Romans. For as they fled, the Britons circled back in the narrow pathways and inflicted a massacre on the pursuers. While they were withdrawing in this manner, Hyder, the son of Nu, hurried with five thousand men to help them. That encouraged the Britons to resist, and they strove like men to hit powerful blows on those whom they had a little before shown their backs to, now opposing them with their chests. The Romans fought back, and as often as they leveled the Britons, they were also leveled by them. The Britons wanted military action with all their heart, but they gave little thought to the result of an action when they began it. The Romans, however, acted more wisely, for Petreius Cocta, in the style of a good commander, prudently instructed them now to attack, now to retreat, and thereby threatened the Britons with great loss.

When Boso realized this, he separated from the others several men whom he knew to be more valiant, and addressed them in this way: "Since we began this battle without Arthur's knowledge, we must take care not to end up the worse for our attempt. For if we suffer that reversal, we will incur great loss among our soldiers and move our king to curse us. Regain your courage and follow me through the Roman host, so that if fortune favors us, we may kill or capture Petreius." So they spurred their horses, and, penetrating the wedge formations of the enemy with matching force, they came to where Petreius was admonishing his troops. Boso burst in there, seized Petreius by the neck, and, as he had planned, fell to the ground with him. The Romans closed in to tear Petreius away from his adversaries. But the Britons ran together to give Boso help. There was great killing among them, with shouts and clamor, while one side sought to free their leader and the other to hold on to him. Men were wounded on both sides, throwing opponents down and being thrown down. There one could see who would prevail with the spear, who with the sword, who with the knife. At last the Britons, moving in close formation and bearing up under the attack of the Romans, retired with Petreius to the security of their battle-line. And they made an unexpected attack on the Romans, who, bereft of their general, were now mostly weakened, scattered, and showing their backs to them. As the Romans rushed off, the Britons hit them from behind, felled those who were hit, stripped those who were felled, and slew those they had stripped, as they went after the others. They also took many prisoners to present to the king. When they had terrorized enough, the Britons returned to their camp with their spoils and prisoners.

Reporting what had happened to them, they handed over to Arthur Petreius Cocta and their other prisoners, in the gladness of victory. He congratulated them and promised them honors and promotions, since they had performed so valiantly in his absence. But desiring to lead the captives to confinement, he called aside those who might conduct them to Paris the next day and deliver them to the city guards, to keep them till he gave other orders regarding them. He commanded Duke Cador and Bedivere the Cupbearer and two of his military leaders, Borellus and Richerius, with their retinue, to guide them until they came where there was no fear of a rescue by the Romans. But the Romans happened to discover that plan and on the orders of the emperor selected fifteen thousand of their men to move ahead of the British march that night. Once they met the Britons, they were told to hold their ground, in order to free the captives. They assigned as leaders Vulteius Catellus and Quintus Carucius, who were Senators, and Evandrus, the King of Syria, and Sertorius, the King of Libya. With the soldiers already mentioned they took the commanded journey that night and, having reached a site with suitable hiding places, lay concealed where they thought the Britons would pass.

When morning came, the Britons got underway with their captives, and soon they drew near that spot, not aware what traps the shrewd enemy had set. But when they had begun to pass by, the Romans appeared without warning and fell upon them—who were anticipating nothing of the sort—and penetrated their ranks. But the Britons, though they had been unexpectedly attacked and finally scattered, regrouped and fought back like men. They stationed some of their men around the prisoners, while they dispatched others into the throng to engage the enemy. Richerius and Bedivere they put in command of the force assigned to guard the prisoners. Cador, Duke of Cornwall, and Borellus were put in charge of the others. But the entire Roman force burst forward in confusion; without bothering to group their men by squadrons, but succeeding with all their might, they slaughtered the Britons as they were trying to organize their troops and defend themselves. Much weakened as a result, the Britons would shamefully have lost those they were escorting if fortune had not sped to bring them welcome aid.

For Guitard, the Duke of Poitou, as soon as the entrapment was known, came up with three thousand men. Confident in their help, the Britons prevailed at last and gave back to the heartless waylayers a counter-massacre. Yet they lost many of their own men in the first engagement. They lost that distinguished leader of Maine, Borellus, who, while confronting Evandrus, the King of Syria, spewed out his life with his blood with the Syrian's lance fixed in his throat. They lost, too, four noble lords: Hirelgas of Periron, Maurice Cador of Cahors, Aliduc of Tintagel, and Her, the son of Hider—men not to be easily matched in bravery. But they did not slacken in courage or show despair, but pressed forward with every effort, trying both to keep the prisoners and to overthrow the enemy. At length, the Romans, being unable to bear the contest with them, sped from the field and headed for their camp. Yet the Britons kept in pursuit and inflicted great slaughter. They seized very many, and did not rest until, after Vulteius Catellus and Evandrus, the King of Syria, were slain, they utterly routed the remnant. Victory being theirs, they sent the prisoners whom they were convoying on to Paris and returned to their king with the ones they had just taken. They assured the king of supreme victory, since, though they were but a few, they had gained a triumph over an enormous attacking enemy.

Lucius Hiberius suffered these reverses with bitterness. He turned his mind—stung with mixed torments—now here, now there, debating whether to engage in the fighting already begun with Arthur or, having withdrawn to Autun, to await the assistance of the Emperor Leo. At length he yielded to fear, and the next night, heading for Autun, he entered Langres with his army. When Arthur learned of this, wanting to get ahead of the Roman march that night, he bypassed the city on his left and entered a valley called

Saussy, which Lucius was about to cross. Desiring to organize his soldiers by troops, he ordered one legion under the command of Morvid to be in reserve so that, if necessary, he would know where he could retreat and, after regrouping his squadrons, again do battle with the enemy. He distributed the others into seven divisions, assigning to each division five thousand, five hundred and fifty-five men fully equipped with arms. A part of these divisions was organized as cavalry, the other part as infantry. The order was given them that, while an infantry group was attempting an attack, cavalry were to attack in the same place, obliquely and in close formation, to scatter the enemy. The infantry were drawn up in the British manner, in a square, with a right and a left wing. Placed in command of the first of these divisions were Auguselus, the King of Albany, and Cador, the Duke of Cornwall, the first for the right wing and the second for the left. For the second division Arthur named two other outstanding generals, Gerin of Chartres and Boso of Rydychen (which is called Oxford in the Saxon tongue). For the third he named King Aschil of Denmark and King Loth of Norway; for the fourth Duke Hoel of the Armoricans and Gawain, his own nephew. Four divisions were stationed behind as support. In charge of the first Arthur appointed Kay the Seneschal and Bedivere the Cupbearer; of the second Duke Holdin of Flanders and Duke Guitard of Poitou; of the third Iugenis of Leicester, Jonathal of Dorchester, and Cursalem of Caistor; of the fourth Urbgennius of Bath. Following these the king chose for himself a legion that he wanted to be available to him, placed at a location where he raised up his golden dragon as a standard to which the wounded and battle-weary might in necessity flee, as to a fort. In that legion of his there were six thousand, six hundred and sixty-six men.

When all was in order, he addressed his troops in these words: "My countrymen, who have made Britain the mistress of thirty kingdoms, I pay tribute to your valor, which I judge to be not failing but rather flourishing more and more. You were unexercised in battle for five years, when you were given to the sweets of idleness rather than to the practice of arms, yet you have not degenerated from inborn worth but persevered, and you have put the Romans to flight. Provoked by their own pride, they wanted to deprive you of liberty; advancing with a greater number, they began to wage battle; unable to withstand an engagement with you, they have shamefully retreated to this city. You can meet them as they now leave this city and head for Autun through this valley and fall upon them like unsuspecting sheep. Surely they were thinking that the sloth of Eastern races is in you, when they desired to make your country a tributary and to make slaves of you. Could they be ignorant of the wars you waged with the Danes and the Norwegians and the leaders of the Gauls, whom you have subdued to my power and liberated from their shameful rule? We who prevailed in harder conflict shall surely prevail in this easier fight, if with equal passion we labor to crush those half-men. What great honors each of you will possess if as faithful soldiers you obey my will and my orders! For once we have beaten them we will aim straight for Rome and will capture the city we have aimed for and will take possession of what we have captured. You shall therefore have the gold, the silver, the palaces, the towers, the forts, the cities, and the other riches of the conquered." Even as he was speaking, they all gave their assent with one shout, ready as long as Arthur lived to accept death first rather than abandon the field by flight.

But Lucius Hiberius, learning about the stratagems being prepared against him, chose not to flee, as he had wanted to do, but having recovered courage, proposed to confront them in that valley. He called his generals and spoke to them in these words: "Venerable fathers, to whose command the kings of East and West ought to be subject, be mindful of our ancestors, who, in order to vanquish the enemies of the Republic, did not shrink from shedding their blood, but, leaving an example of valor and arms to their descendants, fought as if God had destined them not to die in battle. Thus they triumphed most often and, by triumphing, escaped death, since for none was any other death destined than that which came by the providence of God. So the Republic grew, their valor grew, and whatever decency, honor, and generosity are usually found in the noble flourished longer in them and promoted them and their descendants to lordship over the whole world. Desiring then to rouse the same spirit in you, I urge you to revive the gallant courage of your ancestors and, persevering in that, seek out your enemy in the valley where they lie in wait for you and fight to win from them what is yours. Do not suppose I have retreated to this city because I shrink from them or from a contest with them. I think rather that they are attacking foolishly and that we should surprise the attackers and, with great devastation, attack them as they rush forward in uncoordinated ranks. Since they have now done something other than we had thought, let us also do something unexpected. Let us go after them and attack them audaciously. Or if they should regain themselves, let us fight back with one heart and withstand the first attack, and so we shall surely triumph. For in many battles, whoever could stand in the first engagement has most often made off with the victory."

When he finished speaking these and many other words, all showed approval with one assent, holding up both faces and hands in an oath, and they hastened to arm. Once armed, they left Langres and approached the valley where Arthur had stationed his troops. They too formed twelve wedge-shaped divisions, and all infantry. These, drawn up as wedges in the Roman style, each contained six thousand, six hundred and sixty-six soldiers. They appointed their own commanders to each of them, so that by their command the divisions might both attack and repulse attacks. Of the first, therefore, they put in charge Lucius Catellus and Ali Fatima, the King of Spain; of the second Hirtacius, the King of the Parthians, and Marius Lepidus, Senator; of the third Boccus, the King of the Medes, and Gaius Metellus, Senator; of the fourth Sertorius, the King of Libya, and Quintus Milvius, Senator. These four columns were stationed in the front line. After these another four followed, of which they made Serses, the King of the Itureans, commander of the first; of the second Pandrasus, the King of Egypt; of the third Politetes, the Duke of Bithynia; of the fourth Teucer, the Duke of Phrygia. Behind these were yet another four divisions, and to the command of the first of these, they appointed Quintus Carucius, Senator; of the second Lelius Hostiensis; of the third Sulpicius Subuculus; of the fourth Mauricius Silvanus. Lucius Hiberius, moreover, moved among them here and there, reminding and instructing them how they should conduct themselves. In their midst he ordered a golden eagle, which he carried as a standard, to be securely placed, and he counseled that anyone whom misfortune might isolate should try to return to it.

Finally they stood on opposite sides—here the Britons, there the Romans —with weapons raised. When the sound of the battle-trumpets was heard, at once the division led by the King of Spain and Lucius Catellus boldly plunged into the division led by the King of Scotland and the Duke of Cornwall, but could by no means separate that closely joined body of men. The division led by Gerin and Boso raced up to the Roman division that was attacking fiercely, and, while the other British division was resisting, as I have said, they made an attack on the Romans with a sudden cavalry charge. Having broken that line, they encountered the division which the King of the Parthians was leading against the division of Aschil, King of the Danes. Immediately troops engaged everywhere and, penetrating one another's ranks, waged a mighty combat. Terrible slaughter took place among them in the midst of loud cries; and, beating the earth with head and heels, everywhere they coughed out their life with their blood.

First a loss was inflicted on the Britons, because Bedivere the Cupbearer was slain and Kay the Seneschal mortally wounded. For while Bedivere was fighting Boccus, King of the Medes, he was pierced by that one's lance among the enemy troops and collapsed, slain. When Kay the Seneschal tried to avenge him, he was surrounded by the troops of the Medes and received his death wound. Yet like a good soldier, with a flank that he was leading, he opened a way through slain and routed Medes and would have retreated to his own lines with his division still intact, if he had not encountered the division of the King of Libya, whose assault wholly dispersed the men whom Kay was leading. But he withdrew with a few men and fled to the golden dragon with Bedivere's body. How great the lamentations of the men of Normandy when they saw the body of their Duke Bedivere torn to pieces with so many wounds! How great the cries of anguish of the men of Anjou as by many means they dressed the wounds of Kay, their leader! But there was no call for mourning, since everywhere the battle-lines bloodily rushing at one another gave them no chance to groan, but forced them to defend themselves.

Therefore Hirelgas, the nephew of Bedivere, greatly moved by his death, gathered three hundred of his men around himself and, like a boar in a pack of dogs, making a sudden cavalry dash through the enemy ranks, sought the place where he had seen the standard of the King of the Medes, little thinking what might befall him while he avenged his uncle. When he reached that place, he killed that king and carried his corpse back to his fellow warriors. When this body was brought next to the body of the Cupbearer, Hirelgas tore it apart. Then with a tremendous shout he urged the troops of his fellow citizens to rush against the enemy, to attack with repeated attacks while courage burned freshly in them and while the breast trembled in those fearful ones, and, while menacing them face to face, they were organized in their division more wisely than the others and could more cruelly and more often inflict a loss.

Stirred by his exhortation, the Britons attacked the enemy at every point, and so great slaughter came to both sides. For on the side of the Romans, not counting many others, there fell King Ali Fatima, Micipsa of Babylon, and Senators Quintus Milvius and Marius Lepidus. There fell, on the side of the

Britons, Duke Holdin of Flanders and Leodegarius of Boulogne, and three lords of Britain: Cursalem of Caistor, Guallauc of Salisbury, and Urbgennius of Bath. Then the troops they were leading fell back much weakened, till they reached the line of the Armorican Britons, which Hoel and Gawain were leading. This line, like a burning flame, made an assault on the enemy. Those who had retreated were renewed, and the Armorican line forced the enemy, who shortly before were in pursuit, to flee. Always pursuing, the Armorican line now unhorsed those in flight, now slew them, now kept on slaughtering until it came to the Roman commander's division. When Lucius saw the distress of his allies, he hastened to give them assistance. At the start of that engagement the Britons lost strength. Chinmarchocus, the lord of Tréguier, fell, and with him went two thousand men. There also fell three notable chieftains: Riddomarcus, Bloctonius, and Iaginvius of Bodloan, whose valor was so great that, had they been princes of kingdoms, ages to come would celebrate their fame. For while they made that attack with Hoel and Gawain, the enemy they threatened did not escape, but they ripped life from them by sword or lance. Yet after reaching the line commanded by Lucius, being everywhere surrounded by Romans, they fell with the lord and soldiers I have named.

Hoel and Gawain—past ages have given birth to no better men—heard of the massacre of their troops and pressed on more strongly, now here, now there, one on this side, the other on that; charging through, they attacked the Roman commander's wedge formation. Gawain, always fiery in courage, sought the opportunity of engaging with Lucius. As he made the attempt, like an audacious soldier, he rushed forward, and as he rushed forward, he unhorsed the enemy, and as he unhorsed them, he slew them. Hoel, no less a man, thundered on the other side. He exhorted his comrades, struck at the enemy, took their blows unafraid, and did not fail at any hour, but repeatedly was hit and hit back. It could not easily be said which of the two outdid the other.

Gawain, however, by hewing down troops, as has been told, found at last the opportunity he wanted and attacked the Roman commander and engaged with him directly. But Lucius, vigorous with youth, had much bravery, much energy, much valor, and he desired nothing more than to encounter a soldier who forced him to test what he could do in arms. Confronting Gawain therefore, he was glad to enter combat with him, and he gloried, for he had heard so much of Gawain's great fame. As the battle was long waged between them, they dealt powerful blows, extending their shields against the attacks, and each labored to bring on the death of the other. While they fought very ferociously in this way, suddenly the Romans recovered and made an attack on the Armoricans. Supporting their commander by killing, they hurled back Hoel and Gawain and their troops, until they came unexpectedly before Arthur and his division. He had heard of the massacre just done to the Britons and had rushed forward with his own legion. He drew out his excellent sword Caliburn and in a loud voice inspired his soldiers with these words, saying: "What are you doing, men? Why do you let these womanish creatures go off uninjured? Do not let one of them escape! Remember your right arms, exercised in so many battles, that have subdued thirty kingdoms to my power! Remember your ancestors, whom the Romans, while they were stronger, made vassals! Remember your

liberty, which those half-men, mere weaklings compared with you, desire to
steal! Don't let one get away alive, not one! What are you doing?"

Shouting these and many other taunts, Arthur attacked the enemy. He
overthrew, he killed, and whomever he met, he slew either him or his horse
with one blow. They fled from him as from a ferocious beast, a lion
provoked by savage hunger to devour whatever chance offers. Their arms
did not prevent Caliburn, wielded in the right hand of so able a king, from
making them spit out their souls with their blood. Bad luck led two kings,
Sertorius of Libya and Politetes of Bithynia, to meet Arthur, and he cut off
their heads and sent them to Hell. When they saw their king fight in this
way, the Britons gained greater courage, attacked the Romans with a single
spirit, and assaulted with close-packed squadrons. As the infantry attacked
on one side, the cavalry on the other side tried to unhorse and penetrate the
enemy ranks. Still the Romans fought back strongly, and under the command
of Lucius they labored to give the Britons retaliation for the slaughter done
by their renowned king. As a result they fought with as great force on each
side as if they had just begun to fight.

On this side Arthur was again and again, as I have said, thrusting at the
enemy and urging the Britons to stand their ground. But on the other side
Lucius Hiberius both admonished his Romans and led them many times into
brilliant deeds of valor. And he himself did not cease to wield his sword, but
as he circled through his troops, he killed with lance or sword any enemy
that chance presented to him. Appalling slaughter occurred on each side, for
now the Britons, now the Romans, in turn prevailed. Then, as this fight was
being waged, Morvid, the Earl of Gloucester, dashed forward with the
legion that, as I noted above, was in the hills, and from the rear he rushed
upon the unwitting enemy. Rushing he entered their lines and scattered
them, causing great ruin. Then many thousands of Romans fell. And finally
the commander, Lucius, was caught among the troops and killed, pierced by
some unknown soldier's lance. Though with great labor, the unrelenting
Britons pressed on and got the victory.

The Romans were dispersed: some of them, impelled by fear, chose secret
byways and woods; some, towns and forts; and all fled to whatever might
be the safest places. The Britons strained on after and crushed them with
pitiful carnage, capturing and stripping them, as most of the Romans held
their hands out like women to be bound, hoping to get a little more life. This
outcome was ordained by the providence of God, since the Roman ancestors
in ancient times had harassed the Britons' ancestors with hostile oppressions,
and now the Britons were trying to defend the liberty the Romans wanted
to take from them and were denying the tribute unjustly demanded of them.

In victory Arthur ordered that the bodies of his lords be separated from
the bodies of the enemy and, having been separated, that they be prepared
royally and carried thus to abbeys nearby, to be honorably buried there. But
Bedivere the Cupbearer was carried by the men of Normandy with great
lamenting to his own city of Bayeux, which Bedivere the First, his grand-
father, had built. There in a certain cemetery that was in the western part of
the city, next to the wall, he was honorably laid to rest. Kay was carried to
Chinon—a town that he himself had built—gravely wounded, and a little
after he died of that wound. As became the Duke of Anjou, he was buried in
a wood belonging to a monastic community there, not far from the main
town. And Holdin, the Duke of Flanders, was taken to Flanders and buried

in his city of Thérouanne. But other lords and chieftains, as Arthur had ordered, were borne to nearby abbeys. Merciful also to his enemies, he ordered the natives to bury them, and the body of Lucius to be conveyed to the Senate, with the message that nothing else was to be paid from Britain. Until the following winter he stayed on in that region and was free to subdue the cities of the Burgundians.

Then as summer approached, when he wanted to go to Rome and had just begun to cross the mountains, it was announced to him that his nephew Modred, to whose guardianship he had entrusted Britain, was wearing its crown in tyranny and treachery, and that Queen Guinevere, having broken the oath of her prior nuptials, had been joined to him in unconscionable lust. Geoffrey of Monmouth will not speak about this, my noble duke. But since he finds it told in the British work previously mentioned, and since he heard it from Walter of Oxford, a man well schooled in many histories, he will make public, though in an ordinary style and briefly, what battles that illustrious king engaged in with his nephew when he returned to Britain after his victory over the Romans.

When the infamy of this notorious crime reached his ears, Arthur postponed the invasion he had wanted to make against Emperor Leo, and having sent Duke Hoel of the Armoricans with an army of Gauls to pacify those districts, he immediately returned to Britain with only the kings of the islands and their armies. But that criminal traitor Modred sent Chelric, the Duke of the Saxons, to Germany, so that there he might league with himself those he could and might quickly return with any allies he could muster. For by agreement Modred had promised that he would give Chelric that part of the island which extends from the River Humber to Scotland, and whatever Hengist and Horsa had possessed in Kent in the time of Vortigern. Chelric had carried out his command and had already landed with eight hundred ships full of armed pagans. He had given a pledge to the traitor and was obeying him as his king. Modred had also allied with himself the Scots, the Picts, the Irish, and anyone who he knew from experience hated his uncle. They were about eight hundred thousand in all, both pagans and Christians.

Relying on their help and on the multitude of his own army, Modred met Arthur landing in the port of Richborough. Battle having been engaged, he devastated those coming ashore. King Auguselus of Albany and Gawain, the nephew of the King, with countless others, fell that day. But Ywain, the son of Urian, succeeded Auguselus in the kingdom and afterward in those battles distinguished himself by many acts of valor. Finally, though they got to the shore with great difficulty and killing on both sides, Arthur's men put Modred and his army to flight. Practiced through rigorous conquests, they had ordered their troops wisely, partly as cavalry to fight, so that when an infantry division intended to attack or resist, the cavalry would rush in there from an angle and try to penetrate the enemy ranks and so put them to flight. That perjurer, having regrouped his troops from all quarters, entered Winchester the next night. When this was made known to Queen Guinevere, she instantly despaired, fled from York to Caerleon, and among the nuns in the church of the Martyr Julius embraced their way of life and vowed to live in chastity.

But Arthur raged with tougher anger, since he had lost so many hundreds of his fellow soldiers, and on the third day, having buried the slain, he approached the city of Winchester and besieged the scoundrel who was sheltered inside. That one was unwilling to desist from what he had begun, but animating in every way those who followed him, he came with his troops and arranged to fight his uncle. Once the contest had begun, there was much slaughter on both sides, but finally more was borne by Modred's side, which forced him with humiliation to abandon the field. Taking little care about what burial might be given to his slain, he quickly fled, conveyed by boat, on his way toward Cornwall. Arthur suffered torment that Modred had so often escaped, and at once went after him into that country, to the River Camblan, where Modred awaited his approach.

Supremely audacious and always swift to attack, Modred immediately divided his soldiers into squadrons, wishing rather to conquer or die than flee any longer as he had done before. Sixty thousand of his allies still remained loyal to him, from which he made six divisions, and in each one he placed six thousand, six hundred and sixty-six armed men. Moreover, he made one division from the remaining soldiers, and, after generals were appointed for each of the other divisions, he took this one under his own command. Having organized these divisions, he encouraged each of them, promising them the possessions of their enemies if they held on to victory. Arthur also positioned his army on the opposite side, and he divided it into nine divisions of infantry, with a right and left wing, square-shaped, and with leaders assigned to each. He urged them to kill the perjurers and thieves who, at the command of his betrayer, had been drawn from distant regions to this island and wanted to take their honors from them. He also said that Modred's allies were mongrel barbarians from many kingdoms, unwarlike and ignorant in the practice of war, who could not at all resist Arthur's forces, who were powerful men practiced in many conquests—provided Arthur's men chose to attack boldly and fight manfully.

After Arthur and Modred had urged their troops on in this way, the two lines rushed together in a sudden burst. They joined in battle, striving to give blow after blow. At that place there occurred on both sides such killing, such groans of the dying, such furies of the attackers that it is tragic to describe. For everywhere they wounded or they were wounded, they killed or they were killed. After they had spent much of the day in this manner, Arthur finally rushed with his one division, in which he had put six thousand, six hundred and sixty-six men, into that squadron where he knew Modred to be. By opening a way with swords, he entered it and caused frightening bloodshed. Then that abominable traitor fell and many thousands with him. And yet the rest did not flee because of his death, but joining from every field, they tried to resist with as much bravery as was theirs. The hardest of fighting was waged between them, in which almost all the leaders present on both sides fell with their troops. On Modred's side there fell Chelric, Elaf, Egbrict, and Bruning, who were Saxons; Gillapatric, Gillamor, Gillasel, Gillarvus, who were Irish; Scots also and Picts, with almost all whom they commanded. On Arthur's side Odbrict, the King of Norway, fell; Aschil, the King of Denmark; Cador Limenich; Cassibellaunus; with many thousands of their men, who were Britons or from other races they had led with them. Furthermore, the glorious King Arthur was mortally wounded, and was carried from there to the Isle of Avalon, so that his wounds might be healed. To Constantine, his cousin, who was the son of Duke Cador of Cornwall, he granted the crown of Britain, in the year of Our Lord 542.

chapter V

CHRÉTIEN de TROYES: LANCELOT, *or* THE KNIGHT OF THE CART

William W. Kibler

Although nearly all of what Geoffrey of Monmouth wrote concerning Arthur is believed to be unsubstantiated and fictional, his contemporaries (and perhaps Geoffrey himself) believed that he was writing history. Chrétien de Troyes was the first writer who consciously used the myth of Arthur as the basis for long fictional narratives. *Lancelot*, like most of Chrétien's works, had its roots in the soil of the British Isles. In particular, it seems related to a Celtic abduction tale, the *aithed*, in which a mysterious stranger claims a married woman, makes off with her through a ruse or by force, and carries her off to his otherworldly home. Her husband pursues the abductor and, after overcoming seemingly impossible odds, penetrates the mysterious kingdom and rescues his wife. However, this material is only distantly related to the *Lancelot* as we have it—the role of Lancelot himself, for example, is nowhere to be found—and the precise manner by which the Celtic materials reached the French-speaking world is unclear.

In the prologue to his first romance, *Erec and Enide*, Chrétien tells us that he "*tret d'un conte d'avanture / une molt bele conjointure*" (creates from an adventure tale a very beautiful arrangement). In the opening lines of *Lancelot* he writes that the Countess Marie of Champagne, his principal literary patroness, gave him the *matiere* (material) and *san* (sense) for his romance. Critics generally agree that the *matiere* referred to Chrétien's source story, perhaps given him orally and in a loosely connected manner by the Countess, and that the *san* was the interpretation or meaning to be given to this matter. Both statements give proof of a conscious literary artistry on the part of Chrétien; and the fact that he signed all his works, in a period when many literary productions remained anonymous, is another indication of the pride of accomplishment of a great writer. In a deliberate fashion, and with often unappreciated artistry, Chrétien gathered together the threads of a tradition to weave his beautiful fabric. From Geoffrey and the Norman-French poet

Wace before him, as from oral tradition, he could have taken little more than the names of characters, perhaps some rudiments of story lines or characterizations, and a general tone. It was his genius alone to assemble these various fictions into a coherent form that would guarantee them their immense and lasting success.

What little we know of Chrétien's biography must be drawn from allusions found in his work, or what can be surmised from a careful study of them. His name does not appear in any official records, and neither his life nor his works can be dated with certainty. In the prologue to *Erec and Enide* our author refers to himself as *Crestiens de Troies* (line 9), from which we can assume that he was born or at least spent the better part of his formative years in Troyes, one of the leading cities in the region of Champagne. At Troyes he was most assuredly associated with the court of the Countess Marie of Champagne, to whom he dedicated his *Lancelot*. This Marie, a daughter of Eleanor of Aquitaine by her first marriage, to Louis VII of France, was married in 1159 to Henry the Liberal, Count of Champagne. Sometime after Count Henry's death in 1181 Chrétien shifted patrons and began his never-to-be-completed romance *Perceval* for Philip of Flanders. The *Perceval* was no doubt begun before Philip's departure for the Third Crusade in September of 1190.

Chrétien's literary career probably began no earlier than the mid-1150s and ended around 1190. In the prologue to his second major romance he tells us that he had previously composed some adaptations of Ovidian materials as well as a poem treating the Tristan legend, which he enigmatically refers to as being "about King Mark and Isolde the Blond." All of this early material, with the exception of an adaptation of the Philomela story (*Metamorphoses*, Book 6), has been lost. After honing his technique on the adaptations, he created his first masterpiece when he turned from Rome to the Celtic world for his inspiration and wrote *Erec and Enide*. This fine psychological story of a knight and his new bride is the first extant literary work to incorporate the Arthurian material. Its success was followed by *Cligès*, which, though set in part at Arthur's court, is principally an adventure romance based on Greco-Byzantine material.

After *Erec* and *Cligès* Chrétien composed two of his greatest romances, *Lancelot* and *Yvain*. Then finally, toward the end of his career, he wrote his most enigmatic work, *Perceval*, or the *Conte du Graal* (Story of the Grail). *Perceval* was left unfinished, just as *Lancelot* was turned over to Godefroy of Lagny to complete.

A romance such as *Lancelot* may at first appear ill composed and loosely structured to a reader who is raised on the realistic novel. The plot is based on the motif of the quest, and the various adventures are all related to the expiation of Lancelot's great sin against the courtly code: his two-step hesitation before mounting the cart of infamy. Thus each of his adventures demands that he serve women unhesitatingly, for having shown the slightest preference for knightly honor over amorous duty. The *Lancelot* is not "unified" in the modern sense but shows rather a cohesiveness based on the principle of analogy. Scenes that may have no direct bearing on the development of the central intrigue nonetheless serve the meaning of the story as analogues of other actions. The complex interrelationship of the individual episodes, in which a later scene may serve to clarify an earlier one, demands a greater effort on the part of readers, requiring them to reread or reflect upon earlier episodes in the light of later ones before the sense can manifest itself clearly. For those with patience and an openness to an unfamiliar esthetic, the reading will prove most rewarding.

Bibliographic note: A detailed bibliography up to the mid-1970s can be found in Douglas Kelly, *Chrétien de Troyes, An Analytic Bibliography* (Grant & Cutler, 1976). A good general introduction to Chrétien can be found in Jean Frappier, *Chrétien de Troyes, the Man and His Work* (English translation by Raymond J. Cormier, Ohio University, 1982), and U. T. Holmes, *Chrétien de Troyes* (Twayne, 1970). Important recent studies in English include Douglas Kelly, *Sens and Conjointure in the "Chevalier de la Charrette"* (Mouton, 1966); Norris Lacy, *The Craft of Chrétien de Troyes: An Essay on Narrative Art* (Brill, 1980); and L. T. Topsfield, *Chrétien de Troyes: A Study of the Arthurian Romances* (Cambridge University, 1981). This translation is based on my new edition of the Guiot manuscript, B.N. 794 (Garland, 1981); line numbers from that text are indicated periodically throughout the translation in brackets.

Lancelot, or *The Knight of the Cart*

Since my lady of Champagne wishes me to begin a romance, I shall do so most willingly, like one who is entirely at her service in anything he can undertake in this world. I say this without flattery, though another might begin his story with the desire to flatter her; he might say (and I would agree) that she is the lady who surpasses all women who are alive, just as the foehn that blows in May or April surpasses the other winds. Certainly I am not one intent upon flattering his lady. Will I say, "As the polished diamond eclipses the pearl and the sard, the countess eclipses queens"? Indeed not; I'll not say anything of the sort, though it be true in spite of me. I will say, however, that her command has more importance in this work than any thought or effort I might put into it.

Chrétien begins his book about the Knight of the Cart; the source and the meaning are furnished and given him by the countess, and he strives carefully to add nothing but his effort and diligence. Now he begins his story.

On a certain Ascension Day King Arthur was in the region near Caerleon and held his court at Camelot, splendidly and luxuriantly as befitted a king. After the meal the king did not stir from among his companions. There were many barons present in the hall, and the queen was among them, as were, I believe, a great number of beautiful courtly ladies, skillful at conversing in French. And Kay, who had overseen the feast, was eating with those who had served. While Kay was still at table, there appeared before them a knight, who had come to court equipped and fully armed for battle. The knight came forward in his splendid armor to where the king was seated among his barons. Instead of the customary greeting he declared, "King Arthur, I hold imprisoned knights, ladies, and maidens from your land and household. I do not bring you news of them because I intend to return them to you; rather, I want to inform you that you have neither wealth nor power enough to ensure their release. And know you well that you will die before you are able to come to their aid."

The king replied that he must accept this, if he could not do anything about it, but that it grieved him deeply.

Then the knight made as if to leave: he turned and strode from the king until he reached the door of the great hall. But before descending the stairs, he stopped and proffered this challenge: "Sir, if at your court there is even one knight in whom you have faith enough to dare entrust the queen to accompany her into these woods where I am going, I give my oath that I will await him there and will deliver all the prisoners who are captive in my land—if he is able to win the queen from me and bring her back to you."

Many there in the palace heard this, and all the court was in turmoil. Kay, who was eating with the servants, also heard this challenge. He left his meal, came directly to the king, and spoke to him in indignation: "My king, I have served you well, in good faith and loyally. But now I take my leave; I shall go away and serve you no more; I've neither the will nor desire to serve you any longer."

The king was saddened by what he heard; but when he was able to reply he said to him at once: "Is this in truth or jest?"

"Fair king," replied Kay, "I have no need to jest—I take my leave in truth. I ask no further wages or recompense for my service; I have firmly resolved to depart without delay."

"Is it out of anger or spite that you wish to leave?" asked the king. "Sir seneschal, remain at court as you have in the past, and be assured that there's nothing I have in all this world that I'd not give you at once to keep you here."

"Sir," he replied, "no need for that. For each day's stay I wouldn't take a half-liter of purest gold."

In desperation King Arthur went to his queen and asked, "My lady, have you no idea what the seneschal wants from me? He has asked for leave and says that he will quit my court. I don't know why. But what he wouldn't do for me, he'll do at once if you beg him. Go to him, my dear lady; though he deign not stay for my sake, pray him to stay for yours and fall at his feet if necessary, for I would never again be happy if I were to lose his company."

The king sent his queen to the seneschal. She went and found him with the other barons; when she had approached him, she said, "Sir Kay, I'm most upset at what I've heard tell of you—you must know this. I've been informed, and it saddens me, that you wish to leave the king's service. What gave you this idea? What feelings compel you? I no longer see in you the wise and courtly knight that once I knew. I want to urge you to remain: Kay, I beg of you—stay!"

"My lady," he said, "I beg your pardon, but I could never stay."

The queen once again implored him, as did all the knights together with her. Kay replied that she was wasting her efforts asking for what would not be granted. Then the queen, in all her majesty, fell down at his feet. Kay begged her to rise, but she replied that she would not do so: she would never again rise until he had granted her wish. Thereupon Kay promised her that he would remain, but only if the king and the queen herself would grant in advance what he was about to request. "Kay," said she, "no matter what it may be, both he and I will grant it. Now come and we shall tell him that on this condition you will remain."

Kay accompanied the queen, and together they approached the king. "My lord," said the queen, "with great pains I have retained Kay. But I bring him to you with the assurance that you will do whatever he is about to ask."

The king was overwhelmed with joy and promised to grant Kay's request, no matter what he might demand. "My lord," said Kay, "know then what I want and the nature of the gift that you have promised me; I consider myself most fortunate to obtain it with your blessing: you have agreed to entrust to me the queen whom I see here before me, and we shall go after the knight who is awaiting us in the forest."

Though it saddened the king, he entrusted her to Kay, for never was he known to break his word; but his anger and pain were written clearly upon his face. The queen was also very upset, and all those in the household insisted that Kay's request was proud, rash, and mad. Arthur took his queen by the hand and said to her: "My lady, there is no way to prevent your going with Kay."

"Now trust her to me," Kay insisted, "and don't be afraid of anything, for I'll bring her back quite safe and sound."   [196]

The king handed her over to Kay, who led her away. The members of the court followed after the two of them; not a soul remained unmoved. You must know that the seneschal was soon fully armed. His horse was brought to the middle of the palace yard; beside it was a palfrey, as befitted a queen: it was neither restive nor high-spirited. Weak, sad, and sighing, the queen approached the palfrey; she mounted, then said beneath her breath for fear she might be heard: "Ah! My friend, if you knew, I don't believe you'd ever let Kay lead me even a single step away." (She thought she had spoken in a whisper, yet she was overheard by Count Guinable, who was near her as she mounted.)

As she was led away by Kay, every man and woman who was present at court and saw this lamented as if she were already lying dead in her bier; no one thought she would ever return alive. In his rashness the seneschal led her toward where the knight was waiting; yet no one was inspired by his grief to attempt to follow him until my lord Gawain said loudly to his uncle the king: "My lord, it surprises me that you have done such a foolish thing. However, if you will accept my advice, you and I, with any others who might wish to come, should hurry after them while they are yet near. I cannot refrain myself from setting out at once in pursuit. It would be unseemly if we didn't follow them at least until we know what will become of the queen and how well Kay will acquit himself."

"Let us be off, fair nephew," said the king. "Your words are nobly spoken. Since you have suggested this course, order our horses to be brought forth, bridled and saddled and ready to mount."

The horses were led out immediately, saddled and fully equipped. The king mounted first, my lord Gawain after him, then the others as quickly as they could. Everyone wanted to be among the party, and each went as it pleased him: some with arms, and many unarmed. My lord Gawain was armed for battle and had ordered two squires to accompany him, leading in hand two war horses. As they were nearing the forest, they recognized Kay's horse coming out and saw that both reins were broken from the bit. The horse was riderless, its stirrup-leathers stained with blood; the rear part of its saddle was broken and in pieces. Everyone was upset by this; they nudged one another and exchanged comprehending glances. My lord Gawain was riding well in advance of the others; it was not long before he saw a knight approaching slowly on a horse that was sore and tired, breathing hard and lathered in sweat. The knight greeted my lord Gawain first, and my lord Gawain then returned his greeting. The knight, who recognized my lord Gawain, stopped and said, "My lord, do you not see how my horse is bathed in sweat and in such state that he is no longer of use to me? And I believe these two war-horses are yours. Now I beg you, with the promise to return you the service and favor, to let me have one or the other at your choice, either as a loan or gift."

Gawain replied, "Choose whichever of the two you prefer."

But the unknown knight, who was in desperate need, did not take the time to choose the better, or the more handsome, or the larger; rather, he leapt upon the one that was nearest him, thus making his choice. And the horse he had been riding fell dead, for that day it had been overridden and hardspent, and had suffered much. The knight galloped straightway back into the forest, and my lord Gawain followed after him in hot pursuit until he reached the bottom of a hill.

After he had ridden a great distance, Gawain came upon the war-horse that he had given the knight. It was now dead. Gawain saw that the ground had been trampled by many horses and was strewn with the fragments of many shields and lances. It clearly appeared that a pitched battle had been waged there between many knights; Gawain was bitterly disappointed not to have been present. He did not tarry long, but passed quickly beyond until by chance he again caught sight of that same knight, now alone and on foot, although still fully armed—with helmet laced, shield strung from his neck, and sword girded. He had overtaken a cart.   [320]

In those days carts were used as are pillories now; where each large town now has three thousand or more carts, in those times they had but one. Like our pillories, that cart was for all criminals alike, for all traitors and murderers, for all those who had lost trials by combat, and for all those who had stolen another's possessions by larceny or snatched them by force on the highways. The guilty person was taken and made to mount in the cart and was led through every street; he had lost all his feudal rights and was never again heard at court, nor invited or honored there. Since in those days carts were so dreadful, the saying first arose, "Whenever you see a cart and cross its path, make the sign of the cross and remember God, so that evil will not befall you."

The knight, on foot and without his lance, hurried after the cart and saw, sitting on its shaft, a dwarf who held a driver's long switch in his hand. The knight said to the dwarf, "Dwarf, for God's sake, tell me if you have seen my lady the queen pass by this way?"

The uncouth, low-born dwarf would give him no information; instead he said, "If you want to get into this cart I'm driving, by tomorrow you'll know what has become of the queen."

The dwarf continued on his way without slowing down even an instant for the knight, who hesitated but two steps before climbing in. He would regret this moment of hesitation and be accursed and shamed for it; he would come to consider himself ill-fortuned. But Reason, who does not follow Love's command, told him not to get in, and chastised and counseled him not to do anything for which he might incur shame or reproach. Reason, who dared tell him this, spoke from the lips, not from the heart; but Love, who held sway within his heart, urged and commanded him to climb into the cart at once. Because Love wished it, he jumped in; since Love ruled his action, the shame did not matter.

My lord Gawain quickly spurred on after the cart and was astonished to find the knight seated in it. Then he said, "Dwarf, if you know anything about the queen, tell me."

The dwarf answered, "If you think as little of yourself as this knight sitting here, then get in beside him and I'll drive you along with him."

When my lord Gawain heard this, he thought it was madness and said that he would not get in, for it would be a poor bargain to trade a horse for a cart. "But go wherever you will and I will follow after."   [394]

So they set off on their way—the one on horseback, the two others in the cart, and all on the same path. About nightfall they came to a fortified town that, I want you to know, was very elegant and beautiful. All three entered through a gate. The people marveled at the knight who was being transported in the dwarf's cart. They did not hide their feelings, but all—rich and poor, young and old—mocked him loudly as he was borne through the streets; the knight heard many a vile and scornful word at his expense. Everyone asked, "How will this knight be put to death? Will he be flayed or hanged, drowned or burned upon a fire of thorns? Say, dwarf—you're driving him—tell us what he's guilty of? Is he convicted of theft? Is he a murderer? Did he lose in single combat?"

The dwarf held his silence and answered not a one of them. Followed constantly by Gawain, the dwarf took the knight to his lodgings: a tower keep that was on the opposite side of town and level with it. Meadows stretched out beyond where the keep stood on a high granite cliff that fell sharply off into the valley. Gawain, on horseback, followed the cart into the keep. In the great hall they met an attractively attired girl, the fairest in all the land. They saw that she was accompanied by two comely and beautiful maidens. As soon as the maidens saw my lord Gawain, they greeted him warmly and inquired about the other knight: "Dwarf, what ill has this knight done whom you drive around like a cripple?"

Instead of answering he had the knight get down from the cart, then left; no one knew where he went. My lord Gawain dismounted; then several valets came forward to relieve both knights of their armor. The girl had two miniver-lined cloaks brought forward for them to wear. When the supper hour came, the food was splendidly prepared. The girl sat at table beside my lord Gawain. Nothing would have made them wish to change their lodging to seek better, for the girl did them great honor and provided them fair and pleasant company all through the evening.

After they had eaten their fill, two long, high beds were set up in the hall. Alongside these was a third bed, more resplendent and finer than the others, for, as the tale affirms, it had every splendor one could wish for in a bed. When it came time to retire for the night, the girl took both of the guests to whom she had offered lodging and showed them the two spacious and comfortable beds, saying, "These two beds over here are made up for you; but only the one who has earned the privilege may sleep in this third bed nearest us. It was not prepared for you."

The knight who had arrived in the cart answered that he held her injunction in perfect contempt. "Tell me," he said, "why we are forbidden to lie in this bed?"

The girl, having anticipated this question, replied without hesitation: "It is not for you to ask or inquire. A knight who has ridden in a cart is shamed throughout the land; he has no right to be concerned with what you've asked about, and he certainly has no right to lie in it, for he might soon regret it. Nor did I have it arrayed so splendidly for you to lie upon; you would pay dearly for even thinking of doing so."

"You will see about that in due time," he said.

"Will I?"

"Yes."

"Then let's see!"

"By my head," said the knight, "I don't know who will pay dearly for this, but I do know that I intend to lie down in this bed and rest as long as I like, whether you like it or not."

As soon as he had removed his armor, he got into the bed, which was half an ell longer and higher than the other two. He lay down beneath a gold-starred coverlet of yellow silk; the fur that lined it was not skinned miniver, but sable. The coverlet over him was suited for a king; the mattress was not thatch, nor straw, nor old matting.

Just at midnight a lance like a bolt of lightning came hurtling at him point first and nearly pinned the knight through his flanks to the coverlet, to the white sheets, and to the bed in which he was lying. On the lance was a pennon that was all ablaze; it set fire to the coverlet, the sheets, and the entire bed. The iron tip of the lance grazed the knight's side; it removed a little skin, but he was not actually wounded. The knight sat up, put out the flame, then grabbed the lance and hurled it to the middle of the hall. Yet in spite of all this he did not get out of the bed; instead he lay back down and slept just as soundly as he had before.   [534]

The next morning at daybreak the girl of the keep had preparations made for mass, then awoke the knights and bade them rise. When mass had been celebrated for them, the knight who had been seated in the cart came to the window that overlooked the meadow and gazed worriedly out across the fields below. The girl had come to the window nearby, where my lord Gawain spoke with her awhile in private. (I assure you that I don't know what words they exchanged.) But as they were leaning on the window ledge, they saw down in the meadows below a bier being carried along the riverbank; a knight was lying in it, and beside it three girls were weeping bitterly. Behind the bier they saw a crowd coming, at the head of which rode a tall knight escorting a beautiful lady, who was riding to his left. The knight at the other window recognized that it was the queen; as long as she was in view he gazed attentively and with pleasure at her. When he could no longer see her, he wanted to throw himself from the window and shatter his body on the ground below; he was already half out the window when my lord Gawain saw him and, after dragging him back inside, said to him, "For pity's sake, sir, calm down! For the love of God, never think such foolish thoughts again; you're wrong to hate your life!"

"No, it is right he should," countered the girl, "for won't the news of his disgrace in the cart be known to all? He certainly should want to be killed, for he's better off dead than living. Henceforth his life is shamed, scorned, and wretched."

Thereupon the knights requested their armor, which they donned. Then the girl had a special touch of courtesy and generosity: having mocked and ridiculed the knight sufficiently, she now gave him a horse and lance as token of her esteem and sympathy.

The knights took leave of the girl with proper courtesy. Having thanked her, they then set off in the direction they had seen the crowd taking and were able to pass through the castle yard without anyone speaking to them. They rode as quickly as possible to where they had seen the queen, but they were unable to overtake the crowd, since it was moving at a rapid pace. Beyond the meadows they entered into an enclosed area and found a beaten path. They rode along in the forest until mid-morning, when they encountered a girl at a crossroads.   [607]

They both greeted her, imploring and praying her to tell them, if she knew, where the queen had been taken. She replied courteously, saying, "If you promise me enough, I can show you the right road and direction and can name for you the land where she is going and the knight who is taking her. But whoever would enter into that land must undergo great tribulations; he will suffer much before getting there."

My lord Gawain said to her, "So help me God, miss, I pledge my word that if it should please you I will put all my strength into your service, if only you will tell me the truth."

The knight who had ridden in the cart did not say that he pledged her all his strength, but rather swore (as one whom Love has made strong and bold for any endeavor) to do anything she might wish without hesitation or fear, and to be entirely at her command in everything.

"Then I shall tell you," said she. And she spoke to them as follows: "By my faith, lords, Meleagant, a huge and mighty knight and the son of the King of Gorre, has carried her off into the kingdom from which no foreigner returns. In that land he must remain in exile and servitude."

Then the knight asked further, "Dear girl, where is this land? Where can we find the road that leads there?"

"You will be told," she replied, "but you must know that you will encounter difficulties and treacherous passes, for it is no easy matter to enter there without the permission of the king, whose name is Bademagu. Nonetheless, it is possible to enter by two extremely perilous ways, two exceptionally treacherous passes. One is named 'The Underwater Bridge,' because the bridge is below the water, with as much running above it as beneath— neither more nor less, since the bridge is precisely in the middle; and it is but a foot and a half in width and of equal thickness. This choice is certainly to be shunned, yet it is the less dangerous. And it has many more perils about which I say nothing. The other bridge is more difficult and so much more dangerous that it has never been crossed by man, for it is like a trenchant sword; therefore everyone calls it 'The Sword Bridge.' I have told you the truth as far as I can give it to you."

Then he asked her further, "Miss, would you deign to show us these two ways?"

And the girl replied, "This is the right way to the Underwater Bridge, and that way goes straight to the Sword Bridge."

Thereupon the knight who had been driven in the cart said, "Sir, I willingly share with you: choose one of these two ways and leave me the other; take whichever you prefer."

"In faith," said my lord Gawain, "both passages are exceedingly perilous and difficult. I cannot choose wisely and hardly know which to take; yet it is not right for me to delay when you have given me the choice: I take the Underwater Bridge."

"Then it is right that I go to the Sword Bridge without complaint," said the other, "which I agree to do."

The three then parted, commending one another gently to God's care. When the girl saw them riding off, she said, "Each of you must grant me a favor at my choosing, whenever I ask it. Take care not to forget that."

"In truth, we'll not forget, fair friend," the two knights replied. Then they went their separate ways.   [710]

The Knight of the Cart was lost in thought, a man with no strength or defense against Love, who torments him. His pensiveness was so deep that he forgot who he was; he was uncertain whether or not he truly existed; he was unable to recall his own name; he did not know if he were armed or not, nor where he was going nor whence he came. He remembered nothing at all save one creature, for whom he forgot all others; he was so intent upon her alone that he did not hear, see, or pay attention to anything. His horse carried him swiftly along, following not the crooked way, but taking the better and more direct path. Thus unguided it bore him onto a heath. In this heath was a ford, and across the ford was an armed knight who guarded it; with him was a girl who had come on a palfrey. Though by this time it was mid-afternoon, our knight had not grown weary of his unceasing meditations. His horse, by now quite thirsty, saw the good clear water and galloped toward the ford. From the other side the guardian cried out, "Knight, I guard the ford and I forbid you to cross it!"

Our knight did not hear or pay attention to this, for he was still lost in his thoughts; all the while his horse kept galloping toward the water. The guard cried out loudly enough to be heard: "You would be wise not to take the ford, for that is not the way to cross!" And he swore by the heart within his breast to slay him if he entered the ford.

Yet the knight heard him not, and so the guard shouted to him a third time: "Knight, do not enter the ford against my order, or by my head I'll strike you the moment you set foot in it!"

The knight, still wrapped in his thoughts, heard nothing. His horse leapt quickly into the water, freed himself from the bit, and began to drink thirstily. The guardian swore that the knight would pay for this and that neither his shield nor the hauberk on his back would ever save him. He urged his horse to a gallop, and from the gallop to a run; he struck our knight from his steed flat into the ford that he had forbidden him to cross. The knight's lance fell into the stream and his shield flew from round his neck. The cold water awakened him with a shock; he leapt startled to his feet, like a dreamer from sleep. He regained his sight and hearing and wondered who could have struck him. Then he saw the guard and shouted to him, "Varlet, tell me why you struck me when I didn't know you were before me and had done you no wrong?"

"In faith, you have indeed wronged me," he answered. "Did you not show me no respect when I shouted to you three times as loudly as I could not to cross the ford? You certainly must have heard at least two of my warnings, yet you entered in spite of me, and I said that I would strike you as soon as you set foot in the water."

To that the knight replied, "May I be damned if ever I heard you or if I ever saw you before! It's quite possible you did warn me not to cross the ford—but I was lost in my thoughts. Rest assured that you'll regret this if I ever get even one hand on your reins!"

The guardian of the ford replied, "What good would that do you? Go ahead and grab my reins if you dare. I don't give a fistful of ashes for your haughty threats!"

"I'd like nothing better than to seize hold of you right now," he retorted, "no matter what might come of it!"

Thereupon the guardian advanced to the middle of the ford. The unknown knight grabbed the reins with his left hand and a leg with the right. He pulled and tugged at him until the guard cried out, for it felt as if his leg was being yanked from his body. He implored him to stop: "Knight, if it pleases you to fight me on equal terms, then remount your horse and take your lance and shield and come joust with me."

"Upon my word, I won't do it. I think you'll try to run away as soon as you're free from my grasp."

When the other heard this, he was greatly shamed, and answered, "Sir knight, mount your horse and have no fear, for I give you my solemn oath that I'll not flee. You have cast shame upon me and I am offended."

The unknown knight replied, "First you will pledge me your word: I want you to swear to me that you will not flinch or flee, and that you will not touch or approach me until you see me remounted. I shall have been very generous indeed to set you free, when now I have you."

The guardian of the ford had no choice but to give his oath. When the knight heard his pledge, he went after his lance and shield, which had been floating in the ford, going along with the current, and were by now a good distance downstream. Then he returned to get his horse; when he had overtaken it and remounted, he took the shield by the straps and braced the lance against the saddletree.

Then the two spurred toward each other as fast as their steeds could carry them. The knight whose duty it was to guard the ford reached the other knight first and struck him so hard that he completely splintered his lance. The other dealt him a blow that sent him tumbling flat beneath the water, which closed completely over him. Then the Knight of the Cart withdrew and dismounted, confident that he could drive away a hundred such before him. He drew his steel-bladed sword from his scabbard, and the other knight sprang up and drew his fine, flashing blade. Again they engaged in hand-to-hand struggle, protected behind their shields, which gleamed with gold.

Their swords flashed repeatedly; they struck such mighty blows and the battle was so lengthy that the Knight of the Cart was ashamed in his heart and said that he would be unable to meet the trials of the way he had undertaken, since he needed so long to defeat a single knight. Had he met a hundred such in a valley yesterday, he felt certain they would have had no defense against him, so he was exceedingly distressed and angry to be so weak today that his blows were wasted and his day spent. Thereat he rushed the guardian of the ford until he was forced to give way and flee, though loath to do so; he left the ford's passage free. Our knight pursued him until he fell forward onto his hands; then the rider of the cart came up to him and swore by all he could see that he would rue having knocked him into the ford and having disturbed his meditations.

Upon hearing these threats, the girl whom the knight of the ford had brought with him was most fearful and begged our knight for her sake not to kill the other. But he said that in truth he must; he could not show the mercy she asked since the other had shamed him so. Then he came up to him, with sword drawn. Frightened, the guardian said, "For God's sake and mine, show me the mercy I ask of you!"

"As God is my witness," replied the Knight of the Cart, "no person has ever treated me so vilely that, when he begs me for mercy in God's name, I would not show him mercy at once for God's sake, as is right. Since I would do wrong to refuse what you have asked in His name, I will show you mercy; but first you will swear to become my prisoner wherever and whenever I summon you."

With heavy heart he swore this to the knight, whereupon the girl said, "Sir knight, since in your goodness you have granted him the mercy he requested, if ever you have released a captive, release this one now to me. If you free him for me, I swear to repay you in due course whatever you would be pleased to request that is within my power to grant."

And then the knight understood by the words she spoke who she was, and he released his prisoner to her. She was troubled and upset, for she feared he had recognized her, which she did not want him to do. But he was eager to be off, so the girl and her knight commended him to God and asked his leave, which he granted.   [930]

Then he continued on his way until near nightfall, when he beheld a most comely and attractive girl approaching. She was splendidly attired and greeted him properly and graciously. He replied, "May God keep you well and happy."

"Sir," she then said, "my lodging nearby is set to welcome you if you will accept my hospitality. But you may lodge there only if you agree to sleep with me—I make my offer on this condition." Many would have thanked her five hundred times for such an offer, but he became quite downcast and answered her very differently: "I thank you most sincerely for your kind offer of hospitality; but, if you please, I would prefer not to sleep with you."

"By my eyes," said the girl, "on no other condition will I lodge you."

The knight, when he saw he had no choice, granted her what she wished, though it pained his heart to do so. Yet if it wounded him now, how much more it would do so at bedtime! The girl who accompanied him would likewise suffer disappointment and sorrow; perhaps she would love him so much that she would not want to let him go. After he had granted her her wish, she led him to the finest bailey from there to Thessaly. It was enclosed round about by high walls and a deep moat. There was no one within, save him whom she had been awaiting.

For her residence she had had a number of fine rooms outfitted, as well as a large and spacious hall. They reached the lodging by riding along a river-bank, and a drawbridge was lowered to let them pass. They crossed over the bridge and found the tile-roofed hall open before them. They entered through the opened door and saw a table covered with a long, wide cloth; upon it a meal was set out. There were lighted candles in candelabra and gilded silver goblets, and two pots, one filled with red wine and the other with a heady white wine. Beside the table, on the end of a bench, they found two basins brimming with hot water for washing their hands. On the other end they saw a finely embroidered white towel to dry them. They neither saw nor found valet, servant, or squire therein. The knight lifted the shield from round his neck and hung it on a hook; he took his lance and laid it upon a rack. Then he jumped down from his horse, as did the girl from hers. The knight was pleased that she did not want to await his help to dismount.

As soon as she was dismounted, she hastened to a room from which she brought forth a short mantle of rich material that she placed upon his shoulders. Though the stars were already shining, the hall was not at all dark: a great light from the many large, twisted-wax candles banished all darkness from the room. Having placed the mantle over her guest's shoulders, the girl said, "My friend, here are the water and the towel; no one else offers them to you, for you see that there is no one here except me. Wash your hands and be seated when it pleases you; the hour and food require it, as you can see. So wash now, then take your place."

"Most willingly."

Then he sat down and she took her place beside him, which pleased him greatly. They ate and drank together until it was time to leave the table. When they had risen from eating, the girl said to the knight, "Sir, go outside and amuse yourself, if you don't mind; but if you please, only stay out until you think I'm in bed. Don't let this upset or displease you, for then you may come in to me at once, if you intend to keep the promise you made me."

He replied, "I will keep my promise to you and will return when I believe the time has come."

Then he went out and tarried a long while in the courtyard, until he was obliged to return, for he could not break his promise. He came back into the hall, but he could not find his would-be lover, who was no longer there. When he saw she had disappeared, he said, "Wherever she may be, I'll look until I find her."

He started at once to look for her on account of the promise he had given her. As he entered a room, he heard a girl scream out loudly; it was that very girl with whom he was supposed to sleep. Then he saw before him the opened door of another room; he went in that direction and right before his eyes he saw that a knight had attacked her and was holding her nearly naked across the bed. The girl, who was sure he would help her, screamed, "Help! sir knight—you are my guest—if you don't pull this other knight off me, I'll never find anyone to pull him away! And if you don't help me at once, he'll shame me before your very eyes! You are the one who is to share my bed, as you've already sworn to me. Will this man force his will upon me in your sight? Gentle knight, gather your strength and help me at once!"

He saw that the other held the girl uncovered to the waist, and he was troubled and embarrassed to see that naked body touching hers. Yet this sight evoked no lust in our knight, nor did he feel the least touch of jealousy. Moreover, two well-armed knights guarded the entrance with drawn swords; behind them were four men-at-arms, each holding an ax—the kind that could split a cow's backbone as easily as a root of the juniper or broom.   [1095]

The knight hesitated at the doorway and said, "My God, what can I do? I have set off in pursuit of nothing less than the queen, Guinevere. I must not have a hare's heart if I am in quest of her. If Cowardice lends me his heart and I follow his command, I'll never attain what I pursue. I am disgraced if I don't go in to her. Indeed I am greatly shamed even to have considered holding back—my heart is black with grief. I am so shamed and filled with despair that I feel I should die for having delayed here so long. May God never have mercy on me if there's a word of pride in anything I say, and if I would not rather die honorably than live shamed. If the way to her were free and those fiends were to let me cross to her unchallenged, what honor would there be in it? To be sure, the basest man alive could save her then! And still I hear this poor victim who constantly implores my aid, reminding me of my promise and reproaching me most bitterly!"

He approached the doorway at once and thrust his head and neck through; as he looked up toward the gable, he saw swords flashing toward him and drew back swiftly. The knights were unable to check their strokes and both swords shattered as they struck the ground. With the swords shattered, he was less afraid of the axes. He leapt in among the knights, jabbing one man down with his elbows and another after him. He struck the two nearest him with his elbows and forearms and beat them both to the ground. The third swung at him and missed, but the fourth struck him a blow that ripped his mantle and chemise and tore open the white flesh of his shoulder. Though blood was pouring from his wound, our knight took no respite, and without complaining of his wound he redoubled his efforts until he managed to grab the head of the knight who was trying to rape his hostess. (Before he leaves, he will be able to keep his promise to her.) He forced him up, in spite of the other's resistance; but meanwhile the knight who had missed his blow rushed upon our knight as fast as he could with his ax raised to strike—he meant to hack the knight's skull through to the teeth. But our knight skillfully maneuvered the rapist between himself and the other, and the axman's blow struck him where the shoulder joins the neck, splitting the two asunder. Our knight seized the ax and wrested it free; he dropped the man he'd been holding to look once more to his own defense, for the two knights were fast upon him and the three remaining axmen were again most cruelly assailing him. He leapt to safety between the bed and the wall and challenged them: "Come on, all of you! As long as I'm in this position, you'll find your match, even if there were twenty-seven of you! You'll never get the better of me."

As she watched him, the girl said, "By my eyes, you needn't worry from now on, since I am with you." She dismissed the knights and men-at-arms at once, and they immediately left her presence without question. Then the girl continued, "You have defended me well, sir, against my entire household. Now come along with me." They entered the hall hand in hand; yet he was not pleased, for he would gladly have been free of her.

A bed had been prepared in the middle of the hall, with smooth, full, white sheets. The bedding was not of cut straw or rough quilted padding. A covering of two silk cloths of floral design was spread over the mattress. The girl lay down upon the bed, but without removing her chemise. The knight was at great pains to remove his leggings and take off his clothes. He was sweating from his efforts; yet in the midst of his sufferings his promise overpowered him and urged him on. Is this duress? As good as such, for because of it he had to go sleep with the girl. His promise urged him on. He lay down with great reluctance; like her, he did not remove his chemise. He carefully kept from touching her, moving away and turning his back to her. Nor did he say any more than would a lay brother who has taken a vow not to speak when lying in bed. Not once did he look toward her or anywhere but straight before him. He could show her no favor. But why? Because his heart, which was focused on another, felt nothing for her; not everyone desires or is pleased by what is beautiful and fair. The knight had but one heart, and it no longer belonged to him; rather, it was promised to another, so he could not bestow it elsewhere. His heart was kept fixed on a single object by Love, who rules all hearts. All hearts? Not really, only those she esteems. And whomever Love deigns to rule should esteem himself the more. Love esteemed this knight's heart and ruled it above all others and gave it such sovereign pride that I would not wish to find fault with him here for rejecting what Love forbids him to have and for setting his purpose by Love's commands.

The girl saw clearly that he disliked her company and would gladly be rid of her, and that he would never seek her favors, for he had no desire to touch her. "If it does not displease you, sir," she said, "I will leave you and go to bed in my own room so you can be more at ease. I don't believe that the comfort of my presence is pleasing to you. Do not consider me ill bred for telling you what I believe. Now rest well this night, for you have kept your promise so fully that I have no right to ask even the least thing more of you. I'm leaving now and I wish to commend you to God."

With these words she arose. This did not displease the knight; on the contrary, he was glad to have her go, for his heart was devoted fully to another. The girl perceived this clearly; she went into her own room, disrobed completely, and lay in her bed saying to herself: "Of all the knights I have ever known this is the only one I would value the third part of a penny, for I believe he is intent upon a quest more dangerous and difficult than any ever undertaken by a knight. May God grant him success in it!"   [1278]

Thereupon she fell asleep and lay abed until the light of day appeared. As dawn broke, she rose quickly from her bed. The knight awoke, arose, then dressed and armed himself without waiting for anyone. The girl arrived in time to find him fully dressed.

"I hope a good day has dawned for you," she said when she saw him.

"The same to you, dear lady," replied the knight. And he added that he was in a hurry to have his horse brought forth.

The girl had it led to him and said, "Sir, if you dare to escort me according to the customs and usages that have been observed in the Kingdom of Logres since long before our days, I will accompany you some distance along this way." The customs and practices at this time were such that if a knight encountered a girl alone—be she lady or maidservant—he would as soon cut his own throat as treat her dishonorably, if he prized his good name. And should he assault her, he would be forever disgraced at every court. But if she were being escorted by another, and the knight chose to do battle with her defender and defeated him at arms, then he might do with her as he pleased without incurring dishonor or disgrace. This was why the girl told him that she would accompany him if he dared to escort her according to the terms of this custom and to protect her from those who might try to do her ill. "I assure you," he replied, "that no one will ever harm you unless he has first defeated me."

"Then," she said, "I wish to accompany you."

No sooner had she ordered her palfrey to be saddled than it was done; then it was brought forth along with the knight's horse. Both mounted without waiting for a squire's help and rode off rapidly. She spoke to him, but he paid no heed to what she said and refused to speak himself; to reflect was pleasing, to speak was torment. Love frequently reopened the wound she had dealt him; yet he never wrapped it to let it heal or recover, for he had no wish to find a doctor or to bandage it, unless the wound grew deeper. Yet gladly he sought that certain one. . . .

They kept to the tracks and paths of the main road without deviating until they came to a spring in the middle of a meadow. Beside the spring was a flat rock on which someone (I don't know who) had left a comb of gilded ivory. Not since the time of the giant Ysoré had anyone—wise man or fool—seen such a fine comb. In its teeth fully half a handful of hair had been left by her who had used it.

When the girl noticed the spring and the flat rock, she took a different path, since she did not want the knight to see them. And he, delighting in and savoring his pleasant meditations, did not immediately notice that she had led him from the main path. But when he did notice, he was afraid of being tricked, believing she had turned aside to avert some danger. "Stop!" he said to her. "You've gone astray; come back here! I don't think anyone ever found the right way by leaving this road."

"Sir," the girl said, "I'm certain we'll do better to go this way."

And he replied, "I don't know what you're thinking, miss, but you can plainly see that this is the beaten path. Since I have started along this road, I'll take no other! So if it pleases you, come with me, for I plan to continue along this way." They rode on together until they neared the stone and saw the comb. "Never in all my life," said the knight, "have I seen a finer comb than this!"

"Give it to me," the girl requested.

"Gladly, miss," he answered. Then he bent down and picked it up. As he held it, he gazed steadfastly at the hair until the girl began to laugh. When he noticed her laughing, he asked her to tell him why, and she replied, "Don't be so curious; I'll tell you nothing for the moment."

"Why?" he asked.

"Because I don't want to."

Upon hearing this reply, he begged her as one who feels that lovers should never betray one another in any way: "If you love anyone in your heart, miss, in his name I beg and urge you not to hide your thoughts from me."

"Your appeal is too powerful," she said. "I'll tell you and hide nothing from you: I'm as sure as I have ever been that this comb belonged to the queen—I know it. Believe me when I assure you that the bright, beautiful, shining hair you see entangled in its teeth has come from the queen's own head. They never grew in any other meadow."

The knight replied, "In faith, there are many kings and queens; which one do you mean?"

"Upon my word, sir, the wife of King Arthur."

On hearing this, the knight did not have strength enough to keep from falling forward and was obliged to catch himself upon the saddle-bow. When the girl saw this, she was amazed and terrified, fearful he might fall. Do not reproach her for this fear, because she thought he had fainted. Indeed he had come quite near fainting, for the pain he felt in his heart had driven away his speech and the color from his face. The girl dismounted and ran as quickly as she could to aid and support him, because she would not have him fall for anything. When he saw her, he was ashamed and said to her, "Why have you come here before me?"

Do not suppose that the girl would reveal the true reason. He would be ashamed and troubled, and it would cause him pain and anguish were she to reveal the truth. Therefore she hid the truth and said with utmost tact, "Sir, I came to get this comb. That's why I dismounted. I wanted it so much I couldn't wait any longer."

He was willing for her to have the comb, but first he removed the hair, being careful not to break a single strand. Never will the eye of man see anything so highly honored as those strands, which he began to adore, touching them a hundred thousand times to his eyes, his mouth, his forehead, and his cheeks. He expressed his joy in every way imaginable and felt himself most happy and rewarded. He placed the strands on his breast near his heart, between his chemise and his skin. He would not have traded them for a cart loaded with emeralds and carbuncles; nor did he fear that ulcers or any other disease could afflict him; he had no use for magic potions mixed with pearls, nor for drugs against pleurisy, nor for theriaca, nor even for prayers to St. Martin and St. James! He placed so much faith in these strands of hair that he felt no need for any other aid.

But what were these strands like? I'd be taken for a fool and liar were I to describe them faithfully: when the Lendi fair is at its height and all the finest goods are gathered there, this knight would not accept them all—it's the absolute truth—should it prevent his finding this hair. And if you still demand the truth, I'd say that if you took gold that had been refined a hundred thousand times and melted down as many, and if you put it beside these strands of hair, the gold would appear, to one who saw them together, as dull as the darkest night compared to the brightest summer day of all this year. But why should I lengthen my story?   [1495]

The girl remounted at once, still holding the comb; and the knight rejoiced and delighted in the strands that he held to his breast. Beyond the plain they entered a forest and took a sidetrack that eventually narrowed to where they were obliged to continue one behind the other, since it was impossible to ride two horses abreast. The girl preceded her escort along the path.

At the very narrowest place along the trail they saw a knight coming toward them. The girl recognized him the moment she saw him and said to her escort, "Sir knight, do you see that man coming toward us fully armed and ready for battle? He fully intends to carry me off with him without meeting any resistance. I know he thinks this, because he loves me (though in vain) and has implored me for a long while, both in person and by messenger. But my love is not for him; there is no way I could love him. God help me, I'd rather die than ever love him at all! I know he's as happy at this moment as if he'd already won me. But now I'll see what you can do! I'll see if you are bold and if your escort can bring me safely through. If you can protect me, then I shall be able to say without lying that you are a bold and worthy knight."

He answered only, "Go on, go on," which was as much as to say, "I'm not worried by anything you've told me. You've no cause to be afraid."

As they went along conversing thus, the single knight was rapidly approaching them at full gallop. He hastened so because he was confident of success and considered himself very fortunate to see the one he most loved. As soon as he drew near her, he greeted her with words of his heart on his tongue, saying, "May the girl whom I most desire, who gives me the least joy and the greatest pain, be well come from wherever she is coming."

It was fitting that she not be so stingy with her words as to refuse to return his greeting—from her tongue, if not from her heart. The knight was elated to hear the girl respond, though it cost her little effort and was not allowed to stain her lips. And had he fought brilliantly that moment at a tournament he would not have esteemed himself so highly nor felt that he had won as much honor or renown. Out of pride and vanity he reached for her bridle rein. "Now I shall lead you away with me!" he said. "Today's fine sailing has brought my ship to a good port. Now my troubles are ended: after shipwreck I've reached port; after trial, happiness; after pain, health. At this moment all my wishes are fulfilled, since I have found you under escort and will be able to take you away with me now without incurring dishonor."

"Don't be too confident," she said, "for I'm being escorted by this knight."

"Then you have poor protection indeed!" said he. "I intend to take you at once. This knight would sooner eat a whole hogshead of salt, I believe, than dare to try to wrest you from me. I don't think I've ever met a man I couldn't defeat to get you. Since now I have you here so opportunely, I intend to lead you away before his very eyes, in spite of anything he may do to try to stop me."

Our knight did not become angered by all the boasting he had heard; rather, without impudence or pride he began to challenge him, saying, "Sir, don't be too hasty and don't waste your words. Speak more reasonably. Your rights will not be denied you once you win them. But just remember that this girl has come here under my safekeeping. Now let her be; you've detained her much too long and she has no reason to fear you."

The other granted that he would rather be burned alive than fail to carry her off in spite of her knight. He said, "It would not be good if I were to allow you to take her from me. Consider it settled: I must fight. But if we wish to do combat properly, we cannot by any means do it here on this path. Let us go rather to a main road, or to a meadow or heath."

The other replied that this suited him perfectly: "Indeed I grant your request, for you are quite right that this path is too narrow—my horse would be so hampered here that I'm afraid he'd break his leg before I could turn him about." Then with very great effort and attentive not to injure his steed, he managed to wheel him about. "I'm very angered indeed that we've not met in an open place where other men could witness which of us fights better. But come along, let's go look; we'll find a wide clearing nearby."

They rode until they reached a meadow in which there were knights, ladies, and ladies-in-waiting playing at many games, for the place was delightfully pleasant. Not all were occupied in idle sport; some were playing backgammon and chess, while others were occupied in various games of dice. Most were engaged in these diversions, though some others were playing at childhood games—rounds and dances and reels, singing, tumbling, and leaping. A few were struggling in wrestling matches.   [1648]

Across the meadow from the others was an elderly knight mounted on a Spanish sorrel. His saddle and trappings were of gold, and his armor was of grey mesh. One hand was placed smartly on one of his hips as he watched the games and dances. Because of the warm weather, he was clad in his chemise, with a rich mantle trimmed in vair thrown over his shoulders. Opposite him, beside a path, were more than twenty armed knights seated on good Irish steeds. As the three riders neared them, they abandoned their sport, and their shouts could be heard throughout the meadows: "Look at that knight, just look! It's the one who was driven in the cart. Let no one continue his play while he's among us. Damned be anyone who seeks to amuse himself or dares to play as long as he is here!"

While they were speaking in this manner, the old knight's son (the one who loved the girl and already considered her his) approached his father and said: "Sir, I'm bursting with joy! Let anyone who wishes to hear this harken to it: God has granted me the one thing I have always most desired. He could not have rewarded me more if he had had me crowned king, nor would I have been as grateful, nor would I have gained as much, for what I have been granted is fair and good."

"I'm not sure it's been granted you yet," said the old knight to his son.

"You're not sure!" snapped his son. "Can't you see, then? By God, sir, how can you have any doubts when you see me holding her fast? I met her just now as she was riding along in this forest from which I've just come. I believe God was bringing her to me, so I took her as my own."

"I'm not yet sure that that knight I see following you will agree to this. I think he's coming to challenge you for her." While these words were being exchanged, the others abandoned their dancing; they stopped their games and sport out of spite and hatred for the knight they saw approaching. And this knight unhesitatingly followed swiftly on the heels of the girl. "Knight," he said, "give up this girl, for you've no right to her. If you dare fight me, I'll defend her against you here and now."

Then the old knight said: "Was I not right? My son, don't keep the girl any longer; let her go."

The son was not at all pleased and swore that he would never give her up: "May God never again grant me joy if I give her up to him. I have her and intend to keep her as my own. Before I abandon her to him I'll break my shield strap and all its armlets; I'll have lost all faith in my strength and weapons, in my sword and lance!"

"I'll not let you fight," retorted his father, "no matter what you say. You place too much faith in your own prowess. Now do as I order."

The son answered proudly, "Am I a child to be cowed? Of this I boast:

though there are many knights in this wide world, there's not one for as far as the sea stretches who is so mighty that I'd abandon her to him without a fight. I'm sure I can bring any knight to quick submission."

"I have no doubt, fair son," said his father, "that you believe this, so greatly do you trust in your own strength. But I do not consent and will not consent this day to have you test yourself against this knight."

"Were I to do as you say, I would be shamed," said the son. "May anyone who'd take your advice and abandon the field without fighting bravely be damned! It's true when they say it's bad business to deal with friends: it is better to trade elsewhere since you intend to cheat me. I can see that I could better test my courage in some far-off place, where no one would know me and attempt to dissuade me from my intention, as you do who seek to bring me low. I am all the more upset because you have found fault with me, for as you well know, when anyone reproaches a person's intent, this sparks and inflames him all the more. May God never again grant me joy if I should hesitate because of you. No, in spite of your wishes, I intend to fight!"

"By the faith I owe the holy apostle Peter," said his father, "I can clearly see that pleading is to no avail. I'm wasting my time chastising you. But before long I'll come up with a way to force you to do my will, whether you want to or not, for I'll get the best of you." Thereupon he called all his knights. When they came to him, he ordered them to seize his son, who would pay no attention to him: "I'll have him bound before I'll let him fight. You are all my liegemen and owe me esteem and loyalty. By whatever you hold from me, respect my order and my wish. My son has acted rashly, it seems to me, and with unbridled pride in opposing my desires."

They answered that they would seize him and that he would never want to fight as long as they held him; and they said that they would force him to release the girl in spite of his wishes. Then they all seized him by grabbing him by the arms and around the neck.

"Now don't you feel like a fool?" asked his father. "Admit the truth: you no longer have the power to fight or joust, and no matter how much you might be upset, your feelings will do you no good now. Give in to what I want; you'll do well to follow my advice. And do you know what I am thinking? In order to lessen your disappointment, you and I, if you want, will follow this knight today and tomorrow, through the forest and across the plain, each of us on ambling steed. We might soon find him to be of such character and bearing that I would permit you to fight him as you desire."

Then the son agreed against his will, for he had no choice. The other knight, seeing no other solution, reluctantly accepted this proposal, provided they both would follow him.   [1814]

When the people who were gathered in the meadow saw this, they all said, "Did you see that? The knight who was in the cart has won such honor this day that he is leading away my lord's son's lady, and my lord permits it. We may truthfully say that he believes there is some merit in the man to let him lead her off. A hundred curses on anyone who stops his play on his account! Let's return to our games!" Then they resumed their games and returned to their rounds and dances.

The knight turned and rode out of the meadow at once. He took the girl with him and both set off with dispatch. The son and father followed at a distance. Through a mowed field they rode until mid-afternoon, when in a most picturesque setting they found a church with a walled cemetery alongside the chancel. Being neither a boor nor fool, the knight entered the church on foot to pray to God; the girl looked after his horse until his return. When he had said his prayer and was returning, he saw an elderly monk coming directly toward him. As they met, the knight asked him politely to explain what was within these walls. The monk answered that there was a cemetery.

"As God is your help, please take me there."

"Gladly, sir." Then he led him into the cemetery, among the most beautiful tombs that could be found from there to Dombes, or even to Pamplona. Upon each were carved letters forming the names of those who were to be buried in the tombs. The knight himself began to read through the list of names and discovered: "Here will lie Gawain, here Lionel, and here Yvain." After these three there were many resting places bearing the names of many fine knights, the most esteemed and greatest of this or any other land. Among the tombs he found one of marble, which seemed to be more finely worked than all the others. The knight called to the monk and asked: "What is the purpose of all these tombs here?"

"You have seen the letters," he replied. "If you have comprehended them well, then you know what they say and the meaning of the tombs."

"Tell me what that largest one is for?"

The hermit replied, "I'll tell you all there is to know: this sarcophagus surpasses all others that have ever been made. Never has anyone seen a more elaborate or finely carved tomb; it is beautiful without and even more so within. But do not be concerned about that, for it can never do you any good and you will never see inside, because if anyone were to wish to open the tomb, he would need seven large and very strong men to open it, since it is covered by a heavy stone slab. You can be sure that to lift it would take seven men stronger than you or I. On it are carved letters that say: 'He who will lift this slab by his unaided strength will free all the men and women who are imprisoned in the land from which no one returns: since first they came here, no cleric or nobleman has been freed. Foreigners are kept prisoners, while those of this land may come and go as they please.'"

The knight went at once and seized hold of the slab and lifted it without the least difficulty, more easily than ten men could have done by putting their combined strength to the task. The monk was so astounded that he nearly fainted when he saw this marvel, for he never thought to see the like of it in all his life. "Sir," he said, "now I am most eager to know your name. Will you tell me?"

"Upon my word, I will not," answered the knight.

"Indeed, this weighs heavily upon me," said the other. "But to tell me would be a worthy action, and you could be rewarded well. Who are you? Where are you from?"

"I am a knight, as you see, born in the Kingdom of Logres—I think that is enough. Now, if you please, it is your turn to tell me who will lie in this tomb."

"Sir, he who will free all those held captive in the kingdom from which none escape."

When the monk had told him all there was to know, the knight commended him to God and to all His saints, then returned to the girl as quickly as he could. The elderly, grey-haired monk accompanied him from the church till they reached the road. As the girl was remounting, the monk told her all that the knight had done while inside and begged her to tell him his name, if she knew it. She assured him that she did not know it, but one thing was certain: there was not a living knight his equal as far as the four winds blow.   [1954]

The girl left the monk and hurried after the knight. The two who had been following them arrived then and found the monk alone before the church. The old knight said: "Sir, tell us if you have seen a knight escorting a girl."

The monk answered, "It will be no trouble to tell you all I know, for they have just this moment left here. While the knight was inside he did a most marvelous thing by lifting the stone slab from the huge marble tomb, alone and with no effort at all. He is going to rescue the queen. There is no doubt that he will rescue her and all the other people with her. You who have often read the letters inscribed on the stone slab know well that this is so. Truly no mortal knight who ever sat in a saddle was as worthy as he."

Then the father said to his son, "My son, what do you think? Is he not exceedingly bold to have performed such a deed? Now you can clearly tell whether it was you or I who was in the wrong. For all the wealth in Amiens I'd not have wanted you to fight with him. Yet you resisted mightily before you could be swayed from your purpose. Now we can return, for it would be madness to follow them beyond this spot."

"I agree with that," replied his son; "we are wasting our time following him. Let us return as soon as you are ready." He acted very wisely in turning back.

The girl rode on beside the knight; she was eager to get him to pay attention to her and learn from him his name. She asked him to tell her; time and time again she begged him until in his annoyance he said to her: "Did I not tell you that I am from the Kingdom of Arthur? I swear by God and His might that you'll not learn my name." Then she asked him for leave to turn back, which he gladly granted her. Thereupon the girl left and the knight rode on alone until it was very late.

After vespers, about compline, as he was riding along he saw a knight coming out of the woods after hunting. He had his helmet strapped on and the venison God had permitted him to take was tied over the back of his iron-grey hunter. This vavasor rode swiftly up to the knight and prayed him to accept lodging. "Sir," said he, "it will soon be night and is already past the time when it is reasonable to think of lodging. I have a manorhouse nearby where I will take you. I will do my best to lodge you better than you've ever been lodged before. I'll be happy if you'll accept."

"For my part, I am very happy to accept," said the knight.

The vavasor immediately sent his son ahead to make ready the house and hasten the supper preparations; and the youth loyally and willingly did as he was bid, riding off rapidly. The others, in no hurry, continued their easy pace until they reached the house. This vavasor had married a very accomplished lady and was blessed with five beloved sons (three mere youths and two already knighted) as well as two beautiful and charming daughters, who were still unmarried. They were not natives of this land, but were held captive there, having been imprisoned for a long while away from their homeland of Logres.

As the vavasor led the knight into his courtyard, his wife ran forward to meet him, and his sons and daughters all hastened out and vied with one another to serve him. They greeted the knight and helped him dismount. The sisters and five brothers almost ignored their father, for they knew that he would want it so. They made the stranger welcome and honored him. When they had relieved him of his armor, one of his host's two daughters took her own mantle from off her shoulders and placed it about his neck. I do not intend to give you any details about the fine dinner he was served; but after the meal they showed no reluctance to converse about many topics. First, the vavasor began to ask his guest who he was and from what land, but did not ask him his name. Our knight answered at once, "I am from the Kingdom of Logres and have never before been in this land."

When the vavasor heard this, he and his wife and all his children were most astonished. They were all very upset and began to say to him: "Woe that you were ever here, fair sir, for you will suffer for it: like us you will be reduced to servitude and exile."

"And where then are you from?" the knight asked.

"Sir, we are from your land. Many good men from your land are held in servitude in this country. Cursed be the custom, and those who promote it, that dictates that all foreigners who enter here must stay, prisoners in this land. Anyone who wishes may come in, but once here he must remain. Even for you there is no hope: I don't think you'll ever leave."

"Indeed I will," said he, "if I am able."

The vavasor said, "What! Do you believe you can escape?"

"Yes, if God is willing. And I'll do everything within my power."

"Then all the others would be able to leave without fear, for when one person can escape this imprisonment without trickery, all the others, I assure you, will be able to leave unchallenged." The vavasor then remembered that he had been told that a knight of great goodness was coming boldly into the land to seek the queen, who was being held by Meleagant, the king's son. He thought, "Indeed, I am quite convinced that this is he; I shall tell him so." Then he spoke: "Sir, do not hide your purpose from me. For my part I swear to give you the best counsel that I know. I myself stand to gain by any success you might have. For your good and mine tell me the truth. I am convinced that you came into this land to seek the queen among this heathen people, who are worse than Saracens."

"I came for no other purpose," replied the knight. "I do not know where my lady is imprisoned, but I am intent upon rescuing her and am thus in great need of counsel. Advise me if you can."

"Sir," said the vavasor, "you have chosen a most difficult path. The one on which you are presently engaged will lead directly to the Sword Bridge. You must heed my advice. If you will trust me, I'll have you led to the Sword Bridge by a safer route."

Eager to take the shortest route, he inquired, "Is that path as direct as the one before me?"

"No," said his host, "it is longer, but safer."

"Then I have no use for it. Tell me about this path, for I am set to take it."

"Indeed, sir, it will never profit you. If you take this path I advise you against, you will come tomorrow to a pass where you might easily be harmed. It is called the Stone Passage. Do you want me to give you some idea of how bad a pass it is? Only one horse can go through there at a time; two men could not go abreast through it, and the pass is well defended. Do not expect them to surrender it to you when first you get there; you'll have to endure many a sword's blow and return full measure before you can pass through."

When he had told him all this, one of the knighted sons of the vavasor came forward and said, "Sir, I will go with this knight, if it is not displeasing to you." Thereupon one of the young boys rose and said: "And I'll go too!" Their father willingly gave leave to both. Now the knight would not have to travel alone; and he thanked them, being most happy for the company.   [2186]

Then they broke off their conversation and showed the knight to his bed so that he might sleep, if he wished. As soon as he could see the day, he arose, and those who were to accompany him noticed this and immediately got up. The knights donned their armor, took their leave, and rode off with the young boy before them. They traveled on together until they came to the Stone Passage right at mid-morning. In the middle of the pass was a battlement in which a man always stood guard. While they were yet a good distance away, the man in the tower saw them and shouted loudly, "Enemy approaching! Enemy approaching!"

Then immediately a mounted knight appeared upon the battlement, armed in unspotted armor and surrounded by men-at-arms carrying sharp battle-axes. As our knight was nearing the pass, the mounted knight reproached him bitterly for having ridden in the cart: "Vassal! You acted boldly, yet like a naive fool, in coming into this land. A man who has ridden in a cart should never enter here. And may God never reward you for it!"

Thereupon the two spurred toward each other as fast as their horses would carry them. The knight whose duty it was to guard the pass split his lance with the first blow and let both pieces fall. The other took aim at his throat just above the upper edge of his shield and tossed him backwards flat upon the stones. The men-at-arms leapt to their axes, yet they deliberately avoided striking him, for they had no desire to injure either him or his horse. The knight saw clearly that they did not wish to wound him in any way and harbored no desire to harm him, so without drawing his sword he passed beyond them unchallenged, with his companions after him.

"Never have I seen such a good knight," the younger son said to his brother, "and never was there anyone to equal him. Has he not performed an amazing feat by forcing passage through here?"

"Fair brother," the older son replied, "for God's sake, hurry now to our father and tell him of this adventure!" The younger son swore that he would never go tell him and would never leave this knight's company until he had been dubbed and knighted by him. Let his brother deliver the message if he was so eager to do so!

The three then rode on together until mid-afternoon, when they encountered a man who asked them who they were. They answered, "We are knights going about our business."

And the man said to the knight who seemed to him to be lord and master of the others, "Sir, I would like to offer lodgings to you and to your companions as well."

"It is impossible for me to accept lodging at this hour," replied our knight. "Only cowardice permits one to tarry or relax when he has undertaken such a task as I have; and I am engaged in such a task that I will not take lodging for a long while yet."

Upon hearing this, the man replied, "My house is not at all nearby, but rather a long distance ahead. I promise that you will be able to lodge there at a suitable hour, for it will be late when you reach it."

"In that case I will go there," said the stranger. The man who was their guide then set off before them, and the others followed after. When they had been riding for some while, they encountered a squire galloping full speed toward them on a nag that was as fat and round as an apple. The squire called out to the man, "Sir, sir, come quickly! The men of Logres have raised an army against the people of this land and the skirmishes and fighting have already begun. They say that a knight who has fought in many places has invaded this land, and they cannot keep him from going wherever he wishes, whether they like it or not. All the people in this land say that he will soon free them and defeat our people. Now take my advice and hurry!"

The man quickened his pace to a gallop. The others, who had likewise heard this, were filled with joy and eager to help their countrymen. "Sir," said the vavasor's son, "listen to what this servant has said! Let's go to the aid of our people who are fighting their enemies!"

Their guide hurried off without waiting for them and made his way to a fortress that stood mightily on a hill. He rode until he reached the entrance, with the others spurring after him. The bailey was surrounded by a high wall and moat. As soon as they had entered, a gate was lowered upon their heels so they could not get out again. "Let's go! Let's go!" they shouted. "Let's not stop here!" They hastened after the man until they reached a passage that was not closed to them; but as soon as the man they were pursuing had gone through, a gate slammed shut behind him. They were most distressed to find themselves trapped within and thought they must be bewitched. But the knight about whom I have the most to say had a ring upon his finger whose stone had the power to break any spell, once he gazed upon it. He placed the ring before his eyes, looked at the stone, and said: "Lady, lady! By the grace of God I greatly need you to come now to my aid." This lady was a fairy who had given him the ring and had cared for him in his infancy, so he was certain that she would come to succour him wherever he might be. But he could see from his appeal and from the stone in the ring that no spell had been cast here; and he realized perfectly well that they were trapped and locked in.

They came now to the barred door of a low and narrow postern gate. All three drew their swords and struck so many blows that they hacked through the bar. Once out of the tower they saw the fierce battle raging in the meadows below, with a full thousand knights at least on either side, not counting the mass of peasants. Whey they came down into the meadows, the vavasor's son spoke with wise and measured words: "Sir, before entering the fray we would do well, I believe, to have one of us go learn which side is made up of our countrymen. I'm not sure which side they are on, but I'll go ask if you want."

"I wish you would go quickly," he said, "and return just as quickly." He went quickly and returned quickly. "It has turned out well for us," he said. "I've seen for certain that our men are on the near side."

Then the knight rode straight into the melee. He jousted with a knight he encountered coming at him and hit him such a blow in the eye that he struck him dead. The vavasor's younger son dismounted, took the dead knight's horse and armor, and outfitted himself properly and skillfully. When he was armed, he remounted at once and took up the shield and the long, straight, and colorfully painted lance; at his side he hung the sharp, bright sword. Into battle he followed his brother and their lord, who had been defending himself fiercely throughout the melee—breaking, cleaving, and splitting shields, helmets, and hauberks. Neither wood nor iron was any defense for those he attacked, as he knocked them dead or wounded from their horses. With unaided prowess he routed all he met, and those who had come with him did their share as well. The men of Logres marveled at the deeds of this unknown knight and asked the vavasor's son about him. They persisted in their questioning until they were told, "My lords, this is he who will lead us out of exile and free us from the great misery we have been in for so long. We owe him great honor because, to free us, he has already traversed many a treacherous pass and will cross many more to come. Though he has done much already, he has much yet to do."

When the news had spread throughout the crowd, everyone was filled with joy; all heard, and all understood. From the elation they felt sprang the strength that enabled them to slay many of their enemies. Yet it seems to me that the enemy was defeated more by the efforts of a single knight than by those of all the others combined. Were it not already so near nightfall the enemy would have been fully routed; but the night grew so dark that the armies were obliged to separate.   [2436]

As the armies separated, all the prisoners from Logres pressed excitedly about the knight, grabbing his reins from every side and saying, "Fair sir, you are welcome indeed!" And everyone added, "Sir, in faith, you'll be sure to take your lodging with me! Sir, by God and His Holy Name, don't stay anywhere but with me!" What one said, they all said, because young and old alike wanted him to stay with them. "You will be better provided for at my house than anywhere else," they all said. Everyone crowded about him there was saying this and trying to pull him away from the others, because each wanted to host him; they nearly came to blows.

He told them all that it was foolish to quarrel so. "Stop this bickering," he said, "for it won't help me or you. Rather than quarrel among ourselves, we should aid one another. You should not argue over who will lodge me, but should be intent upon lodging me somewhere that will bring honor to everyone and will help me along my way."

Yet each kept repeating: "At my house—no, at mine!"

"You're still talking foolishly," said the knight. "In my opinion the wisest of you is a fool for arguing this way. You should be helping me along, but all you want to do is turn me aside. By all the saints invoked in Rome, I'm as grateful now for your good intentions as I would have been if all of you, one after another, had provided me as much honor and service as one can give a man. As surely as God gives me health and happiness, your good intentions please me as much as if each of you had already shown me great honor and kindness. So may the intentions be counted for the deed!"

In this manner he persuaded and appeased them all. They brought him to the house of a very well-to-do knight that was situated along the road he was to take, and everyone took pains to serve him. They all honored and served him and showed how happy they were for his presence; because of their great respect for him, they entertained him until bedtime.   [2496]

In the morning, when it was time to depart, everyone wanted to accompany him and all offered him their services. But it was not his pleasure or will to have anyone accompany him except the two he had brought there with him. He took these two and no others. They rode that day from early morning until dusk without encountering adventure. Late in the evening as they were riding rapidly out of a forest, they saw the manorhouse of a knight. His wife, who seemed a gentle lady, was seated in the doorway. As soon as she caught sight of them, she rose up to meet them. With a broad and happy smile she greeted them: "Welcome! I want you to accept lodgings in my house. Dismount, for you have found a place to stay."

"My lady, since you command it, by your leave we'll dismount and stay this night at your house."

When they had dismounted, the lady had their horses cared for by the members of her fine household. She called her sons and daughters, who came at once: young boys, who were courteous and proper knights, and comely daughters. Some she asked to unsaddle and groom the horses, which they willingly did without a word of protest. At her request the girls hastened to help the knights remove their armor; when they were disarmed, they were each given a short mantle to wear. Then they were led straightway into the magnificent house. The lord of the manor was not there, for he was out in the woods hunting with his two sons. But he soon returned, and his household, showing proper manners, hastened to welcome him at the gate. They untied and unloaded the venison he was carrying and said as they reached him, "Sir, you don't know it yet, but you are entertaining three knights."

"May God be praised!" he replied.

The knight and his two sons were delighted to have this company, and even the least member of the household did his best to do what had to be done. Some hastened to prepare the meal, others to light the tapers; still others fetched the towels and basins and brought generous amounts of water for washing their hands. They all washed and took their places. Nothing to be found therein was unpleasant or objectionable.

While they were partaking of the first course, there appeared before them at the outside door a knight who was prouder than the proudest bull. He was armed from head to foot and sat upon his charger, with one foot fixed in the stirrup but the other, for style, thrown jauntily over his steed's flowing mane. No one noticed him until he was right before them and said, "I want to know which one of you was so proud and foolish and so empty-headed as to come into this land, believing he can cross the Sword Bridge? He's wasting his strength; he's wasting his steps."

Unruffled, our knight answered confidently, "I am he who wishes to cross the Sword Bridge."

"You! You? What ever gave you that idea? Before undertaking such a thing you should have thought how you might end up, and you should have recalled the cart you climbed into. I don't know whether you feel shamed for having ridden in it, but no one with good sense would have undertaken such a great task after having shown himself so blameworthy."

To these insults our knight did not deign to reply a single word; but the lord of the manor and all those with him were rightly astounded beyond measure at this. "Oh God! What a misfortune!" thought each to himself. "Damned be the hour when a cart was first conceived of and built, for it is a vile and despicable thing. Oh God! What was he accused of? Why was he driven in the cart? For what sin? For what crime? He will be reproached forever for it. Were he innocent of this reproach, no knight in all the world could match him in boldness; and if all the world's knights were assembled in a single place, there'd not be a more genteel or handsome one, if the truth be told." Concerning this, everyone agreed.

The intruder continued his haughty words, saying, "Knight, hear this, you who are going to the Sword Bridge: if you wish, you can cross over the water quite safely and easily. I will have you taken quickly across in a boat. However, if I decide to exact the toll once I have you on the other side, then I'll have your head if I want it; or, if not, it will be at my mercy."

Our knight answered that he was not seeking trouble: he would never risk his head in this manner, no matter what the consequences. Whereupon the intruder continued, "Since you refuse my aid, you must come outside here to face me in single combat, which will be to the shame and grief of one of us."

"If I could refuse, I'd gladly pass it up," said our knight to taunt him, "but indeed, I'd rather fight than have something worse befall me."

Before rising from where he was seated at table, he told the youths who were serving him to saddle his horse at once and to fetch his armor and bring it to him. They hurried to do as he commanded. Some took pains to arm him; others brought forward his horse. And you can rest assured that, as he was riding off fully armed upon his horse and holding his shield by the armstraps, he could only be counted among the fair and the good. The horse suited him so well that it seemed it could only be his own—as did the shield he held by the armstraps. The helmet he had laced upon his head fit him so perfectly that you'd never have imagined he'd borrowed it or wore it on credit; rather, you'd have said—so pleasing was the sight of him—that he had been born and raised to it. All this I'd have you believe on my word.

Beyond the gate, on a heath where the battle was to be held, the challenger waited. As soon as the one saw the other, they spurred full speed to the attack and met with a clash, striking such mighty thrusts with their lances that they bent like bows before flying into splinters. With their swords they dented their shields, helmets, and hauberks; they split the wood and broke the chainmail, and each was wounded several times. Every blow was in payment for another, as if in their fury they were settling a debt. Their sword blows often struck through to their horse's croups; they were so drunk in their blood-thirst that their strokes fell even on the horses' flanks, and both were slain. When their steeds had fallen, they pursued one another on foot. In truth they could not have struck more mightily with their swords had they hated one another with a mortal passion. Their payments fell more swiftly than the coins of the gambler who doubles the wager with each toss of the dice. But this game was quite different: there were no dice cast, only blows and fearful strokes, vicious and savage.

Everyone—the lord, his lady, their daughters and sons—had come forth from the house and assembled to watch the battle on the broad heath. When he saw his host there watching him, the Knight of the Cart blamed himself for faintheartedness; then, as he saw the others assembled there observing him, his whole body shook with anger, for he was convinced he should have defeated his adversary long since. With his sword he struck him a blow near the head, then stormed him, pushing him relentlessly backward until he had driven him from his position. He forced him to retract and pursued him until the intruder had almost lost his breath and was nearly defenseless.

Then our knight recalled that the other had reproached him most basely for having ridden in the cart; he pummeled and assailed him until no strap or lacing remained unbroken around his neckband. He knocked the helmet from his head and the ventail flew off. He pressed and beleaguered him so that he was compelled to beg for mercy. Like the lark, which is unable to find cover and is powerless before the merlin that flies more swiftly and attacks it from above, the intruder to his great shame was forced to plead for mercy, since he could not better his adversary. When the victor heard his foe pleading for mercy, he did not strike or touch him, but said, "Do you want me to spare you?"

"That's a smart question," he retorted, "such as a fool would ask! I've never wanted anything as much as I now want mercy."

"Then you shall have to ride in a cart. Say anything you wish, but nothing will move me unless you mount the cart for having reproached me so basely with your foolish tongue."

But the proud knight answered him, "May it never please God that I ride in a cart!"

"No?" said the other. "Then you shall die!"

"Sir, my life is in your hands. But in God's name I beg your mercy, only don't make me climb into a cart! There is nothing I wouldn't do except this, no matter how painful or difficult. But I know I'd rather be dead than be so shamed. No matter what else you could ask of me, however difficult, I'd do it to obtain your mercy and pardon."   [2778]

Just as he was asking for mercy, a girl came riding across the heath on a tawny mule, with her mantle unpinned and hair disheveled. She was striking her mule repeatedly with a whip, and no horse at full gallop, to tell the truth, could have run faster than that mule was going. The girl addressed the Knight of the Cart: "May God fill your heart with perfect happiness and grant you every wish."

Delighted to hear this greeting, he replied, "May God bless you and grant you happiness and health!"

Then she announced her purpose: "Sir knight, I have come from far off in great distress to ask a favor of you, for which you will earn the greatest reward I can offer. And I believe that a time will come when you will need my assistance."

"Tell me what you wish," he answered, "and if I have it, you will receive it at once, so long as it is not impossible."

"I demand the head of this knight you have just defeated. To be sure, you have never encountered a more base and faithless knight. You will be committing no sin but rather will be doing a good and charitable act, for he is the most faithless being who ever was or ever will be."

When the defeated knight heard that she wanted him killed, he said to his conqueror, "Don't believe a word she says, because she hates me. I pray you to show mercy to me in the name of the God who is both Father and Son, and who caused His daughter and handmaiden to become His mother."

"Ah, knight!" said the girl. "Don't believe this traitor. May God give you as much joy and honor as you desire, and may He give you success in the quest you have undertaken!"

Now the victorious knight hesitated and reflected upon his decision: should he give the head to this girl who has asked him to cut it off, or should he be touched by pity for the defeated knight? He wishes to content them both: Generosity and Compassion demand that he satisfy them both, for he is equally generous and merciful. Yet if the girl carries off the head, Compassion will have been vanquished and put to death; and if she must leave without it, Generosity will have been routed. Compassion and Generosity hold him doubly imprisoned, with each in turn spurring him on and causing him anguish. One wants him to give the head to the girl who asked for it; the other urges Pity and Kindness. But since the knight has begged for mercy, will he not have it? Indeed he must, for no matter how much our knight hates another, he has never refused to grant mercy once—but only once—when that knight has been defeated and forced to plead with him for his life. So he will not refuse mercy to this knight who now begs and implores him, since this is his custom. Yet will she who desires the head not have it? She will, if possible.

"Knight," he said, "you must fight with me again if you wish to save your head. I will have mercy enough on you to let you take up your helmet and arm yourself anew as best you are able. But know that you will die if I defeat you again."

"I could wish no better and ask no other mercy," replied the knight.

"I shall give you this advantage," added the Knight of the Cart, "that I will fight you without moving from this spot I have claimed."

The other knight made ready, and they soon returned hotly to the fight, but he was defeated now with more ease than he had been the first time.

The girl immediately shouted, "Don't spare him, sir knight, no matter what he says, for he would certainly never have spared you even the first time! If you listen to his pleas, you know he'll deceive you again. Cut off the head of this most faithless man in the whole kingdom and give it to me, fair knight. It is right that you give it to me, because that day will yet come when I shall reward you for it. If he could, he would deceive you again with his false promises."

The knight, seeing that his death was at hand, cried out loudly for mercy, but his cries and all the arguments he could muster were of no avail to him. Our knight grabbed him by the helmet, ripping off all the fastenings; the ventail and the white coif he struck from his head. The knight struggled till he could no more: "Mercy, for the love of God! Mercy, noble vassal!"

"Having once set you free, I'll never again show mercy, even if it were to ensure my eternal salvation."

"Ah!" said he. "It would be a sin to believe my enemy and slay me thus!"

All the while the girl, eager for him to die, was urging the knight to behead him quickly and not to believe his words. His blow fell swiftly: the head flew out onto the heath, the body crumpled. The girl was pleased and satisfied. The knight grasped the head by the hair and presented it to her. She was overjoyed and said, "May your heart find great joy in whatever it most desires, as my heart has now in what I most hated. I had only one sorrow in life: that he lived so long. I have a recompense awaiting you, which will come when you most need it. Rest assured that you will be greatly rewarded for this service you have done me. I am going now, but I commend you to God, that He might protect you from harm." Thereupon the girl took her leave, and each commended the other to God.   [2941]

A very great joy spread through all those who had seen the battle in the heath. They all happily removed the knight's armor and honored him as best they knew how. Then they washed their hands once again, for they were eager to return to their meal. Now they were much happier than ever, and the meal passed amid high spirits.

After they had been eating for some time, the vavasor remarked to his guest, who was seated beside him: "Sir, we came here long ago from the Kingdom of Logres, where we were born. We want you to find great honor, fortune, and happiness in this land, for we ourselves and many others as well stand to profit greatly if honor and fortune were to come to you in this land and in this undertaking."

"May God hear your prayers," he replied.

When the vavasor had finished speaking, one of his sons continued, saying, "We should put all our resources in your service and offer you more than promises. If you have need of our help, we should not wait to give it until you ask for it. Sir, do not worry that your horse is dead, for there are many more strong horses here. I want you to have whatever you need that we might give you: since you need it, you will ride off on our best horse to replace your own."

"I gladly accept," replied the knight.

With that they had the beds prepared and went to sleep. They arose early the next morning, outfitted themselves, and were soon ready to be off. As they left, the knight did not forget any politeness: he took leave of the lady and the lord, then of all the others. But I must tell you one thing so that nothing will be omitted: our knight did not wish to mount upon the borrowed horse that had been presented him at the gate. Instead (I would have you know) he had one of the two knights who had accompanied him mount it, and he mounted that knight's horse, since thus it pleased and suited him. When each was seated on his horse, the three of them rode off with the blessings of their host, who had served and honored them as best he could.

They rode straight on until night started to fall, reaching the Sword Bridge in the late afternoon, about vespers. At the foot of that very dangerous bridge they dismounted their horses and saw the treacherous water, black and gurgling, dark and thick, as horrifying and frightening as if it were the Devil's stream, and so perilous and deep that there's nothing in the whole world that, if it were to fall into it, would not be lost as surely as if it had fallen into the frozen sea. The bridge across was unlike any other: there never was nor ever will be another like it. Were you to ask me for the truth, I'd say that never has there been such a treacherous bridge and unstable crossing. The bridge across the cold waters was a sharp and gleaming sword—but the sword was strong and stiff and as long as two lances. On either side were large stumps into which the sword was fixed. No one need fear falling because of the sword's breaking or bending, for it was forged well enought to support a heavy weight.

What caused the two knights who accompanied the third to be most discomfited, however, was that they thought there were two lions or two leopards tethered to a large rock at the other end of the bridge. The water and the bridge and the lions put them in such a state that they were trembling in fear. "Sir," they said, "be forewarned by what you see before you! This bridge is vilely constructed and joined together, and vilely built. If you don't turn back now, it will be too late to repent. There are many things that should only be undertaken with great foresight. Suppose you should get across—but that could never happen, no more than you could contain the winds or forbid them to blow, or prevent the birds from singing their songs; no more than a man could reenter his mother's womb and be born again; all this could not be, any more than one could drain the oceans—if you should get across, could you be sure that those two wild lions that are chained over there would not kill you and suck the blood from your veins, eat your flesh, and then gnaw upon your bones? It takes all my courage just to look at them! If you are not careful, I assure you they'll kill you: they'll break and tear the limbs from your body and show no mercy. So take pity on yourself and stay here with us. It is wrong to put yourself knowingly in such certain danger of death."

He reassured them with a laugh: "My lords, receive my thanks for being so concerned about me. It is sincere and springs from love. I know that you would never wish me to fall into any misfortune, but my faith in God is so strong that He will protect me always. I have no more fear of this bridge and this water than I do of this solid earth, and I intend to prepare myself to undertake a crossing. I would rather die than turn back!"

They did not know what more to say to him; both sighed deeply and wept with compassion. The knight prepared himself as best he could to cross the chasm, and he did a most unusual thing in removing the armor from his hands and feet—he certainly wouldn't be whole and uninjured when he reached the other side! Yet he could get a better grip on the sword, which was sharper than a scythe, with his bare hands and feet, so he left nothing on his feet—neither shoes, mail leggings, nor socklets. It mattered not to him if he should injure his hands and feet: he'd rather maim himself than fall from the bridge into the water from which there was no escape.

He crossed in great pain and distress, wounding his hands, knees, and feet. But Love, who guided him, comforted and healed him at once and turned his suffering to pleasure. He advanced to the other side on hands, feet, and knees. Then he remembered the two lions that he thought he had seen while he was still on the other side. He looked, but there was not so much as a lizard to do him harm. He raised his hand before his face, gazed at his ring, then looked again. (Since he had found neither of the lions that he thought he'd seen, he believed there must be some sort of enchantment; yet there was no living thing there.)

The two knights on the other shore rejoiced to see that he had crossed, as well they should; but they were unaware of his injuries. The knight considered himself most fortunate not to have been more seriously wounded; he was able to staunch the flow of blood from his wounds by wrapping them with his chemise. 	 [3137]

Now he saw before him a tower more mighty than any he had ever seen before; there was no way it could have been finer. Leaning on a window ledge was King Bademagu, who was most scrupulous and keen in every matter of honor and right and who esteemed and practiced loyalty above all other virtues. And resting there beside him was his son, who strove constantly to do the opposite, since disloyalty pleased him, and he never tired of baseness, treason, and felony. From their vantage point they had watched the knight cross the bridge amid great pain and hardship. Meleagant's face reddened with anger and wrath; he knew well that he would be challenged now for the queen. But he was such a knight that he feared no man, no matter how strong or mighty. Had he not been treasonous and disloyal, one could not have found a finer knight; but his wooden heart was devoid of kindness and compassion.

Yet what caused Meleagant to suffer so made his father the king pleased and happy. The king knew with certainty that he who had crossed the bridge was far better than any other knight, for no one would dare cross who harbored within himself Cowardice, which shames those who have it more than Nobility brings them honor. Nobility cannot do as much as Cowardice and Sloth, for it's the truth—and never doubt it—that evil is easier done than good.

I could tell you many things about these qualities if we could linger here, but I must return to my matter and turn toward something else, and you will hear how the king addressed and instructed his son. "Son," said he, "it was by chance that you and I came here to lean upon this window ledge, and we have been repaid by witnessing with our own eyes the very boldest deed that has ever been conceived. Now tell me if you don't esteem the knight who performed such a wondrous feat? Go make peace with him and surrender the queen. You will gain nothing by fighting with him, and are likely to suffer greatly for it. So let yourself be known as wise and noble, and send him the queen before he comes to you. Honor him in your land by giving him what he came to seek before he asks it of you—for you know quite well that he is seeking Queen Guinevere. Don't let anyone find you obstinate or foolish or proud. Since he has entered alone into your land, you must offer him hospitality, for a gentleman must welcome, honor, and praise another gentleman and never snub him. He who does honor is honored by it. Know you well that honor will be yours if you honor and serve him who without any doubt is the best knight in the world."

"May I be damned if there is not another as good or even better than he!" retorted his son. (The king had unwisely overlooked Meleagant, who thought himself not a bit inferior to the other.) "Perhaps you want me to kneel before him with hands joined and become his liegeman and hold my lands from him? So help me God, I'd rather be his liege than return Guinevere to him! She'll certainly never be handed over by me without a fight, and I'll defend her against all who are fool enough to come seeking her!"

Then the king answered him at once, "Son, you would do well not to be so stubborn. I urge and advise you to hold your peace. You know that it would cast shame upon this knight not to win the queen from you in battle; there can be no doubt that he would rather regain her through battle than generosity, for it would enhance his fame. In my opinion he's not sought after her in order to have her given peaceably to him but because he wants to win her in battle. So you would do well to keep him from having the battle. It hurts me to see you play the fool: but if you ignore my advice, I won't care if he gets the better of you. You stand to suffer greatly for your obstinacy, since this knight need fear no one here but yourself. I offer him peace and protection on behalf of myself and all my men. I have never acted disloyally or practiced treason or felony, and I will no more do so for your sake than for that of a total stranger. I don't want to give you any false hopes: I intend to assure the knight that everything he needs in the way of armor and horses will be provided him, since he has shown such courage in coming this far. He need fear for his safety from no man but you alone; and I want you to know that, if he can defend himself against you, he need fear no other."

"For the moment I am content to listen and say nothing," replied Meleagant. "You may say what you will, but I'm not bothered by anything you've said. I don't have the cowardly heart of a monk or do-gooder or almsgiver, nor do I care to have any honor that requires me to give him what I most love. His task won't be so easily and quickly accomplished and will turn out quite differently than you and he think. Even if you aid him against me, we'll not make our peace with you. If you and all your men offer him safe-conduct, what do I care? None of this causes me to lose heart. In fact it pleases me greatly, so help me God, that he has no one to fear but myself. Nor do I ask you to do a thing for me that might be interpreted as disloyalty or treason. Be a gentleman as long as you please, and let me be the villain!"

"What, will you not change your mind?"

"Never!" he replied.

"Then I've nothing more to say. Do your best. I shall leave you and go speak with the knight. I want to offer him my aid and counsel in every matter, for I am entirely in his camp."   [3302]

Then the king went down and ordered his horse saddled. A huge war-horse was brought to him, which he mounted by the stirrup. He ordered three knights and two men-at-arms, no more, to accompany him. They rode down from the castle heights until they neared the bridge and saw the knight, who was tending his wounds and wiping the blood from them. The king presumed that he would have him as a guest for a long while as his wounds were healing, but he might as well have expected to drain the sea.

King Bademagu dismounted at once, and the knight, though he was seriously wounded and did not know him, rose to greet him. He showed no sign of the pain he felt in his feet and hands. The king observed his self-control and hastened to return his greeting, saying, "Sir, I am astounded that you have fought your way into this land among us. But be welcome here, for no one will undertake this feat again. Never has it happened and never will it happen that anyone but you will have the courage to face such danger. Know that I esteem you the more for having done this deed that no one before you dared even conceive. You will find that I am most agreeable, loyal, and friendly toward you; I am the king of this land and freely offer you my counsel and aid. I'm quite certain that I know what you are seeking here: you have come to seek the queen, I presume?"

"Sir," replied the wounded knight, "you presume correctly—no other duty brings me here."

"My friend, you will have to suffer before you win her," said the king, "and you are already grievously hurt, to judge by the wounds and blood I see. You won't find the knight who brought her here generous enough to return her without battle, so you must rest and have your wounds treated until they are fully healed. I shall provide you the ointment of the Three Marys—and better, if such be found—for I am most anxious about your comfort and recovery. The queen is securely confined, safe from the lusts of men, even from that of my son (much to his chagrin), who brought her here with him. I've never known anyone so crazed and mad as he! My heart goes out to you and, so help me God, I will gladly provide you everything you need. Though he'll be angry with me for it, he'll never have such fine arms that I'll not give you some equally good, and a horse that suits your needs. I shall protect you against everyone, no matter whom it might displease; you need fear no one except him alone who brought the queen here. No one has ever threatened another as I threatened him, and I was so angry at his refusal to return her to you that I all but chased him from my land. Though he is my son, you needn't worry, for unless he can defeat you in battle he can never, against my will, do you the least harm."

"Sir," he answered, "I thank you! But I'm wasting too much time here— time I don't want to waste or lose. I'm not hurt at all, and none of my wounds are causing me pain. Take me to where I can find him, for I'm ready to do battle with him now in such armor as I'm wearing."

"My friend, it would be better for you to wait two or three weeks for your wounds to heal; a delay of at least a fortnight would do you good. And I would never permit and could never countenance your fighting in my presence with such arms and equipment."

"If it pleases you," he replied, "I would have no arms but these, and gladly would I do battle in them. Nor do I seek even the slightest respite, postponement, or delay. However, to please you I will wait until tomorrow; but no matter what anyone may say, I'll not wait any longer!" Thereupon the king confirmed that all would be as the knight wished. He had him shown to his lodging and prayed and commanded those who were escorting the knight to do everything to serve him; and they saw to his every need.

The king, who would gladly arrange peace if he could, went meanwhile to his son and spoke to him in accordance with his desire for peace and harmony. "Fair son," he told him, "reconcile yourself to this knight without a fight. He has not come into this land to amuse himself or to participate in the hunt, but rather has come to seek his honor and to increase his renown. I have seen that he is in great need of rest. Had he taken my advice, he would have put off for several months at least the battle he is already eager to have. Are you afraid of incurring dishonor by returning the queen to him? Have no fear of this, for no blame can come to you from it; on the contrary, it is a sin to keep something to which one has no right. He would willingly have done battle here without delay, even though his hands and feet are gashed and wounded."

"You are a fool to be concerned," said Meleagant to his father. "By the faith I owe St. Peter, I'll not listen to your advice in this affair. Indeed I should be torn apart by horses if I did as you suggest. If he is seeking his honor, so do I seek mine; if he is seeking his renown, so do I seek mine; if he is eager for battle, I am a hundred times more so!"

"I plainly see that you have your mind set on madness," said the king, "and you will find it. You shall try your strength against the knight tomorrow, since you will have it so."

"May no greater trial than this ever come to me!" said Meleagant. "I would much rather it were for today than tomorrow. See how I am acting more downcast than usual: my eyes are troubled and my face is very pale. Until I do battle I won't feel happy or at ease, nor will anything pleasing happen to me."   [3474]

The king recognized that no amount of advice or pleading would avail, so reluctantly he left his son. He selected a strapping fine horse and good weapons, which he sent to the one who needed them. In that land there lived an aged man and excellent Christian: no more loyal man could be found in all the world—and he was better at healing wounds than all the doctors of Montpellier. That night he summoned all his knowledge to care for the knight, since such was the king's command.

Already the news had spread to the knights and maidens, to the ladies and barons from the whole land round about. Both friend and stranger rode swiftly through the night until dawn, coming from every direction as far away as a hard day's travel. By daybreak there were so many crowded before the tower that there wasn't room to move. The king arose that morning worried about the battle; he came directly to his son, who had already laced his Poitevin helmet upon his head. He could arrange no further delay and was unable to establish peace; though the king did all in his power to make peace, he was unable to achieve anything. So the king ordered that the battle was to take place in the square before the keep, where all the people were gathered.

The king sent at once for the foreign knight, who was led into the square, filled with people from the Kingdom of Logres. Just as people are wont to go to hear the organs at churches on the great feasts of Pentecost and Christmas, so in like manner they had all assembled here. The foreign maidens from the kingdom of King Arthur had all fasted three days and gone barefoot in hairshirts so that God might give strength and courage to their knight, who was to do battle against his enemy on behalf of the captives. In like manner the natives of this land prayed that God might give honor and victory in the battle to their lord.

Early in the morning, before the bells of prime had rung, the two champions were led fully armed to the center of the square on two iron-clad horses. Meleagant was handsome and bold: his arms, legs, and feet rippled with muscles, and his helmet and shield complemented him perfectly. But no one could take his eyes from the other—not even those who wished to see him shamed—and all agreed that Meleagant was nothing in comparison with him.

As soon as both had reached the center of the square, the king approached and did his best to postpone the battle and establish peace, but again he was unable to dissuade his son. So he said to them, "Rein in your horses at least until I have taken my place in the tower. It will not be too much to delay that long for my sake."

Downcast, he left them and went straight to where he knew he'd find the queen, for she had begged him the night before to be placed somewhere where she might have a clear view of the battle. He had granted her request and went now to find and escort her, for he strove constantly to do her honor and service. He placed her before a window while he reclined at another, beside and to the right of her. Together with the two of them were many knights, courtly ladies, and maidens of this land. There were also many captive maidens, who were intent upon their prayers and petitions, and many prisoners, both men and women, who were all praying for their lord, because to him and to God they had entrusted their help and deliverance.

Then at once the two combatants had the people fall back. They seized their shields from their sides and thrust their arms through the straps; they spurred forward until their lances pierced fully two arm's lengths through their opponent's shield, which broke and splintered like flying sparks. Quickly their horses squared off head to head and met breast to breast. Shields and helmets clashed together and rang round about like mighty claps of thunder. Not a breast-strap, girth, stirrup, rein, or flap could support the shock; even the sturdy saddle-bows split. Nor did they feel any shame in falling to the ground when all this gave way beneath them.

They leapt at once to their feet and without wasting words rushed together more fiercely than two wild boars. What good were challenges? Like hated enemies they struck mighty blows with their steel-edged swords; savagely they slashed helmets and gleaming hauberks, as blood rushed out from beneath the gashed metal. The battle was a mighty one as they stunned and wounded one another with powerful and treacherous blows. They withstood many fierce, hard, long assaults with equal valor, such that it was never possible to determine who was in the right. Yet it was inevitable that the knight who had crossed the bridge would begin to lose strength in his wounded hands. Those who sided with him grew most concerned, for they saw his blows weakening and feared he would be defeated; they were certain now that he was getting the worst of it, and Meleagant the better. A murmur ran through the crowd.   [3633]

But looking from the windows of the tower was a clever maiden, who recognized within her heart that the knight had not undertaken the battle for her sake, nor for that of the common people assembled in the square: he would never have agreed to it had it not been for the queen. She felt that if he realized that the queen herself was at the window watching him, it would give him renewed strength and courage. If only she could learn his name, she would willingly shout out for him to look about himself a little. So she came to the queen and said, "For God's sake and your own, my lady, as well as for ours, I beg you to tell me the name of this knight, if you know it—because it may be of some help to him."

"In what you have requested, young lady," replied the queen, "I perceive no wicked or evil intention, only good. I believe the knight is called Lancelot of the Lake."

"Praise God! You've made me so happy; my heart is full of joy!" exclaimed the girl. Then she rushed forward and shouted to him, in a voice that everyone could hear: "Lancelot! Turn around to see who is watching you!"

When Lancelot heard his name, he turned at once and saw above him, seated in one of the tower loges, that person whom he desired to see more than anyone else in the whole world. From the moment he beheld her, he began to defend himself from behind so he would not have to turn or divert his face or eyes from her. Meleagant pursued him with renewed eagerness, elated to think that now he had him defenseless. The men of that kingdom were likewise elated, but the foreign prisoners were so distraught that many of them could no longer stand, and sank to their knees or fell prostrate upon the ground. Thus were felt both joy and sorrow in full measure.

Then the girl shouted again from the window: "Ah! Lancelot! What could make you behave so foolishly? Once you were the incarnation of all goodness and prowess, and I don't believe that God ever made a knight who could compare with you in valor and worthiness! Yet now we see you so distracted that you're striking blows behind you and fighting with your back turned. Turn around and come over here where you can keep the tower in sight, for seeing it will bring you strength and help."

Lancelot was shamed and vexed and despised himself because he well knew that for a long while now he'd been getting the worst of the fight— and everyone present knew it too! He maneuvered around behind his enemy, forcing Meleagant to fight between himself and the tower. Meleagant struggled mightily to regain his position, but Lancelot carried the fight to him, shoving him so powerfully with his full weight behind his shield when he tried to get to the other side, that he caused him to stagger twice or more in spite of himself. Lancelot's strength and courage grew because Love aided him, and because he had never before hated anything as much as this adversary. Love and mortal Hatred, the greatest ever conceived, made him so bold and courageous that Meleagant realized that this was deadly serious and began to fear him exceedingly, for Meleagant had never before faced such a bold knight, nor had any knight ever before injured him as this one had. He withdrew willingly and kept his distance, dodging and avoiding his hated blows.

Lancelot did not waste threats upon him, but drove him steadily with his sword toward the tower where the queen was seated—he often served and did homage to her—until he had driven him in so close that he had to desist, for he would have been unable to see her, had he advanced a step farther. Thus Lancelot constantly drove him back and forth at will, stopping each time before his lady the queen, who had so inflamed his heart that he gazed upon her continually. And this flame so stirred him against Meleagant that he could drive and pursue him anywhere he pleased: he was driven mercilessly, like a man blinded or lame.

The king, seeing his son so pressed that he could no longer defend himself, took pity on him. He intended to intervene if possible; but to proceed properly he must first ask the queen. "My lady," he began by saying, "I have always loved, served, and honored you while you have been in my care, and I have always been prompt to do anything that I felt would be to your honor. Now I wish to be repaid. But I want to ask you a favor that you should only grant me through true affection: I clearly see that my son is getting the worst of this battle; I don't come to you because I am sorry to see him defeated, but so that Lancelot, who has the power to do so, will not kill him. Nor should you want him slain—though it is true that he deserves death for having so wronged both you and Lancelot! But for my sake I beg you in your mercy to tell Lancelot to refrain from slaying him. Thus you might repay my services, if you see fit."

"Fair sir, because you request it, I wish it so," replied the queen. "Even if I felt a mortal hatred for your son, whom I do not love, yet you have served me well, and because it pleases you, I wish Lancelot to restrain himself."

These words, which had not been spoken in a whisper, were overheard by Lancelot and Meleagant. One who loves totally is ever obedient and willingly and completely does whatever might please his love. Thus Lancelot, who loved more than Pyramus (if ever a man could love more deeply), must do her bidding. No sooner had the last word flowed from her mouth—no sooner had she said, "Because it pleases you, I wish Lancelot to restrain himself"—than nothing could have made Lancelot touch Meleagant or make any move to defend himself, even had the latter attempted to kill him. He did not move or touch him; but Meleagant, shamed and out of his mind with rage at hearing he had sunk so low that his father had had to intervene, struck Lancelot repeatedly.

The king hurried down from the tower to reproach him; he stepped into the fray and shouted to his son at once: "What! Is it right for you to strike him when he doesn't touch you? You are unspeakably cruel and savage, and your rashness condemns you! Everyone here knows for certain that he has vanquished you."

Beside himself with shame, Meleagant then said to the king, "You must be blind! I don't think you can see a thing! Anyone's blind who doubts that I've defeated him!"

"Then find someone who believes you!" said the king. "All these people know full well whether you're lying or speaking the truth. We know the truth." Then the king ordered his barons to restrain his son. They immediately did his bidding and pulled Meleagant away. But no great force was necessary to restrain Lancelot, for Meleagant could have done him serious harm before he would ever have touched him. Then the king said to his son, "So help me God, now you must make peace and hand over the queen! You must call an end to this whole dispute."

"Now you're talking like an old fool! I hear nothing but nonsense. Go on! Get out of our way and let us fight!"

And the king replied that he would intervene indeed, for he was certain that Lancelot would kill his son if he were to let them continue fighting.

"Him, kill me? Hardly! I'd kill him at once and win this battle if you'd let us fight and not interrupt us!"

"By God," said the king, "nothing you say will have any effect on me!"

"Why?" he challenged.

"Because I don't wish it! I refuse to lend credence to your folly and pride, which would only kill you. It takes a real fool to seek his own death, as you do, without realizing it. I am well aware that you detest me for wanting to protect you. I don't believe that God will ever let me witness or consent to your death, because it would break my heart."

He reasoned with his son and reproached him until a truce was established. This accord affirmed that Meleagant would hand over the queen on the condition that Lancelot would agree to fight him again one year and no more from that day on which he would be challenged. Lancelot readily consented to this condition. With the truce, all the people hastened around and decided that the battle would take place at the court of King Arthur, who held Britain and Cornwall; there they decided it would be. And the queen was obliged to grant, and Lancelot to promise, that if Meleagant were to defeat him there, no one would prevent her return with him. The queen confirmed this, and Lancelot consented. So upon these conditions the knights were reconciled, separated, and disarmed.   [3898]

It was the custom of this land that when one person left, all the others could leave. They all blessed Lancelot, and you can be sure that great joy was felt then, as well it should be. All those who had been held captive came together, greatly praising Lancelot and saying, so that he might hear, "Sir, in truth, we were very elated as soon as we heard your name, for we were quite certain that soon we would all be freed."

There were a great many people celebrating there, and everyone was striving to find some way to touch Lancelot. Those who were able to get nearest were happy beyond words. There was great joy, but sadness too: those who had been freed were given over to happiness; but Meleagant and his followers shared none of their joy; rather, they were sorrowful, downcast, and dejected. The king turned away from the square, leading Lancelot, who begged to be taken to the queen, away with him.

"I am not reluctant to take you there," said the king, "for it seems to me to be a proper thing to do. If you wish, I'll show you the seneschal Kay as well."

Lancelot was so overjoyed that he nearly cast himself at the king's feet. Bademagu led him at once into the hall where the queen had gone to await him. When the queen saw the king leading Lancelot by the hand, she stood up before the king and acted as if she were angered. She lowered her head and said not a word.

"My lady," said the king, "this is Lancelot, who has come to see you."

"Me? Sir, he cannot please me. I have no interest in seeing him."

"My word, lady," exclaimed the king, who was very noble and courtly. "What makes you feel this way? Indeed you are much too disdainful of one who has served you well, who has often risked his life for you on this journey, and who rescued you and defended you against my son, Meleagant, who was most reluctant to give you up."

"Sir, in truth he has wasted his efforts. I shall always deny that I feel any gratitude toward him."

You could see Lancelot's confusion, yet he answered her politely and like a perfect lover: "My lady, indeed this grieves me, yet I dare not ask your reasons."

Lancelot would have poured out his woe if the queen had listened, but to pain and embarrass him further she refused to answer him a single word and passed instead into a bedchamber. Lancelot's eyes and heart accompanied her to the entrance; his eyes' journey was short, for the room was near at hand, yet they would gladly have entered in after her, had that been possible. His heart, its own lord and master, and more powerful by far, was able to follow after her, while his eyes, full of tears, remained outside with his body.

The king whispered to him: "Lancelot, I am amazed that this has happened. What can this mean when the queen refuses to see you and is so unwilling to speak with you? If ever she was pleased to speak with you, she should not now be reticent or refuse to listen to you, after all you have done for her. Now tell me, if you know, what reason she has to treat you this way."

"Sir, I never expected this sort of welcome. But clearly she does not care to see me or listen to what I have to say, and this disturbs me greatly."

"Of course," said the king, "she is wrong, for you have risked death for her. So come now, my fair friend, and go speak with the seneschal Kay."

"I am very eager to do so," replied Lancelot.

The two of them went to the seneschal. When Lancelot came before him, the seneschal addressed him first, saying: "How you have shamed me!"

"How could I have?" answered Lancelot. "Tell me what shame I've caused you."

"An enormous shame, because you have completed what I was unable to complete and have done what I was unable to do."

At that the king left the two of them and went out of the room alone. Lancelot asked the seneschal if he had suffered greatly.

"Yes," he answered, "and I am still suffering. I have never been worse off than I am now, and I would have been dead long ago had it not been for the king who just now left us, who in his compassion has shown me such kindness and friendship. Whenever he was aware I needed anything, he never failed to arrange to have it prepared for me, as soon as he knew of my need. But each time he tried to help me, his son Meleagant, who is full of evil designs, deceitfully sent for his own physicians and ordered them to dress my wounds with ointments that would kill me. Thus I've had both a loving father and a wicked stepfather: for whenever the king, who did everything he could to see that I would be quickly healed, had good medicine put on my wounds, his son, in his treachery and desire to kill me, had it removed straightway and some harmful ointment substituted. I am absolutely certain that the king did not know this, for he would in no way countenance such base treachery.

"And you aren't aware of how kindly he has treated my lady: never since Noah built his ark has a tower in the march been as carefully guarded as he has had her kept. Though it upsets his son, he has not let even Meleagant see her except in his own presence or with a company of people. The good king in his kindness has always treated her as properly as she could require. No one but the queen has overseen her confinement; she arranged it so, and the king esteemed her the more because he recognized her loyalty. But is it true, as I've been told, that she is so angry with you that she has publicly refused to speak to you?"

"You have been told the truth," replied Lancelot, "the whole truth. But for God's sake, can you tell me why she hates me?"

Kay replied that he did not know and was extremely amazed by her behavior.

"Then let it be as she orders," said Lancelot, who could not do otherwise. "I must take my leave and go seek my lord Gawain, who has come into this land having sworn to me to go directly to the Underwater Bridge."

Lancelot left the room at once, came before the king, and asked his leave to depart. The king willingly consented; but those whom Lancelot had delivered from imprisonment asked what was to become of them. Lancelot replied, "With me will come all those who wish to seek Gawain, and those who wish to stay with the queen should remain. They need not feel compelled to come with me."

All who so wished accompanied him, happier than they'd ever been before. There remained with the queen many maidens, ladies, and knights, who were likewise filled with joy. Yet all of those remaining would have preferred to return to their own country rather than stay in this land. The queen only retained them because of the imminent arrival of my lord Gawain, saying that she would not leave until she had heard from him.

Word spread everywhere that the queen was freed, that all the captives were released, and that they would be able to leave without question whenever it might please them. When people came together, they all asked one another about the truth of this matter and spoke of nothing else. They were not at all upset that the treacherous passes had been destroyed. Now people could come and go at will—this was not as it had been!

When the local people who had not been at the battle learned how Lancelot had fared, they all went to where they knew he was to pass, for they thought that the king would be pleased if they captured and returned Lancelot to him. Lancelot's men had all removed their armor and were quite bewildered to see these armed men approaching. It is no wonder that they succeeded in taking Lancelot, who was unarmed, and returned with him captive, his feet tied beneath his horse. "Lords, you do us wrong," said the men of Logres, "for we are traveling under the king's safe-conduct. We are all under his protection."

"We know nothing of this," replied the others. "But captive as you are, you must come to court."

Swift-flying rumor reached the king, saying that his people had captured and killed Lancelot. On hearing this, Bademagu was greatly upset and swore by more than his head that those who had killed him would die for it. He said that they would never be able to justify themselves, and if he could catch them, he'd have them hanged, burned, or drowned at once. And should they try to deny their deed, he would never believe them, for they had brought him such grief and had caused him such shame that he himself would bear the blame for it unless he took vengeance—and without a doubt he would.

The rumor spread everywhere. It was even told to the queen, who was seated at dinner. She nearly killed herself when she heard the lying rumor of Lancelot's death. She thought it was true and was so greatly perturbed that she was scarcely able to speak. Because of those present, she spoke openly: "Indeed, his death pains me, and I am not wrong to let it, for he came into this land on my account, and therefore I should be grieved." Then she said to herself in a low voice, so she would not be overheard, that it would not be right to ask her to drink or eat again, if it were true that he for whom she lived were dead. She arose at once from the table, and was able to give vent to her grief without being noticed or overheard. She was so crazed with the thought of killing herself that she repeatedly grabbed at her throat. Yet afterward she confessed in conscience, repented, and asked God's pardon; she accused herself of having sinned against the one she knew had always been hers, and who would still be, were he alive. Anguish brought on by her own lack of compassion destroyed much of her beauty. Her lack of compassion, the betrayal of her love, combined with ceaseless vigils and fasting, caused her to lose her color.

She counted all of her unkindnesses and called them each to mind; she noted every one, and repeated often: "Oh misery! What was I thinking, when my lover came before me and I did not deign to welcome him, nor even care to listen! Was I not a fool to refuse to speak or even look at him? A fool? No, so help me God, I was cruel and deceitful! I intended it as a joke, but he didn't realize this and never forgave me for it. I believe that it was I alone who struck him the mortal blow. When he came happily before me and expected me to receive him joyfully, and I shunned him and would never even look at him—was this not a mortal blow? At that moment when I refused to speak, I believe I severed both his heart and his life. Those two blows killed him, I think, and not any highway brigands.

"Ah God! Will I be forgiven this murder, this sin? Never! All the rivers and the sea will dry up first! Oh misery! How it would have brought me comfort and healing if once, before he died, I had held him in my arms. How? Yes, quite naked next to him, in order to enjoy him fully. Since he is dead, I am wicked not to kill myself. Can my life bring me anything but sorrow if I live on after his death, since I take pleasure in nothing except the woe I bear on his account? The sole pleasure of my life after his death—this suffering I now court—would please him, were he alive. A woman who would prefer to die rather than to endure pain for her love is unworthy of it. So I am happy indeed to mourn him unceasingly. I prefer to live and suffer life's blows than to die and be at rest." [4244]

The queen mourned thus for two days, without eating or drinking, until it was thought she was dead. Many there are who would prefer to carry bad news than good, and so the rumor reached Lancelot that his lady and love had succumbed. You need not doubt that he was overcome with grief, and everyone can understand that he was sorrowful and depressed. He was so saddened (if you care to hear and know the truth) that he disdained his very life: he intended to kill himself at once, but not before he'd unburdened his soul. He tied a sliding loop in one end of the belt he wore around his waist, and said to himself, weeping, "Ah death! How you have sought me out and overcome me in the prime of life! I am saddened, but the only pain I feel is the grief in my heart—an evil, mortal grief. I want it to be mortal so that, if it please God, I shall die of it. And if it doesn't please God that I should die of grief, could I not die in another way? Indeed I shall, if he lets me loop this cord about my neck! In this manner I am sure that I can force Lady Death to take me, even against her will. Though Death, who seeks out only those who don't want her, does not want to come to me, my belt will bring her within my power, and when I control her she will do my bidding. Yet she will be too slow to come because of my eagerness to have her!"

Then, without waiting, he put the loop over his head until it was taut about his neck; and to be sure of death, he tied the other end of the belt tightly to his saddle horn, without attracting anyone's attention. Then he let himself slip toward the ground, intending to be dragged by his horse until he was dead. He did not care to live another hour. When those who were riding with him saw him fallen to the ground, they thought he had fainted, for no one noticed the loop that he had tied around his neck. They lifted him up at once, and when they had him in their arms, they discovered the noose, which had made him his own enemy when he had placed it around his neck. They cut it immediately, but it had been pulled so tight around his throat that he could not speak for a long while. The veins of his neck and throat were nearly severed. Even had he wanted, he could no longer harm himself.

He was so distraught at being stopped that he was aflame with anger and would have killed himself had he not been watched. Since he could no longer harm himself physically, he said, "Ah! vile, whoring Death! Why didn't you have the strength and power to slay me before my lady's death? I suppose it was because you wouldn't deign to do a good turn to anyone. You did this out of treachery, and you will never be anything but a traitor. Ah! What kindness! What goodness! How wonderful you've been with me! But may I be damned if I ever welcome this kindness or thank you for it!

"I don't know which hates me more: Life, who wants me, or Death, who refuses to take me! Thus they both destroy me: but it serves me right, by God, to be alive despite myself, for I should have killed myself as soon as my lady the queen made known her displeasure. She did not show it without reason—there was certainly a good cause, though I do not know what it was. Yet had I known, I would have reconciled myself to her in any way she wished, so that before her soul went to God she might have forgiven me. My God! What could this crime have been? I think that perhaps she realized that I had mounted into the cart. I don't know what else she could have held against me. This alone was my undoing.

"But if she hated me for this crime—oh God! how could this have damned me? One who would hold this against me never truly knew Love; for there is nothing known that, if prompted by Love, should be contemptible; rather, anything that one can do for his lady-love should be considered an act of love and courtliness. Yet I did not do it for my lady-love. Ah me! I don't know what to call her. I don't know whether I dare name her my 'lady-love.' But I think that I know this much of Love: if she had loved me, she would not have esteemed me the less for this act, but would have called me her true love, since it seemed to me honorable to do anything for her that Love required, even to mounting into the cart. She should have ascribed this to Love, its true source. Thus does Love test her own, and thus does she know her own. But by the manner of her welcome I knew that this service did not please my lady. Yet it was for her alone that her lover performed this deed for which he has often been shamed, reproached, and falsely blamed. I have indeed done that for which I am blamed, and from sweetness I grow bitter, in faith, because she has behaved like those who know nothing of Love and who dip honor into shame; yet those who dampen honor with shame do not wash it, but soil it. Those who condemn lovers know nothing of Love, and those who do not fear her commands esteem themselves above Love. There is no doubt that he who obeys Love's command is uplifted, and all should be forgiven him. He who dares not follow Love's command errs greatly." [4396]

Thus Lancelot lamented, and those beside him who watched over and protected him were saddened. Meanwhile word reached them that the queen was not dead. Lancelot took comfort immediately and, if earlier he had wept bitterly over her death, now his joy in her being alive was a hundred thousand times greater.

When they came within six or seven leagues of the castle where King Bademagu was staying, news that was pleasing came to him about Lancelot—news that he was glad to hear: that Lancelot was alive and was returning hale and hearty. He behaved most properly in going to inform the queen. "Fair sir," she told him, "I believe it, since you have told me. But were he dead, I assure you that I could never again be happy. If Death were to claim a knight in my service, my joy would leave me altogether."

Thereupon the king left her. The queen was most eager for the arrival of her joy, her lover. She had no further desire to quarrel with him about anything. Rumor, which never rests but runs unceasingly all the while, soon returned to the queen with news that Lancelot would have killed himself for her, had he not been restrained. She welcomed this news and believed it with all her heart, yet never would she have wished him ill, for it would have been too much to bear.

Meanwhile Lancelot came riding swiftly up. As soon as the king saw him, he ran to kiss and embrace him; his joy so lightened him that he felt as if he had wings. But those who had taken and bound Lancelot cut short his joy. The king cursed the hour in which they had come and wished them all dead and damned. They answered only that they thought he would have wanted Lancelot.

"Though you may think that," replied the king, "nonetheless it displeases me. Worry not for Lancelot—you have brought him no shame. No! But I, who promised him safe-conduct, am dishonored. In all events the shame is mine, and you will find it no light matter if you try to escape me."

When Lancelot perceived his anger, he did his very best to make peace and was finally able to do so. Then the king led him to see the queen. This time the queen did not let her eyes lower toward the ground but went happily up to him and had him sit beside her, honoring him with her kindest attentions. Then they spoke at length of everything that came into their minds; they never lacked for subject matter, which Love supplied them in abundance. When Lancelot saw how well he was received, and that anything he said pleased the queen, he asked her in confidence: "My lady, I wonder why you acted as you did when you saw me the other day and would not say a single word to me. You nearly caused my death, yet at that moment I didn't have enough confidence to dare to ask you, as now I am asking you. My lady, if you would tell me what sin has caused me such distress, I am prepared to atone for it at once."

The queen replied, "What? Were you not ashamed and fearful of the cart? By delaying for two steps you showed your great unwillingness to mount. That, to tell the truth, is why I didn't wish to see you or speak with you."

"In the future may God preserve me from such a sin," said Lancelot, "and may He have no mercy upon me if you are not completely right. My lady, for God's sake, accept my penance at once; and if ever you could pardon me, for God's sake tell me so!"

"Dear friend, may you be completely forgiven," said the queen. "I absolve you most willingly."

"My lady," said he, "I thank you. But I cannot tell you in this place all that I would like to. If it were possible, I'd gladly speak with you at greater leisure."

The queen indicated a window to him with a glance, not by pointing. "Tonight when everyone within is asleep, you can come speak with me at this window. Make your way first through the orchard. You cannot come inside or be with me: I shall be inside and you without. It is impossible for you to get inside, and I shall be unable to come to you, except by words or by extending my hand. But for love of you I will stay by the window until the morrow, if it pleases you. We cannot come together because Kay the seneschal, suffering from the wounds that cover him, sleeps opposite me in my room. Moreover, the door is always locked and guarded. When you come, be careful lest some informer see you."

"My lady," said Lancelot, "I will do everything possible so that no one will observe my coming who might consider it evil or speak badly of us." Having set their tryst, they separated joyfully.   [4532]

On leaving the room, Lancelot was so full of bliss that he did not recall a single one of his many cares. But night was slow in coming, and this day seemed longer to him, for all his anticipation, than a hundred others or even a whole year. He ached to be at the tryst, if only night would come. At last dark and somber night conquered day's light, wrapped it in her covering, and hid it beneath her cloak. When Lancelot saw the day darkened, he feigned fatigue and weariness, saying that he had been awake a long while and needed repose. You who have behaved in like manner will be able to understand that he pretended to be tired and went to bed because there were others in the house; but his bed had no attraction for him, and nothing would have made him sleep. He couldn't have slept, nor had he the courage, nor would he have wanted to dare fall asleep.

He crept out of bed as soon as possible. It bothered him not at all that there was no moon or star shining outside, nor any candle, lamp, or lantern burning within the house. He moved slowly, careful not to disturb anyone; everyone thought he had slept the whole night in his bed. Alone and unobserved, he went straight to the orchard. He had the good fortune to discover that a part of the orchard wall had recently fallen. Through this breach he quickly passed and continued until he reached the window, where he stood absolutely silent, careful not to cough or sneeze, until the queen approached in a spotless white gown. She had no tunic or coat over it, only a short mantle of rich cloth and marmot fur.

When Lancelot saw the queen leaning upon the window ledge behind the thick iron bars, he greeted her softly. She returned his greeting promptly, since she had great desire for him, as did he for her. They did not waste their time speaking of base or tiresome matters. They drew near to one another and held each other's hand. They were troubled beyond measure at being unable to come together, and they cursed the iron bars. But Lancelot boasted that, if the queen wished it, he could come in to her—the iron bars would never keep him out. The queen responded, "Can't you see that these bars are too rigid to bend and too strong to break? You could never wrench or pull or bend them enough to loosen them."

"My lady," he said, "don't worry! I don't believe that iron could ever stop me—nothing but you yourself could keep me from coming in to you. If you grant me your permission, the way will soon be free; but if you are unwilling, then the obstacle is so great that I will never be able to pass."

"Of course I want you with me," she replied. "My wishes will never keep you back. But you must wait until I am lying in my bed, so that you will not be endangered by any noise, for we would be in real trouble if the seneschal sleeping here were to be awakened by us. So I must go now, for if he saw me standing here he'd find no good in it."

"My lady," said Lancelot, "go then, but don't worry about my making any sound. I plan to separate the bars so smoothly and effortlessly that no one will be aroused."

Thereupon the queen turned away, and Lancelot prepared and readied himself to unbar the window. He grasped the iron bars, strained, and pulled, until he had bent them all and was able to free them from their fittings. But the iron was so sharp that he cut the end of his little finger to the quick and severed the whole first joint of the next finger; yet his mind was so intent on other matters that he felt neither the wounds nor the blood flowing from them.

Although the window was quite high up, Lancelot passed quickly and easily through it. He found Kay still asleep in his bed. He came next to that of the queen; Lancelot bowed low and adored her, for he did not place as much faith in any saint. The queen stretched out her arms toward him, embraced him, clasped him to her breast, and drew him into the bed beside her, looking at him as tenderly as she could, prompted by Love and her heart. She welcomed him for the sake of Love; but if her love for him was strong, he felt a hundred thousand times more for her. Love in other hearts was as nothing compared with the love he felt in his. Love took root in his heart, and was so entirely there that little was left for other hearts.

Now Lancelot had his every wish: the queen willingly sought his company and affection, as he held her in his arms, and she held him in hers. Her love-play seemed so gentle and good to him, both her kisses and caresses, that in truth the two of them felt a joy and wonder, the equal of which has never been heard or known. But I shall let it remain a secret forever, since it should not be written of: the most delightful and choicest pleasure is that which is hinted, but never told.

Lancelot had great joy and pleasure all that night, but the day's coming sorrowed him deeply, since he had to leave his love's side. So deep was the pain of parting that rising was a true martyrdom, and he suffered a martyr's agony: his heart repeatedly turned back to the queen where she remained behind. Nor was he able to take it with him, for it so loved the queen that it had no desire to quit her. His body left, but his heart stayed. Lancelot went straight to the window, but he left enough of his body behind to stain and spot the sheets with the blood that dripped from his fingers. As Lancelot departed he was distraught, full of sighs and full of tears. It grieved him that no second tryst had been arranged, but such was impossible. Regretfully he went out the window through which he had entered most willingly. His fingers were badly cut. He straightened the bars and replaced them in their fittings so that, from no matter what angle one looked, it did not seem as if any of the bars had been bent or removed. On parting, Lancelot bowed low before the bedchamber, as if he were before an altar. Then in great anguish he left. [4719]

On the way back to his lodging he did not encounter anyone who might recognize him. He lay down naked in his bed without awakening anyone. And then at dawn, to his surprise, he noticed his wounded fingers; but he was not the least upset, for he knew without doubt that he had cut himself pulling the iron bars from the window casing. Therefore he did not grow angry with himself, since he would rather have had his two arms pulled from his body than not to have entered through the window. Yet, if he had so seriously injured himself in any other manner, he would have been most upset and distressed.

In the morning the queen was gently sleeping in her curtained room. She did not notice that her sheets were stained with blood, but thought them still to be pure white, fair, and proper. As soon as he was dressed, Meleagant came into the room where the queen had been sleeping. He found her awake and saw the sheets stained with fresh drops of blood. He nudged his men and, as if suspecting some evil, looked toward the seneschal Kay's bed. There, too, he saw bloodstained sheets—because, you can surmise, his wounds had reopened during the night. "My lady," said Meleagant, "now I've found the proof I've been seeking! It's certainly true that a man is a fool to take pains to watch over a woman—all his efforts are wasted. And the man who makes the greater effort loses his woman more quickly than he who doesn't bother. My father did a fine job of protecting you from me! He has guarded you carefully from me, but in spite of his efforts the seneschal Kay has looked closely upon you this night and has done all he pleased with you. This will be easily proven!"

"How?" she asked.

"I have found blood on your sheets—clear proof, since you must be told. This is how I know, and this is my proof: that on your sheets and his I have found blood that dripped from his wounds. This evidence is irrefutable!"

Then, for the first time, the queen noticed the bloody sheets on both beds. She was dumbfounded, shamed, and red-faced. "As the Lord Almighty is my protector," she said, "this blood you see on my sheets never came from Kay . . . my nose bled last night—it must have come from my nose." She felt as if she were telling the truth.

"By my head," replied Meleagant, "all your words are worth nothing! There is no need for lies, for you are proved guilty and the truth will soon be known." Then he spoke to the guards who were there: "Lords, don't move. See that the sheets are not removed from the bed before my return. I want the king to acknowledge my rights when he sees this for himself."

Meleagant sought out his father, the king, then let himself fall at his feet, saying, "Sir, come and see something that you would never have expected. Come and see the queen, and you will be astounded at what I have found and proved. But before you go there, I beg you not to fail me in justice and righteousness. You are well aware of the dangers to which I have exposed myself for the queen; yet you oppose me in this and have her carefully guarded for fear of me. This morning I went to look at her in her bed, and I saw enough to recognize that Kay lies with her every night. By God, sir, don't be disturbed if this angers me and I complain, for it is most humiliating to me that she hates and despises me, yet lies every night with Kay."

"Silence!" said the king. "I don't believe it!"

"Sir, then just come and see what Kay has done to the sheets. If you don't believe my word and think that I am lying to you, the sheets and spread, covered with Kay's blood, will prove it to you."

"Let us go then," said the king. "I want to see this for myself: my eyes will teach me the truth." The king went at once into the room, where he found the queen just getting up. He saw the bloody sheets on her bed and those on Kay's bed as well. "Lady," he said, "you are in a terrible plight if what my son says is true."

"So help me God," she answered, "not even about a dream has such an awful lie been spread! I believe the seneschal Kay is so courteous and loyal that it would be wrong to mistrust him, and I have never offered my body for sale or given it away. Kay is certainly not a man to insult me like this— and I have never had the desire to do such a thing, and never will!"

"Sir, I shall be most grateful to you," said Meleagant to his father, "if Kay is made to pay for his offense in such a manner that shame is cast upon the queen as well. It is for you to dispense the justice that I seek. Kay has betrayed King Arthur, his lord, who had faith enough in him that he entrusted to him what he most loved in this world."

"Sir, now permit me to reply," said Kay, "and I shall acquit myself. May God never absolve my soul after I leave this world if ever I lay with my lady. Indeed I would much rather be dead than to have committed such a base and blameworthy act against my lord. May God never give me healing for these wounds I bear, but may Death take me at once, if I ever even contemplated such an act! I know that my wounds bled profusely this night and soaked my sheets. This is why your son suspects me, but he certainly has no right to."

Meleagant answered him, "So help me God, the demons and the living devils have betrayed you! You became too excited last night, and no doubt because you overtaxed yourself your wounds were reopened. No lies can help you now. The blood in both beds is proof—it is there for all to see. One must by right pay for a sin in which he has been openly caught. Never has a knight of your stature committed such an impropriety, and you are shamed by it."

"Sir, sir," Kay pleaded with the king, "I will defend my lady and myself against your son's accusations. He causes me grief and torment but is clearly in the wrong."

"You are in too much pain to do battle," replied the king.

"Sir, with your permission, I am ready to fight him in spite of my injuries to prove that I am innocent of that shame of which he accuses me."   [4900]

Meanwhile the queen had sent secretly for Lancelot. She told the king that she would provide a knight to defend the seneschal against Meleagant in this matter, if his son would dare accept the challenge. Meleagant replied without hesitation, "I am not afraid to do battle to the finish with any knight you might select, even if he were a giant!"

At this moment Lancelot entered the hall. There was such a mass of knights that the room was filled to overflowing. As soon as he arrived, the queen explained the situation so that all, young and old, could hear: "Lancelot," she said, "Meleagant has accused me of a shameful act. I am considered guilty by all who have heard this accusation, unless you force him to retract it. He asserts that Kay slept with me this night, because he has seen my sheets and Kay's stained with blood. He says that the seneschal will be proved guilty unless he can defend himself in single combat, or find another to undertake the battle on his behalf."

"You have no need to beg for help as long as I am near," said Lancelot. "May it never please God that anyone should doubt either you or Kay in such a matter. If I am worth anything as a knight, I am prepared to do battle to prove that Kay never so much as conceived of such a deed. I will undertake the battle on his behalf and defend him as best I can."

Meleagant sprang forward and declared: "As God is my Savior, I'm quite satisfied with this arrangement. Let no one ever think otherwise!"

"My lord king," spoke Lancelot, "I am knowledgeable in trials, laws, suits, and verdicts. When a man's word is doubted, an oath is required before the battle begins."

Sure of himself, Meleagant replied immediately, "I'm fully prepared to swear my oath. Bring forward the holy relics, for I know that I'm in the right."

"No one who knows the seneschal Kay," countered Lancelot, "could ever mistrust him on such a point."

They called for their armor at once and ordered their horses to be fetched. They donned their armor when it was brought them, and their valets armed their horses. Next the holy relics were brought out. Meleagant stepped forward with Lancelot beside him. They both knelt, and Meleagant stretched forth his hand toward the relics and swore his oath in a powerful voice: "As God and the saints are my witnesses, the seneschal Kay slept this night with the queen in her bed and took his full pleasure with her."

"And I swear that you lie," said Lancelot, "and I further swear that he never slept with her or touched her. And if it please God, may He show His righteousness by taking vengeance on whichever of us has lied. And I will take yet another oath and will swear that, if on this day God should grant me the better of Meleagant, may He and these relics here give me the strength not to show him any mercy, no matter whom it may grieve or hurt!" King Bademagu could find no cause for joy when he heard this oath.

After the oaths had been sworn, the horses, fair and good in every respect, were led forward, and each knight mounted his steed. Then they charged headlong toward one another as fast as their horses could carry them. As their steeds rushed full speed, the two vassals struck each other two such mighty blows that each was left holding only the half of his lance. They thrust each other to the ground, but neither remained there defeated. They both rose up at once with drawn swords to strike with all the might of their naked blades. Burning sparks flew from their helmets toward the heavens. So enraged were they in their assaults with unsheathed blades that, as they thrust and parried and struck one another, there was no desire to rest, nor even to catch their breath. The king, gravely concerned, summoned the queen, who had gone up into the tower loge to observe the battle. He asked her in the name of God the Creator to let them be separated.

"Whatever suits and pleases you," replied the queen. "In faith, you would be doing nothing that would displease me."

As soon as Lancelot heard what the queen had replied to King Bademagu's request, he had no further desire for combat and abandoned the fight altogether. But Meleagant struck and slashed at him unceasingly, until the king forced his way between them and restrained his son, who swore that he had no intention of making peace: "Peace be damned! I want to fight!"

"You will be wise to keep silent and do as I say," the king answered him. "Certainly no shame or harm will come to you for taking my advice. So do what is right. Don't you remember that you have arranged to do battle with Lancelot in the court of King Arthur? And can you doubt that it would be a far greater honor to defeat him there than anywhere else?" The king said this in an attempt to appease his son, and eventually he was able to calm him and separate them.

Lancelot, who was very eager to find my lord Gawain, then asked leave of the king, and next of the queen. With their permission he rode off rapidly toward the Underwater Bridge. He was followed by a large company of knights, but he would have been happier if many of those with him had remained behind. [5053]

They rode for several full days until they were about a league from the Underwater Bridge. But before they could get near enough to see the bridge, a dwarf came forth to meet them. He was riding on a huge hunter and brandishing a whip to encourage and incite his steed. Promptly he inquired, as he had been ordered, "Which one of you is Lancelot? Don't hide him from me, I am one of your party. You must tell me in perfect confidence, because it is for your profit that I ask."

Lancelot spoke for himself, saying, "I am he whom you are seeking."

"Ah, Lancelot! Brave knight! Quit these men and place your faith in me. Come along with me alone, for I wish to take you to a very wonderful place. Let no one watch which way you go. Have them wait at this spot, for we shall return shortly."

Suspecting no deceit, Lancelot ordered his companions to remain behind, and he himself followed the dwarf, who was betraying him. His men who are awaiting him there could wait forever, because those who have captured him and hold him prisoner have no intention of returning him. His men were so distressed at his failure to return that they did not know what to do. They all agreed that the dwarf had deceived them, and they were very upset, but felt it would be folly to seek after him. They approached the search with heavy hearts, because they did not know where they might find him or in which direction to look. They discussed their predicament among themselves: the wisest and most reasonable men agreed that they should proceed first to the Underwater Bridge, which was nearby, then seek Lancelot afterward with the aid of my lord Gawain, should they succeed in finding him.

They proceeded toward the Underwater Bridge and, upon reaching it, saw my lord Gawain, who had slipped and fallen into the deep water. He was bobbing up and down, in and out of sight. They approached and reached out to him with branches, poles, and crooked sticks. Gawain had only his hauberk on his back, and on his head his helmet, which was worth ten of any others. He wore chainmail greaves rusted with sweat, for he had been sorely tried and had endured and overcome many perils and challenges. His lance, his shield,

and his horse were on the far bank. Those who dragged him from the water
feared for his life, since he had swallowed a lot of water, and they heard no
word from him until he had heaved it up. But when he had cleared his chest
and throat and had regained his voice enough to make himself understood,
he began to speak. His first question to those before him was whether they
had any news of the queen. Those who answered him said that she never left
the presence of King Bademagu, who served and honored her well.

"Has anyone come recently into this land to seek her?" inquired my lord
Gawain.

"Yes," they replied, "Lancelot of the Lake, who crossed the Sword
Bridge. He rescued her and freed her and all of us along with her. But a
humpbacked, sneering dwarf tricked us—with insidious cleverness he has
kidnapped Lancelot, and we don't know what he's done with him."

"When was this?" my lord Gawain asked.

"Sir, today, quite near this spot, as we were coming with Lancelot to find
you."

"And what has Lancelot done since coming into this land?"

They began to tell him, giving every detail and not omitting a single
word. And they told Gawain that the queen was awaiting him and had
sworn that nothing would make her leave this land until she had seen him.
My lord Gawain inquired of them, "When we leave this bridge, will we go
to seek Lancelot?"

They all thought it best to go first to the queen: Bademagu would make
provisions for seeking Lancelot. They believed that his son Meleagant, who
hated him profoundly, had had him taken prisoner. If the king knew his
whereabouts, he would have him freed no matter where he was; therefore
they could delay their search. They all concurred in this suggestion, and so
they rode on together until they neared the court, where they found King
Bademagu and the queen. Together with them was the seneschal Kay, along
with that traitor, overflowing with deceit, who had villainously caused all of
those who were approaching to be anxious about Lancelot. These knights
felt deceived and defeated, and could not hide their grief.

The news of this misfortune was not pleasing to the queen, yet she tried
to act as cordially as she could. For the sake of my lord Gawain she managed
to appear cheerful. However, her sorrow was not so well hidden that a little
didn't appear. She had to express both joy and sorrow, since her heart was
empty because of Lancelot, yet toward my lord Gawain she felt great
happiness. Everyone who heard of the disappearance of Lancelot was overcome with grief and sorrow. The king would have been cheered by the
arrival of my lord Gawain and by the pleasure of his acquaintance had he not
felt such grief and pain and been so overwhelmed by sorrow at the betrayal
of Lancelot. The queen urged King Bademagu to have him sought throughout his land, both high and low, without a moment's delay. My lord
Gawain, Sir Kay, and everyone else without exception likewise urged him
to do this. "Leave this to me," said the king, "and say no more about it, for I
am long since persuaded. You need beg me no further to have this search
begun."

Every knight bowed low before him. The king straightway sent wise and
prudent men-at-arms as messengers throughout his land to ask news of

Lancelot wherever they went. Though they sought everywhere for information, they were unable to learn a thing. When they found no trace of him, they returned to where the other knights were staying—Gawain, Kay, and all the others, who said they would set off to seek him themselves, fully armed and with lances ready. They would send no one else in their stead.

One day, after eating, they were all assembled in the hall arming themselves (they had by now reached the moment set for their departure) when a young man entered there. He passed among them until he stood before the queen. She had lost the rosy tint in her cheeks, and all her color had faded because of her deep sorrow for Lancelot, of whom she had heard no news. The youth greeted her and the king who was near her, and afterwards he greeted all the others, including Sir Kay and my lord Gawain. In his hand he held a letter that he extended toward the king, who took it. To avoid any misunderstanding, the king had it read aloud so everyone could hear. The reader well knew how to communicate everything he found written on the parchment, and said, "Lancelot sends greetings to the king as his noble lord, and like one who is willingly and completely at his command he thanks him for the honor and services he has rendered him. And he wishes you to know that he is strong and in good health, and that he is with King Arthur, and that he bids the queen to come there—this he orders—with my lord Gawain and Sir Kay." The letter bore such seals as to cause them all to believe that the message was true. They were happy and full of joy. The whole court resounded with gaiety, and their departure was set for the next day at dawn. [5275]

When morning came, they outfitted themselves and made ready. They arose, mounted, and set forth. The king escorted them amid great joy and exultation a good bit of the way. When he had accompanied them beyond the frontiers of his land, he took leave first of the queen, then of the others as a group. On bidding him farewell, the queen very graciously thanked him for his many services. She embraced him and offered him her service and that of her husband—she could make no finer promise. My lord Gawain likewise pledged to serve him as his lord and friend, as did Sir Kay. Having promised this, they all set off at once on their way. King Bademagu commended the queen and the two knights to God; after these three he bid farewell to all the others, then returned home.

The queen and the crowd accompanying her did not delay a single day, but rode on until the welcome news reached King Arthur of the imminent arrival of his queen. News of his nephew Gawain kindled great joy and happiness in his heart, for he thought that the queen, Sir Kay, and all the common people were returning because of his daring. But the truth was quite other than they assumed. The whole town emptied to greet them; everyone went forth to meet them and each one, knight and commoner alike, said: "Welcome to my lord Gawain, who has brought back the queen and many another captive lady, and who has returned many a prisoner to us!"

"My lords, I am due no praise," Gawain said to them. "Your praise must stop at once, because none of this is of my doing. I am ashamed to be honored so, for I did not get there soon enough and failed because of my delay. But Lancelot was there in time and to him fell greater honor than any knight has ever received."

"Where is he then, fair sir, since we do not see him here with you?"

"Where?" replied my lord Gawain then. "Why, at the court of King Arthur—isn't he here?"

"In faith, he is not, nor is he anywhere in this land. We have heard no news of him since my lady was led away."

Then for the first time my lord Gawain realized that the message that had betrayed and deceived them was forged. They had been tricked by the message and were once again plunged into sadness. They arrived at court full of sorrow, and the king immediately asked what had happened. There were many who were able to give him an account of all that Lancelot had accomplished, how the queen and all the captives had been rescued by him, and how through deceit the dwarf had stolen him away from them. This news vexed the king, overwhelming him with grief and anguish. But his heart was so elated at the queen's return that his grief soon gave way to joy; now that he had what he most desired, he gave little thought to the rest.

It was while the queen was out of the country, I believe, that the ladies and the maidens who lacked the comfort of a husband came together and decided that they wished to be married soon. In the course of their discussions they decided to organize a splendid tournament, in which the Lady of Pomelegoi would be challenged by the Lady of Noauz. The women would refuse to speak to those who fared poorly, but to those who did well they promised to grant their love. They announced the tourney and had it cried throughout all the lands nearby, and those distant as well. They had the date of the tournament heralded well in advance so that there might be more participants.

The queen returned while preparations for the tournament were still being made. As soon as they learned of the queen's return, most of the ladies and maidens hastened to court to urge the king to grant them a favor and do their bidding. Even before learning what they wanted, he promised to grant them anything they might desire. Then they told him that they wished him to permit the queen to come to observe their tournament. Being unable to refuse anything, the king said that if the queen wished to attend, it would please him. Overjoyed at this, the ladies went before the queen and stated at once: "Our lady, do not refuse us what the king has already granted."

"What is it? Don't hide it from me."

"If you are willing to come to our tournament," they replied, "he will not try to stop you or refuse you his permission." So the queen promised to attend, since Arthur had given his permission.

The ladies immediately sent word throughout the realm that the queen would be in attendance on the day set for the tournament. The news spread far and wide and everywhere; it spread so far that it reached the kingdom from which no man had been able to return (though now whoever wished could enter or leave and never be challenged). The news spread through this kingdom and was repeated so often that it reached a seneschal of the faithless Meleagant—may hellfires burn the traitor! This seneschal was guarding Lancelot, imprisoned at his castle by his enemy Meleagant, who hated him with a mortal hatred.   [5431]

Lancelot learned of the date and hour of the tourney, and immediately his eyes filled with tears and all joy left his heart. The lady of the manor saw how sad and pensive he was and questioned him privately: "Sir, for the love of God and your soul, tell me truthfully why you have changed so. You no longer eat or drink, nor do I see you happy or laughing. You can confide your thoughts and what is troubling you in me."

"Ah, my lady! If I am saddened, for God's sake don't be surprised. Indeed I am greatly troubled because I am unable to be there where everything that is good in this world will be: at that tourney where everyone, I am sure, is gathering. However, if God has granted you the kindness to let me go there, you can be assured that I shall feel compelled to return afterward to my imprisonment here."

"Indeed," she answered, "I would willingly do this if I did not feel that it would cost me my life. I am so afraid of the might of my lord, the despicable Meleagant, that I dare not do it, for he would utterly destroy my husband. It is no wonder that I dread him so, for as you well know he is a most wicked man."

"My lady, if you are afraid that I will not return at once to your keeping after the tourney, I shall take an oath that I will never break and shall swear that nothing will ever keep me from returning to imprisonment here as soon as the tournament has ended."

"In faith," she said, "I will do it on one condition."

"My lady, what is that?"

"Sir," she answered, "that you will swear to return and will, moreover, assure me that I shall have your love."

"My lady, upon my return I will certainly give you all that I have."

The lady responded with a laugh, "It seems to me that you have assigned and given to another this love I have asked of you. Nevertheless, I shall not disdain to receive whatever I can have. I'll hold to what I can and will accept your oath that you will honor me by returning to imprisonment here."

In accordance with her wishes Lancelot swore by Holy Church that he would not fail to return. Thereupon the lady gave him her husband's red armor and his marvelously strong, brave, and handsome steed. Armed in his magnificent new armor, Lancelot mounted and rode forth until he reached Noauz. He selected this camp for the tournament and took his lodging just outside the town. Never had such a noble knight chosen such lowly lodgings, but he did so because he did not wish to stay anywhere he might be recognized. Many fine and worthy knights had assembled within the castle walls, yet there were even more outside. Indeed, so many had come when they learned that the queen would attend that not one in five was able to find lodging within: for every one who might ordinarily have come, there were seven who attended only because of the queen. The many barons were housed in tents, shelters, and pavilions stretching for five leagues round about. And so many ladies and maidens were present that it was a marvel to behold.

Lancelot had placed his shield before the door of his lodging place and, in order to relax, had removed his armor and was stretched out on an uncomfortably narrow bed, with thin matting covered by a coarse hemp cloth. While he was lying in this hovel, a barefooted young fellow in shirt-sleeves came running up. He was a herald-at-arms who had lost his cloak and shoes gambling in the tavern, and who was now barefoot and exposed to the cool air. He noticed the shield before the door and began to examine it, but there was no way for him to recognize it or to know who bore it. Seeing the open door, he entered and found Lancelot lying on the bed. As soon as he saw him, he recognized him and crossed himself. But Lancelot warned him not to tell a soul about this; if he mentioned having seen him, the boy would rather have his eyes put out or neck broken than receive the punishment Lancelot would give him.

"Sir," replied the herald, "I have always esteemed you highly and still do. As long as I live, no amount of money will ever make me do anything that might cause you to be unhappy with me." He hurried out of the house and ran off shouting: "The one is come who will take their measure! The one is come who will take their measure!" The youth shouted this everywhere he went, and people hastened up from every side to ask him what this meant. He was not so rash as to tell them, but continued shouting as before. This is when the expression was coined: "The one is come who will take their measure." The herald who taught us this is our master, for he was the first to say it.

Already the crowds had assembled on every side: the queen with all her ladies and the knights with their many men-at-arms. The most magnificent, the largest, and the most splendid viewing stands that had ever been seen had been built there on the tournament field, since the queen and her ladies were to be in attendance. All the ladies followed the queen onto the platform, for they were eager to see who would do well or poorly in the combat. The knights arrived by tens, by twenties, by thirties—here eighty and there ninety, a hundred or more here, two hundred there. So great was the crowd gathered before and about the stands that the combat was begun.

Knights clashed whether or not they were already fully armed. There seemed to be a forest of lances there, for those who had come for the pleasure of the tourney had brought so many that everywhere one turned one saw only lances, banners, and standards. Those who were to joust moved down the lists, where they encountered a great many companions of like mind. Others, meanwhile, made ready to perform other knightly feats. The meadows, fields, and clearings were so packed with knights that it was impossible to guess how many there were. Lancelot did not participate in this first encounter; but when he did cross the meadow and the herald saw him coming onto the field, he could not refrain from shouting: "Behold the one who will take their measure! Behold the one who will take their measure!"

"Who is he?" they all asked. But the herald refused to answer.

When Lancelot entered the fray, he alone proved the match of twenty of the best. He began to do so well that no one could take his eyes from him, wherever he might go. A bold and valiant knight was fighting for Pomelegoi, and his steed was spirited and swifter than a wild stag. He was the son of the king of Ireland, and he fought nobly and well, but the unknown knight pleased the onlookers four times as much. They all troubled themselves over the question, "Who is this knight who fights so well?"

The queen summoned a clever, pretty girl to her and whispered, "Miss, you must take a message, quickly and without wasting words. Hurry down from these stands and go at once to that knight bearing the red shield; tell him in secret that I bid him to 'do his worst.'"*

---

*Chrétien employs a pun here: the Old French expression *au noauz* can mean "Do one's worst" or "Onward for Noauz!"

The girl swiftly and discreetly did as the queen asked. She pursued the knight until she was near enough to tell him in a voice that no one could overhear, "Sir, my lady the queen bids me tell you to 'do your worst.'" [5654]

The moment he heard her, Lancelot said that he would gladly do so, as one who wishes only to please the queen. Then he set out against a knight as fast as his horse would carry him, but when he should have struck him, he missed. From this moment until dark he did the worst he could, because it was the queen's pleasure. The other knight, attacking him in turn, did not miss, but struck Lancelot such a powerful blow that Lancelot wheeled and fled and did not turn his horse against any knight the rest of that day. He would rather die than do anything unless he were sure that it would bring him shame, disgrace, and dishonor, and he pretended to be afraid of all those who approached him. The knights who had praised him before now laughed and joked at his expense. And the herald, who used to say, "This one will beat them all, one after another!" was very disspirited and embarrassed on becoming the butt of the knights' jibes. "Hold your peace now, friend," they said mockingly. "He won't be taking our measure any more. He's measured so much that he's broken that measuring stick you bragged so much about!"

"What is this?" many asked. "He was so brave just a while ago; and now he's so cowardly that he doesn't dare face another knight. Perhaps he did so well at first because he'd never jousted before. He just flailed about like a madman and struck so wildly that no knight, however expert, could stand up to him. But now he's learned enough about fighting that he'll never want to bear arms again as long as he lives! His heart can no longer take it, for there's no bigger coward in the world!"

The queen was not upset by anything she heard. On the contrary, she was pleased and delighted, for now she knew for certain (though she kept it hidden) that this knight was truly Lancelot. Thus throughout the day until dark he let himself be taken for a coward. When darkness brought an end to the fighting, there was a lengthy discussion over who had fought best that day. The son of the king of Ireland felt that beyond any doubt he himself deserved the esteem and renown; but he was terribly mistaken, for many there were equal to him. Even the Red Knight pleased the fairest and most beautiful of the ladies and maidens, for they had not kept their eyes on anyone that day as much as on him. They had seen how he had done at first—how brave and courageous he had been. But then he had become so cowardly that he dared not face another knight, and even the worst of them, had he wanted, could have defeated and captured him. So the ladies and knights all agreed that they would return to the lists the following day, and that the young girls would marry those who won honor then.

Once this was settled, they all returned to their lodgings, where they gathered in little groups and began to ask: "Where is the worst, the lowliest, and the most despicable of knights? Where has he gone? Where has he hidden himself? Where might we find him? Where should we seek him? Cowardice has probably chased him away, and we'll never see him again. He's carried Cowardice off with himself, so that there cannot be another man in the world so lowly! And he's not wrong, for a coward is a hundred thousand times better off than a valorous, fighting knight. Cowardice is a facile thing, and that's why he's given her the kiss of peace and taken from her everything he has. To be sure, Courage never lowered herself enough to try to find lodging in him. Cowardice owns him completely. She has found a host who loves and serves her so faithfully that he has lost all his honor for her sake." All night long those given to slander gossiped in this manner. Though the one who speaks ill of another is often far worse than the one he slanders and despises, this did not keep them from having their say.

When day broke, all the knights donned their armor once more and returned to the fighting. The queen, with her ladies and maidens, came back to the stands, and together with them were many knights without armor who had either been captured on the first day or had taken the cross, and who were now explaining to them the heraldry of the knights they most admired.

"Do you see the knight with the gold band across a red shield?" they inquired. "That's Governal of Roberdic. And do you see the one behind him who has fixed a dragon and an eagle side by side on his shield? That's the son of the king of Aragon, who has come into this land to win honor and renown. And do you see the one beside him who rides and jousts so well? One half of his shield is green with a leopard upon it, and the other half is azure. That's Ignaures the Covetous, a handsome man who pleases the ladies. And the one with the pheasants painted beak to beak upon his shield? That is Coguillant of Mautirec. And do you see those two knights beside him on dappled horses, with dark lions on gilded shields? One is called Semiramis, the other is his companion—they have painted their shields to match. And do you see the one whose shield has a gate painted upon it, through which a stag seems to be passing? In faith, that is King Yder."

Such was the talk in the stands: "That shield was made in Limoges and was brought by Pilades, who is always eager for a good fight. That shield, with matching harness and stirrups, was made in Toulouse and brought here by Sir Kay of Estral. That one comes from Lyons on the Rhone—there's none so fine under heaven!—and was awarded to Sir Taulas of the Desert for a great service. He bears it well and uses it skillfully. And that other shield there, on which you see two swallows about to take flight, yet which stay fast to take many a blow of Poitevin steel, is an English model, made in London. It is carried by Sir Thomas the Young."

In this manner they pointed out and described the arms of those they recognized; but they saw no sign of that knight whom they held in such low esteem. So they assumed that he had stolen off in the night, since he did not return that day to the combat. When the queen, too, did not see him, she determined to have him sought through the lists until he was found. She knew of no one she could trust more to find him than that girl she had sent the day before with her message. So she summoned her at once and said to her, "Go, miss, and mount your palfrey. I am sending you to that knight you spoke to yesterday. You must seek until you find him. Make no delay! Then tell him once again to 'do his worst.' And when you have so instructed him, listen carefully to his reply."

The girl set off without hesitation, for the evening before she had carefully taken note of the direction he went, knowing without a doubt that she would once again be sent to him. She rode through the lists until she saw the knight, then went at once to advise him to continue "doing his worst" if he wished to have the love and favor of the queen, for such was her command. "Since she so bids me," he replied, "I send her my thanks."

The girl left him at once. As he entered the field, the young men, the squires, and the men-at-arms began jeering: "What a surprise! The knight with the red armor has returned! But what can he want? There's no one in the world so lowly, so despicable, and so base. Cowardice has him so firmly in her grip that he can do nothing to escape her."

The girl returned to the queen, who would not let her go until she had heard that reply which filled her heart with joy, for now she knew beyond a doubt that that knight was the one to whom she belonged completely, and she knew, too, that he was fully hers. She told the girl to return at once and tell him that she now ordered and urged him to "do the best" that he could. The girl replied that she would go at once, without delay. She descended from the stands to where her serving-boy was waiting for her, tending her palfrey. She mounted and rode until she found the knight, and she told him immediately, "Sir, my lady now orders you to 'do the best' you can."

"Tell her that it would never displease me to do anything that might please her, for I am intent upon doing whatever she may desire." [5893]

The girl hurried back as quickly as she could with her message, for she was certain that it would please the queen. As she approached the viewing stands, eager to deliver her message, the queen stood up and moved forward to meet her. But in order not to betray her own eagerness, the queen did not go down to her, but waited at the head of the steps. The girl started up the steps, and as she neared the queen she said, "My lady, I have never seen a more agreeable knight, for he is perfectly willing to do whatever you command of him. And, if you ask me the truth, he accepts the good and the bad with equal pleasure."

"In faith," she replied, "that well may be."

Then the queen returned to the window to observe the knights. Without a moment's hesitation Lancelot thrust his arm through the shield straps, for he was inflamed with a burning desire to show all his prowess. He neck-reined his horse and let it run between two ranks. Soon all those deluded, mocking men, who had spent much of the past night and day ridiculing him, would be astounded—they had laughed, sported, and had their fun long enough!

With his shield on his arm, the son of the king of Ireland came charging headlong across the field at Lancelot. They met with such violence that the son of the king of Ireland wished to joust no more, for his lance was splintered and broken, having struck not Irish moss but firm dry shield-boards. Lancelot taught him a lesson in this joust, striking his shield from his arm, pinning his arm to his side, then knocking him off his horse to the ground. Knights from both camps rushed forward at once, some to help the fallen knight and others to worsen his plight. Some, thinking to help their lords, knocked many knights from their saddles in the melee. But Gawain, who was there with the others, never entered the fray all that day, for he was content to observe the prowess of the knight with the red shield, whose deeds seemed to make everything the other knights did pale by comparison. The herald, too, found new cause for happiness and cried out for all to hear: "The one is come who will take their measure! Today you will witness his deeds; today you will see his might!"

At this moment Lancelot wheeled his horse and charged toward a magnificent knight, striking him a blow that carried him to the ground a hundred feet or more from his steed. Lancelot performed such deeds with both his lance and sword that all the spectators marveled at what they saw. Even many of the knights participating in the jousts watched him with admiration and delight, for it was a pleasure to see how he caused both men and steeds to stumble and fall. There was scarcely a knight he challenged who was able to remain in the saddle, and he gave the horses he won to any who wanted them. Those who had been mocking him now said, "We are ashamed and mortified. We made a great mistake to slander and disdain him. Truly he is worth a thousand of the likes of those on this field, since he has vanquished and surpassed all the knights in the world, so that there now remains no one to oppose him."

The young women who were watching him in amazement all said that he was destroying their chances for marriage. They felt that their beauty, their wealth, their positions, and their noble births would bring them little advantage, for surely a knight this valiant would never deign to marry any one of them for beauty or wealth alone. Yet many of them swore that if they did not marry this knight, they would not take any other lord or husband in this year. The queen, overhearing their boastful vows, laughed to herself. She knew that the knight they all desired would never choose the most beautiful, nor the fairest among them, even if one were to offer him all the gold of Arabia. Yet the young women had but one thing in mind: they all wanted to have that knight. And they were already as jealous of one another as if they had married him, because they believed him to be so skilled in arms that they could not conceive of any other knight, no matter how pleasing, who could have done what he had done.

Indeed he had fought so well that when it came time for the two camps to separate, those on both sides agreed that there had never been an equal to the knight who bore the red shield. It was said by all, and it was true. But as the tournament was breaking up, our knight let his shield, lance, and trappings fall where the press was thickest and hastened away. His departure was so furtive that no one in all that great crowd noticed it. He rode on swiftly and purposefully in order to keep his pledge to return directly to that place from where he had come.   [6039]

On their way from the tournament everyone inquired after him, but they found no trace, for he had left so as not to be recognized. The knights, who would have been overjoyed to have had him there, were filled instead with great sorrow and distress. But if the knights were saddened that he had left in this fashion, the young women, when they learned of it, were far more upset and swore by St. John that they would refuse to marry in this year: if they could not have the one they wanted, they would take no other. Thus the tournament ended without any one of them having taken a husband.

Lancelot returned to his prison without delay. The seneschal into whose charge he had been entrusted reached home some two or three days before Lancelot's return and inquired after his whereabouts. The lady who had outfitted Lancelot with her husband's magnificent red armor, his trappings, and his horse, told her husband truthfully how she had sent their prisoner to take part in the jousting at the tournament of Noauz.

"My lady," said the seneschal, "truly you could have done nothing worse! Great misfortune will surely befall me because of this, for I know that my lord Meleagant will treat me worse than a fierce giant would if I were shipwrecked on his lonely island. I shall be destroyed and ruined as soon as he hears of this. He will never show me pity!"

"Dear husband, do not be distraught," replied the lady. "There is no need to be so fearful. He will not fail to return, for he swore to me by the saints above that he would be back as quickly as possible."

The seneschal mounted his horse and rode at once to his lord, to whom he related the whole of this adventure. Meleagant was reassured when the seneschal told him how Lancelot had sworn to his wife to return to prison.

"He will never break his oath," said Meleagant. "This I know. Nonetheless I am greatly troubled by what your wife has done, for there was no way that I wanted him to be at the tournament. But go back now and see to it that when he returns he is guarded so securely that he will never be able to escape from prison or have any freedom of movement. Send me word as soon as this is done."

"It shall be as you command," said the seneschal. When he reached his castle, he found Lancelot returned, a prisoner once more at his court. The seneschal sent a messenger straight to Meleagant to inform him that Lancelot had returned.

Upon hearing this, Meleagant engaged masons and carpenters who did as he ordered, whether willingly or by constraint. He summoned the best in the land and told them to work diligently until they had built him a tower. Meleagant knew an island set within an inlet on one shore of the land of Gorre, where there was a broad, deep arm of the sea. There he ordered that the stone and wood for constructing the tower be brought. The stone was shipped in by sea, and the tower was completed in less than two months. It was thick-walled and solid, broad and tall. When it was ready, Meleagant had Lancelot brought there and placed within the tower. Then he ordered that the doorways be walled up, and he forced all the masons to swear that they would never speak of this tower to anyone. He had it sealed so that there remained no door or opening, save only a small window, through which Lancelot was given niggardly portions of poor fare to eat at fixed hours. Now Meleagant had everything he wished, and all was done just as the traitorous felon had ordered.   [6146]

Meleagant next went directly to Arthur's court. As soon as he arrived, he came before the king and, filled with arrogance and perfidy, addressed him in these words: "My king, I have agreed to single combat against Sir Lancelot at your court and in your presence, but I do not see him anywhere! However, to fulfill my promises, I hereby offer him my challenge before your assembled court. If Lancelot is present, let him come forward and swear to meet me here in your court one year from this day. I do not know whether anyone here has told you under what circumstances this combat was arranged, but I see knights here who were at our pledging and who can tell you everything if they are willing to acknowledge the truth. And if Lancelot should attempt to deny this, I'll not hire any second to defend me, but oppose him myself."

The queen, who was seated at court beside the king, leaned toward him and said, "Sir, do you know who this is? He is Meleagant, who captured me while I was in the protection of the seneschal Kay, and who thereby caused him great shame and suffering."

"My lady," the king replied, "I have clearly understood that this is the man who held my people prisoner."

The queen spoke no further. The king now turned to Meleagant and said, "My friend, so help me God, we've had no news of Lancelot, which grieves us deeply."

"My lord king," said Meleagant, "Lancelot assured me that I would not fail to find him here, and I am pledged not to undertake this combat except at your court. I want all of the barons here present to bear witness that I now summon him to be present here one year from this day, in accord with the pledges we gave when we first agreed to this combat."

On hearing these words my lord Gawain arose, for he was deeply troubled by what had been said. "Sir," he spoke, "Lancelot is nowhere to be found in this land; but we shall have him sought and, if it please God, he will be found before the year is out—unless he is imprisoned or dead. But should he fail to appear, let me assume the combat, for I am willing. I will take up my arms for Lancelot at the appointed day, if he is not here before then."

"By heavens!" said Meleagant. "In the name of God, King Arthur, grant Gawain this battle. He wants it and I urge it, for I know of no knight in the world against whom I'd rather test myself, unless it is Lancelot himself. But know for certain that if I cannot fight against one of these two, I'll not accept any substitute or fight against anyone else."

And the king said that he would grant the challenge to Gawain if Lancelot failed to return in time.   [6225]

Having received this promise, Meleagant left King Arthur's court and rode until he reached that of his father, King Bademagu. In order to appear noble and distinguished before him, he haughtily assumed an air of importance. This day the king was hosting a festive celebration in his capital city of Bath. The court was assembled in all its splendor to celebrate his birthday. People of every sort came there to be with him, and the palace was overflowing with knights and maidens. There was one among them (she was Meleagant's sister) about whom I'll gladly tell you more later; I do not wish to speak further of her now, however, since it is not part of my story to tell of her at this point, and I do not want to inflate or confuse or alter my story but develop it in a proper and straightforward manner. So now I shall tell you that upon his arrival Meleagant addressed his father in a loud voice, which commoner and noble alike could hear: "Father, as God is your salvation, please tell me truthfully whether one who has made his prowess feared at King Arthur's court is to be considered worthy and whether he should be filled with great joy."

Without waiting to hear more, his father answered these questions: "My son, all good men should honor and serve one who has shown himself worthy in this fashion, and keep his company." Then his father cajoled him and urged him to say why he had asked this, what he was seeking, and from where he had come.

"Sir, I don't know whether you recall the terms of the agreement that was established when you made peace between Lancelot and myself. But you must remember, I'm sure, that we were both told before many witnesses to

be ready in one year's time to meet again at King Arthur's court. I went
there at the appointed time, armed and equipped for battle. All that was
required of me I did: I sought Lancelot and inquired after him, but I was
unable to find any trace of him. He had turned and fled! So I arranged to
have Gawain pledge his word that there would be no further delays. Even if
Lancelot is no longer alive and fails to return within the fixed term, Gawain
himself has promised to fight me in his stead. Arthur has no knight more
praiseworthy than Gawain, as is well known. But before the elderberries
blossom, I will see when we fight whether his deeds match his fame. The
sooner we fight the better!"

"Son," said his father, "now indeed you have shown yourself a fool to
everyone here. Those who did not know it before have learned it now by
your own words. True it is that a great heart is humble, but the fool and the
braggart will never be rid of their folly. Son, I'm telling you this for your
own good: you are so hard and dry of character that there is no trace of
gentility or friendship in you. You are filled with folly and your heart lacks
all mercy. This is why I find fault with you; this will bring you down. If
one is of noble heart, many will bear witness to it at the appropriate time; a
gentleman need not praise his courage to magnify his act, for the act is its
own best praise. Self-flattery does not enhance your renown at all; rather, it
makes me esteem you the less. Son, I chastise you, but to what avail? It is of
little use to advise a fool, and he who tries to rid a fool of his folly wastes his
efforts. The goodness that one preaches, if it is not transformed into works,
is wasted—wasted, lost, and gone forever."

Meleagant was beside himself with fury and rage. I can assure you
truthfully that no man alive was ever as full of wrath as he was; and in his
anger the last bond between father and son was broken, for he did not mince
words with his father, but raged, "Are you dreaming or deluded to say that
I'm crazy to have told you of my triumph? I thought I'd come to you as to
my lord, as to my father; but that doesn't seem to be the case, and I feel
you've treated me more odiously than I deserve. Nor can you give me any
reason for having done so."

"Indeed I can."

"What then?"

"That I see nothing in you but lunacy and madness. I know only too well
that heart of yours, which will yet bring you to great harm. Damned be
anyone who could ever believe that Lancelot, this perfect knight who is
esteemed by all but yourself, would ever flee out of fear of you! Perhaps he's
been buried in some underground cell or locked up in a prison, whose gate is
so tightly kept that he cannot leave without permission. I assure you I'd be
sorely angered if he were injured or dead. It would be a great loss indeed if a
person so skilled, so handsome, so valiant, and so just were to perish before
his time. May it please God that this not be so!"   [6373]

With these words Bademagu grew silent; but all that he had said had been
heard and carefully noted by one of his daughters—the one I mentioned
earlier in my story—and she was not at all pleased to hear such news of
Lancelot. It was evident that he was being kept locked up, since no one had
heard anything from him. "May God never have mercy upon me," she
swore, "if ever I rest before I know for certain what has become of him."

She stole noiselessly away and ran immediately to mount her comely and smooth-gaited mule. For my part I can assure you that she had no idea which way to turn upon leaving the court. Yet instead of inquiring, she took the first path she found. She rode swiftly along, uncertain of her destination, guided by chance, without servant or knightly escort. She sought far and wide in her eagerness to reach her goal, but her search was not destined to be brief. Yet she could not stop long in any one place if she wished to accomplish properly what she had set out to do: release Lancelot from prison if she could find him and manage it. And I believe that she will have traversed many a country before hearing anything of him. But what good is it for me to tell of her nightly lodgings and daily wanderings? She traveled so many roads over mountains, through valleys, high and low, that a month or more passed without her having been able to learn more than she already knew—which was less than nothing.

One day as she was riding sad and pensive through a field, she saw in the distance beside the shore near an inlet—a tower! But for a league on any side there was not any house, or cabin, or hut. Meleagant had had it built in order to keep Lancelot, but his sister knew nothing of that. As soon as she saw it, she fixed her sights upon it and never turned away; and her heart promised her that this was what she had sought for so long. Now her search was ended; after many tribulations Fortune had guided her to the right path.

The girl rode straight up to the tower, then circled it, listening carefully to see whether she might hear something that would bring her joy. She examined the tower from bottom to top and saw that it was tall and wide. But she was amazed to find no opening in it, except for a small and narrow window. Nor was there any stair or ladder to enter this high tower. She reasoned that this was deliberate and that therefore Lancelot was within, and she was determined to find out for sure or never eat again. She was going to call out his name and was about to say "Lancelot!" when she heard a weak voice from within the tower that caused her to hold her tongue.

The voice was filled with deepest doom and was calling for death. Lamenting piteously, it longed for death; in its suffering it asked only to die; life and its own body no longer held any value for it. Feebly, in a low and trembling voice, it lamented: "Ah, Fortune, how cruelly your wheel has now turned for me! Once I was on the top, but now I've been thrown down to the bottom; once I had everything, now I have nothing; once you wept to see me, now you laugh at me. Poor Lancelot, why did you trust in Fortune when she abandoned you so quickly? In no time at all she has cast me down from high to low. By mocking me, Fortune, you behave despicably—but what do you care? All has come to naught, no matter what. Ah! Holy Cross, Holy Spirit! I am lost! I am damned! How totally destroyed I am!

"Ah, most worthy Gawain, unequaled in goodness, how I marvel that you've not come to rescue me! Certainly you are unchivalrous to have delayed so long. You should come to the aid of one you once loved so dearly. Indeed I can say with certainty that there's no hideaway or secluded place on either side of the sea that I'd not have spent seven years or even ten to seek out had I known you to be imprisoned there. But why am I bothering with this? You are not brave enough to expose yourself to hardships on my account. Peasants are right to say that it's hard to find a good friend any more: in times of trial it is easy to test one's friends. Alas! I've been a prisoner for over a year now, and you are a faithless friend indeed, Gawain, to have left me to linger here so long.

"Yet if you don't know that I'm imprisoned here, then it's unfair of me to accuse you so. Indeed that must be the case—I'm sure of it now! And I was wrong and unreasonable to have such thoughts, for I know that you and your men would have searched to the ends of the earth to release me from this evil confinement, had you but known the truth. And you would do it out of the love and friendship you bear me—yes, this is what I truly believe. But I'm wasting my breath. It can never happen! May Meleagant, who has brought me to this shame, be damned by God and St. Sylvester! Out of envy he has done me all the evil he could conceive—he's surely the most wicked man alive!" [6529]

With these words he took comfort and grew silent, as grief gnawed away at his life. The girl stood staring at the ground as she listened to everything he said. Knowing that her search was ended, she hesitated no more. She shouted "Lancelot!" with all her strength and more. "Fair knight in the tower there, speak to a friend who loves you."

But the one within was too weak to hear her. She shouted louder, and louder still, until Lancelot with his last bit of strength heard her and wondered who could be calling him. Though he knew he was being called, still he did not recognize the voice—he thought perhaps it was some ghost. He looked all about him, but saw only himself and the tower walls. "My God," he wondered, "what am I hearing? I hear words but I see nothing. This is truly amazing! Yet I'm awake and not asleep. If it were a dream, I would probably think it was a lie; but I am awake, and therefore it troubles me."

Then with great effort Lancelot arose and moved slowly, step by step, toward the tiny crevice. When he reached the opening, he wedged his body in, from top to bottom and on each side. He looked out in every direction and finally saw the girl who had called to him. Though he saw her now, he did not recognize her. She, however, knew him at once and spoke: "Lancelot, I have come from afar seeking you. Now, thank God, my search is ended, for I have found you. I am the one who asked a favor of you as you were going to the Sword Bridge. You granted it to me willingly when I requested it: I asked for the head of the defeated knight, because I bore him no love. For that boon and that service I have exposed myself to these hardships; because of them I will get you out of here!"

"My thanks to you," said the prisoner upon hearing her words. "The service I did you will be well repaid if I am freed from this place. If you are able to free me, I swear to you that with the aid of the Apostle Paul I will be yours from this day forth. As God is my witness, the day will never come on which I fail to do everything that you may be pleased to request from me. Whatever you ask from me you shall have immediately, if I am able to do it."

"Have no doubt, my friend, that you will be set free this very day. I would not leave, not even for a thousand pounds, without seeing you released before daybreak. Afterward I will put you at ease, in great comfort and repose: whatever I have that is pleasing, if you want it, will be given to you. Don't be worried: I must leave you for a short while to find something to use to enlarge this window enough so that you can escape through it."

"May God help you find it," he said in heartfelt agreement. "Here inside I have plenty of rope, which the soldiers gave me to haul up my food—stale barley bread and stagnant water that have ruined my health!"

Then the daughter of King Bademagu found a solid pickax, as strong as it was sharp. She brought it to Lancelot, who in spite of his weakened body hammered and pounded and struck and dug until he was able to crawl easily through the crevice. How very relieved and happy he was—you can be sure—to be out of that prison and able to leave that place where he had been confined for so long! At last he was free and at large, and even if all the gold in the world were gathered together and piled mountain high and offered to him, he would never choose to go back in.   [6636]

Now Lancelot was free, but he was still so weak that he staggered on his feeble limbs. Gently, so as not to cause him injury, the girl helped him mount her mule ahead of her, and they set off in great haste. She kept off the main roads deliberately, so that they would not be seen. They rode on cautiously, fearful that if they traveled openly someone might recognize them and do them harm, and this she was anxious to prevent. Therefore she avoided narrow passes, and they finally reached a retreat where, because of its beauty and charm, she had often stayed. The castle and its occupants were all in her service; the place was well-equipped, secure, and very private. There Lancelot would be safe. As soon as he had arrived, she had him undressed and gently stretched out upon a beautiful, thickly cushioned couch. She then bathed and cared for him so well that I could not tell you half of all the good she did. She handled and treated him as gently as she would her own father, completely reviving and healing him and giving him new life. No longer was he starved and weak. Soon he was strong and fair, no less handsome than an angel, and able to rise.

When he arose, the girl found him the most beautiful robe she had and dressed him in it. Lancelot slipped it on with more joy and grace than a bird in flight. He kissed and embraced the girl, then said to her fondly: "My dear friend, to God and to you alone, I give thanks for being healed and healthy. Because you have made possible my escape, I give you my heart, my body, my aid, and my possessions to take and keep whenever you wish. For all that you have done, I am yours. Yet I have been absent now for a great while from the court of King Arthur, who has honored me greatly, and I have much still to do there. Therefore, my sweet noble friend, I must beg your leave with love. If it is pleasing to you, I am most eager to go there."

"Beloved Lancelot, fair gentle friend," replied the girl, "I grant your request, for I seek only what is for your honor and good, both now and forever."

She gave him the most marvelous horse that anyone had ever seen, and he leapt swiftly into the saddle without even touching the stirrups. When he had mounted, they heartily commended one another to the ever truthful God. Lancelot set off on his way, so overjoyed that, I swear, nothing I could ever say would convey to you how happy he was to have escaped from that place where he had been imprisoned. He repeated over and over to himself that that despicable traitor who had held him prisoner was about to become the victim of his own deceits and be damned by his own doing.

"I am free in spite of him!" exclaimed Lancelot. Then he swore by the heart and body of the Creator of this world that Meleagant would never escape with his life if ever he succeeded in overpowering and capturing him—no, not for all the riches from Babylon to Ghent. He had been too deeply shamed. [6725]

And it would come to pass that Lancelot would avenge himself, for this very Meleagant, whom he had been threatening and he was eager to encounter, had reached the court this same day without having been summoned. Upon his arrival he sought out and found my lord Gawain. Then the evil, proven traitor inquired whether Lancelot had been found or seen—as if he himself knew nothing of him! (And he did not, in fact, although he thought that he did.) Gawain replied that he had not seen him, nor had he come to court since Meleagant had been there last.

"Since it is you whom I have found here," said Meleagant, "come forward and keep your promise to me. I will wait for you no longer."

"If it is pleasing to God, in whom I place my trust," answered Gawain, "I shall shortly keep my promise to you. I am confident that I shall acquit myself well. It is like casting dice; and with God and St. Foy on my side, I shall cast more points than you, and before it's over I shall pocket all the wagers."

Then Gawain ordered a carpet to be spread out before him. His squires quickly did as he commanded, carrying out his bidding without complaint or question. After they had taken the carpet and placed it where he had ordered, Gawain stepped upon it at once and summoned three valets in his suite, still unarmed themselves, to bring him his armor. These young men were his cousins or nephews, I'm not sure which, and were truly brave and well bred. The three youths armed him so fittingly that no one in the world could have found fault with anything they did. After arming him, one among them went to fetch a Spanish warhorse, which could run more swiftly through open field and woodland, over hill and dale, than could the fine Bucephalus. The renowned and worthy Gawain, the most skilled knight ever to be blessed by the sign of the cross, mounted his magnificent steed. He was about to grasp his shield when he beheld Lancelot dismounting before him. He had never expected to see him here!

Lancelot had appeared so suddenly that Gawain stared in wonder at him, and I do not exaggerate when I tell you that he was as astonished as if Lancelot had just fallen at his feet from a cloud. When he saw that it was indeed Lancelot, no other duty could have kept Gawain, too, from dismounting and going forth to welcome him with outstretched arms. Gawain greeted him, then embraced and kissed him; he was filled with joy and relieved at having found his companion. You must never doubt me when I assure you that Gawain would not have wanted to have been chosen a king if it meant losing Lancelot.

Soon King Arthur and everyone at court knew that Lancelot, whom they had been seeking for so long, had returned healthy and safe—to the great displeasure of one among them. The court, which had long been anxious about him, came together in full assembly to celebrate his return. Young and old alike rejoiced in his presence. Joy dissipated and obliterated the grief that had reigned there; grief fled and joy appeared, eagerly beckoning again to all. And was the queen not there to share in this joy? Indeed she was, and among the first. Heavens, and where else would she be? Never had she experienced greater joy than that she now felt at his return—how could she have stayed away? To tell the truth, she was so near him that she could scarcely restrain her body (and nearly didn't!) from following her heart to him. Where then was her heart? Welcoming Lancelot with kisses. Why then was the body reticent? Was her joy not complete? Was it laced with anger or hatred? No indeed, not in the least; rather, she hesitated because the others present—the king and his entourage, who could see everything—would immediately perceive her love if, before their very eyes, she were to do all that her heart desired. And if Reason did not subdue these foolish thoughts and this love-madness, everyone present would understand her feelings. O, height of folly! In this way Reason encompassed and bound her foolish heart and thoughts and brought her to her senses, postponing the full display of her affections until she could find a better and more private place, where they might reach a safer harbor than they would have now.

The king gave Lancelot every honor, and, when he had welcomed him properly, said, "My friend, I've not heard in many a year such welcome news of anyone as that of you today. But I have no idea what land you've been in for so long. All winter and all summer I have had you sought high and low, yet you were nowhere to be found."

"Indeed, fair sir," answered Lancelot, "in but a few words I can tell you everything just as it happened to me. Meleagant, the wicked traitor, has kept me imprisoned since the day the prisoners were released from his land. He has forced me to live shamefully in a tower by the sea. He had me captured and walled in there, and there I would still be suffering, were it not for a friend of mine, a girl for whom I had once done a small favor. For that tiny favor she has given me a huge reward; she has done me great honor and great good. Now, however, without further delay, I wish to repay him for whom I have no love. He has long sought and pursued me, and has treated me with shame and cruelty. He has come here to court to seek his payment, and he shall have it! He need wait no longer for it, because it's ready. I myself am prepared for battle, as is he—and may God never again give him cause for boasting!"

Then Gawain said to Lancelot, "My friend, it would cost me little to repay your creditor for you. I am already equipped and mounted, as you can see. Fair gentle friend, do not refuse me this favor I eagerly beg of you."

Lancelot replied that he would rather have both his eyes gouged from his head than to be so persuaded. He swore never to let Gawain fight for him. He had given his own pledge to fight Meleagant, and he himself would repay what he owed. Gawain saw that nothing he might say would be to any avail, so he loosed his hauberk and lifted it from his shoulders, then disarmed himself completely. Lancelot immediately donned these same arms, so eager was he for his debt to be repaid and canceled. He was determined not to rest until he had repaid the traitor.   [6914]

Meleagant, meanwhile, was stunned beyond belief at everything he had just witnessed with his own eyes. He felt his heart sink within and nearly lost his mind. "Indeed," he said to himself, "what a fool I was not to check before coming here to be certain that Lancelot was still secure within my prison tower. Now he has gotten the better of me. Ah, God, but why should I have gone there? There was never any reason to suspect that he could have escaped. Was the wall not solidly constructed and the tower tall and strong? There was no flaw or crack through which he could slip without help from outside. Perhaps someone gave away my secret? But even granted that the walls cracked before their time and crumbled and fell, would he not have been buried under them and killed, his body crushed and dismembered? Yes, by God, if they had fallen he would surely have died within. Yet I am positive that those mighty walls would not crack before the last drop of water in the oceans had dried up and the mountains been leveled, unless they were destroyed by force. All this is impossible. There must be another anwer: he had help in escaping; otherwise he'd not be free. I have no doubt that I've been betrayed. So I must accept the fact that he is out. If only I had taken more precautions, it would never have happened, and he would never again have come to court! But now it is too late to feel sorry for myself. The peasant, who doesn't like to lie, spoke the truth in his proverb: it is too late to lock the barn door after the horse has been stolen. I know that I shall be brought to shame and greatly vilified unless I endure great trials and sufferings. What trials and sufferings? So help me God, in whom I place my trust, I'll fight my best for as long as I am able against the knight I have challenged."

Thus he gathered his courage and now asked only that they be brought together on the field of battle. I don't believe there'll be a long delay, for Lancelot is eager to meet him, anticipating a quick victory. But before either charged the other, the king asked that they go down below the tower onto the heath, the fairest from there to Ireland. They did as he ordered, going there without delay. The king, accompanied by milling crowds of knights and ladies, followed. No one remained behind; and the queen with her fair and beautiful ladies and maidens crowded the windows to watch Lancelot.

On the heath was the finest sycamore that ever grew, spreading wide its branches. About it, like a woven carpet, was a beautiful field of fresh grass that never lost its green. From beneath the beautiful sycamore gushed a sparkling spring of rapid-running water over a bed of beautiful stones that shone like silver. The water flowed off through a pipe of purest, rarefied gold and ran down across the heath into a valley between two woods. Here it suited the king to take his place, for he found nothing that displeased him.

After King Arthur ordered his people to keep their distance, Lancelot rode angrily toward Meleagant like a man bursting with hatred. But before striking a blow, he shouted in a loud, bold voice: "Come forward, I challenge you! And be assured that I will not spare you!"

Then he spurred his horse hotly, pulling back to a spot about a bowshot's distance. Now they charged toward one another as swiftly as their horses could run; each knight struck the other's sturdy shield so forcefully with his lance that it was pierced through. Yet neither knight was wounded. They rode past, then wheeled about and returned full gallop to strike more mighty blows on their strong, good shields. Each was a courageous, bold, and valiant knight, and each rode a swift and powerful steed. Their mighty thrusts hammered the shields they bore at their sides, piercing them through with lances that forced their way right to the bare flesh, without breaking or splitting. With powerful blows they drove one another to the ground. Breast-straps, girths, stirrups—nothing could keep them from being tumbled backward from their saddles onto the bare earth. Their frightened horses reared and plunged, bucking and biting: they too wished to kill each other!

The fallen knights leapt up as quickly as they could. They drew their swords, with their mottoes engraved upon them. Protecting their faces with their shields, they sought how best to injure one another with their sharp steel blades. Lancelot was unafraid, for he was twice as skilled at fencing as Meleagant, having practiced it since his youth. Both struck such powerful blows to the shields and gold-plated helmets that they split and broke. But Lancelot relentlessly pursued Meleagant and gave him a mighty blow that severed the steel-covered right arm, so that his enemy could no longer shield himself. When Meleagant felt the loss of his right arm, he determined to sell his life dearly. If he could grasp the opportunity, he would avenge himself, for he was nearly insane with anger, spite, and pain. His situation was hopeless if he could not find some evil trick to destroy Lancelot. He rushed toward him, thinking to take him by surprise, but Lancelot was on his guard and with his trenchant sword opened Meleagant's belly so wide that he would not be healed for months. A second blow slashed his helmet, knocking the nasal into his mouth and breaking three teeth.

Meleagant was so enraged that he couldn't speak a word, not even to ask for mercy, because his foolish heart, which bound him and held him prisoner, has so besotted him. Lancelot approached, unlaced Meleagant's helmet, and cut off his head. Never again would Meleagant deceive him: he had fallen in death, finished. But I assure you now that no one who was there and witnessed this deed felt any pity whatsoever. The king and all the others there rejoiced greatly over it. Then the happiest among them helped Lancelot remove his armor and led him away amid great joy.

My lords, if I were to tell any more, I would be going beyond my matter. Therefore I draw to a close: the romance is completely finished at this point. The clerk Godefroy of Lagny has put the final touches on *The Knight of the Cart*; let no one blame him for completing the work of Chrétien, since he did it with the approval of Chrétien, who began it. He worked on the story from the point at which Lancelot was walled into the tower until the end. This much only has he done. He wishes to add nothing further, nor to omit anything, for this would harm the story.   [7112]

Here ends the romance of *Lancelot of the Cart*.

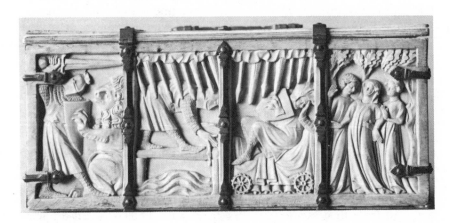

Lancelot crossing the Sword Bridge. From an ivory casket, French, fourteenth century. Metropolitan Museum of Art. Gift of J. Pierpont Morgan, 1917.

chapter VI

SIR GAWAIN AND THE GREEN KNIGHT

James J. Wilhelm

Sir Gawain and the Green Knight is not only the finest Arthurian romance in English literature, but also a work of commanding literary merit. This fourteenth-century tale deals with the timeless themes of love, honor, heroism, and the human will to survive in a world that is often perplexing, changeable, and violent.

In his *Anatomy of Criticism* Northrop Frye suggests that all literature can be grouped under headings of religious affirmation, romantic fantasy, or realistic presentation. *Sir Gawain* simultaneously exhibits all three modes of expression. On the one hand it can be read as a religious parable that extols humility and integrity against the vices of pride, lust, and recklessness. Certainly the dominant symbol of the green sash must be viewed as a token of Gawain's humble acceptance of his all-too-human flaw of wanting to survive at any price.

The fantastic element is also conspicuous in the story, since the tale contains magical acts and unreal creatures, such as trolls and fairies. Morgan the Fay, who is herself a member of the mythic world, is the presiding genius of the story. Her desire to test Arthur's court and to shock Guinevere (supposedly because the Queen exposed her love affair with the knight Guiomar) impels the action, in which the Green Knight is in many ways simply her tool. Behind Morgan is the wizard Merlin (Part Four, Stanza 19) and the entire world of Celtic myth.

Realistic elements also abound, especially in the basic vocabulary, with its highly precise words for butchering an animal or dressing a knight in armor. No novelist of the nineteenth century ever showed a firmer handling of detail. In its outlook, too, the poem celebrates the "real" every bit as much as it does the ideal or the imaginary. What causes Sir Gawain to abandon his rigid code of morality is simply his desire to save his own skin—and this frank simplicity is also the thing that saves him. For, as the Green Knight says at the last encounter, Gawain's lack of integrity "didn't arise for an artful object or amorous fling—/ No! You just loved your life! And I blame you the less for it" (2367–68).

By employing these three very different modes of expression almost simultaneously, the poet is able to establish striking juxtapositions. The blood and gore of the hunting scenes alternate with the slick French manners of the boudoir. Prayers to Christian divinities are uttered in heathen places. The poet is able to hold these diverse strands together because of the strict unity that he employs. Part One sets up the motif of the beheading challenge and its first enactment. Part Two introduces the motif of the exchange of presents between a host and a guest. Part Three alternates panels showing the overt aggression of the hunt with the suppressed sensuality of the beautiful hostess's temptations. Part Four brings together the two central motifs, which can be found widely in folklore, as the violence of the hunt finds its last echo in the abortive beheading, and the potentially lascivious secrets of the boudoir are finally revealed as merely the innocent acceptance of a sash.

Everything ends happily in *Sir Gawain*, as it should in a fairy tale. The hero also learns a lesson, as he should in a religious parable. And finally the reader is exposed, along with the hero, to a series of traumatic experiences that lead to a catharsis that brings one close to the true meaning of humility. If we read the poem correctly, surely we feel pity for the once-unassailable Gawain, that paragon of virtue, and terror toward the mysteries that threaten him and us all, whether they spring from supernatural sources or the human heart.

Only a very great writer could achieve a successful conclusion for so complex a design. Unfortunately we do not know the author's name, since none is appended to the single fourteenth-century manuscript in which the poem survives. There it occurs with two other works written in alliterative verses (*Patience* and *Purity*) and another composed in rhymed stanzas (*The Pearl*). These three poems are also written in a dialect of the Midlands of England, probably from around Stafford, and treat moral or religious themes.

The so-called "Gawain-poet" may well have written all four pieces, but he made of *Sir Gawain and the Green Knight* something greater than a traditionally moral work of art. The dangerous ramifications of the courtly game of love are clearly delineated (in contrast to Chrétien's *Lancelot*, where they are exalted), and Arthur's court is portrayed as refined to the point of effeteness. To Gawain, his sash at the end of the story is a religious icon, but to the other courtiers it is little more than the latest French fashion. Still, the morality of the work never intrudes upon the poem's esthetic structure, and *Sir Gawain* transcends a literature that is merely didactic to join the mainstream of the imaginative literature of all times.

Bibliographic note: The following book contains a complete summary of criticism and scholarship to 1977: Malcolm Andrew, *The "Gawain"-Poet: An Annotated Bibliography, 1839–1977* (Garland, 1979). Three important critical studies are: Larry D. Benson, *Art and Tradition in "Sir Gawain and the Green Knight"* (Rutgers University, 1965); John Burrow, *A Reading of "Sir Gawain and the Green Knight"* (Barnes and Noble, 1966); and Donald R.

Howard, *The Three Temptations* (Princeton University, 1966). See also Marie Borroff, *"Sir Gawain and the Green Knight": A Stylistic and Metrical Study* (Yale University, 1962). For analogues with earlier literature, see Chapter 39 of R. S. Loomis, ed., *Arthurian Literature in the Middle Ages* (Oxford, 1959).

The text translated here was edited by J. R. R. Tolkien and E. V. Gordon, rev. Norman Davis (Oxford, 1967). I have consulted almost every previous translation, but especially those of Marie Borroff (Norton, 1967) and John Gardner (University of Chicago, 1965). For the many cruxes I tend to follow the Oxford text and its notes. In the translation I do not try to reproduce the alliteration of the original exactly; I frequently reduce it, just as I suppress one of the rhymes in the so-called "wheel of the bob," the last five lines of every stanza. No other poem that we know of contains this unique construction, and the work is similarly unique in its free handling of meter, alliteration, and diction.

Note on the opening stanza: Following the tradition established by Latin chronicles and the Anglo-Norman *Roman de Brut*, by Wace, in the 1100s, the poet links Britain to a founder named Felix Brutus, whose roots reach back through Rome to Troy. The traitor in line 3 is apparently Antenor, while the Ticius of line 11 is unknown (sometimes the name is emended to Tirius, for whom the Tyrrhenian Sea was supposedly named).

Sir Gawain and the Green Knight

PART ONE

1.

After the siege and the assault had ceased at Troy,
The citadel was shattered and burned to cinders and shards,
And the traitor who wove out his tapestry of treason
Was tried for his treachery, which was proved beyond doubt;
Then Aeneas the kingly and his high-born kinsmen
Prevailed over many powers, becoming the possessors
Of well-nigh all of the wealth of the western lands.
Next royal Romulus reached out ambitiously for Rome;
With pomp and with pride, he founded that place first,
Honoring it with his own name, which it even now bears.   10
Ticius went into Tuscany and erected some towers;
King Longbeard in Lombardy lifted up dwellings,
And over the French flood-waves great Felix Brutus
Established Britain with eagerness upon its many
     Spreading hills,
Where war and ruin and wonder
At times have overspilled;
And there have been swift turnings
Of the blissful and the ill.

2.

And when Britain had been built by this noble baron,   20
Bold men were bred there who relished their battling,
Who incited insurgence in many times gone by.
More miracles have occurred more often on British meadows
Than on any others that I've heard tell of till now.
And of all the British founders who have ever flourished here,
Surely Arthur was the most heroic, as I have heard.
And so I aim to narrate an earthly adventure
That many men consider a marvelous thing to view,
An otherworldly exploit of Arthurian wonder.
If you will listen to this lay just a little while,   30
I shall tell it at once, as I have heard it told round,
      In my own song,
The way it was set and established
In a story stout and strong,
That's been locked in loyal letters
Through our land for very long.

3.

This king lay at Camelot around Christmastime
With many a gracious lord, the best of his liegemen,
Assuredly all royal brethren of the Round Table,
With rich revels and innumerable games arranged.   40
There tussled many champions in tourneys at times;
They jousted, these gentle knights, with great jocularity,
Then crowded into court to sing and dance to carols.
And then the feast flowed unbroken for a good fifteen days
With all of the fun and the food that one could fancy;
Such noise and enjoyment were invigorating to hear,
Delightful all the day long, with dancing during the night.
The height of happiness was attained in those chambers and halls
By those lords and ladies—the loveliest of lives, they thought.
With all the delights of the world they dwelled together,   50
The most celebrated knights to recognize Christ himself,
And the loveliest ladies who have ever enjoyed their lives,
And the most courteous king who ever controlled a court.
All of these fair-haired people still had their precious primes
      To fulfill—
The happiest folk under heaven,
With the king of greatest good will.
It would be far too taxing to number
All the hardy host on that hill.

4.

While the New Year was young, having just now entered,   60
Double portions that day were served to all of the diners.
When the king came in with his counts into the hall
As the chanting in the chapel had hushed to its close,
An outcry was uttered by the clerics and by others:
"Noel!" they announced, calling it again and again.
Then the regal party ran around to pass out their gifts,
Hawking them with high-pitched calls, giving them out by hand,
Debating very busily about all their barterings.
The ladies laughed loudly—even when they were losers—

While the winners felt no wrath, *that* you may well trust.   70
They made all this merriment right up until mealtime,
When they washed themselves well and then went on to their seats,
With the grandest barons above, for so it seemed best.
Queen Guinevere very gaily was gathered among them,
Dressed up on the dais, which was decked all around
With expensive silk sidings, and a ceiling above
Made of drapes from Toulouse and Turkestan—indeed!
They were embroidered and embellished with the best of gems
That could be purchased with pounds to meet the price
    On any selling day.   80
The prettiest lady that one may describe,
She gleamed there with eyes of grey;
To have seen one fairer to the sight—
That no one could truly say.

5.

But Arthur would not sit down until they were served:
He was so jolly in his youthfulness—and just a bit juvenile.
He wanted life to be lighthearted, liking much less
To loll around for very long, or a long time to sit.
This way his young blood and restless brain kept him busy.
Then also, another affair concerned him as much: 90
For he had established the noble custom that he never would sup
On a high and holy day until he had first heard
An unusual account of some adventuresome affair,
Or some major miracle in which he might believe:
About aristocrats and arms and other such achievements;
Or unless somebody begged him for some brave-hearted knight
To join in a joust, with each to lay in jeopardy
A life for a life, thereby allowing the other
To have the fairer share if Fortune should so favor him.
This was always the king's custom when he was in court,   100
At every fancy feast among the finest fellows
    In his hall.
He stood firm in his place
Appearing proud and tall,
But early in this New Year,
He loosed merriment for all.

6.

So he appeared in that place, the proud king himself,
Talking before the High Table about delicate trifles.
And there Gawain the good was seated next to Guinevere,
While Sir Agravain Hard-hand on the other side was sitting—   110
Both sons of the king's sister and stout knights for sure.
Bishop Baldwin led off the guests on the board up above,
While Yvain, the son of Urien, ate with him there.
They were seated this way on the dais, and scrupulously served,
With many a sterling sire set along the sideboards.
In came the first course to the crackling sound of trumpets,
While many a bright-colored banner was furling close by.
The kettledrums clamored, accompanied by courtly pipes,
Blending wild warblings with loudly awakened alarms
That lifted hearts high as they heard those crescendoes.   120

Dainties were doled out with other dearly bought foods—
A harvest of wholesomeness, heaped high on so many platters
That scarcely were places found before all those people
To set down the silver vessels with the various entrees
      Upon the cloth.
Every person reached as he pleased,
Not feeling one bit loath.
No—twelve dishes for every pair;
Good beer and bright wine both!

7.

Now of the service I'll supply no further details,   130
But well you might wager that there was no want there.
Then another noise, all new, drew suddenly nigh
That now might allow noble Arthur to gather some nurture.
For scarcely had the music ceased for a single second
And the first course been courteously doled around to the court,
When there rushed through the door an extremely awesome rider,
One of the greatest on earth, in measure enormous,
From his neck to his nates looking nearly square and thick,
While his loins and his limbs were long and very huge.
Half a giant from the ground up I'd guess him to be,   140
But still wholly human I'd have to declare him—
The grandest master in girth who ever galloped!
For the back and the breast of his body were very broad,
Though his stomach and his waistline were supremely slim;
And his facial features were like his figure—very neat
      And clean.
Yet one truly wondered at the hue
Of his countenance when seen;
For he acted like a thing bewitched
And was, head to toe, ink-green.   150

8.

All colored green were this creature and his clothes.
He sported a very tight straight-coat that stuck to his sides,
With a lovely mantle on top and a lining within
Whose fur clearly was trimmed with a facing that was fair,
And with elegant ermine embellishing it and the hood,
Which hung loose from his locks, lying over his shoulders.
He also sported tight stockings of the very same color,
Which clung to his calves, and below, cleanly polished spurs
Of burnished gold set on bases of richly barred silk;
And shoeless beneath his shanks this chevalier rode.   160
All of his gear was, I swear, a gorgeous green:
Both the bosses on his belt and the brilliant, shiny stones
That were elaborately arranged on the noble array
Of his saddle and on his own clothes spun from silk.
It would be much too tiring to tell even half the details
That were embroidered above: the birds and the butterflies,
With the gay, gaudy green and the gold interwoven
On the hangings from the breast-band, the horse's crupper,
The bosses on its bit, with their enameled metal,
The stirrups that he stood on, stained the same color,   170
And the bows and the panels of his princely saddle,

Which always gleamed and glimmered with its greenish stones.
The steed that he sat on shared the same color,
    It's true:
A green horse, huge and heavy,
A stallion hard to subdue;
In its bordered bridle, it was quick
Its master's will to pursue.

9.

Very gaily was this gallant man decked out in green,
The hair of him and his horse having the same sheen.   180
Beautifully flowing tresses folded over his shoulders.
A beard as big as a bush spread out over his breast
That with the heavy hair falling down from his head
Was clipped all around just a bit above the elbows,
So that half of his arms were hidden underneath,
The way a king's heavy coat may cover his torso.
The mane of that mighty horse resembled it very much;
It was nicely curled and well-combed, with many a knot
Of golden thread twisted in among the fair green:
Here a strand of green hair, and there a strand of gold.   190
Its tail and its tuft were twins in their coloring,
And both were bound with bands of bright-shining green,
Which adorned the tail's point with preciously priced stones.
Then a thong was bound tight with a high triple knot
From which many bright bells of burnished gold were ringing.
Such a foal in a field or a fellow to ride upon it
Was never observed in that open hall before that hour
    By any man alive.
He looked as lithe as lightning,
Said those who saw him arrive.   200
It seemed no mortal might
His deadly blows survive.

10.

And yet he had no helmet, and no hauberk either,
No breastplate or other parts pertaining to armor,
No shaft or no shield to shove or to strike with,
But in one of his hands he was holding a branch of holly,
Which is greatest in its greenery when all the groves are bare.
In his other he held an ax, immense and appalling,
A battle-ax quite awful to describe—if anyone could.
The large head measured the full length of an ell-yard;   210
Its handle had the hues of green steel and of gold;
That blade had a bright burnish, and also a broad edge
As well-shaped for shearing as any sharpened razor.
The stern one gripped it by its stiff and steely shaft,
Which was wound around with iron down to the wand's end,
And all engraved with enchanting designs in emerald.
A lacing was looped around it and locked at the head,
And down the shaft it swept in tight-clinging circles,
With innumerable, intricate tassels attached to it
On buttons of emerald that were embroidered most elegantly.   220
This horseman hurtled up and hove into the hall,
Dashing forward to the dais and fearing no danger,

Not saluting a single soul, but surveying them all.
The very first word that he hurled out then was: "Where
Is the commander of this crowd? I would quite gladly
Summon him to my sight, and with His Honor speak words
    Rational and sound."
On the knights he beamed his eyes,
Rolling them all around;
He paused—to ascertain   230
Who claimed the seat of renown.

11.

The group there kept gawking a long time to gather more,
For everyone was marveling at exactly what it might mean
That a champion and his charger could acquire such a sheen,
Growing green as the grass—even greener, it seemed—
Glowing brighter than green enamel gleaming upon gold.
All who stood there were stupefied; they stepped a bit nearer,
With all the world's wonder as to what works he'd perform.
For they'd witnessed a lot of weird things, but never one like this!
Many of the followers charged it to phantoms and fairies,   240
And so these aristocrats were a bit anxious about answering;
Yes, astonished by that voice, they sat there all stone-still,
While silence like a swoon swept through that hall,
As if everyone was slipping into slumber. They censored
    Any words coming out,
And because of courtesy, I think—
Not because of fear or doubt—
So the king whom they all obeyed
Could speak up to that lout.

12.

Then Arthur before the dais acknowledged the adventurer   250
And warmly welcomed him, for he was never weak-kneed,
Saying, "Good sir, I extend a greeting to my gathering.
I'm the head of the household here; Arthur's my name.
Step down now gently, and stay a while, I ask you;
And whatever you want—we shall see that it's fulfilled."
"No!" said the stranger. "So help me He who rules on high!
It was not my intention to interrupt your amusements;
But because the praise of you, prince, is puffed so high,
And your manor and your men are considered so magnificent,
The most stalwart ever to ride on steeds in steel-gear,   260
The most valiant and virtuous of the variety of humans,
Tough lads to try one in a gentleman's many tests,
And politeness is practiced here—so it's been prated—
Your celebrity summons me here now in this season.
Please be assured by the branch that I am bearing
That I'm passing in peace, wanting no prickly words.
For if I'd come here with comrades in a quarrelsome mood,
I wouldn't have left my hauberk at home—or my helmet either—
And my shield and my sharp spear shining all bright,
And other weapons to wield—please know this well.   270
No, because I want no warfare, I wore my soft garments.
And if you're as bold as all the barons bandy it,

You'll graciously grant me the little game that I ask
    By right."
Arthur then responded,
Saying, "Sir kindly knight,
If true battle is your care,
You will not lack your fight."

13.

"No, in full faith! I'm not spoiling for any fight!
Why, around on these benches I see just beardless babies!   280
If I were suited in my armor, on top of my strong steed,
There'd be no man here to match me; their muscles are too weak.
No, in this court I crave just a little Christmas pastime,
For it's New Year and Yuletide—and the people here are young.
If any human here considers himself husky enough
With a bold brain in his head—as well as some boiling blood—
So that he'd exchange with me one stiff stroke for another,
I'll give him as a gift this gorgeous battle-ax—
This haft, which is heavy indeed, to handle as he chooses.
And I'll undergo the first thrust, unarmed as I am now.   290
And if any churl is so childish as to challenge what I say,
Let him leap down lightly here and latch on to this tool.
I'll quit-claim it forever; he can keep it as his catch.
And I'll suffer his swiping—standing stiff on this floor—
If you'll grant me the chance to give him another glance
    My way.
Yet he can have a little respite
For twelve months and a day.
Now hurry, and let's see quickly
If someone will have his say."   300

14.

If they were astonished at first, they now acted even stiller,
Those householders in the hall, the high and the low.
The man on his stallion swung around on his saddle
And roguishly rolled his red eyes all about,
Bending his bristly brows, which were beaming all green,
And, wagging his beard, while waiting for someone to answer.
When no one would counter his charge, he coughed just a bit,
And, pulling himself up pompously, he proclaimed:
"What! Is this Arthur's house," said the accuser then,
"Whose fame goes flowing throughout so many fiefdoms?   310
Well, where's your derring-do now, your dashing conquest?
Your bluster and bravado, your big-sounding words?
Now all the revel and renown of the Table Round
Are overwhelmed by the words of one creature's speech,
And from fear, all fierceness fades without a blow!"
With this he guffawed so loud that the good king grieved.
The blood shot for shame up into Arthur's cheeks
    And hair.
He grew as angry as the wind,
As did all those who were there.   320
But the king, always keen to act,
Answered that tough man's dare,

15.

Saying, "My fond fellow, by God, your asking is foolish,
But he who requests what's wrong shall reap his will.
I'm sure that no person here is put off by your proud words.
Give me your great-ax, for the sake of our Lord God,
And the boon that you beg for soon shall be bestowed."
Lightly Arthur leaps down and lunges toward that hand,
While fiercely the other fellow falls to his feet.
Now Arthur grabs the great-ax, gripping it by the haft,   330
And swinging it sternly, takes some practice swipes.
The grim one stands his ground, in all of his grandeur,
Huger than any thane in the house by a head-length or more.
With an unsmiling face, he stands there, stroking his beard,
And with a deliberate look, he draws down his collar,
No more nervous or unsettled by Arthur's warming strokes
Than if some buddy from the benches had brought him a draught
    Of wine.
Gawain, who sat by the queen,
To Arthur's ear inclined: 340
"I beg you, sir, here and now:
Please let this match be mine.

16.

"Would you please, kindly sir," said Gawain to the king,
"Let me jump up from this bench and join you over there?
Without breaking protocol, I'd abandon this board
And if my liege-lady here doesn't greatly dislike it,
I'll come share your counsel before this courtly throng.
For I find it unthinkable, if the truth may be told,
That when such a weird request is raised in your halls,
You alone should have the yearning to undertake it yourself,   350
While so many bold warriors are warming these benches,
Who, I know, stand second to none in fighting spirit
And who cut the finest figures on the fields in the fray.
I'm the weakest of all, I'm aware—the feeblest in wit.
The loss of my life would surely be the least important.
My only claim to fame is that I call you my close kin.
My body has no blessing except what comes from your blood;
And since this is all a foolish fuss, it shouldn't fall upon you.
For since I've asked for it first, it is fittingly mine.
And if I annoy you by my nagging, this noble court should   360
    Give me the blame."
The nobles whispered together;
And since they felt the same,
To spring their sceptred king,
To Gawain they gave the game.

17.

Then the king commanded the knight to come and join him;
And the knight arose all ready and reached him fast,
Kneeling down to his lord, laying hands on the lethal weapon.
Arthur lightly yielded it, and then lifted up his hand,
Bestowing God's blessing, and bidding him urgently   370
To employ heart and hands in a very hardy way:
"Take care, my cousin," said the king; "make just one carving.

For if you deal with him deftly, I know, without a doubt
That you'll absorb any tap that he'll administer later."
Gawain approached the adversary with ax in hand,
Facing him most fiercely—not the least bit afraid.
Then the Giant in Green muttered grimly to Sir Gawain:
"Let's reformulate our agreement before we go further.
First, I'll query you, kind sir, as to how you are called,
And please tender me a retort in a way I can trust."   380
"In God's faith," said the good knight, "Gawain is my name.
I'll be handing you a hack soon—whatever happens after—
And twelve months from this Yuletime, I will take another
By whatever weapon you want, and without any second
        Alive."
The other one responds:
"Sir Gawain—God let me thrive!—
I am wonderfully content
To take any dent you drive.

18.

"Bigod," said the Green Knight, "Sir Gawain, I am glad   390
To acquire from your armed fist what I asked for here,
And you've already recited with a reasoning that's right
And careful all of the clauses I claim from your king—
Except for promising me, good sir, by your sworn pledge,
That you'll search for me yourself wherever you suspect
You'll find me on earth's face, to gather such fees
As you'll pay me here today before this powerful party."
"Where will I find you?" asked Gawain. "Where do you live?
I don't know your homestead—by Him who created me!—
No, I don't know, knight, either your court or your name.   400
Tell me this truly; tell me what you are called,
And I'll use all my wits to wend my way toward you.
This I openly swear on my own self-assured oath!"
"That's enough for a New Year. You need say no more,"
Said the vassal shining verdant to Gawain the valiant;
"To tell you the truth, when I've taken your tap,
And you've had your swift swipe, I'll instruct you then
About houses and homesteads and how I am called;
Then you can question my customs—and keep to your promise.
And if my spirit's snuffed, you'll surface all the safer,   410
For you can tarry on this turf without traveling any farther—
        So relax!
It's time to take up your tool
And show how you can hack."
"Yes, indeed, milord," said Gawain,
Stroking upon the ax.

19.

The Green Knight got ready right away on that ground,
Bending his neck a bit forward to lay bare the flesh,
Stringing his long, lovely strands up over his scalp,
Exposing his naked nape to the need at hand.   420
Gawain gathers up the ax, gripping it tightly,
And placing his left foot before him on the floor,
He brings it down brusquely upon the bare-skinned neck,

So that the sharpened blade shatters through the bones.
It shears the shaft of the neck, splitting it in two,
With the edge of bright iron biting into the earth.
The fair head flips from its foundation to the floor,
And the crowd begins to kick it as it caroms their way.
Blood spurts from the base, shining bright upon the green,
But the fellow doesn't fail or falter one bit.   430
No, he starts up swiftly upon his solid shanks
And reaches out roughly where the courtiers are ranked
To gather back his head, which he heaves then on high.
Then he strides to his stallion, snatching at its bridle,
Stepping up into the stirrups and standing aloft.
Then, dangling the head by its hairs in one of his hands,
The stranger sits very steadily in his saddle,
As if nothing had bothered him one bit—but yet he had
        No head.
He twisted his torso around,   440
That ugly trunk that bled.
The onlookers had some doubts
Before the next words were said.

20.

Holding the head straight outward in one hand,
He directed the face toward the great dons on the dais.
It opened its eyelids and ogled them all around,
Then muttered from the mouth these words that you must hear:
"All right, Gawain! Be so good as to go as you promised
And try faithfully to find me, my fine fellow,
As you have sworn in this hall, and these knights have heard.   450
Come to the Green Chapel, I command you, to suffer
A dent like the one you've dealt me—for you deserve
To be promptly repaid on the approaching New Year's morn.
Numerous people know me as the Knight of the Chapel Green.
So if you want faithfully to find me, you shall not fail.
And so, come! Or else, be called a craven coward!"
With a violent jerk, he veered away on the reins
And hurtled through the hall-door with his head in his hand,
While a fire, as from flint, flickered up from his horse's hooves.
To what land he launched out—nobody there could learn;   460
Nor did they have any notion as to his native place.
        What then?
The king and Gawain next
Laughed and grinned again;
The affair was widely proclaimed
A marvel by all men.

21.

Though Arthur, the artful king, felt a bit anxious at heart,
He let no semblance be seen, but loudly issued instead
To his most becoming queen this courteous speech:
"My dear lady, you should not be dismayed today;   470
This cleverness is customary at Christmastime,
With performances of plays, pastimes, and songs,
As well as the deft dances of knights and damsels.
And so to my supper I shall now address myself,

For a wonder I have witnessed—*that* no one will deny."
He glanced over at Gawain and graciously said to him,
"Hang up your hatchet, sir; you have hewn quite enough."
The tool was tied to a tapestry over the throne,
Where all men might marvel at it with great amazement
And prattle about the prodigy, having viewed the living proof. 480
Then they fell to their food, these fond friends together,
This king and his companion, where men catered carefully
With the plentiful portions that to princely men fall!
With all manner of fine meats—and minstrelsy to boot—
In good spirits they spent that day, till its end sped
    Through the land.
Now be very mindful, Sir Gawain,
That, if in danger you stand,
You see to the very end
Any enterprise at hand. 490

PART TWO

1.
This exchange of exploits Arthur experienced early
In the young year; how he yearned to hear such vaunts!
Though words once were lacking, as they went to their seats,
The court now swelled with serious talk—overspilled!
Gawain was glad to begin those games in that hall,
But if this story turns serious, you shouldn't feel surprised,
For though men have merry minds when they've drunk very much,
The seasons run rather swiftly and experience many shiftings:
The outset and the outcome are seldom in one accord.
And so the Yuletide rolled by, and the young year came on, 500
And one season, as established, succeeded another.
After Christmas there came the cold of crabby Lent,
Which tests the human flesh with fish and simpler foods.
And then the world's weather wrestles against the winter.
Chill clings to the earth, while clouds go billowing upward.
Sheerly sprinkles the rain in showers that are warm,
Falling upon fair plains where the spring flowers swell,
And the ground and the groves burgeon under gowns of green.
Birds busy themselves with their building and beautifully warble
In the solace of the soft summer that slowly steals in 510
    Over hill and shore.
Then blossoms sprout on boughs
That are lined with blooms galore,
While all throughout the woodland
Bird-notes show that birds adore.

2.
Next comes the season of summer with its softened winds,
When Zephyrus sighs over the seedlings and the sedges;
Full of pleasure are the plants that spring up all around,
As the dampening dew drops gently from their leaves,
And then they bask in the blissful blush of the sun. 520
Ah, but then Harvest comes hurrying, making all things harsh,
Warning them that, against the winter, they must wax all ripe.

He drives up the dust in the middle of a drought,
Making it fly up over the fair face of the earth.
Wrathful winds wrestle with the sun high up in the heavens;
Leaves fall, loosened from lindens, then drift to the ground,
And all grey is the grass that was green just a bit before.
Then everything ripens and rots that once rose high,
And so the year yields, with the passing of yesterdays,
And winter winds round again, as the world-order demands—   530
        No lie!
Now the moon of Michaelmas
Hangs with wintry pledges high.
His own voyage most annoying
Gawain ponders by and by.

3.

Up to All Hallows Day with Arthur he abided,
When the king arranged a great revel for his relative's sake,
With plenty of pomp and partying at the Table Round.
Courtiers acting courteous and very becoming women
Felt a sympathy inside, out of love for that fond sire,   540
But nevertheless, they accentuated their amusement,
And, though joyless, invented jests for that gentleman.
After dinner, Sir Gawain dolefully addressed his dear uncle
About the perilous passage; he very plainly explained:
"My liege, the lord of my life, I now must leave you.
You know the terms of my trial. I'm not going to try
To tell you a lot about it—just a trifle.
You know that I'm bound to bear up my burden tomorrow,
To seek out the knight in green—and may God guide me!"
Then the select of that circle sequestered a bit: 550
Sir Yvain and Sir Erec, and many another aristocrat:
Sir Dodinal the Savage, with the Duke of Clarence,
And Lancelot and Lionel along with Lucan the good,
Sir Bors and Sir Bedivere—both mighty barons—
And many another manly one, like Mador of the Gate.
All of this courtly company drew closer to the king
To advise the arch-ruler with anxiousness at heart.
A somber sorrow was stealing through that inner sanctum
That a gallant man like Gawain should go on that errand
And suffer some baleful blow, feeling his brave hand   560
        Fall weak.
But Gawain feigned a happy face
And asked, "Should I now retreat?
Whether destiny looms dear or dark,
What can a man do but seek?"

4.

He stayed there all of that day, getting dressed in the morning,
Asking early for his arms, all of which were conveyed to him.
The servants spread a silken carpet over the floor,
Which had many a gold garment there gleaming upon it.
The stalwart one stepped onto the rug and took hold of the steel,   570
Slipping into a jacket that was spun from rich Turkish silk,
And donning a fancy hood that was fastened tight at the throat,
Which had a brilliant fur lining bound up inside.

Then they fitted some footwear over the hero's feet.
His legs were lined with lovely greavings of steel,
Which had kneeplates appended, polished all bright,
That were knit around the kneecaps with knots of gold.
Then costly cuisse-pieces craftily enclosed
His thick, brawny thighs, with many a thong attached.
Next body-armor embroidered with burnished rings   580
Circumscribed that courtier with very costly material.
He had beautifully shining bracers on both his arms,
And wore strong, gaudy elbow-guards and gloves of iron;
And all of that gorgeous gear was guaranteed to help
      Turn any tide.
With a fashionable overcoat
And gold spurs to jab with pride,
He was girded by a silken belt
With a trusty sword at his side.

5.

When he was suited in his steel, his armor looked superb.   590
The slightest lacing or loop was lustrous with gold.
Fully harnessed this way, he heard the high mass sung,
As it was offered and honored at the high altar.
Then he went to the king and all his courtly companions,
And lovingly took his leave from those ladies and lords.
They kissed him, walked with him, commending him to Christ.
Then Gringolet was geared up, girt round with a saddle
That glistened all gaily with many a golden fringe;
It was all newly nailed, newly furbished for that mission.
The bridle was barred around and bound with the brightest gold.   600
The sheen of the breast-cloth and its haughty side-skirts,
The crupper and caparison accorded with the saddle-bow,
For a rich field of red was arrayed with golden studs
That glittered and glistened like the glints of the sun.
Then our hero grabbed his helmet and hastily kissed it;
It was strongly stapled together and stuffed within.
He put it high on his head and hooked it behind,
Letting a band of cloth cover over the visor,
Which was embroidered and bound with the best of all gems
Set on broad, silken borders with birds at the seams,   610
Such as popinjays that were painted among periwinkles
And turtledoves entangled with true-loves so thickly
That it would take a seamstress seven winters to sew them
      In any town.
The band was of even greater price
That circumscribed his crown,
With diamonds that were finely cut
And glittered brightly around.

6.

Then they showed him the shield that was of shiny scarlet
With the pentangle depicted in pure golden hues.   620
He swung it by its strap, slung it over his shoulders,
And it seemed to fit that fighter perfectly.
Now why the pentangle is proper for this noble prince
I intend to inform you, despite the interruption:

It's a sign that Solomon established some time ago
As a token of truthfulness, which it bears title to,
For it is a figure that is formed out of five points,
And every line overlaps and locks in another
In a way that's entirely endless; therefore Englishmen
Call it everywhere, I hear, "the endless knot."   630
And so it was appropriate for this knight and his armor,
For Gawain was famous as a good man, as pure as is gold,
Always faithful in five things, each in a fivefold way,
Always devoid of villainy, and endowed in the finest virtues
    Most duly;
He carried on his shield and coat
This pentangle painted newly—
That man who was gentle in his speech
And who kept his word most truly.

7.

First of all, he was always faultless in his five senses,   640
And secondly he never failed in using his five fingers,
And his earthly faith was founded upon the five wounds
That Christ suffered on the Cross, as the Creed informs us;
And whenever this baron was embroiled in a battle,
His every thought was on that, above all other things.
Indeed, all of his daring he derived from the five delights
That the charming queen of heaven had from her boy-child.
And for this reason the royal man quite rightly had the queen
Embellished in her image on the inside of his shield,
So that when he viewed it, his vigor never wavered.   650
And the fifth group that I find the fighter employing were:
Free-giving and Good Fellowship, before all of the others;
His Chastity and his Courtesy were never corrupted;
And his Pity surpassed all the rest. These five points
Were more firmly fixed in him than in any other fellow.
Yes indeed, all of these five fives were ingrained in this knight,
And each one linked to the next, so that there was never an end;
They were fastened securely by the five points that never failed,
And they never swerved to one side or broke asunder.
No ending at any nook do I find anywhere,   660
Wherever the design began or glided to an end.
And so on this shiny shield, that knot stood painted
Royally with reddish gold upon a red-gules field.
This is the Pentangle Perfect—which is known to every person
    Of good lore.
Now Gawain the gay was fully geared
And his lance he lightly bore.
He issued them all a fond "Good day"—
He thought: for evermore.

8.

He stuck his spurs into his steed, and they sprang on the way   670
So fast that sparks went flashing, as from flint, out behind.
And all who saw him depart sighed sincerely within,
And uttered indeed the same old saws to one another
In compassion for the courtier: "By Christ! it's a shame
That you, my lad, shall be lost, who lived so nobly.

In faith, it's not easy to find your equal here on earth.
It would have been wiser if you'd waited more warily,
And later on, you'd be dubbed a dashing duke.
I believe you'd have made an unsurpassed leader of legions
And would have shone brightly instead of being snuffed out,　　680
Beheaded by some beast because of unbridled pride.
Who'd ever think that our Arthur would embark on such an exploit
As to yield to the gibberish of knights in a Yuletide jest!"
A great deal of warm water was wept from those eyes
As that handsome young hero ambled away from their haunt
　　　That day.
He didn't make any stops,
But went swiftly on his way.
Many a winding road he took,
As I've heard the old books say.　　　　　　　　690

9.

Now this regal noble rides through the realm of Logres,
Sir Gawain, the champion of God—no mere gamester he!
Usually solitary, he sleeps alone with the stars
And seldom does he find any food one might call the finest.
He had no friend except for his foal in those forests and hills,
And no creature except the Creator there to converse with,
Until he drew near to the northernmost part of Wales.
All of the islands of Anglesey he bore on his left hand
As he passed by the fords that fork into the foothills
Over toward Holy Head; then he gained the higher ground　　700
In the Wilderness of Wirral, where few men are dwelling
Who show a humane heart toward God or any human.
And always, as he went, he asked those whom he encountered
If they'd heard any gossip about some gallant in green
Or if, in the environs, might exist some emerald chapel.
Everyone nodded no. They said that they'd never seen
In all their careers any creature with such a coloring
　　　Of green.
The knight took many pathways strange
In terrain both bleak and mean;　　　　　　　710
And his visage suffered many a change
Before that chapel was seen.

10.

Many a cliff he climbed over in that strange country
Where he rode as a foreigner, far removed from his friends.
At every creek and crossing where that fellow coursed,
He found—quite fantastically—some foe before him,
One who was foul and fierce, with whom he had to fight.
In those mountains he met with such a host of marvels
That it would be too trying to tell even the tenth part.
Sometimes with serpents he struggled, sometimes with wolves,　　720
Sometimes with troll-like creatures who camp in the crags,
Also with bulls and with bears—and even with boars—
And giants who jumped out at him from the jags.
Had he not been strong and unstinting and served his Maker,
He would doubtlessly have been utterly dashed, and then died.
Yet danger was not what worried him; the weather was worse,

For the cold, clear water kept dropping down from the clouds
And freezing even before it fell on the frigid earth.
Almost slain by the sleet, he slept in his iron clothes
More nights than he had need for among the naked rocks,   730
Where cold torrents came crashing down from the crests
And hard icicles were hanging over his head.
And so in peril and pain, and in pitiful danger,
This chevalier coursed the countryside till Christmas Eve,
    All alone.
Then the horseman at that time
To good Mary made a moan
That she should direct his wanderings
And guide him to some home.

11.

By a mountain the next morning he merrily rode   740
Into a wood that was deep and wonderfully wild,
With towering hills on each side and high trees below
Containing a hundred or more huge, hoary oaks
And hazels and hawthorns heavily gnarled together,
While rough, ragged moss ran rampant everywhere.
Above, bevies of down-hearted birds on bare twigs
Were pitifully peeping because of the painful cold.
The rider on the back of Gringolet glided in below them
Through all of the mud and the mire—that lonely man—
Caring about his condition, fearing he might not come back   750
To see again the services for that Sire who on that Eve
Was born from a maiden to mollify all of our miseries.
And so, breathing hard, he begged: "I beseech thee, Lord,
And Mary, who is the mildest mother and dear,
For some haven where I might devoutly hear my mass,
And tomorrow hear matins—very meekly I ask this—
And now I promptly offer my Our Father and my Ave
    And Creed."
He rode on, deep in prayer,
Crying for his misdeeds,   760
And blessed himself several times,
Saying, "Christ's Cross grant me speed!"

12.

The cavalier had just crossed himself for the third time
When quickly through the trees he caught sight of a moated castle
Perched on a mound above a meadow, enmeshed in the boughs
Of tough-rooted tree-trunks that grew around the main trench.
It was the most charming chateau that a chevalier ever saw!
It lorded high on its towering lawn with a park below it,
Where pointed palisades kept everything in their pen,
Enfolding a forest for more than a fine two miles.   770
The hero simply stared at the façade of that stronghold
As it shimmered and shivered among the spangling leaves.
Then he humbly bared his head, and he heartily thanked
Lord Jesus and St. Julian, who are both gentle men,
Who had heard his cry and compassionately conveyed him:
"Now for a lovely lodging," said he. "I long for that still!"
Then he goaded on Gringolet with his gilded spurs

And he chose by chance to approach the chief portcullis.
This course carried him quickly to the head of the bridge
    At last. 780
The drawbridge was sharply lifted,
And the main gate bolted fast;
The walls looked very heavy
To withstand the winter's blast.

13.

The noble stayed on his steed, which drew short at the shore
Of the deep double ditch that fully encircled the dwelling.
The walls reached down into the water wondrously deep
And conversely they climbed to a dizzying crest above
As their hard, well-cut rocks created the cornices
That bulged underneath the battlements in the best of styles; 790
And over them towered the turrets neatly interspersed
With lots of useful loopholes to look through clearly.
Our baron had never laid eyes on a better barbican!
Then inside he could see the impressive inner keep,
Where towers extended tall between thick pinnacles
Whose fancy finials reached fittingly up, fine and long,
Culminating in carved caps that were craftily fashioned.
Then the champion noticed a host of chalk-white chimneys
That were sparkling snow-white upon the citadel's roof.
So many painted pinnacles were pointing up everywhere 800
And clambering in clusters among the crenellations
That the palace appeared indeed to be cut out of paper.
The stolid lord on his steed thought it all quite splendid
If he could just gain entrance into that enclosure
And, while the holidays lasted, find haven in that hostel
    Clean and bright.
He called, and soon there answered
A porter most polite,
Who assumed his place on the wall
And saluted the errant knight. 810

14.

"Kind sir," answered Gawain, "could you convey this message
To the lord of the house: I would deeply like some lodging."
"By Saint Peter, yes!" said the porter. "I can almost promise
You'll be summoned, good sir, to stay as long as you like."
Then he rushed away rapidly, and returned again as fast,
Bringing waves of well-wishers to welcome the knight.
They let down their drawbridge and then they all dashed out
And fell on their knees upon that freezing earth
To welcome that warrior in a way that was most worthy.
They guided him then to the main gate, which was soon yanked open, 820
And he graciously urged them to rise as he rode over the bridge.
Inside, the servants took his saddle as he dismounted,
And many stout-hearted men then stabled his steed.
A drove of mighty dons and squires then descended
To lead the lord lightheartedly into the hall.
When he took off his helmet, there hurried up a group
To hoist it out of the hands of this handsome man.
They also took his sword and his shining shield.

Then he greeted those gracious men most gratefully,
While many proud people pressed forward to honor that prince.   830
They whisked him, still clad in his armed coat, into the court,
Where a fine fire was kindling fiercely upon the hearth.
Then the great duke of that land descended from his den
To face with good manners the foreigner on his floor.
He said, "You are welcome to take whatever you wish
Of what is here; it's your own—to have and to hold
    At your own pace."
"Many thanks," returned Sir Gawain;
"May Christ grant you equal grace!"   840
Like humans who are happy,
The two men then embrace.

15.

Gawain glanced at the lord who had greeted him so kindly
And considered him capable of guarding that castle—
An enormous fellow, by the way, exactly at his prime.
Broad and bright was his beard, with a beaver's color;
Sturdy and straight was his stance upon his strong shanks.
He was frank in his speech, with a face as ferocious as fire,
And he seemed in all truth (or so Sir Gawain supposed)
Just right for leading a lordship with its liegemen.
The host then conducted his guest to a chamber, commanding   850
A servant to be sent to wait sedulously upon him.
A whole host of boys were bound to his beck and call.
They led him into a boudoir where the bedding was splendid,
With curtains of sheerest silk and shiny gold hems,
And coverlets quaint with the most becoming panels,
Brightly lined on the top, with embroidery on the sides.
The draperies ran on ropes with red-gold rings,
And tapestries from Toulouse and Tarsia spread on the walls,
While the floor was covered with fancy rugs for the feet.
There Sir Gawain was stripped of his iron suit   860
And his shiny garments, surrounded by humorous speeches.
Carefully educated esquires gave him expensive robes
To experiment with or exchange or elect the best.
As soon as he selected one, he slipped it on,
And it suited him beautifully with its swirling skirt.
"Primavera" he truly appeared from his springlike expression
To almost all the aristocrats; his limbs were absolutely
Dazzling and adorable as they reflected those hues,
So that Christ never created a more radiant creature,
    They thought.   870
Wherever in the world he went,
It seemed that Gawain ought
To be a prince without a peer
In the fields where menfolk fought.

16.

Before the chimney, where charcoals were burning, a chair
Was prepared for Sir Gawain, made plush with pillows.
Little cushions were placed on the quilt, both carefully sewn,
And then a magnificent mantle they threw over that man
Made of the finest fabric, and embroidered most fancily

With lovely furs inside to serve as a soft lining,   880
And they were made entirely of ermine, as was his hood.
He sat on that settee that seemed very royal indeed,
And warmed himself well—and soon his mood waxed brighter.
Then a table was tossed up on the finest trestles,
Covered with a clean cloth that appeared clear white,
Along with linens and a salt-cellar and some silver spoons.
Gawain washed as he wanted, and then went on to dine.
The servants certainly set themselves to serving him well,
With several fine soups, which were seasoned with the best,
With double servings, as was suitable, and many species of fish—   890
Some baked in bread, some broiled over the coals,
Some boiled, some cooked in stews with savory spices,
And always with subtle sauces that the connoisseur adores.
Very often and freely, that fellow proclaimed it a feast
With great courtesy, while the courtiers teased in a chorus:
        "Be comforted!
Just suffer this penance now,
For soon you'll be better fed!"
Their guest responded with laughter
As the wine went to his head!   900

17.
Then they queried and questioned—but always courteously—
Placing before that prince some private inquiries,
And finally he confessed that he came from the court
Where Arthur the admirable monarch held sway alone—
The rich, royal ruler of the Table Round.
Ah yes, Sir Gawain himself was sitting right there!
He had come to them at Christmastime as chance befell.
When the overlord was informed who this invited man was,
He laughed very loudly, for he liked it a lot;
And all the men of his mansion amused themselves too   910
By partaking of Gawain's presence right then and there.
Soon virtue and valor and the very finest manners
Were attributed to his person. He was always praised.
Before every human on earth, he was hailed as the highest!
Every man very softly then muttered to his mate:
"Soon we'll be seeing the most subtle behavior,
The most sophisticated standards of civilized speech,
And we'll be learning the lore of effortless language,
For we have in this place the paragon of perfect manners.
God has graciously granted us a gift indeed,   920
That a guest such as Gawain is given to us now
When gentlemen, overjoyed at the Savior's birth, join together
        And sing.
An education in etiquette
This knight shall surely bring;
And those who listen well
May gain love's mastering."

18.
When the dinner drew to an end, the dear guest arose;
It was nearing nighttime, for evening had now descended.
Chaplains to the chapel began wending their way   930

To ring the bells roundly, as rightly they should,
In the solemn evensong of that most sacred season.
The great lord attended there, along with his lady,
Who passed by with beauty en route to her private pew.
Gawain jumped up all jovially and went over to join them.
The lord seized his lapel and led him to a seat,
Then kindly took care of him, calling him by name,
Saying that he was the most welcome guest in all the world.
Gawain thanked him thoroughly; they embraced each other
And sat there soberly throughout the high service.   940
Then it intrigued the lady to entertain the invited one;
She departed from her pew, trailed by her pretty maids.
She was the fairest of all in her figure, flesh, and face,
As well as her contour, complexion, and conduct—
Even more gorgeous than Guinevere, so Gawain thought.
She crossed over the chancel to encounter the chevalier,
With another lady leading her by the left hand
Who was far more aged—an ancient one, she appeared—
And highly honored by all those high-born around her.
I must tell you that these two were totally unalike,   950
For if the younger had spirit, the senior one was seared.
A perfect pink complexion suffused the one,
While rough, wrinkled cheeks rolled down upon the other.
The younger wore a kerchief clustered with clearest pearls;
Her breast and her bright throat were laid all bare,
Shining more splendidly than the snow adrift on the hills.
The senior wore a scarf that was encircling her throat,
And her swarthy chin was concealed under chalky veils;
Her forehead was burrowing under silk folds and frills
With laces and lattices and lots of little ornaments,   960
So that only the black brows of that beldame were bared,
With her nose, her naked lips, and her two eyes—
And those two, sour to see, were most sorrowfully bleared.
She was one of the world's most wonderful women, you'd say—
        By God!
Her body was squat and thick,
Her buttocks bulging and broad;
Far lovelier was the lady
Who just behind her trod.

19.

When Gawain glances at that lady who looks so lovely,   970
He takes leave of her lord and lounges over to the two.
He salutes the senior first, scraping very low,
While the lovelier one he locks for a little in his arms,
Kissing her very courteously and chatting cavalierly.
They ask for his acquaintance, and he readily asserts
That he'll act as their obedient if they find this opportune.
They entwine him between them and, talking, they propel
Him into a chamber with charcoals, where they chiefly
Call for some spices that the serving-boys speedily bring
And the most wanted wines—all that they could wish for.   980
The host most hospitably kept hopping all around,
Reminding them that mirth should be made on every side.
He shucked off his hood and hung it upon a hook,

Then prodded them all to compete for its possession
By trying to raise the greatest revelry during that Yule:
"And I shall try, by my faith, with the help of my fond friends
To hustle with the happiest so my hood will not be lost."
And so, with these lighthearted words, the lord enlivened
And gladdened Sir Gawain's heart with gaming in his hall   990
    And great delight.
And when the hour rolled by
To call for the candlelight,
Sir Gawain climbed the stairs,
Bidding them all good night.

20.

On that morning when every mortal mulls over the time
When our Divine Lord for our destiny was born to die,
Joy wells up in everyone in the world on His behalf.
So did it there on that day with its countless delights,
Both at buffet and at the broad board spread on the dais,
Where caterers were serving courses of the finest cuisine.   1000
The aged harridan was sitting there highest in honor,
With the baron attentively by her, so I believe.
Gawain and the gay first lady were grouped together
About in the central section when supper was served,
While others were placed in the hall as was appropriate,
Since every diner was dealt with according to his degree.
There was food, there was fun, there was great frivolity—
So much that it would be tiring to tell the sum
Or to document the details, if I even dared.
Yet I think that our champion and his choice companion   1010
Were drawing such comfort from their company together,
From their sweet sophistication with subtle words,
With their nice and courteous talk—indeed, nothing nasty—
That their pastime surpassed any other palatial game—
    I declare!
Trumpets and kettledrums
And pipings filled the air;
Everyone tended his own thing,
And these two looked after theirs.

21.

Much merriment was made there that day and the next,   1020
And the third one impelled itself as intensely after.
The enjoyment of St. John's Day was a joy to behold,
But that was the end of entertaining—or so each thought.
The guests were planning to go away in the grey morning;
And so they remained wide-awake, imbibing their wine,
And all night long, they danced their devoutly loved carols.
At last, in the wee, wee hours, they whispered good night,
With each one wending his way to his own bedroom.
Gawain bade all goodbye; then the baron grabbed him,
Pulling him into his private chamber by its fireplace,   1030
And there he detained him a while, thanking him deeply
For the very precious privilege that he had provided
By honoring that house with his presence during the holidays,
Enchanting the whole chateau with his lively cheer:

"Indeed, royal sir, for as long as I breathe, I shall relish
The fact that you've been my friend for God's birthday feast."
"Many thanks, good sir," said Gawain, "but in all good faith,
The honor is yours—and may the Yule spirit bless you!
However, I'm here at your will to fulfill your behest
As I'm surely beholden, in matters either high or low,   1040
    With all due right."
The baron takes special pains
To further detain the knight,
But Gawain answers no:
He can't stay another night.

22.

The kindly castellan then inquired concernedly
What dire need had driven him out during this time
To travel so courageously out of the king's court alone
Before the holiday's holly was hauled out of town.
"Indeed, sir," said Gawain, "you certainly speak the truth.   1050
A high mission and a hard one bears me from those halls,
For I've been summoned to search alone for a site
Whose location I don't know where in the world to find.
For all of the land of Logres—may the Lord lend me aid!—
I'm bound to be there by daybreak on New Year's Day.
And so, sir, I'm asking you for assistance now:
Please tell me in all truth if you have ever been told
About any soil where a green sanctuary stands,
Or a knight who keeps it, who is clothed in the color green.
A pact was established with statutes set between us   1060
That I should meet that man at that monument if I could
On New Year's Day, which is now very nearly upon us,
And I'll face up to that fellow, if our Father allows me,
More gladly, by Jesus' grace, than have any other good thing!
And so, if you please, I have a long passage to travel
And I have only three more days to carry it through.
But I affirm I'd rather fall dead than fail in my errand!"
Then laughingly the lord replied, "Linger awhile!
For I'll teach you how to get there before your time is up.
The whereabouts of the church will worry you no longer.   1070
Instead, you can loll in your loft, my lord, at your ease
Till day flushes on the First, and then you can venture forth,
Coming there close to mid-morning, to clear what you
    Have to clear.
Stay awhile! And then rise up
And go on the First of the Year.
We'll direct you to your journey's end,
Which is not two miles from here."

23.

Then Gawain was full of joy and jovially rejoined,
"Now I thank you for this thoroughly—above everything else.   1080
I've accomplished part of my action, and I'm all at your command,
So I'll stay and perform any service that may please you."
Then the sire seized him and set him down at his side,
Paging the ladies to help them prolong their pleasure,
And they all participated in telling pleasant, private jokes.

The lord, who was brimful of friendship, acted frenzied at times,
And nobody knew what he'd say, so out of his wits he was.
Suddenly, in a stentorian voice, he said to his guest,
"You've already agreed to do anything that I ask;
And will you verify your vow at this very time?"   1090
"Yes sir, in all truth," said the trusty knight in return;
"As long as I bask in your bower, I'm bound to your will."
"You've had a terrible trip," said the host, "traveling far,
And been kept awake by me. You're not fully caught up
Either in eating or sleeping—of this I'm sure.
So linger awhile aloft; yes, lie up there and rest
Tomorrow until mass-time, and then meander down
Whenever you want; my wife will be here beside you,
Comforting you with her company till I come back to court.
      Yes, take it slow.   1100
But *I* shall get up early
And to my hunting go."
Gawain assents to this,
Bowing, as knights bow low.

24.
"And still," said the host, "let's set up one stipulation:
Whatever I win out in the woods shall revert to you,
And whatever you gain, be so good as to give it to me.
Let this be our swap, my sweet friend, truly sworn,
Whichever way fortune falls, my partner—fair or foul."
"By God," declared Gawain the good, "I grant it all!"   1110
And I think it's great that this gentleman likes to gamble!"
"Somebody bring us a drink and this bargain is sealed,"
Said the master of the manor, and the masses laughed.
They drank and they flirted and they frolicked freely,
These lords and these ladies, for as long as they liked.
And finally with French mannerisms and many fine words,
They stood and secretly exchanged subtle words,
Kissing very courteously and casting their adieux.
With several servants holding bright, shiny torches,
Everybody was escorted at the end to his chamber,   1120
      Soft and neat.
But before they go to bed,
Their bargains they repeat;
The old keeper of that castle
Surely kept them on their feet!

PART THREE

1.
In the gloom before daybreak, the guests who would journey
Stirred from their slumber and summoned their grooms
And busied themselves with saddling their stallions.
They tended to their gear, tying up their trunks,
And arrayed themselves royally for their riding away.   1130
They leaped on their mounts lightly, lifting the reins,
And they all departed to their desired destinations.
The overlord of that land was far from the last one

To be ready to ride off with his many retainers.
He hurried through his breakfast and then heard his mass
And briskly breezed to the fields at the bugle's cry.
As the morning's glow was glimmering along the horizon,
The man and his minions sat high upon their mounts.
The crafty kennelmen then leashed up their canines
And pulled the pound's doors open, letting them pour forth,   1140
While the bugles kept blaring some solitary blasts.
The beagles bounded out, all barking and baying;
They were chastised and whipped if they strayed in that course
By about a hundred hunters, I've heard—the best
          Who ever might be.
The trainers took their stations
As the bloodhounds were set free;
Bugles blared throughout the wood,
And a roar rose through the trees.

2.

At the chase's first cries, nature's creatures were quaking;   1150
Deer rushed down to the dales, darting with fear,
Then hurtled back to the heights, where they were hastily
Turned around by the beaters with their bold bellowings.
They let the harts with their high heads pass safely by,
As well as the bucks with their broadly branched antlers,
Since the free-giving lord had forbidden in the off-season
Any man to molest one of the masculine deer.
The hinds were hemmed in with a "Hey!" and a "Ho!"
While the does were driven with a din to the glades.
There you could see arrows slipped out and slicing   1160
As the shafts whizzed up under the bends of the boughs,
Then dipped and bit those brown hides under those broad heads.
Ah! they bray and they bleed; they die on those banks!
For the hounds always follow them hot and heavy,
While hunters with high-pitched horns pursue ceaselessly,
With a shrill-sounding cry, as if the steep hills were crumbling.
Any wild ones who managed to get away from the archers
Were pursued and pulled down at the lower posts,
For they were harried on high, then herded to the water.
The kennelmen were very cunning at catching them below,   1170
And the greyhounds were great at getting them quickly
And finishing them off as fast as you could focus
          Your sight.
Our lord was a very merry boy;
He'd ride, and then he'd alight;
Yes, he rode all that day with joy
Till on came the darkening night.

3.

This lord we leave bantering by the lindenwood's borders,
While Gawain the good-hearted lies in his gaudy bed,
Lolling there while daylight is lengthening on the walls,   1180
Safe in his curtained bed with its costly cover.
And while he wallowed in slumber, a wee little noise
He heard at his door, which was delicately opened.
He perked his head up from his pillow and peeked

Around the curtain's corner, which he caught up a bit,
And he warily watched to see who it might be.
It was Madam herself, so marvelous to meditate,
Who slipped past the door, which she stealthily shut
And headed for the bed. How our boy did blush!
He precociously fell back and pretended a profound sleep.   1190
She stepped up silently, stealing toward his side,
Slipped up the curtain's edge, then sidled inside,
Perching very pertly and close beside him,
Lingering on awhile, waiting for him to waken.
Our warrior, however, wallowed on a bit longer,
Mulling in his mind what her actions might mean
Or portend—he pronounced it a bit preposterous;
So he said to himself, "I think it's suitable
To ask very openly just what she is after."
Then he started, and stretched, and turned to her side,   1200
Unlocking his eyelids and looking astonished;
And, to make himself safe with a prayer, he crossed himself
      Right on that bed.
Her chin and cheeks were prettily flushed
As whiteness blended with red;
Through lips both small and laughing
These gentle words she said:

4.

"Good morning, Sir Gawain," was her lilting greeting;
"You're not a smart sleeper! I slipped in here with ease!
And I've caught you right here! If you don't cry surrender,   1210
I'll bind you to this bed—and that you may believe!"
Very teasingly the lady tossed out these taunts.
"Good morning, my charmer," answered Gawain quite graciously,
"I'll do what you please—that I promise you fully.
Yes, I'll yield myself easily, and sue for your mercy.
It's the safest course, I'm sure; so I'm bound to that."
In this way he joked back with some jolly laughter:
"But would you, sweet lady, kindly lend me some leave,
Freeing your fettered guest to allow him to rise—
Then I'll bolt from this bed and be quickly dressed   1220
And prepared to pursue a polite conversation."
"O no, milord!" said that lighthearted lady,
"You'll not get out of bed; here I'll handle you better
By trussing you in tightly on that other side;
Then I can talk with milord, whom I now have trapped,
Since I'm quite assured that you're the great Sir Gawain
Whom the whole world worships wherever you go.
Your gentility and graciousness are grandly sounded
By all lords and all ladies and everyone alive.
And now you are here—ah! and we're all alone!   1230
My husband and his hangers-on are hunting far away.
The servingmen are sleeping downstairs with the maids.
The door is slammed shut, and the bolt has been sprung;
Now I have in my house the hero whom all the world adores
And I'll employ my time while it endures, with an eye
      Toward gathering tales.
My person is at your pleasure,

Your every wish to avail;
Hospitality makes me your servant,
And in nothing shall I fail."   1240

5.

"In good faith," said Sir Gawain, "I feel greatly flattered,
But I'm surely not the person about whom you are speaking.
I'm an unworthy creature—and I know this full well—
Without that perfection that you've just portrayed.
But by God, I'll be glad, if you think it is good,
To arrange some pleasure for your most prized person
Like some speeches or services—it would be sheer joy!"
"In good faith, dear Gawain," replied the gay lady,
"If I scorned or reviled the virtue and the valor
That infatuate the others, it would be most improper,   1250
But there are lots of high ladies who would love to have you
In their clutches, my handsome one, as I have you here:
To dally in delight of your delicate words,
Gaining some consolation to quell their cares—
That they would treasure more than a trove of gold.
But as surely as I adore the Lord in heaven above,
I have wholly in my hands what every woman desires
      By His grace.
She flashed him a merry look,
That lady with her fair face;   1260
And the knight with words immaculate
Parried in every case.

6.

"Madam," said the gentleman, "may Mary reward you!
I've found in all faith a refined spirit in you.
Some men have received fancy favors for their actions,
But my deserts have never matched their great doles.
It's your own great virtue that makes you see virtue in others."
"By Mary," said milady, "I believe that it must be different.
For if I were as worthy as all the women alive,
And all of the wealth of the world were in my hands,   1270
Then I'd shop and search around to find me a sire
With the qualities I've come to admire in you, dear knight:
Your beauty, your debonairness, your smart behavior—
Things I've heard tell of before but never observed—
And so I would choose before all other challengers—*you*!"
"Mercy, dear madam!" said he. "You have a man who's much better!
Still, I'm proud of the price that you put on my worth;
I swear to be a servant, with you as my sovereign,
Your own cavalier, and may Christ kindly guard you!"
So they trafficked in trivia till mid-morning passed,   1280
And the lady allowed as to loving him a lot.
The knight was very gracious—and also on his guard.
The lady said inside, "Even if I were the very loveliest,
He'd show little tenderness because of the terror he faces
      On New Year's Day—
A stroke that will surely stun him
And cannot be waved away."
She begged to leave him then
Since they had had their say.

7.

Then she wished him good cheer and chuckled with a side-glance   1290
As she stood and perplexed him with some very pointed words:
"May He who protects all speech repay you for this pleasure!
Yet to think that you're the brilliant Gawain boggles my mind!"
"But why?" asked the bed-dweller, blurting it out
And fearing he had failed in his flawless behavior.
The lady gently blessed him, and then she said, "It's because
Sir Gawain is considered a knight who's constantly correct,
Who's the paragon of courtly perfection himself;
He couldn't linger very long or engagingly with a lady
Without craving for a kiss with all due courtesy,   1300
And saying so with some trifling phrase at the end of his talk."
Then Gawain retorted, "Is that it? Well, take what you want!
I shall kiss at your command in the best knightly custom,
And more, lest it displease you, so plead no further!"
At that she came nearer, catching him into her arms,
And leaning lovingly over, she kissed his lordly face.
Then they courteously commended each other to Christ,
And she whisked out of the chamber without another word.
He reached out and rose up, rushing into his underwraps,
Calling for his chamberlain and selecting his clothing.   1310
Then, all dressed, he descended to hear the mass;
Later he enjoyed a dinner that was elegantly arranged,
Making merry all day long till the moon at last was rising,
          With jest and game.
Never was a gentleman received
More fairly by more worthy dames,
The old one and the young;
And their happiness matched their fame.

8.

Meanwhile the overlord rode on and on at his pleasure,
Looking for fawnless hinds in the holts and the heaths.   1320
By the time the sun was setting, he had slain such a sum
Of does and other deer that it was dazzling to behold.
Toward evening the hunting-folk eagerly flocked together
And hastily made a heap of the hewn-down game.
The highest hurried up with their henchmen around them
And collected the plumpest corpses piled up there,
And had them cleanly cut up as custom demanded;
At the assaying, they searched for some select innards,
Finding a good two fingers of fat on even the thinnest.
Then they slit the slot and seized the gullet,   1330
Scraping it with a sharp knife and tying it into a knot;
Then they hacked off the legs and stripped away the hide,
Breaking open the belly and scooping out the bowels
Deftly, so as not to destroy the duly tied knot.
Then they seized the gullet and scrupulously separated
The esophagus from the pipe, gouging out the guts;
With sharp knives, they sheared through the hide
And pulled out the shoulders, leaving the skin intact.
Then they broke the breast into two separate bits
And they began to hack again back at the gullet,   1340
Slitting it swiftly right down to the front legs,
Clipping away the clavicle pieces and very cleanly

Removing the membranes rapidly from the rib-cage;
Then, as was customary, they cleaned the ridge of the spine,
All the way to the haunches, which hung together;
Those parts which were pulled up and then completely detached
Have the special and well-suited name of "the numbles,"
       So I find.
At the breaching of the thighs,
They cut the skin behind;   1350
And to separate it swiftly,
The backbone they unbind.

9.

Both the head and the neck they disconnected then
And they swiftly severed the sides away from the chine,
Tossing "the raven's reward" into a rugged thicket.
Then they ran the thick flanks through by the ribs
And hung them up by the hocks of the haunches,
As every fellow claimed the fee that fell to him.
And on the dearly priced pelts they fed the pet hounds,
Letting them feast on livers and lungs and tripe   1360
Blended with bits of bread that were soaked in blood.
Then the bugle's "sound of the kill" blared over the dog-bays,
And they folded their harvest of flesh and headed for home,
Striking strident note after note on their silvery horns.
By the time the daylight had run, the rout had returned
To the comfortable castle, where our cavalier was resting
       By the fire's side
In perfect bliss and ease.
The lord bounced up with a stride,
And Gawain hailed him home;   1370
Their joy was unqualified.

10.

Then the lord commanded his court to convene in the hall,
And the high-born damsels to descend with their domestics,
And before all that assembled audience, he asked his men
To place the venison before all the palace's people.
And he summoned Gawain the goodly to his games,
Tallying for him the total of his great take,
Showing him the fine cutlets that had once fleshed flanks:
"How does our sport please you? Have I won your praise?
Do I have your cordial approval for covering my craft?"   1380
"Yes, indeed," said the invited one, "it's the finest game
That I've spied in seven years in the winter season."
"Well, I give it all to you, Gawain," said he to his guest,
"In accordance with our agreement; it is yours alone."
"Correct and proper," said the guest, "and I'll repay you right now
With everything I've earned in earnest inside your walls.
It shall all be surrendered with the very same good will."
Then Gawain took his host's great neck in his grasp,
And kissed him as courteously as he could do it:
"Here! Take my paltry gain—I've won no further profit.   1390
I'd freely give you something greater if it was here to grant."
"No, that's fine!" replied the host. "A thousand thanks!
But I'd like it even better if you'd just brief me

As to where you garnered this gain with your ingenuity."
"That's not a part of our pact!" replied the knight. "No more!
You've cornered what was in our covenant; no further claim
    Accrues to you."
They chuckled, and they were cheerful;
Their talk was sincere and true.
Very soon they went to dine on   1400
Some delicacies fresh and new.

11.

Afterward by the hearth in a heated hall they lounged
As chamber-boys carried out the choicest of wines,
And once more in their merriment they agreed the next morning
To enact again the agreement that they had earlier made;
Whatever fortune might fling them, what newfangled thing they won—
That earning they'd exchange the ensuing evening.
They came to this accord before all the other courtiers;
Beverages were brought out for a toast at that time;
Then they lovingly uttered their good-nights at last   1410
And everyone bustled off to bed with briskness.
When the cock had crowed and cackled just three times,
The high lord leaped out of bed, along with his lieges;
The morning meal and the mass were duly taken care of,
And the courtiers dressed for the woods before the dawn sprang,
    Off to their chase.
The hunters high with horns
Passed through an open place,
Unleashing among the thorns
The hounds to run their race.   1420

12.

The dogs soon barked after a scent along a bog-side
And the hunters howled out the names of the hounds who sniffed it,
Shouting encouraging cries with strident sounds;
Hearing this, the hounds hurtled forward in haste,
Falling fast on the track, about forty at once;
Then such a yelping and yowling of yappers
Rose up that the rocks all rang around with the sound.
The chasers urged them onward with cheers and with horns.
The pack pushed forward together in a great press
Between a fen in the forest and a fiendish-looking crag;   1430
On a mound by a cliff at the quagmire's side,
Where some rough rocks had once come rumbling down,
They raced after the quarry as the hunters rushed behind;
The men encompassed the mound and the cliff together,
Knowing full well that within it was lurking
A beast that the bloodhounds were now baying out.
The men beat the bushes and bellowed: "Come out!"
It ferociously lunged from the lair on attack—
One of the biggest boars you have ever seen!
It had wandered all alone because of its great age;   1440
And it was grim-looking and quite gigantic,
And ghastly when it grunted; the men soon groaned,
Because at that first thrust, it threw three to the ground,
Then sped away at full speed without further spite.

The men shouted "Hi!"; they yelled "Hey, hey!"
Holding horns to their mouths and recalling the hounds.
Many were the merry mouths of the men and the dogs
Who coursed along after this boar to catch it with cries
     To kill and fell.
The pig often stood at bay   1450
And maimed the pack pell-mell;
It hurt the hounds, and they
Very painfully yowl and yell.

13.

Archers fully armed stepped up then to aim at him,
Showered him with shafts that struck him repeatedly;
But the points couldn't penetrate his powerful shoulders,
And the barbs didn't take a bite away from his brows.
No, the soft-wooded arrows simply split into splinters,
And the arrowheads hopped away harmlessly after a hit.
But as the storm kept stinging him with fiery strokes,   1460
Raving wildly for revenge, he rushed at his tormentors
And gored them most grimly wherever he would go.
Most of them shivered, and then they slinked back.
But the lord on his lithe horse lunged after the boar,
Blowing his bugle like a man who is bent on battle.
He rallied the hounds, riding through the rough brushwood,
Pursuing that pig till the sun began to plummet.
All day long they engaged in activities of this kind
While our kindly courtier lay comfortably in bed:
Sir Gawain safely at home, swaddled in his   1470
     Wealthy gear.
The lady didn't forget
To bring him some morning cheer.
Bright and early she was up
To add spice to his career.

14.

She tiptoed over to his curtain and took a peek in.
Sir Gawain at once offered her a gracious greeting,
And she immediately embarked on another eager talk.
Sitting softly by his side and chuckling at the start,
She addressed him in this way with an amiable look: 1480
"Sir, I find it somewhat strange, since you indeed are Gawain,
A man always genuinely geared toward doing the good,
That you don't pursue the practices of polite society;
If somebody teaches you something, you seem to toss it away;
Certainly you've already let slide my lesson of yesterday,
Where I used the most masterful methods I could employ."
"How's that?" he asked; "indeed, I'm not quite aware of it.
But if what you tell me is true, the transgression's mine."
"I lectured you on kissing," said the lovely lady then;
"And to quickly claim a favor that's been clearly conferred.   1490
This is necessary for a knight concerned with nice behavior."
"My dear," said the dashing man, "do away with such talk.
I dare not ask for any favors, for fear I'd be refused.
If I were denied, I'd be all dismayed about my daring."

"Mercy!" said the merry wife, "but you may not *be* refused!
And you're large enough to latch on to whatever you like—
Provided some woman is plebeian enough to refuse you."
"By God, yes," answered Gawain, "your reasoning is good.
But force is not favored by the people where I come from—
And neither is a gift that is given without gladness.   1500
But I'm at your command, to kiss whenever you please;
You may take it when you want, and whenever you think best,
    Withdraw a pace."
The lady leaned over a bit
And gently brushed his face;
Much speech they then dispensed
About love's grief and grace.

15.

"I would like some wisdom," the worthy woman then said,
"Provided you aren't provoked, to learn about the practices
Of a young and energetic creature such as you are—   1510
As courteous and courageous as you're known to be.
In chivalric affairs, the chief thing that's well chosen
Is the game of love, the true lore of every lord;
For to speak of the striving of all stalwart knights,
Love is the title taken and text of their deeds:
Valiant lords have ventured their very lives for love
And endured for their dowry many doleful hours,
Then later won vengeance with their valor and voided their cares,
And brought bliss into their bower through love's bounty.
You are the knight of your age most known as accomplished;   1520
Your words and high worth are whispered about everywhere;
Yet I have sat by your side now for two whole sessions
And I haven't heard one single syllable slip from your lips
That mentions the art of love, neither more nor less.
Yet you, who are so fine and fastidious in your vows
Ought to be eager to educate some tender young thing
And teach her the tools of the trade of noble love.
Or are you, who are praised for ingenuity, ignorant?
Or maybe you think I'm too slow for your subtleties?
    For shame!   1530
I've come here alone to sit
And bask in your great fame;
Come! Teach me a little wit
While my husband's at his game."

16.

"In good faith," said Gawain, "may God take care of you!
Great is my enjoyment and gigantic my pleasure
To think that one as worthy as you are should come
And expend so much energy on a poor man like me; it encourages
Me that you dawdle away your time with a dull-wit like me;
But to take on the trouble of expounding true love   1540
And teach the terms of that text with its tales of arms
To you, who, I'm sure, have twice the knowledge
Of that art than I do or a hundred like me
Have now or ever will have, as long as I live—

That would be sheer stupidity, my lady, I swear!
I'll strive to satisfy your desires with all my strength,
Since I'm really devoted to you, and forever shall remain
A servant to your person, so save me our Creator!"
In this way the lady tried him and tested him often
To win him over to wooing—whatever else she wanted;   1550
But he put her off so politely there was no improper move
Or no evil expressed on either side. No, there was nothing
      But bliss.
They laughed and sported a long while,
And then she gave him a kiss;
Then she took her gracious leave
When the gentleman granted this.

17.

The hero then stirred and straggled down to his mass,
And next his supper was ready and was superbly served.
He amused himself all day long with the able lady,   1560
While her husband was hunting over the homeland turf,
Pursuing the ill-fated swine, which was sweeping the slopes,
Biting the backs of his finest beagles in two.
When the boar was at bay, the bowmen would break his stance
And, despite his persistence, force him to change position
As fierce arrows kept falling while a following gathered.
Still the swine often forced the stalwart into wavering,
Till finally he was so exhausted, he could escape no more.
Summoning what might he could muster, he managed to reach
A crevice in a cliff where a cold creek was flowing.   1570
He put the slope at his back and scraped the soil,
With froth foaming out of his fierce-looking mouth.
He whet his white tusks; this wait permitted the men,
Who were weary from wearing him down at a distance,
To enclose him in a crowd—yet no one had the courage
      To draw near;
He had hurt so many before
That all were filled with fear
Of being torn apart by those tusks;
He was savage and severe.   1580

18.

Then up swept the seigneur, spurring on his steed,
Spied the standing boar with his men spread in a circle.
He leapt down lightly from his courser's back
And, brandishing a blade, he boldly strode forward,
Wading right through the water to where the beast waited.
The wild one was aware of that weapon in his hand.
He heaved up his bristles and then he horribly snorted.
Many feared that the felon would gore their friend.
The swine then hurtled straight off toward his adversary,
So that baron and boar both fell in one big tumble   1590
In the wild-rushing water. And the boar got the worst.
The man hit the mark well at the shock of their meeting,
Plunging his sword in the soft slot over the breastplate
All the way down to the hilt. It split open the heart.

The snarling one snapped, then slipped away into the water
    Upon his back.
A hundred hounds splashed in,
Biting him blue and black;
Lads bore him then to the shore,
Where the dogs finished off the attack.   *1600*

19.
Then blasts were blown from several blaring horns;
There was a high hallooing as loud as they could make;
The bloodhounds bayed their best as they were bid
By the chief men who presided over the challenging chase.
Then a man who was wise in the ways of woodcraft
Began the skillful butchering of that boar.
First he sliced off the head and set it on a stake;
Then he slit the body roughly straight down the spine;
He scooped out the bowels and broiled them over the embers,
Blending them with breadcrumbs as a boon for his hounds.   *1610*
Then he carved some broad cuts away from the carcass,
Removing the entrails in a way that was just right;
Then he stitched the two sides securely together
And slung them over a strong and sturdy pole.
With the swine swinging, the men then started home.
The boar's head was borne in front of the baron
Who had felled him in that forest, using the force
    Of his strong hand.
Until he could reach Sir Gawain
The time seemed too long to stand;   *1620*
Crying hello, he rushed in,
His day's fee to demand.

20.
Loud with mirth and merry with laughter, the lord,
On seeing Sir Gawain, spoke very sincerely.
He gathered the great ladies and the servants together,
And he showed them his choice cuts and recounted his tale
Of the strength and the size and the savagery
Of the wild pig's struggle away off in those woods.
The courteous guest commended these acts as courageous
And proclaimed he had acted in a manner worthy of praise,   *1630*
Saying that never in his life had he ever laid eyes
On a beast that had such big and such brawny sides!
When the head was exhibited, the guest expressed his awe
At its huge proportions, and he further praised his host.
"Now, Gawain," said the good man, "the game is all yours
By our covenant fixed and fast, as you know for sure."
"That's God's truth," said the guest, "and you'll certainly get
All the wages I've won once more—upon my word!"
Then he grabbed the man's neck and graciously kissed him,
And very soon after he served him a second smack.   *1640*
"Now we're even," said the guest, "right up to this evening
By the agreement arranged when I arrived, with all respect
    To the law."
"By Saint Giles!" exclaimed the host;

"A finer man I never saw!
You'll shortly be a millionaire
If this is the pay you draw!"

21.

Then they tilted up the tables upon their trestles,
Which were covered with cloths, while candlelight flickered
Over the walls, which was cast by torches of wax.   1650
Men set down food and served all around the salon;
Gossip and glee could be found in every group
By the fire and across the floor, and before
And after supper there were many ceremonious songs,
Such as Christmas carols, as well as fresh chansons,
With all the well-mannered mirth a man could imagine,
And always our loyal knight lingered by the lady's side.
She kept glancing at her stalwart guest as if to suggest
That she wanted to please him in some sly, secret way,
So that he was quite agitated and angry within,   1660
But because of his breeding, he could never be boorish;
So he dealt with her delicately, even though this dallying
        Could go awry.
After that parrying in the hall,
The gaming hour passed by;
The lord summoned him to his chamber,
Where the flames were leaping high.

22.

There they dawdled and they drank and discussed once again
The continuance of their covenant till the New Year should come.
The guest regretted he'd have to say goodbye in the morning,   1670
Since the agreed-on hour for departing was approaching.
But the host wouldn't hear of it; he tried to hold him back,
Saying, "I swear on my word, I fully assure you
You'll arrive at the Chapel to carry out your chores,
My dear friend, on New Year's Day before dawning.
So loll around in your bed and enjoy your leisure
While I scour the countryside, keeping our contract,
And hand over whatever winnings I can carry home.
I have tested you twice and found you trustworthy.
But remember for tomorrow: the third time is the best!   1680
Let's be merry while we can and remember our pleasures,
For the losses may fall to us whenever we like."
Gawain graciously agreed to this, and so he stayed on.
Chalices were cheerfully filled, and then they climbed to bed
        By candlelight.
Sir Gawain lay and slept
Soft and sound all night;
While the lord, keeping to his craft,
Arose very early and bright.

23.

After mass he and his men took a very brief meal.   1690
The morning was magnificent as he mounted on his steed,
And the hunters who would go with him got on their horses,
Sitting tall in their saddles before the tower gates.

The fields were beautifully blanketed under a film of frost,
While the sun with ruddy streaks soared up through the cloud-puffs,
Then coasted with radiance along the cumulus crests.
The hunters unleashed their hounds alongside a thicket,
And the rocks around rang clear with the clarion cries.
Some hit on the scent that was left by the hiding fox;
They pursue a tortuous track that tests their wiles. 1700
A small dog was yelping, and his master yelled after;
All sniffing, the fellow hounds now followed his lead.
They rushed in a rabble, having found the right track.
The fox flashed before them; they dashed after him fast;
Once they perceive him, they pursue all the harder,
Cursing at him cruelly with crass indignation.
He twisted and turned through the tangle of thickets,
Hurtling backward to hear alongside the hedgerows.
At last, at the side of a little ditch, he leapt over a fence,
Then stole out stealthily inside a small copse, 1710
Half-outwitting by his wiles those pursuers in the woods.
But he wandered, unaware, right into a pack of whelps,
And three in one throw thrust themselves upon him
    In their coats of grey.
He swerved again most swiftly
And unfailingly got away;
To the woods he ran a-racing,
Filled with woe and with dismay.

24.

What a heavenly thing it was to hear those hounds,
As the whole pack picked up his scent and pursued again! 1720
Such swears the men growled whenever they got a glimpse of him,
As if the clambering cliffs would come crashing down!
The hunters hollered "Halloo!" whenever they met him,
Loudly haranguing him with their howls of scorn;
They threatened him dourly; they dubbed him a thief;
They tailed him continuously, not allowing any tarrying;
They hounded him endlessly, till he headed for the open,
And then he reeled back again, for Reynard has his ruses.
He led them every which-way, that lord and his lieges,
Over hill and hollow till half the afternoon was gone. 1730
Meanwhile our hero at home was wholesomely sleeping
Inside his cozy curtains throughout that cold morning.
But because of love, the lady was unable to languish
Or control the purpose that kept pricking her heart,
And so she got up early, and she went to see him
In a gorgeous gown that swished along the ground
And was lined with pieces of the most precious pelts.
She wore no hood on her head, and yet her hairnet
Was set with rich stones in sections of twenty;
Her enchanting face and throat were entirely exposed, 1740
And her breasts and her back were also remarkably bare.
She slipped through the door and closed it very softly,
Swinging open a window and suddenly addressing the sleeper,
Rebuking him roundly with her regal-sounding words
    And cheer:
"What, sir! How can you sleep

While the morning shines so clear?"
He still drooped deep in slumber,
But every word he could hear.

25.

From the depths of darkened dreams the hero mumbled,   1750
Like one who is gripped by many grievous thoughts:
How destiny would deal him his fate the very next day
At that meeting-place where he would face his match
And have to suffer a swipe with no forswearing;
But as the queenly one came there, he collected his wits,
Swept free of his slumber and swiftly said hello.
The lovely lady swished toward him, laughing sweetly,
Leaned over his handsome face and kissed him lovingly.
He spoke in a friendly way, presenting his finest face.
To him she seemed so gorgeous, so gloriously attired,   1760
So faultless in her features and fair complexion
That a warm joy came welling up within him.
With merry and subtle smiles, they melted in mirth,
And all was bliss and bonhomie that passed between them—
        Full of delight.
They bandied some delicate words
Replete with sweetness and light;
Yet a peril was lurking around them—
Unless Mary took care of her knight!

26.

Because that prized princess was pressing him so far,   1770
Almost to the edge of the hem, it was now essential
To either embrace her love or emphatically deny it.
He was concerned with courtesy, not wanting to be callous,
And even more with sinning or misbehaving, with standing
As traitor to the man who controlled that territory.
"God help me," he vowed, "but that shall never happen!"
With cheerful chuckles, he was able then to check
All those splendid phrases that kept springing from her lips.
For example, she said, "I feel that you deserve censure
If you don't love the lady whom you're lying next to,   1780
Who's more wounded than any other woman in the whole world.
But if you have a lover already—some lass you like better—
And are faithful to that girl and fastened to her so firmly
That you don't want to be loosed—then I'll believe you.
If that's the case, then tell it to me please, I beg you.
In the name of all human love, don't keep hiding the truth
        With guile."
"By St. John," replied the knight
With a very genial smile,
"Right now I don't love a soul,   1790
And I won't for quite a while."

27.

"Ah, *those* words," she answered, "are the wickedest of all!
But your retort is truthful—this I painfully think.

Now just kiss me once sweetly, and I'll steal away,
Lamenting my fate like some lovelorn maiden."
With a sigh, she swooped over and kissed him quite suavely,
Then severing quickly, she said as she stood up,
"Now, precious, please grant me a favor on parting.
Please offer me a little gift—a glove, if you have one—
For memory's sake, my sweet man, to lessen my sorrow."			1800
"Ah, indeed," sighed the hero, "I wish that I had here
The loveliest thing on the earth to offer your love,
For in all sincerity, you have surely deserved
A far greater reward than I can rightly grant.
But to hand you some token that's only a trifle
Would not be to render you a reward that's right—
A mere glove as a show of Sir Gawain's generosity!
Besides, I'm on errand in these strange parts of the earth,
Having no servants with sacks full of civilized presents;
I'm deeply sorry, sweet lady, for your sake right now.			1810
Every person must do what he can. Please don't take it poorly
     And pine."
"Heavens no, my honored guest,"
Said that lady fair and fine,
"But if I can't have a keepsake of yours,
At least you'll have one of mine!"

28.

She held out a ring that was made of reddish gold,
With a sparkling stone that shone high on the band,
Casting brilliant beams resembling the blazing sun.
And you can rest fully assured it was worth a fortune.			1820
But the baron drew back very brusquely, saying,
"For God's sake, good woman, no gifts at this juncture!
I don't have any to offer, and so I can't take any."
She extended it more eagerly; he eluded her offer,
Swearing on his oath that he simply couldn't accept it.
Rueful about his rejection, she very quickly rejoined,
"If you won't take my ring because it's too rich,
And you rebel against being beholden to me,
Then I'll give you my girdle—a much humbler gift."
She loosened a sash that was lightly locked around her,			1830
Circling her waist underneath her shiny chemise;
It was sewn out of green silk with stitchings of gold,
Embroidered around the edges by the most expert hands.
This she offered the hero, earnestly exhorting him
To take it if he would, insignificant as it might be.
But he kept refusing—he could in no way receive
Keepsakes or gold until God sent him grace
To accomplish the act that he was attempting there:
"So therefore, I beg you, without any further bother,
Let's ignore this whole idea; it's a thing that I can't			1840
     Grant you.
I am dearly beholden to your grace
For all the things you do,
And I promise through thick and thin
To remain your servant true."

29.

"Now, is this silk unsatisfactory," the lady asked,
"Because it is so simple? Or so it seems to you?
Well! It's a paltry thing, not appearing very precious,
But if you were aware of the worth contained within it,
You'd place a much higher price on it, I suspect;   1850
For whoever is girded by this green-colored sash
And wears it tightly wrapped around his waist,
No creature under the heavens may cut him down,
And he can't be killed by any earthly cunning."
This made the knight think; the thought sprang to mind
That here was a magic gem against the jeopardy ahead
When he'd arrive at the Chapel to challenge a checkmate.
If he could escape intact, this trick would not be ignoble!
He acquiesced to her alluring, allowing her to speak,
And she beckoned with the belt, begging him to take it.   1860
He surrendered; and so she handed it to him swiftly,
Urging him for her sake to keep the matter secret,
To conceal it carefully from her lord; Gawain concurred:
Except for the two, no human would ever have it
        In his sight.
He thanked her most emphatically,
With all his heart and might;
After that for three straight times
She kissed that stalwart knight.

30.

Then she asked for her leave, and she left him there,   1870
Knowing that there was no more enjoyment to be had from him.
When she had departed, Gawain quickly got dressed,
Putting on some garments that looked grand indeed,
But laying aside the love-token the lady had left for him;
He concealed it carefully where he could find it later.
Then he went very quickly on his way to the chapel,
Where he privately approached a priest and asked him
To listen to his confession and to lend him some learning
About saving his soul when he should abandon this earth.
Then he confessed sincerely, revealing his sins,   1880
Both major and minor, and, begging for mercy,
He prayed to the priest to purify them all.
The cleric absolved him and cleansed him so completely
That the Day of Doom might have dawned the next morning.
Then he went and enjoyed himself with the elegant ladies,
With singing and dancing and every sort of sweetness
On into the darkness, with a delight he'd never known
        Before that day.
All the courtiers were amused
By Gawain; they were heard to say,   1890
"Ah, he was never so happy
As he has been on this day!"

31.

Now let's leave him at his idyll with love all around him.
The lord of that land was still leading on his men,

And had overtaken that fox he had followed so ferociously.
As he darted over a hedge on the track of that dodger,
And heard the hounds bearing down heatedly on the prey,
He saw Reynard come running out of a rugged thicket,
And all of that rabble were riotously hot on his heels.
The baron, aware of the wild one, craftily waited,   1900
Then flashed out his shiny sword and skillfully struck.
The fox flinched away from the blade and would have fled,
But before he could bolt, a hound came bounding after him,
And right in front of the horses' feet, the pack fell on him,
Attacking the wily one with a wild-sounding roar!
The lord swooped in swiftly and scooped him up,
Saving him for a second from those savage jaws;
He held him over his head and called loud halloos
Over the howling chorus of those ravening hounds.
Hunters hastened there with blares of their horns,   1910
Sounding the recall until they reached their master.
As this courtly company were all convening together,
They blared on the bugles that they were bearing at once,
While the hunters without any horns merely shouted halloos.
It was the merriest melody that a man ever heard—
The riotous racket that was raised for Reynard's soul
     With royal notes!
The men reward their hounds then;
They fondle them and they dote;
And then they take old Reynard   1920
And off they strip his coat.

32.

Then finally they hurried homeward, for the night was hovering,
Blowing boisterously upon their blaring horns.
At last the lord leaped down at his much-loved home,
Finding flames in the fireplace inside, his guest beside it,
Gawain the good, who was glad-hearted in every way,
Enjoying the entertainment of the elegant ladies!
He was wearing a robe of blue that brushed the ground,
And his surcoat with its soft fur lining suited him well,
While a hood of similar stuff hung over his shoulders;   1930
Both had borders that were embroidered with bright ermine.
Gawain went over and met his host in the middle of the hall,
And good-heartedly he greeted him, saying graciously,
"Let me first carry out the main clause of the covenant
That we've already agreed on and drunk to as well."
Then he hugged his host, kissing him three whole times,
As energetically and as earnestly as he had ever done.
"By Christ," said his companion, "you've been quite successful
In conducting your business if you won a bargain like that!"
"Yes, but let's forget the terms," retorted the traveler,   1940
"Since I've openly repaid you the whole debt that I owed."
"Mary!" said the other man, "I'm missing all your luck,
Since I've been out chasing all day and all I've achieved
Is this foul little fox-fur—may the Fiend take it!
Now that's a paltry repayment for the precious things
You've so kindly conferred on me—those three kisses
     That are sweet and good."

"Enough!" replied Sir Gawain.
"I thank you by the Holy Wood!"
Then the baron explained to all   1950
How the fox was dispatched for good.

33.
With music and amusements and all the meat one required,
They carried on as contentedly as any human can;
With the laughter of ladies and great lightheartedness,
Gawain and his goodly host both acted very gleeful
Unless some bore in the crowd was besotted or boorish.
Both the master and his minions cracked many a joke
Till the hour arrived for their saying adieu,
And it was finally the best thing to be off to bed.
Then the hero quite humbly begged leave of his host,   1960
The first to give him fond thanks for all of the fun:
"May the Good Lord repay you for all of the pleasures
I've enjoyed here during your genial holiday feast!
I'll count myself one of your court, if you choose,
But tomorrow morning, as you know, I have to move on;
So please lend me some servant who can show me the way,
As you agreed, to the Green Chapel, where God demands
That I suffer on the First the fulfillment of my fate."
"In good faith," said the gentleman, "very gladly
I'll provide you with whatever I promised in the past."   1970
Then he assigned him a servant to set him on the road
And conduct him through the downs to avoid all delay
In ferreting through the forest, so he could arrive favorably
        At the appointed site.
Gawain thanked his host
With all the respect that was right;
And then to the ladies fair
He uttered a fond good-night.

34.
He spoke then with sincerity and offered sad kisses,
Wishing them all his warmest, most well-meaning thanks;   1980
They willingly replied that they all wished him the same,
Recommending him to Christ with great sighs of care.
Then he politely separated himself from the party,
Extending his thanks to all the people he encountered
For their service and solace and the separate pains
They had taken in trying to comfort him by their care.
Every serving-person was sorry for his separation,
As if they had lived with this lord their whole lives through.
Then the lads with their lights led him up to his chamber,
Guiding him to his bed for a good night's sleep.   1990
I won't venture to vouch for a sound sleep or a vexed one,
For he had much to mull over concerning the morning, if he
        Gave it any thought.
So let him lie quietly there,
Close to what he has sought,
And if you'll just be patient,
I'll tell you what daybreak brought.

PART FOUR

1.

Now the New Year draws near, and the night passes on
As the day drives away the dark as the Deity commands.
But wild weather had wakened and raged through the world;   2000
Clouds cast their cold drops down upon the earth,
As bitterness from the north bit whatever lay bare.
The snow fell ferociously, flailing wild creatures;
A blustery blizzard blew down out of the heights
And drove up mountainous snowdrifts in every dale.
Our hero listened to all this as he lay in his bed,
And, though his lids were locked, he slept very little,
Counting away the hours by every crow of the cock.
He got dressed very deftly before the daylight broke,
Since a lamp had been left for him to light his chamber.   2010
He summoned his manservant, who swiftly answered,
Asking him for his armor and his riding apparel.
The man got moving and produced his many garments,
Outfitting Gawain in a fashion that was fitting.
First he wrapped him in underclothes to ward off the cold,
Then his other equipment, all cleaned and cared for,
Then his pauncer and breastplate, polished all clean,
With the rust removed from the rich rings of mail.
Everything was as fresh as at first, and he was grateful,
     Of course.   2020
The man had shined up every piece
Without neglect or remorse
To make it the best from here to Greece;
Then Gawain called for his horse.

2.

While he dressed himself in his most dapper clothing—
His coat with its crest showing the finest craft
Sewn over velvet, with stones of great virtue
Bound and embroidered to the seams and the borders,
With a fine fur lining inside with fancy pelts—
He did not let slip the sash, the lady's souvenir.   2030
No, Gawain did not omit it because of his own good.
After he had circled his strong hips with his sword-belt,
He wrapped her reminder doubly around his waist,
Swiftly and spryly encircling his central part
With the girdle of green that neatly suited that gay one
Over his rich-looking and royal clothing of red.
But he wasn't garbed in the girdle because of its gaudiness,
Or out of pride for its pendants, which were neatly polished,
With glittering gold gleaming at the ends of their tips—
No, he did this to save himself when the time came to suffer   2040
A malicious swipe without any answer of sword
     Or knife.
And so the bold man, dressed,
Descended to the castle life,
And to all that famous household
His gratitude ran rife.

3.

Gringolet, great and huge, was standing all geared up
After his long stabling in a safe and suitable way.
He was prancing in healthy pride, that powerful horse,
While his master stepped up and inspected his sleek coat,   2050
Saying most soberly and swearing on his oath,
"Now here's a staff that understands what is civilized!
Their man maintains them well—may he joyously thrive,
And may his adorable lady enjoy love all her life!
If they cherish their guests with such Christian charity
And govern so generously, may the Good Protector above
Treat them this way too—and the same thing to you all!
And if I live my life for a good while longer,
I'll rightly repay you some reward if I can!"
Then he stepped into his stirrups and sat on high.   2060
His servant handed him his shield, which he slung over his shoulder.
He goaded Gringolet onward with his gilded heels,
And the steed sprang over the stones, no longer content
    To prance.
The master rode on his horse,
Holding his spear and his lance:
"I commend this castle to Christ!
May He keep it from mischance!"

4.

The drawbridge was let down, and the doors of the gates
Were unbolted and unbarred; they both were gaping open.   2070
The hero blessed himself quickly and hurried across the boards,
Praising the porter, who was praying on his knees
That God would protect Gawain and send him a good day.
Then the hero went on his way with his one assistant,
Who had to direct him toward his terrible destination,
Where he would have to suffer that very serious stroke.
They rode along by some banks where the boughs were all bare;
They climbed over cliffs where the cold was closely clinging.
The heavens were holding back, but the low haze was ugly.
Mist swarmed over the moors, then merged with the mountains.   2080
Every hill wore a hat and a hanging mantle of haze.
Brooks boiled up and then broke free from their banks,
Spattering spume against the slopes before cascading.
The road they took through the woods was weaving along at random,
And soon it was time for the sun in that wintry season
    To rise.
They were riding on a high ridge
With snow all before their eyes.
The man who was guiding Gawain
Said, "It's time now for goodbyes.   2090

5.

"I've guided you this far, Gawain, up to this point,
And now you're not very far from that fabulous spot
That you've asked about and sought with special care;
And I'll tell you sincerely, since I now know you somewhat,
And you're a man whom I admire most assuredly,
If you follow my words, things will work out well for you:

The place you're approaching is indeed very perilous.
A wild man inhabits that waste—the worst in the world.
He is savage and strong and loves to swoop down upon you,
And is mightier than any man on this massive earth.   2100
His physique's more formidable than the finest four
In Arthur's house or in Troy or anywhere else.
He governs the games down at his Green Chapel,
A place that nobody passes scot-free on parade
Without being dashed to death by a dent from his hand.
He's a man who acknowledges no mercy or no mean.
If either a chaplain or a churl rides by his chapel,
A monk or a mass-priest or any other mortal,
He'll wipe him out as easily as he'd just walk away.
And so I say, as surely as you sit in that saddle,   2110
If you keep going, you'll be killed by this creature's whim.
That you can trust, even if you had twenty lives
    To dispense.
He has lived here a long, long time
On a field full of violence,
And against his bitter blows
There is never any defense.

6.
"Therefore, good Sir Gawain, let this ogre go!
Ride on some other route, in the Redeemer's name!
Travel through some other turf, where Christ will take care of you,   2120
And I shall hurry home, but I promise you right here
That I shall swear by God and all of his sacred saints,
By the Lord Himself and his holy realm and a hundred oaths
That I'll truly watch over you and never whisper a word
That you ever wanted to run from anyone I know of."
"A great many thanks," answered Gawain, adding grouchily,
"I wish you luck, sir, since you're worried about my welfare,
And I sincerely believe you'd support me if I escaped.
But even if you kept that secret, and I got away safely,
Fleeing out of fear in the fashion you just mentioned,   2130
I'd be a crass-hearted coward and could never be excused.
No! I'm on my way to the Chapel, whatever chance lets fall;
And I'll tell your cherished monster whatever I choose,
Whether Destiny decides to deal me my destruction
    Or to save.
Your man may have a mighty club
That makes him an awesome knave,
But Our Master is good at shaping
Salvation for the brave!"

7.
"Mary," said the other man, "you've made it very clear   2140
That you're intent on dealing destruction for yourself.
Well, if you want to lose your life, I have to let you.
Have here a helmet for your head and a spear for your hand,
And just ride down this road past that rocky slope there,
And you'll come at last to the bottom of the broad vale below.
Then look around a little, and on your left side
You'll spy that very same chapel you've been searching for,

As well as the massive master who maintains it.
Now, on behalf of God—goodbye, my noble Gawain!
I wouldn't go on with you for all of the gold in the ground.   2150
Not one step further will I take in this forest as your friend!"
With that, the guide bent his horse's bridle backward,
Hitting his horse with his heels as hard as he could,
And it leapt with a sudden lunge, leaving our hero
      All alone.
"For God's sake," said Sir Gawain,
"I'm not going to weep or moan.
To God's will I'm obedient,
For I call myself His own."

8.

Then he goaded Gringolet, going onward down the road,   2160
Skirting the stony slopes along the sheer sides,
Riding over rugged ridges that reached down to the dale.
There he carefully eyed the environs and found them eerie.
There was no sign of civilization on any side—
Just slopes that were slanting up steeply everywhere
With roughly crenellated crags bearing ragged rocks;
It seemed to him that their stones scraped against the sky.
Then he hove in his reins, holding his horse back,
And shifted his eyes, searching for the sanctuary.
Strangely to say, he could see nothing on any side   2170
Except a little nob on the land, like a knoll,
A bulge that was swelling slightly on the bank of a brook,
Where a freshet was flowing freely in its furrow,
Bubbling as if it was boiling upon its bed.
The knight nudged his steed forward, approaching the knoll.
Then he leaped down lightly and attached to a linden's
Ragged branches the reins of his royal steed.
Next he meandered over to the mound and moved slowly around it,
Mulling over in his mind exactly what it might mean.
It had one hole at one end, and there was one at the other.   2180
It was overgrown with globs of grass everywhere;
It was concave and hollow within—just some old cavern
Or a crevice in a crag—he couldn't really be
      Very clear.
"Whew, Lord!" said the gentle knight,
"This might be the Chapel, I fear.
The Devil along about midnight
Might mumble his matins here."

9.

"Dear God!" muttered Sir Gawain, "but this place is grim!
This is an ugly oratory, all overrun with weeds!   2190
It's perfect for that weird person who appears all green
To deal out his devotions in the Devil's camp.
Now I'm confident in my five senses that it's the Fiend
Who arranged this appointment for my undoing here!
It's the Chapel of Bad Chance—may a checkmate fall to it!
It's the most cursed cathedral that I've ever come upon!"
With his helmet on his head and a lance in his hand,
He clambered up on the dome of that dismal edifice.

Then from that hillock he could hear, from behind a rock
On the bank beyond the brook, a barbaric sound: 2200
Whzzz! it echoed against the cliff as if to cleave it—
The sound of somebody grinding a scythe at a grindstone.
Whzzz! it whirred and it whirled like water over a mill.
Whzzz! it scraped and it scratched, offensive to the ear.
"By God," exclaimed Gawain, "these goings-on, I believe,
Are arranged, my dear friend, as a very royal reception
    For me!
Ah, well. Let God's will be done!
No good to act cowardly.
I may lose my life, but still 2210
No noise will make me flee."

10.

Then the knight started to shout out very stridently:
"Who's the agent who arranges the appointments here?
Gawain the gallant has now arrived on your ground!
If anyone wants a word with him, let him appear
Either now or never, and say what he will need."
"Wait awhile," said someone above from the other shore,
"And you'll get very promptly everything that I promised!"
That person didn't stop his scraping for a single second,
But kept whetting and whirring on for a little while; 2220
Then around a rock and out of a burrow he rambled,
Hurtling from his hiding-place with his hideous weapon—
A Danish ax, all neatly honed and ready for an attack,
With a broad-cutting blade that was bent upon the shaft,
Filed by a sharpener, about a good four feet wide
And no less, as you could tell by the lace at its haft.
The strange apparition was appareled in green as at first,
His face and his legs and his locks and his beard,
Except that he now loped along on his own two legs,
Using the shaft as a staff, as it swung at his side. 2230
When he came to the water, he did not want to wade,
And so he hopped over on his ax, then haughtily strode forward,
Looking fierce and grim, onto the field that was filled
    With snow.
Gawain the knight stepped down to meet him,
In no way bending low;
The green one said, "My dear sweet sir,
You have come where you said you'd go.

11.

"Gawain," said the green one, "may God protect you!
Indeed, you are welcome, my man, to my mansion. 2240
And you've timed your travel as a true fellow should,
Acknowledging the agreement arranged between us.
Twelve months ago at this time you took what fell to you,
And promptly on this New Year I'm prepared to repay.
We're all alone in this valley, I assure you;
Not a soul here to separate us from our happy sport.
So take that helmet off your head and have your pay.
Don't try to dicker around any more than I did
When you swiped off my head with a single stroke."

"No, by God," said Gawain, "who granted me my life,   2250
I won't begrudge you a grain for any grief that follows.
But steady yourself to strike, and I'll stand still,
Offering no obstruction to your operation
    In any way."
He bared his neck and bent it,
Pulling his clothes away,
Resolved not to let his fear
At any point hold sway.

12.

Then the man in the green got himself quickly ready,
Lifting his loathsome tool to strike Lord Gawain.   2260
With all the brute force in his body, he bore it up,
As if he meant to maim the hero mercilessly.
If he'd driven it downward as direly as he threatened,
That priceless prince would have perished from the blow.
Gawain glanced up at that gruesome thing that hovered,
And as it started its swoop to split him in two,
His shoulders shrank back from the razor-sharp iron.
With a sudden swerve, his adversary checked his stroke,
Reproaching the prince with some very pompous words:
"You're certainly not Gawain, who's considered so gallant,   2270
And who never feared any fighter either far or wide.
Why, you're flinching out of fear for a harm you only fancy!
I never heard that this hero had such a faint heart!
I didn't flinch or fail when you aimed at me, friend.
I offered you no obstruction in King Arthur's house.
My head flew to the floor, yet I never once faltered.
But before you're hurt, you show you have a cowardly heart.
And so I claim that I'll have to be called the superior knight
    On every score."
Gawain replied, "I did flinch once,   2280
But I won't flinch any more.
Yet if *my* head hits the stones,
It will be hard to restore.

13.

"But be brisk in your business, man; bring this to a head!
Deal out my destiny and do it right away!
I'll suffer your stroke without any further shudder
Till the ax-head hits me; here now is my pledge."
"Get ready then," replied the other, raising his tool
And appearing as angry as if he were half-mad.
He started to swing wildly—yet grazed no skin,   2290
Withholding his heave before it could bring any harm.
Gawain suffered it stoically, not swerving an inch,
Standing as still as a stone or like a stump
That is anchored in the rocky soil by a hundred roots.
Then the man in the green was mocking him merrily:
"Now that you've got your heart again, I can hit you.
Show me some of that chivalry that Arthur showered on you,
And recover your neck from this cut now if you can!"
Gawain very acidly answered him with anger:
"Come on, brave one, strike! You're bragging much too long!   2300

I suspect somehow that your spirit is cringing inside!"
"Ah, so," said the other, "you're talking so sordidly now
That more mincing on your mission is a thing
    I can't allow."
He moved as if to strike,
Twisting both lips and brow;
No wonder if Gawain was grieving,
Since there was no rescue now!

14.

He lifts his ax lightly and then allows it to fall,
With the barb on the blade just grazing the bare neck;   2310
Though he hammers down hard, he inflicts no harm,
Just nicking one side and lightly slicing the skin.
But as the blade brushes against the bright flesh on the neck,
Some scarlet blood spurts downward onto the soil.
When Sir Gawain sees his stains of blood on the snow,
He springs with a sudden leap the length of a spear,
Hastily grabbing his helmet and covering his head.
He swings his shield around from behind his shoulders,
Brandishes his bright sword and speaks up very bravely
(Never since he was a baby born to his mother   2320
Has he been so wholly happy in all this world!):
"Stop blustering, my baron; don't bother me any more!
I've suffered your swing without showing any resistance,
But if you molest me once more, I'll meet you headlong
And fiercely pay back—I promise—with promptness
    Every blow.
I agreed to a single stroke;
The covenant said so
That we formed in Arthur's halls.
Now away, my friend! Yes, go!"   2330

15.

The regal one relaxed, resting upon his ax-blade,
Leaning on the sharp part, with the haft set upon the soil,
And studying the man who was standing there before him.
He observed how that stalwart one stood there unshivering,
Armed and unawed, and he found it very admirable.
Then he spoke sympathetically in a rather stentorian voice,
Addressing that aristocrat with far-echoing words:
"Don't frown so fiercely, my fellow, here on this field.
No man misbehaved here or was unmannerly toward you.
I just carried out the clauses we set at the king's court.   2340
I promised a stroke, which you got; consider yourself paid.
I release you now from all of the rest of my rights.
If I'd been busier, I could have given you a buffet
That was far more aggressive and made you more angry!
My first blow was simply a feint that I made for fun
And caused you no deep cut; I simply carried out
That agreement that we arranged that original evening.
You have truly and trustily maintained your troth,
Giving me all that you gained, like a very good man.
The second feint, my friend, I fashioned for the morning   2350
When you kissed my charming wife—but counted back those kisses.

For those two fond acts I offered you two feints
    Without any mishap.
One true man is true to another
And needs never fear any trap.
But you failed at my third testing
And therefore took my tap.

16.

"It's all because of my beautiful girdle you're bearing,
Which my own wife formed—I know this for a fact;
For I'm conscious of your kisses and other conduct,   2360
Playing games with my spouse. I was the planner myself.
I sent her to tempt you, and truly I've come to think
You're one of the finest fellows to set foot on the earth:
A pearl more precious than any simple white pea
Is our Sir Gawain, by God, next to other gallants.
But you have a small flaw, my friend: you lack some faithfulness.
It didn't arise for an artful object or amorous fling—
No! You just loved your life! And I blame you the less for it."
The other stern knight stood there studiously for a while,
Shuddering inside himself with a shameful rage.   2370
The blood in his body blushed upward into his cheeks,
And he shrank back shamefaced from what was being shown.
The first words then that the fair-haired knight let fly
Were "Curses on cowardice and a covetous heart!
For in that way villainy and vice destroy all virtue."
Then he grasped at his girdle and roughly grabbed it free,
Flinging it frantically over to that foe himself:
"There! That's for falsehood! May it meet a foul fate!
I cringed at your cuts, and my cowardice induced me
To make an accord with avarice, abandoning my nature,   2380
Which always leaned toward loyalty and knightly largess.
Now I'm false and flawed, I who always was fearful
Of treachery and lack of truth; may sorrow overtake them,
    As well as care.
I confess to you, my dear knight,
The wrongs I committed there,
But let me regain your good will,
And from now on, I'll beware."

17.

Then the other party laughed, proclaiming politely,
"Any wrong that you wreaked I now consider repaid.   2390
You've confessed very freely, acknowledging your flaws,
And you've performed your penance at the point of my sword.
I consider you cleansed of your sins, as immaculate
As if you'd never fallen since your very first day;
And I give you, kind sir, this golden-hemmed girdle
Which is as green as my gown, Gawain, so that you may
Meditate on this meeting whenever you move
Among rulers of renown—this is a fine remembrance
Of our affair at this abbey for other adventurous knights.
But come again in this New Year, come back to my castle,   2400
Where for the rest of this rich holiday you can revel
    In a glorious show."

The lord invited him thus,
Saying, "My wife, I know,
Will welcome you most warmly,
Though she was your bitter foe."

18.
"No, I'm sorry," said Sir Gawain, seizing his helmet
And holding it in his hands while he thanked his host;
"I've lingered here far too long; I hope you enjoy good luck
From God, who governs all men with magnanimous grace!   2410
And give my goodbye to your gentle, gracious lady,
And that other aged one, her most honored confidante,
For they cunningly waylaid this warrior with their wiles.
But it's no great wonder whenever a woman outwits
A man and leads him away to mourning or to madness,
For Adam himself was led astray by a woman,
And Solomon by several, and so too was Samson
(Who was doomed by Delilah), not to mention David,
Who was blinded by Bathsheba and suffered a bitter fate.
These were all laid low by women's lies. What great luck   2420
If a lord could simply love them and not believe them!
These former men were the finest who ever followed
The leisurely fates of lovers or lived under heavenly
      Skies of blue.
Yet they were all beguiled
By the women whom they knew;
And if I have been defiled,
Let me be forgiven too.

19.
"But may God repay you for your girdle!" said Sir Gawain.
"I'll wear it with good will—not for its genuine gold   2430
Or the silk in its sewing or the pendants at its side;
Not for its wealth or worthiness or elegant weaving—
But as a sign of my excess, I shall survey it often
Whenever I ride with renown, rehearsing to myself
The frailties and faults of this fickle flesh,
How it eagerly embraces every taint of corruption.
And so whenever pride propels me toward prowess in arms,
One look at this love-token will make my heart feel lowly.
But one thing I beg you, if it doesn't bother you:
Since you're the lord of this land where you have lodged me   2440
Beside you in perfect pleasure—may God repay you
From heaven and the heights where He upholds His throne—
What is your right name? The rest I will ignore."
"Then I'll tell you that truly," said the other there:
"Bertilak de Hautdesert is the name I have around here.
The mighty Morgan the Fay, who lives on my manor,
Whose mastery of magic is manipulated with craft,
Learned to a large degree from the lore of great Merlin—
For indeed she had a long and a lasting love
With that crafty wizard, who is known to your country's knights   2450
      As one of fame;
Therefore Morgan the Goddess
Rightly is her name;

Nobody's so wild against her
That she can't make him tame—

20.

"Well, she guided me in this disguise to your gay halls,
So that I could see if you were all as superb and splendid
As the fame of the Round Table runs with renown.
She produced this paradox in order to puzzle and perplex you,
And to goad poor Guinevere halfway to her grave   2460
As she gaped while I spoke in my most ghastly manner
From the head that I held in my hands right out before her!
She is actually resting at home, that aged lady,
And she's truly your aunt, being Arthur's half-sister,
The daughter of the Duchess of Tintagel, by whom
Uther fathered Arthur, your great ancestral lord.
Now I ask you, dear sir, to come back and see your aunt,
And be merry in my house; my serving-men adore you,
And I wish you well too with all truth, dear sir,
As do all who inhabit God's earth—for your integrity."   2470
But Gawain said no—in no way would he go back.
So, embracing and kissing, they commended each other
To the Prince of Paradise, and they parted right there
        In the cold.
Gawain rides away rapidly
To the fort of Arthur bold,
While the gent in inky green
Slips off to a place untold.

21.

Now Gawain wandered the wild highways of the world
On Gringolet, having regained the grace of life;   2480
Often he accepted lodgings in houses, or slept outside,
And was a victor in many adventures in many vales,
Though I don't have the time to tell them in this tale.
The nick that he had on his neck had healed like new
And he bore his brilliant belt about his body
Obliquely like a baldric that was bound at his side,
Locked under his left arm and laced tightly with a knot
To show that he had slipped badly in some misdeed.
And this way he came to the court, completely sound,
Arousing great revelry when the royal Arthur heard   2490
That Gawain the good was safely home; he considered it grand.
Then the king kissed the knight, as did the queen,
And many a staunch fellow stepped up to salute him,
Asking about his adventures; he answered fascinatingly,
Documenting the dangerous discomforts he'd endured,
The chance he took at the Chapel with its chaplain,
The loving acts of the lady, and lastly her lace.
He exposed for them the nick on his neck all naked,
Which he carried for those connivings that had corrupted
        His fame.   2500
He was troubled when he told this,
Groaning grievously for his blame;
The blood suffused his cheeks
When he showed his mark of shame.

22.

"Look, my lord," said Sir Gawain, fingering the lace,
"This band symbolizes the blame I bear on my neck;
It signifies the sorrowful loss that I have suffered,
Caught by cowardice and covetousness there;
It is a token of the untruthfulness that trapped me,
And I have to wear it for as long as I may live; 2510
For a man can hide his hurt, but never hurl it away,
Since once it is attached, it will not disappear."
The king comforted the knight, and all of the court—
Those lords and ladies who were loyal to the Table—
Laughed loudly at him; very lovingly they agreed
That every member of their brotherhood should wear a baldric,
A slanted belt about him of burnished green,
Out of sympathy for the sake of their sweet friend.
And so the renown of the Round Table was recorded
In this way, and heroes were honored who wore the belt, 2520
As is recounted in the choicest books of romance.
And in this way in Arthur's day this adventure occurred,
As the books about Felix Brutus all bear witness,
That bold baron who, as I've said, established Britain
After the siege and the assault had ceased among
    The Trojan men.
Many adventures of this kind
Have happened long since then.
May He who wore the crown of thorns
Bring us to His bliss. AMEN! 2530

chapter VII

THE ALLITERATIVE
MORTE ARTHURE

Valerie Krishna

The *Alliterative Morte Arthure*, like *Sir Gawain* an anonymous narrative poem and one of the masterpieces of the English alliterative tradition, is nevertheless unique in Arthurian literature. It depicts King Arthur as a warlord, emphasizing his great military victories, in particular his defeat of the fictional Roman emperor "Lucius Iberius," his vast continental conquests, and finally his betrayal and death at the hands of a very human and political Mordred. In its vigorous and enthusiastic celebration of the warlike virtues the *Morte Arthure* is closer in spirit to *Beowulf*, the *Iliad*, or the *Song of Roland* than to most of the Arthurian romances. Unlike Chrétien's knights, who serve the cause of love and display their knightly prowess in a magical, enchanted, or picturesque setting, the knights in the *Morte Arthure* are preoccupied with a more political type of heroism. Loyalty to their overlord, not deference to ladies, motivates them, along with a desire for fame, which is gained not in tournaments but through heroic deeds on the battlefield.

But the poem does not sentimentalize war. Though the poet glorifies his heroes through exaggerated descriptions of superhuman assaults and victories over enormous odds, he is unblinking in his descriptions of the ghastliness of hand-to-hand combat and the finality of death on the battlefield. This is no fairy world in which knights are brought back to life by magic. Arthur's death is real, with no promise or hint of his return.

Also reminiscent of the *Iliad* or *Roland* are the poem's heroic speeches—exhortations to battle and boasts or threats addressed to the enemy (humility is not a strong point with these knights!), elaborate descriptions of knightly costume and armor, and passionate laments for the fallen warriors. Gawain, the greatest of Arthur's warriors, courageous to the point of rashness, is very much like Roland, and in spite of the disastrous consequences of his rashness, his death, like Roland's, is accompanied by stirring elegiac tributes that proclaim the passing of an irreplaceable glory.

Though Gawain is important, the character who dominates the work from beginning to end is King Arthur, and in this the poem is also unusual, since Arthur occupies only a background position in many other Arthurian works. Furthermore, this Arthur is more than a simple heroic warrior-king. He is an ambiguous and not wholly laudable figure, perhaps the most complex Arthur in all of literature. In recent years critics have begun to see this Arthur as a tragic hero—flawed and guilty of hybris—and to consider the poem a kind of primitive tragedy with a strong moral tone. According to this view, the king begins his military campaigns as a just defender of his lands against an oppressor but eventually becomes carried away with his victories, enlarges his ambitions, and becomes in turn an aggressor, who finally contributes to his own downfall through the overextension of his ambitions and conquests.

The work has a symmetrical, rise-and-fall structure resembling that of tragedy, rather than the loose, episodic structure of many medieval works. This "pyramid" shape is underscored throughout by parallel passages, the most notable being Arthur's two prophetic dreams. The first dream, of a battle between a dragon and a bear with the dragon victorious, marks the beginning of the king's rise. The second, of Lady Fortune and her wheel, marks the turn of his fortunes and the beginning of his fall. Similarly, Arthur's altruistic motives in battling the giant of Mont St. Michel (St. Michael's Mount) contrast with the belligerent and aggressive nature of his campaign against the Duke of Lorraine. Yet the poet is careful not only to tie Arthur's fall to the change in his character but to make this change credible by foreshadowing it, giving the story a sense of tragic inevitability. From the beginning Arthur shows traces of pride and incipient rashness, which, fed by his victories, finally overcome the king's prudence, and are the source not only of his aggressive wars in the second part of the poem but also of his final reckless and disastrous battle with Mordred.

Like all Arthurian narratives, the *Alliterative Morte Arthure* is a retelling. Its immediate source is uncertain, but in general outline its story, like other tales in the *Morte* tradition, is another segment of the chronicle version of Arthur's life recounted first by Geoffrey of Monmouth and retold by Wace, Layamon, and other earlier chroniclers. (The *Brut* in the last line probably refers to the Englishman Layamon's poem of about 1205, but might refer to the Norman *Roman de Brut*, by Wace, written around 1155.) The poet has ornamented this basic story with additions from many sources, the most striking being Arthur's dream of Lady Fortune, a combination of two popular medieval motifs—the Wheel of Fortune and the quasi-historical theme of the Nine Worthies (lines 3218 ff.). The *Morte Arthure* is in turn the source of one of the central episodes in *Le Morte Darthur*, and is the most important English work used by Malory in his monumental compilation.

Bibliographic note: Two works that supply more information about the poem are William Matthews's *Tragedy of Arthur: A Study of the Alliterative Morte Arthure* (University of California, 1960) and Karl Heinz Göller's compilation of essays *The Alliterative Morte Arthure* (Brewer, 1981). For the complete poem see the author's *Alliterative Morte Arthure: A New Verse*

Translation (1983); the editors wish to thank the University Press of America for permission to reprint the sections included here. The author's edition of the text was published by Burt Franklin in 1976.

The Alliterative Morte Arthure

Invocation

May great, glorious God, through His singular grace,
And the precious prayers of His peerless Mother,
Help us shun shameful ways and wicked works,
And grant us grace to guide and govern us here,
In this woeful world, through virtuous ways,
That we may hurry to His court, the Kingdom of Heaven,
When the spirit must be split and sundered from the body,
To dwell and abide with Him in bliss forever;
And help me to pour forth some words here and now,
Neither empty nor idle, only honor to Him,   10
And pleasing and helpful to all people who hear.
    You who like to listen and who love to hear
Of lords of the old days and of their dread deeds,
How they were firm in their faith and followed God Almighty,
Hear me closely and hold your silence,
And I shall tell you a tale lofty and true
Of the royal ranks of the Round Table,
The flower of knighthood and all noble lords,
Prudent in their deeds and practiced men-in-arms,
Able in their actions, ever fearful of dishonor,   20
Proper men and polished and versed in courtly ways;
How they gained by battle glories abundant,
Laid low Lucius the wicked, Lord of Rome,
And conquered that kingdom by prowess in arms—
Hark now closely and hear out this tale.

[King Arthur, conqueror and overlord of Britain and of vast territories on the continent, holds court in splendor at Carlisle. A delegation from the Roman emperor Lucius Iberius interrupts the festivities with a demand that Arthur pay tribute to Rome as a vassal of Lucius. Arthur, supported by his prominent nobles, defies the summons, declaring that the emperor is his own vassal. After sending the messengers back with a contemptuous message, Arthur rallies his armies, bids a tender farewell to Guinevere, appoints a reluctant Mordred as regent, and sets sail for the continent to do battle with Lucius (lines 26–755).]

Arthur's First Dream and the Battle with the Giant

    The king was in a great craft with a full force of men,
In a closed cabin, snugly equipped;
Inside on a royal bed he rested awhile,

And with the sighing of the sea he fell into a slumber.
He dreamed of a dragon, dreadful to see,   760
Who came driving over the deeps to drown all his people,
Winging straight out of the western wastes,
Wandering wickedly over the wide waves;
His head and his neck all over the surface
Were rippled with azure, enameled most fair;
His shoulders were scaled in the same pure silver
Spread over all the beast's body in sparkling points;
His belly and his wings of wondrous colors,
In his glittering mail he mounted most high,
And all whom he smote were forfeit forever.   770
His feet were blazoned a beautiful black,
And such a deadly flare darted from his lips
That the sea from the flecks of fire seemed all aflame.
     Then out of the east directly toward him
Up in the clouds came a savage black bear,
With each shank like a pillar and paws most enormous,
Their talons so deadly—all jagged they looked;
With legs all crooked and filthily matted,
Most vilely snarled, and foaming lips,
Rough and repulsive he looked, and worse,   780
His form the foulest that ever was framed.
He stomped, he sneered, then swaggered about;
He bounded to battle with brutal claws;
He bellowed, he roared, so that all the earth rocked,
So lustily he smote it for his own sheer delight.
     Then from afar the dragon charged toward him,
And with his thrusts drove him far off toward the heavens.
He moved like a falcon, fiercely he struck;
He fought all at once with both fire and claw.
Still, the bear seemed the stronger in battle,   790
And savagely slashed him with venomous fangs;
He gave him such blows with his great paws
That his breast and his belly were all bathed in blood.
The bear raged so wildly he rent all the earth,
Which ran with red blood like rain from the heavens.
He would have brought down that serpent by sheer brute force,
Were it not for the fierce fire with which he fought back.
     Then soared the serpent away toward his zenith,
Swooped down from the sky and struck full straight:
Smote the bear with his talons, tore open his back,   800
Which was ten feet in length from the top to the tail.
Thus the dragon crushed the bear and drove him from life;
May he fall in the flood and float off to his fate!
The beasts so wrung the brave king there in the ship's hold,
That he near burst for bale as he lay in his bed.
     Then, worn out with suffering, the good king awoke,
And summoned two sages who attended him always,
In the seven studies the wisest to be seen,
The cleverest of clerics known in all Christendom.
He told them of his torment during the time he slept: 810
"Wracked by a dragon, and such a dread beast;
He has made me most weary—so help me dear God,
Interpret my dream, or I die at once!"

"Sire," said they presently, these sage men of knowledge,
"The dragon you dreamed of, so dreadful to see,
Who came driving over the deeps to drench—not drown—your folk,
Truly and for certain symbolizes you yourself,
Who here sail over the sea with your steadfast knights;
The colors that were painted upon his brilliant wings
Must be all the kingdoms that you have justly conquered;   820
And the tentacled tail with tongues so huge
Signifies these fair folk who in your fleet go forth;
The bear that was vanquished high up in the clouds
Betokens the tyrants who torment your people,
Or that a day of battle must be braved by you alone,
In single-hand combat with some kind of giant,
And you shall gain victory through the grace of our Lord,
As you in your vision were vividly shown.
Of this fearful dream dread you not any more;
Be not troubled, Sir Conqueror, but hearten yourself,   830
As well as these who sail the sea with your steadfast knights."
        To trumpets then briskly they trice up their sails,
And row over the wide waters, this troop, all together;
The fair coast of Normandy they fetch straightway;
Smoothly at Barfleur the stalwarts are landed,
And find there a fleet of friends in abundance,
The flower and the fair folk of fifteen realms;
For kings and chieftains attended him duly,
As he himself had commanded in Carlisle at Christmas.
        Soon as they had reached land and set up their tents,   840
Straightway came a Templar and spoke to the king:
"Near this place is a monster who is plaguing your people,
A huge giant of Genoa, engendered by fiends;
He has devoured more than five hundred folk,
And as many children of freeborn knights;
This has been his sustenance all these seven winters,
And still the sot is not sated, so much it delights him.
In Cotentin country not a clan has he left
Outside the great castles surrounded by walls,
Of which he has not slain fully all the male children,   850
Carried them off to the crag and cleanly devoured them.
The Duchess of Brittany today has he seized
As she rode beside Rennes with her royal knights,
Carried her off to the crag where that creature dwells,
To lie with that lady as long as life lasts.
We pursued them afar, more than five hundred,
Barons and burgesses and high-born knights,
But he gained the crag—she cried out so loud,
I shall never get over my grief for that creature!
She was flower of all France, of full five realms,   860
And one of the fairest that ever was framed;
Lauded by lords as the loveliest gem
From Genoa to Garonne, by Jesu in Heaven!
She was your wife's cousin—own it if you will—
Born of the royalest blood that reigns on this earth.
As a righteous king take pity on your people,
And undertake to avenge them who thus are outraged."
        "Alas!" cries King Arthur, "that so long I have lived!

Had I known of this, things would have gone better.
It befalls me not well, but ill me betides,   870
That thus this fair lady this fiend has destroyed.
I had, rather than own all France these fifteen winters,
I had been close to that creature a furlong's space,
When he captured that lady and carried her off to the crag;
I would have given my life before she had met grief!
Still, will you show me the crag where that cruel creature dwells?
I wish to go to that place and speak face to face,
To come to terms with that tyrant for abuse of these lands,
And make truce for a time till things may go better."
      "Sire, do you see yon headland with those two fires?   880
There lurks that fiend—seek him out when you choose—
On the ridge of the crag, by a cold river,
That guards the cliff with cataracts sheer;
There you can find fated folk beyond number,
And more florins, in faith, than there are in all France,
And more gold which that wretch has guilefully got
Than was in Troy, I swear, at the time it was conquered."
      Then the great king cries out, in pity for the people,
Makes straight for a tent and is tranquil no longer.
He tosses, he writhes, he wrings his hands—   890
Not another living soul could know how he suffered.
He summons Sir Kay, who carries his cup,
And Sir Bedivere the bold, who bears his great sword:
"See that by evensong you be properly armed,
On steeds, by yon thicket, near those soft streams,
For I wish to go on pilgrimage secretly anon,
At the time of supper, when the men are served,
To seek out a saint by yon salt strands,
On St. Michael's Mount, where miracles are made."
      After evensong, King Arthur, alone,   900
Withdrew to his wardrobe and cast off his garb,
And dressed him in a doublet embroidered in gold,
Above that a tunic of Acre on top,
And above that a hauberk of fine chainmail,
And a surcoat of Jerodyn, scalloped in gold.
He clamps on a helmet, gleaming with silver,
The best from Basel, with magnificent trim:
The crest and the coronal compassed so fair
By clasps of pure gold, encrusted with gems,
The vizard, the ventail, enameled so fair,   910
Free of all flaw, with slits framed in silver;
His gauntlet brightly gilded and trimmed at the edge
With seed-pearls and gems of a glorious hue.
He straps on a great shield and calls for his sword,
Saddles him a bay and bounds to the field;
He springs to his stirrup and straddles atop him,
Bridles him firmly and skillfully guides him,
Spurs the bay steed and rides off to the wood,
And there his men await him, all fully armed.
      Then they ride along that river that rapidly rushes,   920
Which the banks overhung with royal boughs;
There the roe and the deer lightheartedly leap
Through brakes and briers to frolic themselves;

The friths were embellished with blooms in abundance,
And with falcons and pheasants of fabulous hues;
There flashed all the birds that fly upon wing,
There sang the cuckoo full clear in the copse—
They give vent to their joy with all manner of mirth.
Sweet was the sound of the nightingales' notes:
They vied with the thrushes, three hundred at once,   930
That such sighing of water and singing of birds
Might soothe the sorrow of one who had never been sound.
    So these folk fare on, alight from their steeds,
And fasten their fine mounts a fair distance off;
With that the king bravely bade his knights
To stay by their steeds and go forward no further:
"I want to search out this saint alone, by myself,
And settle with the master who holds sway on this mount,
And after, you shall do homage, each in turn,
Solemnly, to St. Michael, most mighty in Christ."   940
    The king reaches the crag with its chasms so steep;
He climbs aloft to the crest of the cliff;
He casts up his visor and looks about keenly,
To brace himself, breathes in the cold wind.
Two fires he spies, flaming full high;
He stalks between them a quarter furlong away.
The way by the spring waters he traverses alone,
To find out that fiend in his home ground.

*   *   *   *

    On the side of the smoke straightway he stalked,
And crossed himself faithfully with solemn words,
When, from the side of that creature he reached the sight,
How gruesomely that sot sat gorging himself!
He lay stretched out full length, loathsomely lolling,
The haunch of a man's leg held up by the hip;
His back and his buttocks and his big loins
He baked at the blaze, and breechless he was;
There were such brutal roasts there and pitiful meats,
Human beings and beasts, spitted together,   1050
A cauldron crammed full of christened children,
Some skewered like meat—and the maidens revolved them.
As for this noble king, for the sake of his subjects,
His heart bleeds for pain as he stands there on that plain.
Then he straps on his shield and stands still no longer,
Brandishes his burnished blade by the bright hilt,
Stalks straight toward that sot with a stout heart,
And loudly hails that hulk with haughty words:
"May Almighty God, who is worshiped by us all,
Give you sorrow and suffering, sot, where you lie,   1060
The foulest freak that ever was formed!
Foully you feed yourself—the Fiend have your soul!
This is food unclean, clod, on my oath,
Refuse of all creatures, you cursed wretch!
Because you have murdered these christened children,
And you have made martyrs and sundered from life
Those stabbed here on the heath and crushed at your hands,

I shall mete you out your reward, since you have served well,
Through the might of Saint Michael, who reigns over this mount;
Also for this fair lady, whom you have left lifeless,   1070
And thus befouled in the dust for the sake of your filth:
Get you ready now, dog's son—the Devil take your soul—
For you shall die this day, by dint of my hands!"
Then that sot glared and gruesomely glowered,
Bared his teeth like a hound with hideous fangs;
He gnashed, he snarled fiercely, with scowling face,
In rage at the good king, who confronts him in wrath.
      His hair and his forelock were tangled together,
And from his face spouted foam a half-foot out;
It was flecked all over his features and forehead,   1080
Like the skin of a toad, so that speckled he seemed;
Hook-beaked like a hawk and with a hoar beard,
And furred to his hollow eyes with hanging brows;
Rough as a houndfish to whoever looks hard,
So was the hide of that hulk wholly all over;
Ears had he most huge and hideous to look at,
With eyes full fearsome, and flaming in fact;
Flat-mouthed as a flounder, with fleering lips,
And hunks of flesh in his fangs, foul as a bear;
His beard was bristly and black and hung down to his breast;   1090
He was fat as a sea-hog, with carcass full huge;
And so contorted the flesh of his foul lips,
That the wrinkles, like rebels, writhed out every which-way.
Bull-necked was that being and broad in the shoulders,
Skunk-striped like a swine with bristles full big,
Huge arms like an oak with gnarled sides,
Limbs and loins all loathsome, believe it for sure;
Shovel-footed was that creature and shuffling he seemed,
With legs misshapen, shoved up together,
Thick thighs like a monster, even huger in the haunch,   1100
Fat-swollen as a swine, so unsightly he looks;
He who faithfully gauges the height of that hulk
Will find him five fathoms from forehead to foot.
      Then springs he up wildly on two stout shanks,
And quickly clutches a club of full solid iron;
He would have killed the king with his keen weapon,
But, by Christ's might, in the end the clod failed.
The crest and the circlet, the clasps all of silver
At one clip with his club he struck clean to the ground.
The king throws up his shield and shelters him nimbly,   1110
And with his stout blade he strikes him a blow:
Point-blank in the forehead the savage he smites,
So the bright blade sank into the brain.
The creature clutched at his countenance with his foul claws;
Then fiercely with full force flung out at his face.
The king shifts his footing, gets clear by a hair—
Had he not dodged that stroke, evil had triumphed.
He follows up fiercely and fastens a blow
High up in the haunch with his hardy weapon,
So he buried the blade half a foot in,   1120
And the hot blood of that hulk gushed over the hilt.
Right to the innards of the ogre he thrusts,
Straight up to the genitals, and slashed them asunder.

Then he bellowed, he roared, and frenziedly swung
Full fiercely at Arthur, but struck into the ground.
A sword's length in the sod swiftly he smote,
So that Arthur near swoons from the sweep of his strokes.
But swiftly the king strains himself fiercely,
Thrusts in with the sword so it punctured the groin:
Both the guts and the gore gush out together   1130
And enslime all the grass on the ground where he stands.
Then he casts down the club and lays hold of the king,
On the crest of the crag clutches him in his arms,
Wraps him right round, to rupture his ribs;
So hard he hugs that hero, his heart nearly bursts.
    Then the mournful maidens fell to the earth,
Kneeling and crying, and clasped their hands:
"Christ deliver this knight and keep him from grief,
And let not that fiend fell him from life."
Yet is the monster so mighty he hurls him under;   1140
Wildly they writhe and wrestle together,
Welter and thrash out through the thornbush,
Swiftly tumble and turn and tear their garb;
Ungently from the crest they struggle together—
Sometimes Arthur on top and other times under—
From the height of the mount down to the rough rock,
They slack not till they fall at the shore of the sea.
Then Arthur with a dagger savagely strikes,
And stabs the hulk straight up to the hilt;
The wretch in his death-throes wrings him so hard,   1150
Three ribs in his side he squeezes to splinters.
    Then Sir Kay the courageous rushes up to the king,
Cries, "Alas, we are lost! My lord is laid low!
Felled by a fiend! Evil befalls us!
We will be finished, by my faith, and exiled forever!"
Then they lifted his hauberk and felt underneath it,
His flesh and his thigh and on up to his shoulders,
His flank and his loins and his fair sides,
His back and his breast and his fine arms;
They were happy when they found no flesh torn,   1160
And rejoiced for that day, these noble knights.
    "To be sure," says Sir Bedivere, "it strikes me, by God,
One must seek saints, but seldom to grip them so tight
And to drag down such a relic from these high cliffs
And carry forth a corpse like this to enclose all in silver.
By Michael, of such a fellow I marvel much
That ever our sovereign Lord allows him in Heaven!
If all saints be such who serve our Lord,
I shall never be a saint, by my father's soul!"
    The bold king banters back at Bedivere's words: 1170
"This saint have I searched out, so save me our Lord,
So haul out your sword and thrust him through to the heart;
Be sure of this servant—he has troubled me sore;
I fought not with such a fellow these fifteen winters;
Only on Mount Snowdon have I met such a match;
He was the strongest by far that ever I found;
Had not my fortunes been fair, I had fallen to my fate.
Swiftly strike off his head, set it up on a stake,
And give it to your squire, for he is strong-horsed;

Bear it to King Howell, who is in harsh bondage,   1180
And bid him hearten his spirit, for his foe is felled.
Then carry it to Barfleur and enclose it in iron,
And put it up on the parapet for people to see.
My sword and my great shield lie on the sod,
At the crest of the crag, where first we clashed,
And nearby the club, of full solid iron,
That has killed many Christians on the Breton coast;
Go to that headland and get me that weapon,
And let us set forth for our fleet where it waits on the water;
If you wish any treasure, take what you please;   1190
If I have kirtle and club, I crave nothing else."
Then they climb to the crag, these goodly knights,
And bring him the great shield and his shining sword;
Sir Kay himself bears the club and also the kirtle,
And they set out with the conqueror to show to the kings
What in secret the king had kept hidden to himself,
As bright morn from the mountain mounted on high.
        By then to court had come clamor full great,
And before the noble king the people knelt together:
"Welcome, our liege lord, too long have you been away,   1200
Ruler under God, most great and grand,
To whom grace has been granted and given at God's will;
Now your happy arrival has heartened us all!
In your kingliness you have avenged your vassals:
By the force of your hand the foe is felled,
Who oppressed your people and deprived them of children;
Never was realm in disarray so readily set right!"
        Then the conqueror piously spoke to his people:
"Thank God for this blessing, and no other being,
For it was never man's making, but only God's might,   1210
Or a miracle of His Mother, who is merciful to all."
And with that he swiftly summoned the seamen
To go forth with the townsmen to share out the goods,
All the great treasure that tyrant had taken,
To the folk of that country, clergy and all.
"See it be divided and dealt out to my dear people,
So none complain of their portion—on pain of your lives!"
Then he commanded his kinsman with kingly words
To build a church on the crag where the corpse lay,
And a convent within it for the service of Christ,   1220
In memory of that martyr who rests on the mountain.

[The Emperor Lucius, having raised a great army of barbarians and Saracens, has marched into France. After some initial skirmishes, the armies prepare to face each other (1222–2005).]

The Battle with Lucius

        Then the emperor soon after, with his able knights
And earls, enters the valley in quest of adventure,
And comes on King Arthur, with his armies arrayed.
And at his arrival, to worsen his woe,

Our fair, fearless king comes forth on the field, 2010
With battalions spread full and banners flying.
He had barred the city from every side,
And all the chasms and cliffs with good men-at-arms,
The marsh and the morass and the mountains so high,
With a great multitude of men to bar him the ways.

* * * *

Then Lucius loudly spoke lordly words: 2032
"Think on the wide fame of your great fathers,
And the ravagers of Rome, who ruled with their lords;
And how our ranks overran all that reigned on this earth,
And captured all Christendom by courage in arms—
With every campaign a conquest was gained;
And subdued all the Saracens within seven winters,
All the land from Port Jaffa to the Paradise gates.
For a realm to be rebel, we reck it a trifle: 2040
It is just and right for such a man to be quelled.
Therefore, to arms, and hold back no longer,
For, dread not, without doubt the day shall be ours!"
After these words were spoken, the Welsh king himself
Spotted the foe who had warred on his knights,
And fiercely through the vale he shouts his defiance:
"Viscount of Valence, venomous of deeds,
That feat at Viterbo today shall be avenged;
Unvanquished from this field flee shall I never!"
Then the valiant viscount, noble of voice, 2050
Withdrew from the vanguard that surrounded his steed;
He took up a stout shield, serrated in black,
With a huge dragon, dreadful to see,
Devouring a dolphin, with doleful looks,
As a sign that our leader would be laid low,
And with sweeps of swords done out of his days;
For there is nothing but death where the dragon is raised.
Then the worthy Welsh king readies his weapon,
And with a stern lance he smites him straight,
A span's length of that shaft right in the small ribs, 2060
So both steel and spleen are impaled on the spear.
Blood spurted and splattered as the horse sprang;
The man suddenly sprawls and speaks nevermore.
And thus has Sir Valiant kept to his vows
And vanquished the viscount, who had been called victor.
Then Sir Ewain fitz Urien eagerly rides
In a rush to the emperor to rip down his eagle;
Through his stout troop he swiftly charged,
Hauls out his sword and with a happy face
Promptly cuts down the eagle and gallops away, 2070
Comes back with that bird in his fair hands,
And safely lines up on the front with his fellows.
Now Sir Lancelot makes ready and rushes straight
To Sir Lucius the lord and gruesomely smites him;
Through armor and plate he pierces the mail,
So the proud pennon impales his paunch,
And the point projects behind a half-foot span.

Through hauberk and hip with his hardy weapon,
The steed and the stalwart he strikes to the ground,
Also cuts down a banner and bounds back to his band.   2080
     "I am pleased," says Sir Lot, "yonder lords are dispatched!
It is my turn now, with my lord's leave;
Today my name be laid low and my life henceforth
If some do not fall to their fate who await on the field!"
Then the stalwart stretches his body and strains his bridle,
Strikes into the struggle on a stout steed,
Takes on a giant and slashes him through;
Then boldly this warrior runs down another,
Cuts wide ways, wreaking ruin on knights,
And wickedly wounds all who get in his way.   2090
He fought all the force and in a flash
Felled scores on the field with his fine weapon,
Vanquished and laid low valiant knights,
Charged through the whole valley and withdrew when he chose.
     Thereafter then boldly the bowmen of Britain
Fought with foot-soldiers from afar on those fields;
With flitting arrows they fearlessly forced back the foe,
With feathers fiercely pierce the fine mail;
Such fighting is foul that so rends the flesh,
And that flashes from afar into flanks of steeds.   2100
The Dutchmen hurled their darts against them:
With dread deathblows they slice through shields;
Shafts so swiftly shear through knights,
Cut with iron so clean they cannot even wink.
They so shrink before the sweep of the sharp shafts
That all the troop turned back and scattered at once.
The great stallions spring up and rush right onto weapons,
And soon a whole hundred are stretched out on the heath.
     Still, swiftly the strongest, heathens and all,
All hurtled forth headlong to wreak their woes;   2110
With all the giants in front, engendered by fiends,
They attack Sir Jonathal and other fine knights.
With clubs of hard steel they hammered in helms,
Struck down crests and smashed in skulls,
Slaughtered coursers and caparisoned mounts,
Sliced straight through stalwarts on snow-white steeds;
Neither steel nor stallion could stand up against them,
For they stunned and struck down all who stood in our host,
Till the conqueror came with his keen knights,
And with a fierce countenance lustily cried: 2120
"I expect no Briton to be daunted by so little,
By barelegged boys who have entered the battle!"
     He whips out Caliburn, all freshly whetted,
Hastes to Golapas, who had hurt the most men,
And cleaves him just at the knees cleanly in two.
"Come down," cries the king, "and speak to your comrades!
You are too high by half, I tell you in truth;
You will be handsomer soon, with the help of my Lord."
And with his steel sword he struck off his head.
Stoutly into that struggle he strikes at another,   2130
And sets on seven with his stalwart knights—
Till sixty were so served, ceased they never.

And thus in that skirmish the giants are slain,
Laid low in that battle by lordly knights.
    Then the Romans and the ranks of the Round Table
Arranged themselves in array, rearguard and all,
And on helms went to work with stout weapons of war;
With strong steel they sundered splendid mail,
They arrayed themselves well, these royal men,
And thrust in skillfully on steel-grey steeds, 2140
Fiercely flourished with flashing spears,
Sliced away ornaments fastened on shields;
So many battle-fated are fallen on the field
That each brook on the forest floor flows with red blood.
    Thus swiftly lifeblood is left on the sod,
Swords are broken in two, and dying knights
Loll full length, lurching on lunging steeds;
Worthy warriors' wounds, ruptured ribs,
Faces gruesomely framed in tangled locks
Were all trampled, trod down by steeds in their trappings. 2150
The fairest on earth that ever were framed
Stretched as far as a furlong, a thousand all told.
    By then the Romans were somewhat subdued,
And lingered no longer, but fearfully fled;
Our king with his force follows fast on their heels,
And bears down on the bravest with his best knights;
Sir Kay, Sir Clegis, Sir Cleremond the noble
Take them on at the cliff with skilled men-at-arms,
Fight hard in the forest, hold back no weapon,
And fell at the first rush five hundred at once. 2160
When they saw they were surrounded by our stern knights,
And that, outmatched, our men battled even better,
They fought with all the troop and flourished with spears,
And battled the bravest belonging to France.
Then Sir Kay the keen levels his lance,
Gives chase on a courser and charges a king;
With a spear of Lithuania he rips through his ribs,
So both liver and lungs are impaled on the lance;
The shaft shivered and sailed toward the great lord,
Ripped clear through the shield and came to rest in the man. 2170
But on entry Sir Kay was ignobly attacked
By a coward knight from that great land;
Just as he turned, the traitor struck
Right through the flesh and into the flank,
So the brutal lance ripped open the bowel,
And burst on impact, and broke in the center!
Sir Kay knew full well by that infamous wound
He was doomed by that stroke and done out of his life.
He moves into array and rides into their ranks,
To avenge his own death on that proud man; 2180
Crying, "Guard yourself, coward!" he calls him forth quickly,
And with gleaming sword cleaves him cleanly in two!
"Had you so well dealt that dint with your hands,
I had forgiven you my death, by Christ up in Heaven!"
    He goes to the good king and graciously greets him:
"I am grievously wounded and will never get well;
Do now your rites, as the world demands,

And bring me to burial—I beg nothing more.
Greet well my lady, the queen, if fortune befall you,
And all those fair ladies who belong to her bower;   2190
And my gracious wife, who grieved me never,
Bid her, as worthy woman, to pray for my soul."
The king's confessor came, with Christ in his hands,
And to solace that soul spoke over him prayers;
With a noble heart the knight got to his knees,
And received his Creator, who comforts us all.
        Then the great king cries out with grief in his heart,
And rides into the rout to avenge Sir Kay's death,
Pushes into the press and encounters a prince,
Known as heir of Egypt in those eastern lands,   2200
And with Caliburn cleaves him cleanly asunder;
Slices right through the man, splits the saddle in two,
And right there on the steed's back burst open the bowel.
In his fury he fiercely takes on another,
And the middle of that mighty man, who maddened him mightily,
Through the mail he slits it asunder at center,
So that half of the man falls on the hill,
And the other half, haunch down, is left on the horse—
Of that hurt, I vow, he will never be healed.
He then rushed through the ranks with his rugged weapon,   2210
Slashed through men and shredded mail,
Struck down flags and shattered shields,
Fiercely vented his fury with flashing steel.
He twists and turns madly with all might and main,
Wounded his foes and wreaked ruin on knights,
Fought through the throng thirteen times,
Thrusts fiercely into the thick of it and strikes straight through.
        Then Sir Gawain the good, with his gallant knights,
Moves up to the vanguard by the verge of the wood,
Catches sight of Sir Lucius where he waits in a clearing,   2220
With the lords and the liegemen loyal to him.
The emperor then eagerly asks him at once,
"What do you want, Gawain? Work for your weapon?
I can tell by your trembling you are craving for trouble!
I shall be avenged on your wrath, for all your proud words!"
He whipped out a long sword, and like lightning lunged out,
Like a lord in that glade at Sir Lionel he strikes,
Smites so hard on his head that he shatters his helm,
And laid open the skull a good hand's breadth.
He pitched into the press and highhandedly served them,   2230
Wondrously wounded worthy knights,
Fought with Florent, the finest of swords,
Till the foaming blood flowed clear over his fist.
        Then the Romans rallied, who had been rebuffed,
And on rested steeds put our men all to rout;
When they see their chieftain so hotly aroused,
They chase and chop down our noble knights.
Sir Bedivere was thrust through and his breast gored,
With a hard blade, broad at the hilt;
The noble stout steel sank into his heart,   2240
And he pitched to the earth—pity is the more.

    The conqueror caught sight and came with his force
To rescue the royal ranks of the Round Table,
And to finish the emperor, if fortune allow it;
They ride straight to the eagle, and "Arthur!" they cry.
The emperor then eagerly strikes out at Arthur,
Backhanded at the visor and viciously smites him;
The naked sword wounds him sore on the nose,
And the blood of the brave king gushed over his breast,
And bloodied the broad shield and the bright mail.   2250
The bold king turns his horse by the rich reins,
And with his stout sword deals Lucius a stroke;
Through both armor and breast with his bright blade,
Aslant through the throat with one stroke he slices,
And thus ends the emperor at Arthur's hands.
With that, his fierce force all become frightened,
And they flee to the forest, the few that are left,
In fear of our folk, toward the fresh streams;
The flower of our stalwarts, on steel-grey steeds,
Chased down those men who had never known fear.   2260

                    *   *   *   *

Then heralds hastily, at behest of the lords,
Hunt up the heathens who lie on the heath:
The Sultan of Syria and his steadfast lords,
And sixty of the foremost senators of Rome.
They anoint and array these honored kings,
Then lap them in sixty layers of linen,
And encase them in lead, so they might the less   2300
Decay or crumble, if they could prevent it.
Then enclosed in caskets they will ride clear to Rome,
With their banners above, their badges beneath,
So in all countries they cross men could know
Each king by his colors, in his native land.

                    *   *   *   *

The king himself the coffins consigned to the captives,   2340
And right before his stalwart men spoke these words:
"These are the coffers," said the king, "that will cross the mountains:
The full measure of wealth that you have much craved,
The tax and the tribute of ten score winters,
That was grievously lost in our ancestors' day.
Say to the Senator who governs the city
That I send him the whole sum—assess it as he please!
And bid them never be so bold, so long as my blood reigns,
To wrangle a second time for my spacious lands,
Nor demand tribute or tax by any manner of title,   2350
Save such treasure as this, as long as my day endures!"

[After his victory over Lucius, King Arthur decides to make war on the
Duke of Lorraine, claiming that he is a disloyal vassal. During Arthur's siege
of the city of Metz, Gawain goes off on a foraging expedition and encounters

and fights Priamus, a Saracen knight, in a joust that ends with the two
knights becoming friends and Priamus's mercenary followers deserting the
duke's service. A battle against the duke's forces and the siege of the city end
in victory for the king. Arthur then marches down into Italy, conquering
city after city, in a campaign that ends with the Romans, including an
emissary of the Pope, who offers him the imperial crown. Arthur glories in his
triumph, vowing to become "overlord of all that belongs to this earth"
(2279–3217).]

Arthur's Second Dream
and the News of Mordred's Treachery

Then this noble king, so chronicles say,
Bounds briskly to bed with a blithe heart;
He undresses with ease and loosens his girdle,   3220
And with sleepy languor slips into a slumber.
By the hour after midnight his mood changed completely,
And toward morning he saw wondrous strange dreams;
And when his dread dream had drawn to an end,
The king is frozen with fright as if he should die.
He sends for his sages and tells of his terror:
"Since I was formed, by my faith, so afraid was I never.
So quickly search and translate my dream,
And I shall readily and rightly recount the true story:
      "It seemed I was in a wood, lost and alone,   3230
And knew not at all which way I should go,
For wolves, wild boars, and bloodthirsty beasts
Stalked that wasteland, searching for prey;
There hideous lions were licking their fangs,
In their lust to lap the blood of my loyal knights.
Through that forest I fled to where flowers grew high,
To hide me, in fear of those foul things.
I came on a meadow, surrounded by mountains,
Most delightful on earth that men might behold;
That valley all round was covered all about   3240
And clad clear over with clover and blooms;
The vale was circled with vineyards of silver,
All hung with gold grapes (there never were grander),
Trimmed with arbors and all types of trees,
Fine, fair groves, with flocks grazing beneath.
There were furnished all fruits that flourish on earth,
Nicely fenced in upon those fair boughs;
With no dropping of damp that could damage the blooms,
In the warmth of the day all dry were the flowers.
      "Down from the clouds descended into that dale   3250
A lady dressed richly in damasked robes,
In a surcoat of silk of such a rare hue,
All fretted with fur full to the hem,
And with elegant lappets as long as a yard,
All lovingly lined with layers of gold;
Jewels, gold coins, and other bright gems
On her back and her breast were embroidered all over;

With headdress and coronal richly arrayed,
Another so fair of face could never be found.
  "With her white hands she whirled round a wheel   3260
As if she might suddenly upset it completely;
The rim was red gold set with rare royal stones,
Arrayed with richness and rubies aplenty;
The spokes were all plated with splints of pure silver,
And splendidly spread out a full spear's span.
At the summit was a seat of snow-white silver,
Fretted with rubies, flashing with fire.
Round the rim there clung kings, one after another,
With crowns of pure gold, all cracking apart.
Six from that seat had been struck down abruptly,   3270
Each one in turn, and they cried out these words:
'That I reigned on this wheel I shall rue it forever!
Never monarch mighty like me had ruled on this earth.
When I rode with my retinue I recked nothing more
But to hunt and revel and ravage the people;
And thus I drew out my days, as long as I could endure,
And for that I am ruthlessly damned forever.'
  "The lowest was a little man, who had been thrown beneath;
His loins lay there all lean and loathsome to look at,
His locks grey and long, the length of a yard,   3280
His flesh and his form full foully disfigured;
And one of his eyes was brighter than silver,
And the other was yellower than the yolk of an egg!
'I was lord,' cried that man, 'of lands beyond measure,
And all men bowed before me who drew breath on this earth!
Now not a rag is left me to lay on my body,
And I am suddenly forsaken—let all men see the truth!'
  "The second lord, I swear, who came along in that line,
Seemed more stalwart to me and stronger in arms;
Many times he sighed sadly and these words he spoke: 3290
'On that throne have I sat as sovereign and lord,
And all ladies loved to twine me in their arms;
Now my glories are all lost and laid low forever!'
  "The third was right sturdy and stout through the shoulders,
A tough man to threaten, even thirty together.
His diadem had slipped down, all studded with stones,
And bedecked all with diamonds, adorned to perfection:
'I was dreaded in my day in lands far and wide,
But now am doomed to downfall and death—dole is the more.'
  "The fourth was a fair man, forceful in arms,   3300
The fairest of form that ever was framed:
'I was heroic, by my faith, when I reigned on earth,
Famed in far lands and the flower of all kings;
Now my face has all faded and fate treats me foully,
For I am fallen from far heights and left without friends.'
  "The fifth was a fairer man than most of the others,
A man strong and fierce, with foam at his lips;
He clutched tight at the rim and flexed his arms,
But he faltered and fell from a fifty-foot height;
Still he sprang up and sprinted and spread out his arms,   3310
And, sprawled on those spear-length spokes, speaks these words:

'I was a lord in Syria, set up by myself,
As sovereign and lord of sundry kings' lands;
Now I am abruptly fallen from bliss,
And because of my sins, that seat is bereft me!'
    "The sixth bore a psalter, beautifully bound,
With a cover of silk, splendidly stitched,
A harp, a handsling, and hard flint stones,
And of the sorrows he suffers he soon sent up a cry:
'I was deemed in my day, for deeds of arms,   3320
One of the ablest who ever lived on earth;
But at the peak of my powers I was dropped in the dust
By this meek maid, who moves the whole world.'
    "Two kings were clambering and clawing at the heights,
At the crest of the wheel, which they frantically crave:
'This ruby throne,' they cried, 'henceforth we claim,
As two of the greatest ever graced on this earth!'
Those warriors waxed white as chalk, faces and all,
But that chair at the top they never achieved.
The higher was handsome, with a high brow,   3330
The fairest of face that ever was framed,
And was garbed in a shade of glorious blue,
Flourished all over with gold fleurs-de-lis.
The other was clad in a coat all of pure silver,
With a graceful cross engraved in gold;
Four perfect crosslets surround that cross,
And thus I could tell that king was a Christian.
    "Then I went toward that fair one and greeted her warmly,
And she said, 'Welcome indeed, it is well you are come;
If you were wise, you would worship my will,   3340
Of all the worthy men there ever were in this world,
For all your glory in war through me have you won;
I have been friendly to you, sir, and hostile to others,
Whom you have fought, in faith, and many of your folk,
For I felled Sir Frollo, for all his fierce knights,
And thus the fruits of France are all freely yours.
You shall achieve this chair; I choose you myself
Above all other chieftains honored on earth.'
    "She lifted me smoothly in her slim hands,
And set me gently in the seat and presented me the scepter;   3350
And with a comb deftly she dressed my hair,
So the waving locks curled up round my crown,
Put on me a diadem, dazzling fair bedecked,
Then offered me an orb, all studded with fair stones,
And enameled with azure, earth blazoned thereon,
Encircled with the salt sea on every side,
As a symbol that I truly was supreme on all the earth.
Then she brought me a sword with a most splendid hilt,
And bade me 'Brandish the blade; this sword is my own;
Many a man by its stroke has shed his life's blood,   3360
And while you work with this weapon it will fail you never.'
    "Then she goes off in peace to rest at her pleasure,
To the edge of the forest—a more fruitful was never;
No orchard was so planted for any prince on earth,
And no array so splendid but in Paradise itself.
She bade the boughs bow down and yield to my hands

The best that they bore on their branches so high;
They heeded her behest, the whole lot at once,
The tallest of each grove, I tell you in truth.
She bade me spare not the fruit but sample at will: 3370
'Taste of the finest, you worthy man;
Reach for the ripest and revel yourself;
Rest, royal king, for Rome is your own.
And I shall willingly whirl the well-wheel straightway,
And reach you rich wine in clear-rinsed cups.'
    "Then she went to the well by the edge of the wood,
That welled up with wine and wondrously flowed,
Dipped a cupful, and drew it up deftly,
Then bade me draw deeply and drink it to her.
And thus she led me about the space of an hour,   3380
With all the fondness and love any man could desire;
But exactly at midday her mood changed completely,
And she turned on me with terrible words.
When I entreated her, she drew down her brows:
'King, you cry to no use, by Christ who created me!
You must lose this game and later your life;
You have lived with delight and lands long enough!'
Round she spun the wheel and whirled me under,
So all my limbs then and there were pounded to pieces,
And with the chair my spine was broken asunder.   3390
And I have shivered with chill since this thing befell me.
Then I wakened, truly all worn down with these dreams;
And now you know my woe, speak out as you wish."
    "Sire," said the sage, "your good fortune is passed:
You shall find her your foe—test her out as you wish;
You are now at your zenith, I tell you in truth;
Take what challenge you wish, you will achieve nothing more.
You have spilled much blood and destroyed many men,
All sinless, by your pride, in sundry kings' lands.
Shrive you of your sins and prepare for your end;   3400
You have had a sign, sir king; please you, take heed,
For you shall fall fearfully within five winters.
Found abbeys in France—her fruits are your own—
For Frollo, for Ferrant, and for all those fierce knights
Who in France you have savagely felled on the field.
Take heed of the other kings and search your own heart:
They were renowned conquerors, crowned on this earth.
The most ancient was Alexander, whom all earth bowed before;
The next Hector of Troy, that hardy hero;
The third Julius Caesar, renowned as a giant,   3410
Acclaimed by knights in all battles as mighty;
The fourth was Sir Judas, a jouster most noble,
That unconquered Maccabee, mightiest of strength;
The fifth was Joshua, that gallant man-at-arms,
Who much joy brought to Jerusalem's host;
The sixth, David the peerless, deemed by kings
One of the noblest who ever was knighted;
For with a sling he slew with a stroke of his hands
Goliath the giant, most ferocious on earth,
Then composed in his day all those beloved psalms,   3420
That in the psalter are set down in such a strange tongue.

Of the two clambering kings, I know it in truth,
One shall be called Charlemagne, the great king of France;
He shall be stern and keen, and as conqueror acclaimed,
And shall gain by conquest countries in hosts;
He shall achieve the crown that Christ himself wore,
And the very spear that plunged into His heart,
When He was crucified on the cross, and all those cruel nails
He shall carry like a king into Christian men's keeping.
The other shall be Godfrey, who shall avenge God   3430
On a Good Friday, with his gallant knights.
He shall be made lord of Lorraine, by leave of his father,
And later in Jerusalem achieve great joy,
For he shall win the Cross by his prowess in war,
And then be crowned king and anointed with chrism.
No other duke in his day shall have such a destiny,
Nor suffer such woe when the truth shall be judged.
    "And so Fortune has fetched you to fill out the number:
The noblest nine ever known on the earth.
This shall be read in romance by royal knights,   3440
Renowned and reckoned among ruthless kings,
And you deemed at Doomsday, as deeds of arms go,
One of the ablest ever living on earth.
So many scholars and sovereigns shall speak of your deeds
And preserve your conquests in chronicles forever.
But the wolves in the wood and those wild beasts
Stand for wicked men who wage war on your realms,
And who have dared in your absence to arm against your folk,
With heathens and hosts from barbarous lands.
You will have tidings, I tell you, within ten days,   3450
That some tragedy has taken place since you turned from home.
I urge you: reckon and recount your outrageous deeds,
Or you will too soon repent all your ruinous works.
Mend your heart, king, before you meet with misfortune,
And humbly seek mercy for the sake of your soul."
    Then the great king arose and drew on his garments:
A doublet red with roses, most royal of flowers,
A gorget and a breastplate and a precious girdle;
And he pulls on a hood of most splendid scarlet,
And a round helm from Pavia, preciously set   3460
With jewels from the Orient and magnificent gems,
His gloves gloriously gilded and engraved at the edge
With beads of ruby, bright to behold;
With hunting hound and sword and no other man,
He hastes over a wide mead, with rage in his heart.
He steps softly over a path by the still wood's edge,
And halts on a high road, brooding all alone.
Off in the sunrise he espies there approaching,
Proceeding toward Rome by the readiest way,
A man in a coarse cloak, with clothes rather loose,   3470
With hat and high boots, humble and round;
With flat farthings the man was flourished all over,
And many rags and tatters hung at his hems;
With pouch and with mantle and scallop shells in plenty,
And with staff and with palm, a pilgrim he seemed.
    The man greeted him readily and bade him good morn,

And the king himself, proudly, in the language of Rome,
In Latin all rude he addresses him grandly:
"Where do you wish to go, sir, wandering all alone?
I think it a danger when the world is at war.   3480
Hidden in that vineyard is a foe with his host;
If they see you, I swear, sorrow befalls you;
Unless you have safe-conduct from the king himself,
Knaves will slay you and seize what you have;
And if you keep to the high road, they will catch you as well,
Unless you get help at once from his gallant knights."
        Then Sir Cradok speaks up straight to the king:
"I shall forgive him my death, so help me God,
The lowest groom under Heaven who walks the ground.
Let the fiercest come forth who follows the king: 3490
I shall face him like a knight—may Christ take my soul.
For you will never seize me, or take me yourself,
Though in splendid robes you be richly arrayed;
And for no war will I turn from traveling where I wish,
Nor for no man of this world made on this earth.
But I shall pass in pilgrimage at this pace unto Rome,
To get me a pardon from the Pope himself,
And of the penalties of Purgatory be perfectly absolved.
Then I shall go straight in search of my sovereign lord,
King Arthur of England, that able man;   3500
For he is in this empire, so honest men tell me,
Warring in these eastern parts with his awesome knights."
        "Whence come you, keen man," cried the king then,
"That you know King Arthur and also his knights?
Were you ever in his court when he dwelt in his country?
Your speech is so familiar, it gladdens my heart.
Well are you come and with wisdom you search;
I know you as British knight by your bold speech."
        "I should know the king—he is my kinsman and lord,
And I was named in his court a knight of the chamber;   3510
Sir Cradok was I called in his splendid court,
Chieftain of Caerleon, next to the king.
Now I am harried from my homeland with distress at my heart,
And that castle is captured by barbarous men."
Then the fair king caught him up in his arms,
Threw off his kettle-helm and kissed him straightway,
Cried, "Welcome, Sir Cradok, so help me Christ!
Dear kinsman in blood, you turn my heart cold.
How fares it in Britain with all my brave men?
Are they slaughtered, or burnt, or sundered from life?   3520
Tell me fully what fate has befallen;
I need seek no credentials; I know you as true."
        "Sire, your regent is wicked and wild in his ways,
For he has wrought woe since you went away;
He has captured your castles and crowned himself king,
And raked in all the revenues of the Round Table.
He has carved up the kingdom, passed it round as he wished,
Proclaimed the Danes as dukes and earls,
And dispersed them far and wide to sack your cities;
Joined to Saracens and Saxons on every side,   3530
He has brought together a band of barbaric men,

Sovereigns of Surgenale and hirelings in hosts:
Picts and paynims and practiced knights,
From Ireland and Argyle—outlaw men;
All those louts are now lords who belong to the mountains,
And all have lordship and lands, as much as they like.
And there is Sir Childrik held up as a chieftain;
And that same brutal man is plaguing your people:
They rob your monks and ravish your nuns,
And he rides ready with his rout to ravage the poor;   3540
Humber to Hawick he has in his hand,
And all the country of Kent by covenant bequeathed—
All the lovely castles that belonged to the crown,
The groves, the grey woodlands, and rugged shores,
The same that Hengist and Horsa seized in their time.
At Southampton on the sea are seven score ships,
Freighted full of fierce folk from faraway lands,
To stand up to your army as soon as you strike.
But one more word straight, for you know not the worst:
He has wedded Guinevere and calls her his wife,   3550
And lives in the wild lands of the west marches,
And has got her with child, so say those who have seen.
Of all the men in this world may woe fall on him,
Regent unworthy to watch over women!
Thus has Sir Mordred ruined us all.
So I betook me over these peaks to tell you the truth."
        Then the worthy king, with wrath in his heart,
And with hapless grief, grew ghastly pale.
"By the Cross!" cries the king, "I shall pay him in kind!
He shall too soon repent all his ruinous works!"   3560
Sore wretchedly weeping he went to his tents,
And woefully the worthy king wakens his men,
Summoned with a clarion kings and all,
Calls them to council and makes known their plight:
        "I am treacherously betrayed despite all my true deeds;
All my labor lies in ruins, and I am left none the better.
Woe will befall the man who wrought this betrayal,
If I can only lay hold of him, as I am a true lord.
It is Mordred, the man whom I trusted most.
He has captured my castles and crowned himself king,   3570
With the riches and revenues of the Round Table;
He has made up his retinues of renegade wretches,
And carved up my kingdom for countless lords,
For hirelings and Saracens from all sorts of lands;
He has wedded Guinevere and calls her his wife,
And if a child has appeared, our plight is no better.
On the sea they have gathered seven score ships,
Full of foreign folk to fight none else but me.
So back to Britain the Great it behooves us to hasten,
To crush the man who has caused such grief."   3580

[Upon hearing of Mordred's treachery, Arthur hastens back to Britain and,
on the coast, engages in a sea battle with Mordred's heathen allies. Victorious, he turns now to Mordred (3581–3711).]

Gawain's Last Battle

Still the traitor lurks on land, with knights tried and true,
And to trumpets they trot up on steeds in their trappings,
And come in sight behind shields on the bright shore:
Mordred shrinks not for shame, but shows off with pride.
King Arthur and Gawain both turned toward those men,
Toward sixty thousand men who rode into view.
After the folk were felled, the floodtide had passed,
And there was such sludge in shoals so wide,
The king was loath to land in the low water; 3720
So he stayed on the sea for fear his horses would sink,
And to look after his liegemen and his loyal knights,
So that any lamed or lost would live if they could.
Then Sir Gawain the good seizes a galley,
And glides up at an inlet with his good men-at-arms;
When he landed, in his rage he rushed into the water,
Till he sank to his girdle, in all his gold garb.
He splashes up on the sound, right in sight of those lords,
All alone with his troop—my sorrow is the more.
With banners blazoned with his bearings, the best of his arms, 3730
He bounds up the embankment in his bright array;
He bids his flag-bearer, "Hie you in haste,
To that huge host that waits on the hill,
And I pledge you my word to be right at your heels;
See you shrink from no sword or glittering steel,
But lay low the lustiest and launch them from life!
Be not shaken by their show, but stand your ground.
You have borne my banners in battles so great;
We shall fell the false men—the Fiend have their souls!
Fight hard with this rout and the field shall be ours. 3740
If I overtake that traitor, woe will betide him,
Who contrived this treachery to my true lord;
From such a beginning can come little joy,
And from what in this skirmish is soon to be settled."
Now straightway these men strike out over the sand,
Assail those warriors and lay on their strokes,
Right through shining shield smite those men,
With lances soon split their gleaming spears;
Dire strokes they dealt with stabbing darts:
In the dew's damp many lie dead, 3750
Dukes and peers and new-dubbed knights—
The ablest of Denmark are undone forever.
Then madly those men slash mailcoats asunder,
And lay into the lustiest with cruel blows.
They press into the throng and thrust to the earth
Of the hardiest men, three hundred at once.
And Gawain, his blood boiling, could not hold back:
He grabs up a spear, gallops down on a man,
Who bore scarlet all splendid with droplets of silver,
And thrusts him through at the throat with his bloodthirsty blade, 3760
So the sharpened spear shatters to splinters,
And with that savage stroke, he sinks down to die.
The King of Gotland it was, a good man-at-arms;

And with that, his host all takes to its heels,
All routed for good by gallant knights.
Then they meet the middle ranks, which Mordred commands,
And our men gallop toward them—to their own grief.
For had Sir Gawain had the good luck to hold that green hill,
Doubt it not, he would have gained glory forever.
    But then Gawain, in fact, watches and waits   3770
To wreak his wrath on the wretch who has wrought this war,
And he moves toward Sir Mordred among all his men,
Along with the Montagues and other great lords.
Then Sir Gawain waxed wroth and with iron will
He levels a stout lance and lustily cries,
"Foul-bred bastard, the Fiend have your bones!
A curse on you, wretch, and all your false works!
You shall be dead and undone for your dire deeds,
Or I shall die this day, if destiny have it!"
    Then the foe, with a band of outlaw men,   3780
Drove into a corner our dauntless knights,
Whom that traitor had treacherously singled out himself.
Dukes of Denmark he swiftly disposes,
And Lithuanian leaders with legions in hosts
Surround our men with savage spears;
Hirelings and Saracens from all sorts of lands,
Sixty thousand men, precisely arrayed,
Thickly swarmed in on seven score knights,
Swiftly and slyly by those salt streams.
    Then Sir Gawain dropped tears from his grey eyes,   3790
Out of grief for his good men whom he had to guide:
He knew they were wounded and worn out with fighting,
And, what with anguish and woe, he was at his wit's end.
And then, sorrowing, he spoke with streaming tears:
"We are beset with Saracens from every side;
I sigh not for myself—so help me our Lord—
But to see us caught off guard, my grief is the more.
Be brave this day and yonder dukes shall be yours;
For our dear Lord's sake, dread no weapon now;
We shall finish our fight as faultless knights,   3800
And go on to endless bliss with angels unblemished.
Though we have unwittingly wasted ourselves,
We shall turn it all to good in the glory of Christ.
With the help of these Saracens I give you my word,
We shall feast with our Savior solemnly in Heaven;
In the presence of that peerless Prince above all,
With prophets and patriarchs and apostles most noble,
Before that glorious Face that fashioned us all.
He who ever yields him to yonder sons of jades,
While he still has life and breath and is unbowed by battle,   3810
May he never be saved or succored by Christ,
But may Satan send his soul straight down to Hell!"
    Then grimly Sir Gawain grips his weapon,
And toward that huge host he suddenly hastes,
Swiftly straightens the straps of his stout sword,
Thrusts forth his shield and shrinks back no longer;
All reckless and rabid he rushed in straight,
And bloodied the foe with furious blows,

Till all welled with blood where he rushed by.
And, though in great grief, he wavers but little,   3820
But wreaks, to his glory, the wrath of his lord.
He stabs steeds in the struggle and stalwart knights,
So stout men are left standing stone-dead in their stirrups.
He sunders strong steel, he slashes chainmail—
No men there could stop him, for his sense was distraught.
With the force of his fury he falls into a frenzy,
Assails and strikes down all who stand in his way.
No doomed man on earth ever had such a destiny!
Through the whole host he rushes headlong,
And wounds some of the hardiest who dwell on the earth.   3830
Lashing out like a lion, he slashes them through,
Lords and leaders, who are left in the dust.
Still Sir Gawain wavers but little with woe,
But fells the foe with fearsome strokes,
As if he willfully wished to do away with himself.
Wild and bewildered, he was out of his wits,
And, mad as a wild beast, he rushed on those nearest,
Till all wallowed in blood wherever he went;
Each man could take warning from the wounds of another.
    Then he moves in on Mordred among all his knights,   3840
Smote him mid-shield and thrust him through.
But the traitor swerved slightly from the sharp weapon,
And he slashed him in the ribs a six-inch span.
The shaft shivered and sank into that splendid knight,
So the spurting blood streamed clear to his shank,
And gleamed on his greave, burnished so bright.
They so struggle and shove, Mordred sprawls in the dust;
With the force of the lance, he lands on his shoulders
A furlong off, on the ground, all gruesomely wounded.
Gawain flew after him and flung himself flat;   3850
As his grief was fixed, so followed his fortune:
He whipped out a short knife, sheathed in silver,
And would have slit his throat through, but no chink chanced;
His hand slipped and slid aslant down the mail,
And the other one slyly slung him under.
With a sharp knife the traitor struck,
Through helm and head, up into the brain.
Thus Sir Gawain is gone, that good man-in-arms,
With no rescue at all—rue is the more.
Thus Sir Gawain is gone, who led so many others;   3860
From Gower to Guernsey, all the great lords,
From Glamorgan, from Wales, all worthy knights
With that grievous stroke nevermore will know joy.
    Then King Frederick of Friesland, in faith,
Questions that felon about our fierce knight:
"Knew you ever this knight in your noble land,
And of what kin he came? Declare now the truth.
What man was this with these glorious arms?
With this golden griffon, sprawled now on the ground?
He has grieved us greatly, so help me God;   3870
Struck down our strong men and distressed us full sore.
He was the boldest in battle that ever bore blade,
For he has stunned our troop and destroyed it forever."

Then Sir Mordred speaks with full fair words:
"He was unmatched on earth, sir, on my oath.
He was Gawain the good, most gracious of men,
And the greatest of knights who lived under God,
The man boldest of hand, most blessed in battle,
And the humblest in hall under all the wide heavens;
In leadership the lordliest as long as he lived,   3880
And lauded as a lion in lands far and wide;
Had you known him, sir king, in the country he came from,
His wisdom, his valor, his virtuous works,
His conduct, his courage, his exploits in arms,
You would weep for his death all the days of your life."
Then the traitor freely let fall his tears,
Turned away suddenly and spoke no more,
Rode off crying and cursed the hour
That ever his fate was written to work such woe.
It wrung his heart when he thought on this thing;   3890
For the sake of his blood-ties sorrowing he rides.
When that fugitive wretch recalled to himself
The glory and the good times of the Round Table,
He railed and he rued all his ruinous works.
He rode off with his rout and rested no longer,
In fear of our great king, if he chanced to come.
He hurries to Cornwall, heavy at heart,
Because of his kinsman, who lies cold on the shore.

                    *   *   *   *

When our worthy king learned that Gawain had landed,
He writhes wildly with woe, wringing his hands,   3920
And bids his boats be launched upon that low water.
He lands like a lion with his lordly knights,
Slides aslant into the sludge, straight up to his girdle,
And swiftly splashes ashore with his sword drawn,
Arrays his host and hoists his banners,
And hurries over the wide sand, with rage in his heart.
He dashes quickly to the field where the dead lie,
And, of the traitor's men on mailed mounts,
Truth to tell, a full ten thousand were lost;
And, I swear, on our side just seven score knights,   3930
Along with their leader, lifeless are left.
The king turned over carefully knights and all,
Earls of Africa and Austrian men,
From Argyle and Orkney, Irish kings,
The noblest of Norway, numbers most great,
Dukes of Denmark and new-dubbed knights,
And the Gotland king, in the bright arms,
Who lies groaning on the ground, gored straight through.
The royal king ransacks, with rue in his heart,
And hunts for the heroes of the Round Table,   3940
Spots them all in a heap, apart by themselves,
With mangled Saracens encircled all about,
And Sir Gawain the good, in his glorious arms
Sprawled face down and clutching the grass,
His banners struck down, emblazoned with scarlet,

His blade and his broad shield all bathed in blood.
Never was our goodly king so heavy at heart,
And nothing smote him so sore as that sight itself.
    The good king gazes and grieves in his heart,
Gruesomely groans through grinding tears,   3950
Knelt down to the body, caught it up in his arms,
Cast up his visor and kissed him at once,
Looked at his eyelids that now were locked fast,
His lips like lead and his face white,
And with that, the crowned king cries out aloud,
"Beloved kinsman in blood, cursed am I left;
For now my glory is gone and all my wars ended.
Here lies my promise of ease, my prowess in arms;
My heart and my strength hung wholly on him.
My counselor, my comfort, who carried all my hopes,   3960
King of all knights that lived under Christ,
You were worthy to be king, though I wore the crown.
My good and my glory throughout all this great world
Were won through Sir Gawain, through his wisdom alone.
Alas!" cries King Arthur. "Now swells my sorrow!
I am undone utterly in my own lands.
Ah, dire, dread death, you drag out too long.
Why draw on at such length? You ravage my heart!"
The good king, stricken, sinks into a swoon;
But he staggers up suddenly and kisses him fondly,   3970
Till his thick beard was all bathed in blood,
As if he had butchered beasts and dispatched them from life.
Had not Sir Ewain arrived and other great lords,
His great heart would have burst with grief then and there.
    "Have done!" cried these bold men; "you are losing your reason;
This is bottomless woe, for it will never be better;
It is not worthy, in truth, to be wringing your hands;
To weep like a woman is not deemed wise.
Be manly of mien, as a king must,
And cease this clamor, for love of Christ above!"   3980
"By Christ's blood," cried the king, "cease shall I never!
Till my brain or my breast burst all to bits!
Never did such sharp sorrow sink into my heart,
And grief is close kin to me—my care is the more.
Never was so sorrowful a sight seen by my eyes;
Unsullied, he is destroyed, and all for my sins."
    Down knelt the king and cried aloud;
With careworn countenance he calls out these words:
"Oh great, righteous God, look down on this grief!
See this royal, red blood run over the ground!   3990
It is fit to be shrouded and enshrined in gold,
For it is unstained by sin, so save me our Lord!"
Down knelt the sovereign with sorrow in his heart,
Caught it up carefully in his clean hands,
Placed it in a kettle-helm and covered it fast,
And rode forth with the body toward the place of his birth.
"Here and now I give my oath," cried the king then,
"To Christ and to Mary, Heaven's merciful Queen,
Never again shall I hunt or unleash my hounds,
At any roe or deer that runs about on the earth,   4000

Never let sprint my greyhound or let hunt my hawk,
Nor never see fowl felled that flies upon wing,
Neither falcon nor formel hold on my fist,
Never again with jarfalcon rejoice me on earth,
Nor reign in royal splendor, nor call my Round Table,
Till your death, dear one, be duly avenged.
But ever I'll languish and mourn as long as I live,
Till God and dread death have done their desire!"

[Arthur has Gawain's body conveyed to Winchester and orders it to remain
unburied until he has slain the traitor Mordred (4009-4059).]

Arthur's Last Battle

Now his enemy emerges from out the wood's edge,   4060
With hordes of aliens, awesome to see;
Sir Mordred the Malebranch and a myriad men
Issue out of the forest on every side,
In seven big battalions, precisely arrayed:
Sixty thousand men—the sight was staggering—
All fighting folk from faraway lands,
Tightly formed up in the front line, along those fresh streams.
And all Arthur's army added up, in knights,
To just eight hundred men in all, entered in the rolls.
This was no even match—except for Christ's might—   4070
To take on that multitude in those open lands.
   Then the royal king of the Round Table
Rides round on a fine steed and readies his men:
Arranged his vanguard as he knew best,
And Sir Ewain and Sir Eric and other great lords
Manfully manage the middle-flank next,
With Merrak and Meneduke, mighty of strength;
Idrus and Alimere, able knights both,
Go along with Arthur, with seven score men;
He quickly arrayed his rearguard next,   4080
The rough-and-readiest men of the Round Table.
Thus he fits out his folk and shouts his defiance,
And fires up his men with fearless words:
"I beseech you, sirs, for the sake of our Lord,
That you do well today and dread you no weapon.
Fight fiercely now, and defend yourselves well,
Fell yonder doomed folk and the field shall be ours.
They are Saracens, this lot; may they soon be undone!
Lay into them lustily, for love of our Lord!
If we be destined to die today on this ground,   4090
We shall be hauled up to Heaven before we be half cold.
See you fail in no way to perform like lords:
Lay low this foe before the game finish.
Have no heed of me: hold me of no matter,
But tend to my banners with your bright blades,
So they be amply surrounded by stout men-at-arms,
And held grandly on high for all to behold;
If any man rip them down, rescue them straight;

Now work to my glory, for today my war ends.
You have shared my wealth and my woe, now work to your credit;   4100
May Christ crowned in glory comfort you all,
The noblest creatures that ever a king led.
I bestow on you all my blessing with a blithe heart,
And on all brave Britons—may you find bliss."
    They strike out at sunrise and proceed toward the foe;
Esteemed men and noble put their strength to the test;
Boldly the buglers blazon the trumpets
And cornets grandly, as knights come together.
Thus boldly these brave knights ride out to battle;
A nobler day there never was known,   4110
As when these Britons bravely buckled on shields,
Crossed them as Christians and couched their spears.

*   *   *   *

    Then Sir Mordred the Malebranch and a great mass of men
Engage our middle-rank and grapple together;
He had hidden in the rear, within the wood's edge,
With a whole host on the heath—woe is the more.
He had watched that clash clear to the end,
How our knights had fared by fortune in arms;
He knew our folk were fought out and fated to fall,
And he swiftly decides now to set on the king.   4180
But that churl's son had changed his charge:
His engrailed cross he had cast aside, I swear,
And instead seized three lions of burnished bright silver,
Passant on scarlet, richly studded with stones,
So the king might not know the cunning wretch.
On account of his cowardice he cast off his garb,
But our sovereign spotted him right from the start,
And spoke to Sir Cador these timely words:
"I see the traitor come yonder trotting all hot;
Yonder lord with the lions is like him exactly;   4190
Grief will befall him, if I seize him just once,
For all his treason and treachery, as I am a true lord!
Today Clarent and Caliburn, blade to blade, shall make clear
Which is cleaner of cut or keener of edge;
We shall size up fine steel against fine garb.
It was my great pride, so preciously prized;
It was kept for crownings of sanctified kings;
And on days when I dubbed dukes and earls,
It was borne in procession by the bright hilt;
I never ventured to damage it in deeds of arms,   4200
But kept it ever perfect, at my own pleasure.
Now that I see Clarent uncased, that crown of all swords,
My vault at Wallingford, I know well, is laid waste:
No one knew of that site, but Guinevere herself;
She herself had safekeeping of that splendid blade
And of sealed coffers that belong to the crown,
Holding rings and relics and the Regal of France,
That were found on Sir Frollo, when he was felled on the field."
    Then Sir Marrik, maddened, takes on Mordred straightway,
With a battered mace smites with full might and main;   4210

The edge of his helm he hews asunder,
So the bright red blood ran down his mail.
Mordred pulls back in pain, and his face goes all pale;
He turns at bay like a boar and brutally strikes:
He whipped out the sword that shone like silver,
That was Arthur's own, and Uther, his father's,
And in the vault at Wallingford was wont to be kept,
And with it the dread dog dealt such dire dints
That the other drew far back and dared do no more;
For Sir Marrik was a man scarred by age,   4220
And Sir Mordred was mighty and at the peak of his powers.
None came within range, knight nor other,
Of the sweep of that sword, but surrendered lifeblood.
        Our prince saw this and pressed on fast,
Pushed into the fray with full brute force,
Countered Sir Mordred and scornfully cried,
"Turn, untrue traitor; no more shall you thrive.
By the great God, you shall die by dint of my hands!
No man shall rescue you, nor all the riches on earth!"
And the king with Caliburn heroically smites: 4230
The corners of his shining shield shears right through,
Straight into the shoulder a six-inch span,
So the bright red blood gleamed on the mail.
Mordred shivered and shuddered, but shrank only little;
Then bounded back boldly in his bright garb;
The felon with that fine sword fiercely struck,
And the flesh on the far flank he slashes asunder.
Straight through surcoat and hauberk of splendid mail
He flaps open the flesh a half-foot span.
That dread blow was Arthur's death-wound—dole is the more   4240
That ever the gallant have to die except at God's will.
        Still with his sword Caliburn bravely he strikes,
Thrusts forth shining shield and shelters him well,
And swipes off Mordred's sword hand as he sweeps by!
An inch from the elbow he cleft it clean off—
So Mordred sprawls on the sod and sinks into a faint—
Through armplate of bright steel and shining chainmail,
So both hilt and hand lie on the heath.
Then in a flash he heaves that fiend to his feet,
Runs him through with his blade right to the bright hilt,   4250
So he sprawls on the sword and sinks down to his death.
"In faith," cries the doomed king, "it pains me sore,
For such a false felon to have so fair an end."
When they finished this fight, the field was won,
And the false folk on the field were left to their fate;
To a forest some fled and fell down in the thickets,
But our fierce fighting folk followed right after:
They hunted and hewed down the heathen hounds;
They finished off, in those mountains, Sir Mordred's knights;
No knight got away there, leader or other: 4260
They were cut down on the run—rue is the less.
        But when Arthur erelong comes on Sir Ewain,
And Eric the gracious and other great lords,
He clasped Sir Cador with grief in his heart,
And Sir Clegis and Sir Cleremond, keen men-in-arms,

Sir Lot and Sir Lionel, Sir Lancelot and Lowes,
Marrik and Meneduke, who ever were mighty;
Grieving, he lays them together in the glade,
Looked on their bodies and with a loud voice,
Like a man loath to live, who has lost all his joys,   4270
He stammers, distracted, and all his strength fails;
He casts his eyes to the heavens, and all his hue fades,
Down he sinks suddenly and falls in a swoon;
But he struggled to his knees and sorrowed over and over:
    "King crowned in glory, in care am I left.
All my lordliness down in the dust is laid low!
You who gave me gifts by Your own grace,
Upheld my honor by the might of their hands,
Made me honored near and far, the overlord of earth,
In a wicked time this woe was wrought,   4280
That, through a traitor, all my true lords are destroyed.
Here rests the royal blood of the Round Table,
Undone by a dog—dole is the more!
I can only make my home alone and hopeless on a heath,
Like a woeful widow in want of her man,
Waste away and weep and wring my hands,
For my greatness and my glory are all gone forever,
And I take leave of all lordship for what life I have left.
Here the blood of the Britons has been parted from life,
And here with this battle ends all my bliss."   4290
    Then the ranks of the Round Table all rally round;
To their royal king they ride all together;
Seven score knights assemble most swiftly,
In front of their sovereign, who lies there stricken.
The crowned king then kneels and cries out aloud,
"I gratefully thank Thee, God, for Thy grace,
That gave us strength and skill to surmount these men,
And has granted us the victory over these great lords.
He never sent us shame or stain on this earth,
But mastery evermore over all other monarchs.   4300
We have no leisure now to look out for our lords,
For that loathsome brute has gruesomely lamed me.
Let us go to Glastonbury—nothing else will do now—
Where we may peacefully rest and care for our wounds.
For this lofty day's labor, praise be to the Lord,
Though He has destined and doomed me to die all alone."
    Then at once they wholeheartedly heed his behest,
And proceed toward Glastonbury by the readiest route,
Reach the Isle of Avalon, and Arthur alights,
And goes to a manor there—he could move on no further.   4310
A surgeon of Salerno searches his wounds,
And the king sees from this he will never be sound,
And soon to his steadfast men he speaks these words:
"Do call me a confessor with Christ in his hands;
I must have the Host quickly, whatever else chance.
My kinsman Constantine shall wear the crown,
In keeping with his kinship, if Christ will allow it.
Sir, if you prize my blessing, bury those lords
Who in that struggle with swords were sundered from life;
And then sternly mark that Mordred's children   4320

Be secretly slain and slung into the seas:
Let no wicked weed in this world take root and thrive—
I warn you, by your worth, work as I bid.
I forgive all offenses, for Christ's love in Heaven:
If Guinevere has fared well, fair fortune be with her."
With all his strength, "Into Thy hands . . . ," he said with his last breath,
And gave up his spirit and spoke nevermore.
    The royal blood of Britain then, bishops and all,
Proceed toward Glastonbury, with hearts full of grief,
To bury the brave king and bring him back to the earth,   4330
With all the honor and majesty that any man could have.
Loudly bells they ring and requiem sing,
Intone masses and matins with mournful notes;
Monastics arrayed in their richest robes,
Pontiffs and prelates in precious attire,
Dukes and peers, all dressed in mourning,
Countesses kneeling and clasping their hands,
Ladies forlorn and mournful to look at,
One and all were draped in black, damsels and all,
Who appeared at that sepulcher with streaming tears;   4340
A more sorrowful sight was never seen in their time.
    Thus ends King Arthur, so authors declare,
Of the blood of Hector, the King of Troy's son,
And of Sir Priam the Prince, praised all the earth over;
From Troy the Britons brought all his brave forebears
Into Britain the Greater, so says the *Brut*.

chapter VIII

SIR THOMAS MALORY:
LE MORTE DARTHUR

Laila Zamuelis Gross

Sir Thomas Malory's work *Le Morte Darthur* is probably most responsible for the continued fascination with the romance of Arthur. Although much of a sensational nature has been written about Malory, actually we know only three things about him, and these he tells us himself. He was a knight; he was a prisoner; he "ended" his huge undertaking in 1469, since he specifies the ninth year of the reign of Edward IV.

William Caxton printed *Le Morte Darthur* on July 31, 1485, on his press at Westminster. It is not certain that Caxton commissioned the book or that he even knew Malory. In his preface Caxton presents this book that "treateth of the noble actes, feates of armes of chyvalrye, prowesse, hardynesse, humanyté, love, curtosye, and veray gentylnesse, wyth many wonderful hystoryes and adventures."

The work has been read continuously since then—often with disdain— and it has been refashioned, redone, updated, translated, abridged, and in the nineteenth century even "cleaned up." Yet it has survived magnificently. Though many of these changes and liberties seem unfortunate and even strange, the fact that *Le Morte Darthur* has been reworked so continuously is the strongest testimony to its vitality. (One of the last retellings—John Steinbeck's—rightly was a bestseller.) These "redoings" in a way could be considered natural and appropriate, because what Malory himself did was to translate, abridge, change, and unify long, disparate works, to which he simply refers as the "French book." (Actually one of his sources is English: the *Alliterative Morte Arthure* of which a portion is included in this anthology.)

In the nineteenth century, though read and reworked, Malory was not really appreciated. Oskar H. Sommer in 1889–91 gave us the first edition of the text Caxton had printed. In 1934, however, a fifteenth-century manuscript of Malory differing from Caxton was discovered in the Fellows

Library at Winchester College. The great find had a brilliant scholar—Eugène Vinaver—to edit it. Vinaver's edition, first published in 1947 by the Oxford University Press, helped Malory's genius to be fully recognized at last, and since then critical acclaim of *Le Morte Darthur* has continued to grow. The critical approaches and appraisals have been, understandably, varied, contradictory, and fascinating; the bibliographic note below points to some of them.

The choices of what to include in this anthology from the "whole book" that Malory wrote have been difficult. Ideally, one should read the whole, and that in the original. The first part of what Vinaver titled "Merlin" is included because it seemed that an anthology called *The Romance of Arthur* should offer the tale of Arthur's birth and coronation. "Balin" is in many respects a self-contained tale and interesting for that reason alone. Furthermore, it foreshadows and explains some mysterious features of the "Sangrail"—the Holy Grail. It is also a story full of strange incidents and haunting lines, such as the words spoken by Balin before he kills and is killed by his brother, each unknown to the other: ". . . and so he heard an horn blow as it had been the death of a beast. 'That blast,' said Balin, 'is blown for me, for I am the prize, and yet am I not dead.'" In these words are found both the mystery, and at the same time the explicitness, of Malory. The last section of the work could not be omitted: here Malory has complete command of the story and his inimitable style. It tells of the passing of Arthur and his return as they are told nowhere else. As Benson writes, ". . . the tone of *The Death of Arthur* . . . is one of forgiveness, of final joy, and it shows the ultimate triumph of virtue over vice, if not in the world at large at least in the protagonists themselves" (*Malory's "Morte Darthur,"* p. 235).

Bibliographic note: The text used here is based on Oskar H. Sommer's edition of Caxton (Nutt, 1889–91). The copy of Caxton in the Morgan Library, New York, has also been consulted, as has Rhys's modernization (Dutton, 1906). The spelling is modernized. Words whose meanings have changed are glossed in square brackets the first few times they occur. Also in square brackets are words needed for the sense.

A full bibliography on Malory is Page West Life's *Sir Thomas Malory and the "Morte Darthur": A Survey of Scholarship and Annotated Bibliography* (University of Virginia, 1980). Important critical studies are surveyed in Larry D. Benson's essay "Le Morte Darthur," in *Critical Approaches to Six Major English Works*, edited by Robert M. Lumiansky and Herschel Baker (University of Pennsylvania, 1968). Readers should also consult P.J.C. Field's *Romance and Chronicle: A Study of Malory's Prose Style* (University of Indiana, 1971) and the collection edited by Toshiyuki Takamiya and Derek Brewer, *Aspects of Malory* (Rowman and Littlefield, 1981), as well as Benson, *Malory's "Morte Darthur"* (Harvard University, 1976), Lumiansky, ed., *Malory's Originality* (Johns Hopkins University, 1964), and Edmund Reiss, *Sir Thomas Malory* (Twayne, 1966). An especially important source is Eugène Vinaver's three-volume edition of the Winchester manuscript, with notes (Oxford, 1947; 2nd edition, 1967).

Le Morte Darthur

I. The Birth and Rise of King Arthur

It befell in the days of Uther Pendragon, when he was king of all England and so reigned, that there was a mighty duke in Cornwall that held war against him long time. And the duke was called the Duke of Tintagel. And so by means King Uther sent for this duke, charging him to bring his wife with him, for she was called a fair lady, and a passing wise, and her name was called Igraine.

So when the duke and his wife were come unto the king, by the means of great lords they were accorded both. The king liked and loved this lady well, and he made them great cheer out of measure, and desired to have lain by her. But she was a passing good woman, and would not assent unto the king. And then she told the duke her husband, and said, "I suppose that we were sent for that I should be dishonoured; wherefore, husband, I counsel you that we depart from hence suddenly, that we may ride all night unto our own castle." And in like wise as she said, so they departed, that neither the king nor none of his council were [a]ware of their departing.

All so soon as King Uther knew of their departing so suddenly, he was wonderly wroth. Then he called to him his privy council and told them of the sudden departing of the duke and his wife. Then they asked the king to send for the duke and his wife by a great charge: "And if he will not come at your summons, then may ye do your best; then have ye cause to make mighty war upon him." So that was done, and the messengers had their answers, and that was this shortly: that neither he nor his wife would not come at him. Then was the king wonderly wroth. And then the king sent him plain word again, and bade him be ready and stuff [equip] him and garnish [furnish] him; for within forty days he would fetch him out of the biggest castle that he had.

When the duke had this warning, anon he went and furnished and garnished two strong castles of his, of the which the one hight [was called] Tintagel, and the other castle hight Terrabil. So his wife Dame Igraine he put in the castle of Tintagel, and himself he put in the castle of Terrabil, the which had many issues and posterns out.

Then in all haste came Uther with a great host and laid a siege about the castle of Terrabil. And there he pyght [pitched] many pavilions, and there was great war made on both parties, and much people slain. Then for pure anger and for great love of fair Igraine the King Uther fell sick. So came to the King Uther, Sir Ulfius, a noble knight, and asked the king why he was sick. "I shall tell thee," said the king. "I am sick for anger and for love of fair Igraine that I may not be whole."

"Well, my lord," said Sir Ulfius, "I shall seek Merlin, and he shall do you remedy, that your heart shall be pleased."

So Ulfius departed, and by adventure he met Merlin in a beggar's array, and then Merlin asked Ulfius whom he sought. And he said he had little ado to tell him. "Well," said Merlin, "I know whom thou seekest, for thou seekest Merlin; therefore seek no farther, for I am he, and if King Uther will well reward me, and be sworn unto me to fulfill my desire, that shall be his honour and profit more than mine, for I shall cause him to have all his desire."

"All this will I undertake," said Ulfius, "that there shall be nothing reasonable but thou shalt have thy desire."

"Well," said Merlin, "he shall have his intent and desire. And therefore," said Merlin, "ride on your way, for I will not be long behind."

Then Ulfius was glad, and rode on more than a pace till that he came to King Uther Pendragon, and told him he had met with Merlin. "Where is he?" said the king. "Sir," said Ulfius, "he will not dwell long." Therewithal Ulfius was ware where Merlin stood at the porch of the pavilion's door. And then Merlin was bound to come to the king. When King Uther saw him, he said he was welcome. "Sir," said Merlin, "I know all your heart [in] every deal. So [if] ye will be sworn unto me as ye be a true king anointed to fulfill my desire, ye shall have your desire."

Then the king was sworn upon the four Evangelists. "Sir," said Merlin, "this is my desire: the first night that ye shall lie by Igraine, ye shall get a child on her, and when that is born, that it shall be delivered to me for to nourish there as I will have it. For it shall be your worship, and the child's avail as mickle as the child is worth." "I will well," said the king, "as thou wilt have it."

"Now make you ready," said Merlin; "this night ye shall lie with Igraine in the castle of Tintagel, and ye shall be like the duke her husband; Ulfius shall be like Sir Brastias, a knight of the duke's; and I will be like a knight that hight Sir Jordans, a knight of the duke's. But wait ye make not many questions with her nor her men, but say ye are diseased [tired], and so hie you to bed, and rise not on the morn till I come to you, for the castle of Tintagel is but ten miles hence." So this was done as they devised.

But the duke of Tintagel espied how the king rode from the siege of Terrabil, and therefore that night he issued out of the castle at a postern for to have distressed the king's host. And so, through his own issue, the duke himself was slain or-ever [before] the king came at the castle of Tintagel. So after the death of the duke, King Uther lay with Igraine more than three hours after his death, and begat on her that night Arthur, and or day came, Merlin came to the king and bade him make him ready, and so he kissed the lady Igraine and departed in all haste. But when the lady heard tell of the duke her husband, and by all record he was dead or-ever King Uther came to her, then she marvelled who that might be that lay with her in likeness of her lord. So she mourned privily and held her peace.

Then all the barons by one assent prayed the king of accord betwixt the lady Igraine and him; the king gave them leave, for fain would he have been accorded with her. So the king put all the trust in Ulfius to entreat between them; so by the entreaty at the last the king and she met together. "Now will we do well," said Ulfius; "our king is a lusty knight and wifeless, and my lady Igraine is a passing fair lady; it were great joy unto us all, an [if] it might please the king to make her his queen." Unto that they all well accorded and moved it to the king. And anon, like a lusty knight, he assented thereto with good will, and so in all haste they were married in a morning with great mirth and joy.

And King Lot of Lothian and of Orkney then wedded Margawse, that was Gawain's mother, and King Nentres of the land of Garlot wedded Elaine. All this was done at the request of King Uther. And the third sister, Morgan le Fay, was put to school in a nunnery, and there she learned so much that she was a great clerk of necromancy, and after she was wedded to King Urien of the land of Gore, that was Sir Ywain's le Blanchemain's father.

Then Queen Igraine waxed daily greater and greater, so it befell after within half a year, as King Uther lay by his queen, he asked her, by the faith she owed to him, whose was the child within her body; then was she sore abashed to give answer. "Dismay you not," said the king, "but tell me the truth, and I shall love you the better, by the faith of my body."

"Sir," said she, "I shall tell you the truth. The same night that my lord was dead, the hour of his death, as his knights record, there came into my castle of Tintagel a man like my lord in speech and in countenance, and two knights with him in likeness of his two knights Brastias and Jordans, and so I went unto bed with him as I ought to do with my lord, and the same night, as I shall answer unto God, this child was begotten upon me."

"That is truth," said the king, "as ye say; for it was I myself that came in the likeness, and therefore dismay you not, for I am father of the child." And there he told her all the cause, how it was by Merlin's counsel. Then the queen made great joy when she knew who was the father of her child.

Soon came Merlin unto the king, and said, "Sir, ye must purvey you for the nourishing of your child." "As thou wilt," said the king, "be it." "Well," said Merlin, "I know a lord of yours in this land, that is a passing true man and a faithful, and he shall have the nourishing of your child, and his name is Sir Ector, and he is a lord of fair livelihood in many parts in England and Wales. And this lord, Sir Ector, let him be sent for, for to come and speak with you, and desire him yourself, as he loveth you, that he will put his own child to nourishing to another woman, and that his wife nourish yours. And when the child is born, let it be delivered to me at yonder privy postern unchristened."

So like as Merlin devised, it was done. And when Sir Ector was come, he made fyaunce [promise] to the king for to nourish the child like as the king desired. And there the king granted Sir Ector great rewards. Then when the lady was delivered, the king commanded two knights and two ladies to take the child, bound in a cloth of gold: "and that ye deliver him to what poor man ye meet at the postern gate of the castle." So the child was delivered unto Merlin, and so he bare it forth unto Sir Ector, and made an holy man to christen him, and named him Arthur; and so Sir Ector's wife nourished him with her own pap.

Then within two years King Uther fell sick of a great malady. And in the meanwhile his enemies usurped upon him, and did a great battle upon his men, and slew many of his people. "Sir," said Merlin, "ye may not lie so as ye do, for ye must to the field though ye ride on an horse-litter. For ye shall never have the better of your enemies but if your person be there, and then shall ye have the victory."

So it was done as Merlin had devised, and they carried the king forth in an horse-litter with a great host towards his enemies. And at St. Albans there met with the king a great host of the North. And that day Sir Ulfius and Sir Brastias did great deeds of arms, and King Uther's men overcame the Northern battle and slew many people, and put the remnant to flight. And then the king returned unto London, and made great joy of his victory.

And then he fell passing sore sick, so that three days and three nights he was speechless; wherefore all the barons made great sorrow, and asked Merlin what counsel were best. "There is none other remedy," said Merlin, "but God will have his will. But look ye, all barons, be before King Uther to-morn, and God and I shall make him to speak."

So on the morn all the barons with Merlin came before the king. Then Merlin said aloud unto King Uther, "Sir, shall your son Arthur be king after your days of this realm with all the appurtenance?"

Then Uther Pendragon turned him, and said in hearing of them all: "I give him God's blessing and mine, and bid him pray for my soul, and righteously and worshipfully that he claim the crown upon forfeiture of my blessing." And therewith he yielded up the ghost, and then was he interred as [be]longed to a king. Wherefore the queen, fair Igraine, made great sorrow, and all the barons.

Then stood the realm in great jeopardy long while, for every lord that was mighty of men made him strong, and many weened [thought] to have been king. Then Merlin went to the Archbishop of Canterbury, and counselled him for to send for all the lords of the realm and all the gentlemen of arms, that they should to London come by Christmas, upon pain of cursing. And for this cause: that Jesus, that was born on that night, that he would of his great mercy show some miracle, as he was come to be king of mankind, for to show some miracle who should be rightways king of this realm.

So the Archbishop, by the advice of Merlin, sent for all the lords and gentlemen of arms that they should come by Christmas even unto London. And many of them made them clean of their life, that their prayer might be the more acceptable unto God. So in the greatest church of London— whether it were Paul's or not, the French book maketh no mention—all the estates were long or [ere] day in the church for to pray.

And when matins and the first mass was done, there was seen in the churchyard, against the high altar, a great stone four-square, like unto a marble stone, and in midst thereof was like an anvil of steel a foot on high, and therein stuck a fair sword naked by the point, and letters there were written in gold about the sword that said thus: WHOSO PULLETH OUT THIS SWORD OF THIS STONE AND ANVIL, IS RIGHTWISE KING BORN OF ALL ENGLAND. Then the people marvelled, and told it to the Archbishop.

"I command," said the Archbishop, "that ye keep you within your church, and pray unto God still; that no man touch the sword till the high mass be all done." So when all masses were done, all the lords went to behold the stone and the sword. And when they saw the scripture, some assayed [tried], such as would have been king. But none might stir the sword nor move it.

"He is not here," said the Archbishop, "that shall achieve the sword, but doubt not God will make him known. But this is my counsel," said the Archbishop, "that we let purvey ten knights, men of good fame, and they to keep this sword." So it was ordained, and then there was made a cry, that every man should assay that would, for to win the sword. And upon New Year's Day, the barons let make a joust and a tournament, that all knights that would joust or tourney there might play, and all this was ordained for to keep the lords and the commons together, for the Archbishop trusted that God would make him known that should win the sword.

So upon New Year's Day, when the service was done, the barons rode unto the field, some to joust and some to tourney, and so it happened that Sir Ector, that had great livelihood about London, rode unto the jousts, and with him rode Sir Kay his son, and young Arthur that was his nourished brother; and Sir Kay was made knight at All Hallowmas afore. So as they rode to the joustsward, Sir Kay had lost his sword, for he had left it at his father's lodging, and so he prayed young Arthur for to ride for his sword.

"I will well," said Arthur, and rode fast after the sword; and when he came home, the lady and all were out to see the jousting. Then was Arthur wroth, and said to himself, "I will ride to the churchyard, and take the sword with me that sticketh in the stone, for my brother Sir Kay shall not be without a sword this day." So when he came to the churchyard, Sir Arthur alit and tied his horse to the stile, and so he went to the tent, and found no knights there, for they were at jousting. And so he handled the sword by the handles, and lightly and fiercely pulled it out of the stone, and took his horse and rode his way until he came to his brother Sir Kay and delivered him the sword.

And as soon as Sir Kay saw the sword, he wist [knew] well it was the sword of the stone, and so he rode to his father Sir Ector, and said: "Sir, lo here is the sword of the stone; wherefore I must be king of this land." When Sir Ector beheld the sword, he returned again and came to the church, and there they alit all three, and went into the church. And anon he made Sir Kay to swear upon a book how he came to that sword. "Sir," said Sir Kay, "by my brother Arthur, for he brought it to me."

"How gat ye this sword?" said Sir Ector to Arthur.

"Sir, I will tell you. When I came home for my brother's sword, I found nobody at home to deliver me his sword, and so I thought my brother Sir Kay should not be swordless, and so I came hither eagerly and pulled it out of the stone without any pain."

"Found ye any knights about this sword?" said Sir Ector. "Nay," said Arthur. "Now," said Sir Ector to Arthur, "I understand ye must be king of this land." "Wherefore I," said Arthur, "and for what cause?" "Sir," said Ector, "for God will have it so, for there should never man have drawn out this sword, but he that shall be rightways king of this land. Now let me see whether ye can put the sword there as it was, and pull it out again." "That is no mastery," said Arthur, and so he put it in the stone. Therewithal Sir Ector assayed to pull out the sword and failed.

"Now assay," said Sir Ector unto Sir Kay. And anon he pulled at the sword with all his might, but it would not be. "Now shall ye assay," said Sir Ector to Arthur. "I will well," said Arthur, and pulled it out easily. And therewithal Sir Ector knelt down to the earth, and Sir Kay.

"Alas," said Arthur, "my own dear father and brother, why kneel ye to me?"

"Nay, nay, my lord Arthur, it is not so. I was never your father nor of your blood, but I wot [know] well ye are of an higher blood than I weened [thought] ye were." And then Sir Ector told him all: how he was betaken [entrusted with] him for to nourish him, and by whose commandment, and by Merlin's deliverance. Then Arthur made great dole when he understood that Sir Ector was not his father. "Sir," said Ector unto Arthur, "will ye be my good and gracious lord when ye are king?"

"Else were I to blame," said Arthur, "for ye are the man in the world that I am most beholden to, and my good lady and mother your wife, that as well as her own hath fostered me and kept. And if ever it be God's will that I be king as ye say, ye shall desire of me what I may do, and I shall not fail you. God forbid I should fail you."

"Sir," said Sir Ector, "I will ask no more of you, but that ye will make my son, your foster brother, Sir Kay, seneschal of all your lands."

"That shall be done," said Arthur, "and more, by the faith of my body, that never man shall have that office but he, while he and I live."

Therewithal they went unto the Archbishop, and told him how the sword was achieved, and by whom; and on Twelfth Day all the barons came thither, and to assay to take the sword, who that would assay. But there afore them all, there might none take it out but Arthur. Wherefore there were many lords wroth, and said it was great shame unto them all and the realm, to be over-governed with a boy of no high blood born; and so they fell out at that time, that it was put off till Candlemas, and then all the barons should meet there again. But always the ten knights were ordained to watch the sword day and night, and so they set a pavilion over the stone and the sword, and five always watched.

So at Candlemas many more great lords came thither for to have won the sword, but there might none prevail. And right as Arthur did at Christmas, he did at Candlemas, and pulled out the sword easily, whereof the barons were sore aggrieved and put it off in delay till the high feast of Easter. And as Arthur sped [succeeded] before, so did he at Easter, yet there were some of the great lords had indignation that Arthur should be king, and put it off in a delay till the feast of Pentecost. Then the Archbishop of Canterbury by Merlin's providence let purvey then of the best knights that they might get, and such knights as Uther Pendragon loved best and most trusted in his days. And such knights were put about Arthur as Sir Baudwin of Britain, Sir Kay, Sir Ulfius, Sir Brastias. All these with many other were always about Arthur, day and night, till the feast of Pentecost.

And at the feast of Pentecost all manner of men assayed to pull at the sword that would assay, but none might prevail but Arthur, and pulled it out afore all the lords and commons that were there; wherefore all the commons cried at once: "We will have Arthur unto our king. We will put him no more in delay, for we all see that it is God's will that he shall be our king; and who that holdeth against it, we will slay him." And therewith they all kneeled at once, both rich and poor, and cried Arthur mercy because they had delayed him so long; and Arthur forgave them, and took the sword between both his hands, and offered it upon the altar where the Archbishop was, and so was he made knight of the best man that was there.

And so anon was the coronation made. And there was he sworn unto his lords and the commons for to be a true king, to stand with true justice from thenceforth the days of this life. Also then he made all lords that held of the crown to come in, and to do service as they ought to do. And many complaints were made unto Sir Arthur of great wrongs that were done since the death of King Uther, of many lands that were bereaved lords, knights, ladies, and gentlemen. Wherefore King Arthur made the lands to be given again unto them that owned them. When this was done (that the king had stablished [stabilized] all the countries about London), then he let make Sir Kay seneschal of England; and Sir Baudwin of Britain was made constable; and Sir Ulfius was made chamberlain; and Sir Brastias was made warden to wait upon the north from Trent forwards, for it was that time the most part the king's enemies. But within few years after, Arthur won all the north, Scotland, and all that were under their obeisance. Also Wales—a part of it held against Arthur, but he overcame them all, as he did the remnant, through the noble prowess of himself and his knights of the Round Table.

II. The Book of Balin

After the death of Uther Pendragon, reigned Arthur his son, the which had great war in his days for to get all England into his hand. For there were many kings within the realm of England, and in Wales, Scotland, and Cornwall. So it befell on a time when King Arthur was at London, there came a knight and told the king tidings how that the King Rions of North Wales had reared a great number of people, and were entered into the land, and burnt and slew the king's true liege people.

"If this be true," said Arthur, "it were great shame unto mine estate but that he were mightily withstood." "It is truth," said the knight, "for I saw the host myself." "Well," said the king, "let make a cry: that all the lords, knights, and gentlemen of arms, should draw unto a castle"—called Camelot in those days—and there the king would let make a council-general and a great joust.

So when the king was come thither with all his baronage, and lodged as they seemed best, there was come a damosel, the which was sent on message from the great Lady Lyle of Avalon. And when she came before King Arthur, she told from whom she came, and how she was sent on message unto him for these causes.

Then she let her mantle fall, that was richly furred; and then was she girt with a noble sword whereof the king had marvel, and said: "Damosel, for what cause are ye girt with that sword? It beseemeth [befits] you not."

"Now shall I tell you," said the damosel; "this sword that I am girt withal doth me great sorrow and cumbrance, for I may not be delivered of this sword but by a knight, but he must be a passing good man of his hands and of his deeds, and without villainy or treachery, and without treason. And if I may find such a knight that hath all these virtues, he may draw out this sword out of the sheath. For I have been at King Rions' [where] it was told me there were passing good knights, and he and all his knights have assayed it, and none can speed."

"This is a great marvel," said Arthur, "if this be sooth. I will myself assay to draw out the sword, not presuming upon myself that I am the best knight, but that I will begin to draw at your sword in giving example to all the barons that they shall assay every each one after other when I have assayed it." Then Arthur took the sword by the sheath and by the girdle and pulled at it eagerly, but the sword would not out.

"Sir," said the damosel, "you need not to pull half so hard, for he that shall pull it out shall do it with little might."

"Ye say well," said Arthur; "now assay ye all my barons."

"But beware ye be not defiled with shame, treachery, nor guile. Then it will not avail," said the damosel, "for he must be a clean knight without villainy, and of a gentle strain of father side and mother side."

Most of all the barons of the Round Table that were there at that time assayed all by row, but there might none speed; wherefore the damosel made great sorrow out of measure, and said, "Alas! I weened in this court had been the best knights without treachery or treason."

"By my faith," said Arthur, "here are good knights, as I deem, as any be in the world, but their grace is not to help you; wherefore I am displeased."

Then fell it so, that time, there was a poor knight with King Arthur, that had been prisoner with him half a year and more for slaying of a knight, the which was cousin unto King Arthur. The name of this knight was called Balin, and by good means of the barons he was delivered out of prison, for he was a good man named of his body, and he was born in Northumberland. And so he went privily into the court, and saw this adventure, whereof it raised his heart, and he would assay it as other knights did; but for he was poor and poorly arrayed, he put him not far in press [forward]. But in his heart he was fully assured to do as well, if his grace happed him, as any knight that there was.

And as the damosel took her leave of Arthur and of all the barons, so departing, this knight Balin called unto her, and said, "Damosel, I pray you of your courtesy, suffer me as well to assay as these lords. Though that I be so poorly clothed, in my heart meseemeth I am fully assured as some of these others, and meseemeth in my heart to speed right well." The damosel beheld the poor knight and saw he was a likely man; but for his poor arrayment, she thought he should be of no worship [worth] without villainy or treachery. And then she said unto the knight: "Sir, it needeth not to put me to more pain or labour, for it seemeth not you to speed there as other have failed."

"Ah, fair damosel," said Balin, "worthiness, and good tatches [qualities] and good deeds are not only in arrayment, but manhood and worship is hid within man's person, and many a worshipful knight is not known unto all people, and therefore worship and hardiness is not in arrayment." "By God," said the damosel, "ye say sooth; therefore ye shall assay to do what ye may." Then Balin took the sword by the girdle and sheath, and drew it out easily; and when he looked on the sword, it pleased him much. Then had the king and all the barons great marvel that Balin had done that adventure, and many knights had great despite of Balin.

"Certes," said the damosel, "this is a passing good knight, and the best that ever I found, and most of worship without treason, treachery, or villainy; and many marvels shall he do. Now, gentle and courteous knight, give me the sword again." "Nay," said Balin, "for this sword will I keep, but it be taken from me with force." "Well," said the damosel, "ye are not wise to keep the sword from me, for ye shall slay with the sword the best friend that ye have, and the man that ye most love in the world, and the sword shall be your destruction." "I shall take the adventure," said Balin, "that God will ordain me, but the sword ye shall not have at this time, by the faith of my body." "Ye shall repent it within short time," said the damosel, "for I would have the sword more for your avail than for mine, for I am passing heavy for your sake; for ye will not believe that sword shall be your destruction, and that is great pity." With that the damosel departed, making great sorrow.

Anon after, Balin sent for his horse and armour, and so would depart from the court, and took his leave of King Arthur. "Nay," said the king, "I suppose ye will not depart so lightly from this fellowship. I suppose ye are displeased that I have shewed you unkindness. Blame me the less, for I was misinformed against you, but I weened ye had not been such a knight as ye are, of worship and prowess, and if ye will abide in this court among my fellowship, I shall so advance you as ye shall be pleased." "God thank your highness," said Balin; "your bounty and highness may no man praise half to the value; but at this time I must needs depart, beseeching you alway of your good grace." "Truly," said the king, "I am right wroth for your departing; I pray you, fair knight, that ye tarry not long, and ye shall be right welcome to me, and to my barons, and I shall amend all amiss that I have done against you." "God thank your great lordship," said Balin, and therewith made him ready to depart. Then the most part of the knights of the Round Table said that Balin did not this adventure all only by might, but by witchcraft.

The meanwhile that this knight was making him ready to depart, there came into the court a lady that hight the Lady of the Lake. And she came on horseback, richly beseen [dressed] and saluted King Arthur, and there asked him a gift that he promised her when she gave him the sword. "That is sooth," said Arthur; "a gift I promised you, but I have forgotten the name of my sword that ye gave me." "The name of it," said the lady, "is Excalibur; that is as much to say as Cut Steel."

"Ye say well," said the king; "ask what ye will and ye shall have it, an [if] it lie in my power to give it." "Well," said the lady, "I ask the head of the knight that hath won the sword, or else the damosel's head that brought it. I take no force though [care if] I have both their heads, for he slew my brother, a good knight and a true, and that gentlewoman was causer of my father's death." "Truly," said King Arthur, "I may not grant neither of their heads with my worship; therefore ask what ye will else, and I shall fulfill your desire." "I will ask none other thing," said the lady.

When Balin was ready to depart, he saw the Lady of the Lake, that by her means had slain Balin's mother, and he had sought her three years. And when it was told him that she asked his head of King Arthur, he went to her straight and said: "Evil be you found; ye would have my head, and therefore ye shall lose yours!" And with his sword lightly he smote off her head before King Arthur.

"Alas, for shame!" said Arthur, "why have ye done so? Ye have shamed me and all my court, for this was a lady that I was beholden to, and hither she came under my safe-conduct. I shall never forgive you that trespass."

"Sir," said Balin, "me forthynketh of [I regret] your displeasure, for this same lady was the untruest lady living, and by enchantment and sorcery she hath been the destroyer of many good knights, and she was causer that my mother was burnt, through her falsehood and treachery."

"What cause soever ye had," said Arthur, "ye should have forborne her in my presence. Therefore, think not the contrary; ye shall repent it, for such another despite had I never in my court; therefore withdraw you out of my court in all haste ye may."

Then Balin took up the head of the lady, and bare it with him to his hostelry, and there he met with his squire, that was sorry he had displeased King Arthur, and so they rode forth out of the town. "Now," said Balin, "we must depart. Take thou this head and bear it to my friends, and tell them how I have sped, and tell my friends in Northumberland that my most foe is dead. Also tell them how I am out of prison, and what adventure befell me at the getting of this sword." "Alas!" said the squire, "ye are greatly to blame for to displease King Arthur." "As for that," said Balin, "I will hie me in all the haste that I may to meet with King Rions and destroy him, either else to die therefore; and if it may hap me to win him, then will King Arthur be my good and gracious lord." "Where shall I meet with you?" said the squire. "In King Arthur's court," said Balin. So his squire and he departed at that time. Then King Arthur and all the court made great dole and had shame of the death of the Lady of the Lake. Then the king buried her richly.

At that time there was a knight, the which was the king's son of Ireland, and his name was Lanceor, the which was an orgulous [proud] knight, and counted himself one of the best of the court. And he had great despite at Balin for the achieving of the sword, that any should be accounted more hardy, or more of prowess; and he asked King Arthur if he would give him leave to ride after Balin and to revenge the despite that he had done.

"Do your best," said Arthur. "I am right wroth with Balin; I would he were quit of [repaid for] the despite that he hath done to me and to my court." Then this Lanceor went to his hostelry to make him ready.

In the meanwhile came Merlin unto the court of King Arthur, and there was told him the adventure of the sword, and the death of the Lady of the Lake. "Now shall I say you," said Merlin, "this same damosel that here standeth, that brought the sword unto your court, I shall tell you the cause of her coming: she was the falsest damosel that liveth." "Say not so," said they. [Then Merlin said:] "She hath a brother, a passing good knight of prowess and a full true man; and this damosel loved another knight that held her to paramour, and this good knight her brother met with the knight that held her to paramour, and slew him by force of his hands. When this false damosel understood this, she went to the Lady Lyle of Avalon and besought her of help, to be avenged on her own brother. And so this Lady Lyle of Avalon took her this sword that she brought with her, and told there should no man pull it out of the sheath, but if he be one of the best knights of this realm, and he should be hard and full of prowess, and with that sword he should slay her brother. This was the cause that the damosel came into this court. I know it as well as ye. Would God she had not come into this court, but she came never in fellowship of worship to do good, but always great harm. And that knight that hath achieved the sword shall be destroyed by that sword, for the which will be great damage, for there liveth not a knight of more prowess than he is, and he shall do unto you, my Lord Arthur, great honour and kindness; and it is great pity he shall not endure but a while, for of his strength and hardiness I know not his match living."

So the knight of Ireland armed him at all points, and dressed his shield on his shoulder, and mounted upon horseback, and took his spear in his hand, and rode after a great pace, as much as his horse might go; and within a little space on a mountain he had a sight of Balin, and with a loud voice he cried: "Abide, knight, for ye shall abide whether ye will or nill, and the shield that is tofore you shall not help."

When Balin heard the noise, he turned his horse fiercely, and said: "Fair knight, what will ye with me, will ye joust with me?"

"Yea," said the Irish knight; "therefore come I after you."

"Peradventure," said Balin, "it had been better to have holden you at home, for many a man weeneth to put his enemy to a rebuke, and oft it falleth to himself. Of what court be ye sent from?" said Balin.

"I am come from the court of King Arthur," said the knight of Ireland, "that come hither for to revenge the despite ye did this day to King Arthur and to his court."

"Well," said Balin, "I see well I must have ado with you; that me forthynketh [pains] for to grieve King Arthur or any of his court. And your quarrel is full simple," said Balin, "unto me, for the lady that is dead did me great damage, and else would I have been loath as any knight that liveth for to slay a lady."

"Make you ready," said the knight Lanceor, "and dress you unto me, for that one shall abide in the field." Then they took their spears, and came together as much as their horses might drive, and the Irish knight smote Balin on the shield, that all went shivers of his spear, and Balin hit him through the shield, and the hauberk perished, and so pierced through his body and the horse's croup, and anon turned his horse fiercely, and drew out his sword, and wist not that he had slain him; and then he saw him lie as a dead corpse.

Then he looked by him, and was ware of a damosel that came riding full fast as the horse might ride on a fair palfrey. And when she espied that Lanceor was slain, she made sorrow out of measure, and said: "O Balin, two bodies thou hast slain and one heart, and two hearts in one body, and two souls thou hast lost." And therewith she took the sword from her love that lay dead, and fell to the ground in a swoon. And when she arose, she made great dole out of measure, the which sorrow grieved Balin passingly sore, and he went unto her for to have taken the sword out of her hand, but she held it so fast he might not take it out of her hand unless he should have hurt her, and suddenly she set the pommel to the ground, and rove [stabbed] herself through the body.

When Balin espied her deeds, he was passing heavy in his heart, and ashamed that so fair a damosel had destroyed herself for the love of his death. "Alas," said Balin, "me repenteth sore the death of this knight for the love of this damosel, for there was much true love betwixt them both." And for sorrow he might not longer behold them, but turned his horse and looked toward a great forest, and there he was ware, by the arms, of his brother Balan. And when they were met, they put off their helms and kissed together, and wept for joy and pity.

Then Balan said, "I little weened to have met with you at this sudden adventure. I am right glad of your deliverance out of your dolorous prisonment, for a man told me in the Castle of Four Stones that ye were delivered, and that man had seen you in the court of King Arthur, and therefore I came hither into this country, for here I supposed to find you."

Anon the knight Balin told his brother of his adventure of the sword, and of the death of the Lady of the Lake, and how King Arthur was displeased with him. "Wherefore he sent this knight after me, that lieth here dead, and the death of this damosel grieveth me sore."

"So doth it me," said Balan, "but ye must take the adventure that God will ordain you."

"Truly," said Balin, "I am right heavy that my Lord Arthur is displeased with me, for he is the most worshipful knight that reigneth now on earth, and his love will I get or else will I put my life in adventure, for the King Rions lieth at a siege at Castle Terrabil, and thither will we draw in all haste, to prove our worship and prowess upon him."

"I will well," said Balan, "that we do, and we will help each other as brethren ought to do."

"Now go we hence," said Balin, "and well be we met." The meanwhile as they talked, there came a dwarf from the city of Camelot on horseback, as much [fast] as he might, and found the dead bodies, wherefore he made great dole, and pulled out his hair for sorrow, and said: "Which of you knights have done this deed?" "Whereby askest thou it?" said Balan. "For I would wit [know] it," said the dwarf. "It was I," said Balin, "that slew this knight in my defense, for hither he came to chase me, and either I must slay him or he me; and this damosel slew herself for his love, which repenteth me, and for her sake I shall owe all women the better love." "Alas," said the dwarf, "thou hast done great damage unto thyself, for this knight that is here dead was one of the most valiantest men that lived, and trust well, Balin, the kin of this knight will chase you through the world till they have slain you." "As for that," said Balin, "I fear not greatly, but I am right heavy that I have displeased my lord King Arthur for the death of this knight."

So as they talked together, there came a king of Cornwall riding, the which hight King Mark. And when he saw these two bodies dead and understood how they were dead, by the two knights above said, then made the king great sorrow for the true love that was betwixt them, and said: "I will not depart till I have on this earth made a tomb, and there he pyght [pitched] his pavilions and sought through all the country to find a tomb. And in a church they found one [that] was fair and rich, and then the king let put them both in the earth, and put the tomb upon them, and wrote the names of them both on the tomb, how: HERE LIETH LANCEOR, THE KING'S SON OF IRELAND, THAT AT HIS OWN REQUEST WAS SLAIN BY THE HANDS OF BALIN. And how: HIS LADY, COLOMBE, AND PARAMOUR, SLEW HERSELF WITH HER LOVE'S SWORD FOR DOLE AND SORROW.

The meanwhile as this was a-doing, in came Merlin to King Mark, and seeing all his doing, said: "Here shall be in this same place the greatest battle betwixt two knights that was or ever shall be, and the truest lovers, and yet none of them shall slay other." And there Merlin wrote their names upon the tomb with letters of gold that should fight in that place, whose names were: Lancelot de Lake and Tristram.

"Thou art a marvellous man," said King Mark unto Merlin, "that speakest of such marvels. Thou art a boystous [unpolished] man and an unlikely to tell of such deeds. What is thy name?" said King Mark.

"At this time," said Merlin, "I will not tell, but at that time when Sir Tristram is taken with his sovereign lady, then ye shall hear and know my name, and at that time ye shall hear tidings that shall not please you."

Then said Merlin to Balin, "Thou hast done thyself great hurt because that thou savest not this lady that slew herself, that might have saved her an thou wouldest."

"By the faith of my body," said Balin, "I might not save her, for she slew herself suddenly."

"Me repenteth," said Merlin. "Because of the death of that lady, thou shalt strike a stroke most dolorous that ever man struck, except the stroke of our Lord, for thou shalt hurt the truest knight and the man of most worship that now liveth, and through that stroke three kingdoms shall be in great poverty, misery, and wretchedness twelve years, and the knight shall not be whole of that wound for many years." Then Merlin took his leave of Balin.

And Balin said, "If I wist it were sooth that ye say I should do such a perilous deed as that, I would slay myself to make thee a liar." Therewith Merlin vanished away suddenly. And then Balan and his brother took their leave of King Mark.

"First," said the king, "tell me your name."

"Sir," said Balan, "ye may see he beareth two swords; thereby ye may call him the knight with the two swords." And so departed King Mark unto Camelot to King Arthur, and Balin took the way toward King Rions. And as they rode together, they met with Merlin disguised, but they knew him not.

"Whither ride you?" said Merlin. "We have little to do," said the two knights, "to tell thee." "But what is thy name?" said Balin. "At this time," said Merlin, "I will not tell it thee." "It is evil seen," said the knights, "that thou art a true man that thou wilt not tell thy name." "As for that," said Merlin, "be it as it be may. I can tell you wherefore ye ride this way, for to meet King Rions; but it will not avail you without ye have my counsel." "Ah!" said Balin, "ye are Merlin; we will be ruled by your counsel." "Come on," said Merlin, "ye shall have great worship, and look that ye do knightly, for ye shall have great need." "As for that," said Balin, "dread you not; we will do what we may."

Then Merlin lodged them in a wood among leaves beside the highway, and took off the bridles of their horses and put them to grass and laid them down to rest till it was nigh midnight. Then Merlin bade them rise and make them ready, for the king was nigh them that was stolen away from his host with a three-score horses of his best knights, and twenty of them rode tofore to warn the Lady de Vance that the king was coming, for that night King Rions should have lain with her.

"Which is the king?" said Balin. "Abide," said Merlin; "here in a straight way ye shall meet with him." And therewith he showed Balin and his brother where he rode. Anon Balin and his brother met with the king, and smote him down, and wounded him fiercely, and laid him to the ground; and there they slew on the right hand and the left hand, and slew more than forty of his men, and the remnant fled. Then went they again to King Rions and would have slain him, had he not yielded him unto their grace. Then said he thus: "Knights full of prowess, slay me not, for by my life ye may win; and by my death, ye shall win nothing." Then said these two knights, "Ye say sooth and truth," and so laid him on a horse-litter.

With that Merlin was vanished, and came to King Arthur aforehand, and told him how his most enemy was taken and discomfited. "By whom?" said King Arthur. "By two knights," said Merlin, "that would please your lordship, and tomorrow ye shall know what knights they are." Anon after came the knight with the two swords and Balan his brother, and brought with them King Rions of North Wales, and there delivered him to the porters, and charged them with him. And so they two returned again in the dawning of the day.

King Arthur came then to King Rions and said, "Sir king, ye are welcome; by what adventure come ye hither?" "Sir," said King Rions, "I came hither by an hard adventure." "Who won you?" said King Arthur. "Sir," said the king, "the knight with the two swords and his brother, which are two marvellous knights of prowess." "I know them not," said Arthur, "but much I am beholden to them." "Ah," said Merlin, "I shall tell you: it is Balin that achieved the sword, and his brother Balan, a good knight; there liveth not a better of prowess and of worthiness, and it shall be the greatest dole of him that ever I knew of knight, for he shall not long endure." "Alas," said King Arthur, "that is great pity; for I am much beholden unto him, and I have ill deserved it unto him for his kindness." "Nay," said Merlin, "he shall do much more for you, and that shall ye know in haste." "But, sir, are ye purveyed," said Merlin, "for to-morn the host of Nero, King Rions' brother, will set on you or [ere] noon with a great host, and therefore make you ready, for I will depart from you."

Then King Arthur made ready his host in ten battles [divisions], and Nero was ready in the field afore the Castle Terrabil with a great host, and he had ten battles, with many more people than Arthur had. Then Nero had the vanguard with the most part of his people, and Merlin came to King Lot of the Isle of Orkney, and held him with a tale of prophecy till Nero and his people were destroyed. And there Sir Kay the Seneschal did passingly well, that the days of his life the worship went never from him; and Sir Hervis de Revel did marvellous deeds with King Arthur, and King Arthur slew that day twenty knights and maimed forty.

At that time came in the knight with the two swords and his brother Balan, but they two did so marvellously that the king and all the knights marvelled of them, and all they that beheld them said they were sent from heaven as angels, or devils from hell. And King Arthur said himself they were the best knights that ever he saw, for they gave such strokes that all men had wonder of them. In the meanwhile came one to King Lot and told him [that] while he tarried there Nero was destroyed and slain with all his people. "Alas," said King Lot, "I am ashamed, for by my default, there is many a worshipful man slain, for an we had been together there had been none host under the heaven that had been able for to have matched with us; this fayter [impostor] with his prophecy hath mocked me." All that did Merlin, for he knew well that an King Lot had been with his body there at the first battle, King Arthur had been slain, and all his people destroyed. And well Merlin knew that one of the kings should be dead that day, and loath was Merlin that any of them both should be slain; but of the twain, he had liefer [rather] King Lot had been slain than King Arthur.

"Now what is best to do?" said King Lot of Orkney: "whether is me better to treat with King Arthur or to fight, for the greater part of our people are slain and destroyed?"

"Sir," said a knight, "set on Arthur, for they are weary and forfoughten [exhausted], and we be fresh."

"As for me," said King Lot, "I would every knight would do his part as I would do mine." And then they advanced banners and smote together and all to-shivered [shattered] their spears; and Arthur's knights, with the help of the knight with the two swords and his brother Balan put King Lot and his host to the worse. But always King Lot held him in the foremost front, and did marvellous deeds of arms, for all his host was borne up by his hands, for he abode [stood off] all knights. Alas, he might not endure (the which was great pity) that so worthy a knight as he was one should be overmatched [defeated] that of late time afore had been a knight of King Arthur's, and wedded the sister of King Arthur. And for King Arthur lay by King Lot's wife, the which was Arthur's sister, and gat on her Mordred, therefore King Lot held against Arthur. So there was a knight that was called "the knight with the strange beast," and at that time his right name was called Pellinore, the which was a good man of prowess, and he smote a mighty stroke at King Lot as he fought with all his enemies, and he failed of his stroke, and smote the horse's neck, that he fell to the ground with King Lot; and therewith anon Pellinore smote him a great stroke through the helm and head unto the brows. And then all the host of Orkney fled for the death of King Lot, and there were slain many mothers' sons. But King Pellinore bare the wytte [blame] of the death of King Lot, wherefore Sir Gawain revenged the death of his father the tenth year after he was made knight, and slew King Pellinore with his own hands. Also there were slain at that battle twelve kings on the side of King Lot with Nero, and all were buried in the Church of Saint Stephen's in Camelot, and the remnant of knights and of others were buried in a great rock.

So at the interment came King Lot's wife Margawse with her four sons, Gawain, Agravain, Gaheris, and Gareth. Also there came thither King Urien, Sir Ywain's father, and Morgan le Fay, his wife, that was King Arthur's sister. All these came to the interment. But of all these twelve kings, King Arthur let make the tomb of King Lot passing richly, and made his tomb by his own. And then Arthur let make twelve images of laton [brass] and copper, and overgilt it with gold, in the sign of twelve kings, and each one of them held a taper of wax that burnt day and night; and King Arthur was made in sign of a figure standing above them with a sword drawn in his hand, and all the twelve figures had countenance like unto men that were overcome.

All this made Merlin by his subtle craft, and there he told the king: "When I am dead these tapers shall burn no longer, and soon after the adventures of the Sangrail [Holy Grail] shall come among you and be achieved." Also he told Arthur how Balin the worshipful knight shall give the dolorous stroke, whereof shall fall great vengeance. "Oh, where is Balin and Balan and Pellinore?" said King Arthur. "As for Pellinore," said Merlin, "he will meet with you soon. And as for Balin, he will not be long from you, but the other brother will depart; ye shall see him no more." "By my faith," said Arthur, "they are two marvellous knights, and namely Balin passeth of prowess of any knight that ever I found, for much beholden am I unto him; would God he would abide with me."

"Sir," said Merlin, "look ye keep well the scabbard of Excalibur, for ye shall lose no blood while ye have the scabbard upon you, though ye have as many wounds upon you as ye may have." So after, for great trust, Arthur betook the scabbard to Morgan le Fay, his sister, and she loved another knight better than her husband King Urien or King Arthur, and she would have had Arthur, her brother, slain; and therefore she let make another scabbard like it by enchantment, and gave the scabbard Excalibur to her love. And the knight's name was called Accolon, that after had near slain King Arthur.

After this Merlin told unto King Arthur of the prophecy that there should be a great battle beside Salisbury, and Mordred, his own son, should be against him. Also he told him that Bagdemagus was his cousin, and germane unto King Urien.

Within a day or two King Arthur was somewhat sick, and he let pitch his pavilion in a meadow, and there he laid him down on a pallet to sleep, but he might have no rest. Right so he heard a great noise of an horse, and therewith the king looked out at the porch of the pavilion, and saw a knight coming even by him and making great dole. "Abide, fair sir," said Arthur, "and tell me wherefore thou makest this sorrow." "Ye may little amend me," said the knight, and so passed forth to the castle of Meliot.

Anon after there came Balin, and when he saw King Arthur he alit off his horse, and came to the king on foot, and saluted him. "By my head," said Arthur, "ye be welcome. Sir, right now came riding this way a knight making great mourn, for what cause I cannot tell; wherefore I would desire of you of your courtesy and of your gentleness to fetch again that knight either by force or else by his good will." "I will do more for your lordship than that," said Balin and so he rode more than a pace, and found the knight with a damosel in a forest, and said, "Sir knight, ye must come with me unto King Arthur, for to tell him of your sorrow." "That will I not," said the knight, "for it will scathe [hurt] me greatly, and do you none avail." "Sir," said Balin, "I pray you make you ready, for ye must go with me, or else I must fight with you and bring you by force, and that were me loath to do." "Will ye be my warrant [protector]," said the knight, "an I go with you?" "Yea," said Balin, "or else I will die therefor." And so he made him ready to go with Balin, and left the damosel still.

And as they were even afore King Arthur's pavilion, there came one invisible, and smote this knight that went with Balin throughout the body with a spear. "Alas," said the knight, "I am slain under your conduct with a knight called Garlon; therefore take my horse that is better than yours, and ride to the damosel, and follow the quest that I was in as she will lead you, and revenge my death when ye may." "That shall I do," said Balin, "and that I make a vow unto knighthood." And so he departed from this knight with great sorrow. So King Arthur let bury this knight richly, and made a mention on his tomb, how there was slain Harleus de Berbeus, and by whom the treachery was done, the knight Garlon. But ever the damosel bore the truncheon of the spear with her that Sir Harleus was slain withal.

So Balin and the damosel rode into a forest, and there met with a knight that had been a-hunting, and that knight asked Balin for what cause he made so great sorrow. "Me list not to tell you," said Balin. "Now," said the knight, "an I were armed as ye be, I would fight with you." "That should little need," said Balin; "I am not afraid to tell you," and told him all the cause how it was. "Ah," said the knight, "is this all? Here I ensure you by the faith of my body never to depart from you while my life lasteth."

And so they went to the hostelry and armed them, and so rode forth with Balin. And as they came by an hermitage even by a churchyard, there came the knight Garlon invisible, and smote this knight, Perin de Mount Beliard, through the body with a spear. "Alas," said the knight, "I am slain by this traitor knight that rideth invisible." "Alas," said Balin, "it is not the first despite he hath done me." And there the hermit and Balin buried the knight under a rich stone and a tomb royal. And on the morn they found letters of gold written how Sir Gawain shall revenge his father's death, King Lot, on the King Pellinore.

Anon after this Balin and the damosel rode till they came to a castle, and there Balin alit, and he and the damosel went to go into the castle, and anon as Balin came within the castle's gate the portcullis fell down at his back, and there fell many men about the damosel, and would have slain her. When Balin saw that, he was sore aggrieved, for he might not help the damosel. And then he went up into the tower, and leapt over the walls into the ditch, and hurt him not; and anon he pulled out his sword and would have fought with them. And they all said nay, they would not fight with him, for they did nothing but the old custom of the castle, and told him how their lady was sick, and had lain many years, and she might not be whole but if she had a dish of silver full of blood of a clean maid and a king's daughter. And therefore the custom of this castle is: there shall no damosel pass this way but she shall bleed of her blood in a silver dish full. "Well," said Balin, "she shall bleed as much as she may bleed, but I will not lose the life of her whiles my life lasteth." And so Balin made her to bleed by her good will, but her blood helped not the lady. And so he and she rested there all night, and had there right good cheer, and on the morn they passed on their ways. And as it telleth after in the *Sangrail*: that Sir Percival's sister helped that lady with her blood, whereof she was dead.

Then they rode three or four days and never met with adventure, and by hap they were lodged with a gentleman that was a rich man and well at ease. And as they sat at their supper, Balin overheard one complain grievously by him in a chair. "What is this noise?" said Balin.

"Forsooth," said his host, "I will tell you. I was but late at a jousting, and there I jousted with a knight that is brother unto King Pellam, and twice smote I him down, and then he promised to requite me on my best friend; and so he wounded my son, that cannot be whole till I have of that knight's blood, and he rideth always invisible; but I know not his name." "Ah," said Balin, "I know that knight! His name is Garlon. He hath slain two knights of mine in the same manner; therefore I had liefer meet with that knight than all the gold in this realm, for the despite he hath done me."

"Well," said his host, "I shall tell you: King Pellam of Listenoise hath made do cry in all this country a great feast that shall be within these twenty days, and no knight may come there but if he bring his wife with him, or his paramour; and that knight, your enemy and mine, ye shall see that day." "Then I behote [promise] you," said Balin, "part of his blood to heal your son withal." "We will be forward to-morn," said his host.

So on the morn they rode all three toward Pellam, and they had fifteen days' journey or [ere] they came thither; and that same day began the great feast. And so they alit and stabled their horses, and went into the castle; but Balin's host might not be let in because he had no lady. Then Balin was well received and brought unto a chamber and unarmed him, and there were brought him robes to his pleasure, and [they] would have had Balin leave his sword behind him. "Nay," said Balin, "that do I not, for it is the custom of my country a knight always to keep his weapon with him, and that custom will I keep, or else I will depart as I came."

Then they gave him leave to wear his sword, and so he went unto the castle, and was set among knights of worship, and his lady afore him. Soon Balin asked a knight: "Is there not a knight in this court whose name is Garlon?"

"Yonder he goeth," said a knight, "he with the black face; he is the marvellest knight that is now living, for he destroyeth many good knights, for he goeth invisible."

"Ah well," said Balin, "is that he?" Then Balin advised him long: "If I slay him here, I shall not escape, and if I leave him now, peradventure I shall never meet with him again at such a steven [occasion], and much harm he will do an he live."

Therewith this Garlon espied that this Balin beheld him, and then he came and smote Balin on the face with the back of his hand, and said, "Knight, why beholdest me so? For shame therefor, eat thy meat and do that thou came for."

"Thou sayest sooth," said Balin, "this is not the first despite that thou hast done me, and therefore I will do what I came for," and rose up fiercely and clove his head to the shoulders. "Give me the truncheon," said Balin to his lady, "wherewith he slew your knight." Anon she gave it him, for always she bore the truncheon with her. And therewith Balin smote him through the body, and said openly: "With that truncheon thou hast slain a good knight, and now it sticketh in thy body." And then Balin called unto him his host, saying, "Now may ye fetch blood enough to heal your son withal."

Anon all the knights arose from the table for to set on Balin, and King Pellam himself arose up fiercely, and said, "Knight, hast thou slain my brother? Thou shalt die therefor or thou depart."

"Well," said Balin, "do it yourself."

"Yes," said King Pellam, "there shall no man have ado with thee but myself, for the love of my brother." Then King Pellam caught in his hand a grim weapon and smote eagerly at Balin, but Balin put the sword betwixt his head and the stroke, and therewith his sword burst in sunder. And when Balin was weaponless, he ran into a chamber for to seek some weapon, and so from chamber to chamber, and no weapon he could find, and always King Pellam after him. And at the last he entered into a chamber that was marvellously well dight [furnished] and richly, and a bed arrayed with cloth of gold, the richest that might be thought, and one lying therein; and thereby stood a table of clean gold with four pillars of silver that bore up the table, and upon the table stood a marvellous spear strangely wrought. And when Balin saw that spear, he got it in his hand and turned him to King Pellam, and smote him passingly sore with that spear, that King Pellam fell down in a swoon, and therewith the castle roof and walls broke and fell to the earth, and Balin fell down so that he might not stir foot nor hand. And so the most part of the castle, that was fallen down through that dolorous stroke, lay upon Pellam and Balin three days.

Then Merlin came thither and took up Balin, and got him a good horse, for his was dead, and bade him ride out of that country. "I would have my damosel," said Balin. "Lo," said Merlin, "where she lieth dead." And King Pellam lay so, many years sore wounded, and might never be whole till Galahad, the haughty [noble] prince, healed him in the quest of the Sangrail, for in that place was part of the blood of our Lord Jesus Christ, that Joseph of Arimathea brought into this land, and there himself lay in that rich bed. And that was the same spear that Longius smote our Lord to the heart. And King Pellam was nigh of Joseph's kin, and that was the most worshipful man that lived in those days, and great pity it was of his hurt, for through that stroke, [all] turned to great dole, tray [pain], and tene [sorrow].

Then departed Balin from Merlin, and said, "In this world we meet never no more." So he rode forth through the fair countries and cities, and found the people dead, slain on every side. And all that were alive cried, "O Balin, thou hast caused great damage in these countries; for the dolorous stroke thou gavest unto King Pellam, three countries are destroyed, and doubt not but the vengeance will fall on thee at the last."

When Balin was past those countries he was passing fayn [glad]. So he rode eight days or he met with adventure. And at the last he came into a fair forest in a valley, and was ware of a tower, and there beside he saw a great horse of war, tied to a tree, and there beside sat a fair knight on the ground and made great mourning, and he was a likely man, and a well made. Balin said, "God save you, why be ye so heavy? Tell me, and I will amend it, an I may, to my power."

"Sir knight," said he again, "thou doest me great grief, for I was in merry thoughts, and now thou puttest me to more pain." Balin went a little from him, and looked on his horse; then heard Balin him say thus: "Ah, fair lady, why have ye broken my promise, for thou promisest me to meet me here by noon, and I may curse thee that ever ye gave me this sword, for with this sword I slay myself," and [he] pulled it out. And therewith Balin started unto him and took him by the hand. "Let go my hand," said the knight, "or else I shall slay thee."

"That shall not need," said Balin, "for I shall promise you my help to get you your lady, an ye will tell me where she is."

"What is your name?" said the knight. "My name is Balin le Savage." "Ah, sir, I know you well enough; ye are the knight with the two swords, and the man of most prowess of your hands living." "What is your name?" said Balin. "My name is Garnish of the Mount, a poor man's son, but by my prowess and hardiness a duke hath made me knight, and gave me lands. His name is Duke Hermel, and his daughter is she that I love, and she me, as I deemed." "How far is she hence?" said Balin. "But six mile," said the knight. "Now ride we hence," said these two knights.

So they rode more than a pace, till that they came to a fair castle well-walled and ditched. "I will into the castle," said Balin, "and look if she be there." So he went in and searched from chamber to chamber, and found her bed, but she was not there. Then Balin looked into a fair little garden, and under a laurel tree he saw her lie upon a quilt of green samite and a knight in her arms, fast halsyng [embracing] either [each] other, and under their heads grass and herbs. When Balin saw her lie so with the foulest knight that ever he saw, and she a fair lady, then Balin went through all the chambers again, and told the knight how he found her as she had slept fast, and so brought him in the place where she lay fast sleeping.

And when Garnish beheld her so lying, for pure sorrow his mouth and nose burst out on bleeding, and with his sword he smote off both their heads, and then he made sorrow out of measure, and said: "O Balin, much sorrow hast thou brought unto me, for haddest thou not showed me that sight, I should have passed my sorrow." "Forsooth," said Balin, "I did it to this intent: that it should better thy courage, and that ye might see and know her falsehood, and to cause you to leave love of such a lady. God knoweth, I did none other but as I would ye did to me." "Alas," said Garnish, "now is my sorrow double that I may not endure, now have I slain that I most loved in all my life." And therewith suddenly he rove himself on his own sword unto the hilts.

When Balin saw that, he dressed him thenceward, lest folk would say he had slain them; and so he rode forth, and within three days he came by a cross, and thereon were letters of gold written, that said: IT IS NOT FOR NO KNIGHT ALONE TO RIDE TOWARD THIS CASTLE. Then saw he an old hoar gentleman coming toward him, that said, "Balin le Savage, thou passest thy bounds to come this way; therefore turn again, and it will avail thee." And he vanished away anon.

And so he heard an horn blow, as it had been the death of a beast. "That blast," said Balin, "is blown for me, for I am the prize, and yet am I not dead." Anon withal he saw an hundred ladies and many knights, that welcomed him with fair semblance and made him passing good cheer unto his sight, and led him into the castle, and there was dancing and minstrelsy and all manner of joy.

Then the chief lady of the castle said, "Knight with the two swords, ye must have ado and joust with a knight hereby that keepeth an island, for there may no man pass this way but he must joust or he pass." "That is an unhappy custom," said Balin, "that a knight may not pass this way but if he joust." "Ye shall not have ado but with one knight," said the lady. "Well," said Balin, "since I shall thereto, I am ready, but travelling men are oft weary and their horses too; but though my horse be weary, my heart is not weary; I would be fain there my death should be."

"Sir," said a knight to Balin, "methinketh your shield is not good. I will lend you a bigger; thereof I pray you." And so he took the shield that was unknown and left his own, and so rode unto the island, and put him and his horse in a great boat. And when he came on the other side, he met with a damosel, and she said: "O knight Balin, why have ye left your own shield? Alas, ye have put yourself in great danger, for by your shield ye should have been known; it is great pity of you as ever was of knight, for of thy prowess and hardiness thou hast no fellow living."

"Me repenteth," said Balin, "that ever I came within this country, but I may not turn now again for shame, and what adventure shall fall to me, be it life or death, I will take the adventure that shall come to me." And then he looked on his armour, and understood he was well armed, and therewith blessed him and mounted upon his horse.

Then afore him he saw come riding out of a castle a knight, and his horse trapped all red, and himself in the same colour. When this knight in the red beheld Balin, him thought it should be his brother Balin because of his two swords; but because he knew not his shield, he deemed it was not he. And so they aventryd [leveled] their spears and came marvellously fast together, and they smote each other in the shields, but their spears and their course [charge] were so big that it bore down horse and man, that they lay both in a swoon.

But Balin was bruised sore with the fall of his horse, for he was weary of travel. And Balan was the first that rose on foot and drew his sword, and went toward Balin, and he arose and went against him. But Balan smote Balin first, and he put up his shield and smote him through the shield and tamyd [pierced] his helm. Then Balin smote him again with that unhappy sword, and well nigh had felled his brother Balan, and so they fought there together till their breaths failed. Then Balin looked up to the castle and saw the towers stand full of ladies. So they went unto battle again, and wounded every each other dolefully, and then they breathed ofttimes, and so went unto battle that all the place there as they fought was blood red. And at that time there was none of them both but they had either smitten other seven great wounds, so that the least of them might have been the death of the mightiest giant in this world. Then they went to battle again so marvellously that doubt [frightening] it was to hear of that battle for the great blood-shedding, and their hauberks unnailed [fell apart so] that naked they were on every side.

At last Balan, the younger brother, withdrew him a little and laid him down. Then said Balin le Savage, "What knight art thou? For or now I found never no knight that matched me." "My name is," said he, "Balan, brother unto the good knight Balin." "Alas," said Balin, "that ever I should see this day." And therewith he fell backward in a swoon.

Then Balan yede [went] on all four feet and hands, and put off the helm of his brother, and might not know him by the visage, it was so full hewn and bled. But when he awoke, he said: "O Balan, my brother, thou hast slain me, and I thee; wherefore all the wide world shall speak of us both." "Alas," said Balan, "that ever I saw this day, that through mishap I might not know you, for I espied well your two swords, but because ye had another shield, I deemed ye had been another knight." "Alas," said Balin, "all that made an unhappy knight in the castle, for he caused me to leave my own shield to our both's destruction, and if I might live, I would destroy that castle for ill customs." "That were well done," said Balan, "for I had never grace to depart from them since that I came hither, for here it happed me to slay a knight that kept this island, and since might I never depart; and no more should ye, brother, an ye might have slain me as ye have, and escaped yourself with the life."

Right so came the lady of the tower with four knights and six ladies and six yeomen unto them, and there she heard how they made their moan either to other, and said, "We came both out of one womb—that is to say one mother's belly—and so shall we lie both in one pit."

So Balan prayed the lady of her gentleness, for his true service, that she would bury them both in that same place where the battle was done. And she granted them with weeping it should be done richly in the best manner. "Now will ye send for a priest, that we may receive our sacrament, and receive the blessed body of our Lord Jesus Christ?"

"Yea," said the lady, "it shall be done." And so she sent for a priest and gave them their rites.

"Now," said Balin, "when we are buried in one tomb, and the mention made over us how two brethren slew each other, there will never good knight nor good man see our tomb but they will pray for our souls." And so all the ladies and gentlewomen wept for pity. Then anon Balan died, but Balin died not till the midnight after, and so were they buried both, and the lady let make a mention of Balan how he was there slain by his brother's hands, but she knew not Balin's name.

In the morning came Merlin and let write Balin's name on the tomb with letters of gold, that: HERE LIETH BALIN LE SAVAGE, THAT WAS THE KNIGHT WITH THE TWO SWORDS, AND HE THAT SMOTE THE DOLOROUS STROKE. Also Merlin let make there a bed, that there should never man lie therein but he went out of his wit, yet Lancelot de Lake fordyd [destroyed] that bed through his noblesse. And anon after Balin was dead, Merlin took his sword, and took off the pommel and set on another pommel. So Merlin bade a knight that stood afore him [to] handle that sword, and he assayed, and he might not handle it. Then Merlin laughed.

"Why laugh ye?" said the knight.

"This is the cause," said Merlin: "there shall never man handle this sword but the best knight of the world, and that shall be Sir Lancelot or else Galahad, his son, and Lancelot with this sword shall slay the man that in the world he loved best, that shall be Sir Gawain." All this he let write in the pommel of the sword.

Then Merlin let make a bridge of iron and of steel into that island, and it was but half a foot broad, and there shall never man pass that bridge, nor have hardiness to go over, but if he were a passing good man and a good knight without treachery or villainy. Also the scabbard of Balin's sword Merlin left it on this side the island, that Galahad should find it. Also Merlin let make by his subtlety that Balin's sword was put in a marble stone standing upright as great as a millstone, and the stone hoved [hovered] always above the water and did many years, and so by adventure it swam down the stream to the City of Camelot, that is, in English, Winchester.

And that same day Galahad, the haughty prince, came with King Arthur, and so Galahad brought with him the scabbard and achieved the sword that was there in the marble stone hoving upon the water. And on Whitsunday he achieved the sword as it is rehearsed in *The Book of Sangrail*. Soon after this was done, Merlin came to King Arthur and told him of the dolorous stroke that Balin gave to King Pellam, and how Balin and Balan fought together the marvellest battle that ever was heard of, and how they were buried both in one tomb. "Alas," said King Arthur, "this is the greatest pity that ever I heard tell of two knights, for in the world I know not such two knights." Thus endeth the tale of Balin and of Balan, two brethren born in Northumberland, good knights.

XX. The Piteous Death of Arthur

In May when every lusty heart flourisheth and bourgeoneth, for as the season is lusty to behold and comfortable, so man and woman rejoice and gladden of summer coming with his fresh flowers—for winter with his rough winds and blasts causeth a lusty man and woman to cower, and sit fast by the fire—so in this season, as in the month of May, it befell a great anger and unhap that stinted not till the flower of chivalry of all the world was destroyed and slain; and all was long upon [because of] two unhappy knights, the which were named Agravain and Sir Mordred, that were brethren unto Sir Gawain. For this Sir Agravain and Sir Mordred had ever a privy hate unto the queen Dame Guinevere and to Sir Lancelot, and daily and nightly they ever watched upon Sir Lancelot.

So it mishapped, Sir Gawain and all his brethren were in King Arthur's chamber. And then Sir Agravain said thus openly, and not in no counsel, that many knights might hear it: "I marvel that we all be not ashamed both to see and to know how Sir Lancelot lieth daily and nightly by the queen, and all we know it so; and it is shamefully suffered of us all, that we all should suffer so noble a king as King Arthur is so to be shamed."

Then spoke Sir Gawain, and said: "Brother Sir Agravain, I pray you and charge you move no such matters no more afore me, for wit you well," said Sir Gawain, "I will not be of your counsel." "So God me help," said Sir Gaheris and Sir Gareth, "we will not be knowing, brother Agravain, of your deeds." "Then will I," said Sir Mordred. "I believe well that," said Sir Gawain, "for ever unto all unhappiness, brother Sir Mordred, thereto will ye grant; and I would that ye left all this, and made you not so busy; for I know," said Sir Gawain, "what will fall of it." "Fall of it what fall may," said Sir Agravain, "I will disclose it to the king."

"Not by my counsel," said Sir Gawain, "for an [if] there rise war and wrake [strife] betwixt Sir Lancelot and us, wit you well, brother, there will [be] many kings and great lords [who] hold with Sir Lancelot. Also, brother Sir Agravain," said Sir Gawain, "ye must remember how ofttimes Sir Lancelot hath rescued the king and the queen; and the best of us all had been full cold at the heart root, had not Sir Lancelot been better than we, and that hath he proved himself full oft. And as for my part," said Sir Gawain, "I will never be against Sir Lancelot for one day's deed, when he rescued me from King Carados of the Dolorous Tower, and slew him, and saved my life. Also, brother Sir Agravain and Sir Mordred, in like wise Sir Lancelot rescued you both, and threescore and two, from Sir Tarquin. Methinketh, brother, such kind deeds and kindness should be remembered."

"Do as ye list," said Sir Agravain, "for I will layne [conceal] it no longer." With these words came to them King Arthur.

"Now brother, stint your noise," said Sir Gawain.

"We will not," said Sir Agravain and Sir Mordred.

"Will ye so?" said Sir Gawain. "Then God speed you, for I will not hear your tales or be of your counsel."

"No more will I," said Sir Gareth and Sir Gaheris, "for we will never say evil by that man." "For because," said Sir Gareth, "Sir Lancelot made me knight; by no manner owe I to say ill of him." And therewithal they three departed, making great dole.

"Alas," said Sir Gawain and Sir Gareth, "now is this realm wholly mischieved, and the noble fellowship of the Round Table shall be disparply [dispersed]." So they departed.

And then Sir Arthur asked them what noise they made. "My lord," said Agravain, "I shall tell you that [which] I may keep no longer. Here is I, and my brother Sir Mordred, broke unto my brothers Sir Gawain, Sir Gaheris, and to Sir Gareth, how this we know all, that Sir Lancelot holdeth your queen, and hath done long. And we be your sister's sons, and we may suffer it no longer, and all we wot that ye should be above Sir Lancelot. And ye are the king that made him knight, and therefore we will prove it, that he is a traitor to your person." "If it be so," said Sir Arthur, "wit you well he is none other, but I would be loath to begin such a thing but I might have proofs upon it. For Sir Lancelot is an hardy knight, and all ye know he is the best knight among us all; and but if he be taken with the deed, he will fight with him that bringeth up the noise, and I know no knight that is able to match him. Therefore an [if] it be sooth as ye say, I would he were taken with the deed." For as the French book saith, the king was full loath thereto, that any noise should be upon Sir Lancelot and his queen; for the king had a deeming [suspicion], but he would not hear of it, for Sir Lancelot had done so much for him and the queen so many times, that wit ye well the king loved him passingly well.

"My lord," said Sir Agravain, "ye shall ride to-morn on hunting, and doubt ye not Sir Lancelot will not go with you. Then when it draweth toward night, ye may send the queen word that ye will lie out all that night, and so may ye send for your cooks, and then upon pain of death we shall take him that night with the queen, and outher [either] we shall bring him to you dead or quick."

"I will well," said the king. "Then I counsel you," said the king, "take with you sure fellowship."

"Sir," said Agravain, "my brother, Sir Mordred, and I, will take with us twelve knights of the Round Table."

"Beware," said King Arthur, "for I warn you ye shall find him wight [strong]." "Let us deal [act]," said Sir Agravain and Sir Mordred.

So on the morn King Arthur rode on hunting, and sent word to the queen that he would be out all that night. Then Sir Agravain and Sir Mordred got to them twelve knights, and hid themself in a chamber in the Castle of Carlisle, and these were their names: Sir Colgrevance, Sir Mador de la Porte, Sir Gingaline, Sir Meliot de Logris, Sir Petipace of Winchelsea, Sir Galleron of Galway, Sir Melion of the Mountain, Sir Astamore, Sir Gromore Somir Joure, Sir Curselaine, Sir Florence, Sir Lovel. So these twelve knights were with Sir Mordred and Sir Agravain, and all they were of Scotland, outher of Sir Gawain's kin, either well-willers to his brethren.

So when the night came, Sir Lancelot told Sir Bors how he would go that night and speak with the queen. "Sir," said Sir Bors, "ye shall not go this night by my counsel." "Why?" said Sir Lancelot. "Sir," said Sir Bors, "I dread me ever of Sir Agravain, that waiteth you daily to do you shame and us all; and never gave my heart against no going, that ever ye went to the queen, so much as now. For I mistrust that the king is out this night from the queen because peradventure he hath lain some watch for you and the queen, and therefore I dread me sore of treason." "Have ye no dread," said Sir Lancelot, "for I shall go and come again, and make no tarrying." "Sir," said Sir Bors, "that me repenteth, for I dread me sore that your going out this night shall wrath us all." "Fair nephew," said Sir Lancelot, "I marvel much why ye say thus, sithen [since] the queen hath sent for me; and wit ye well, I will not be so much a coward, but she shall understand I will see her good grace." "God speed you well," said Sir Bors, "and send you sound and safe again."

So Sir Lancelot departed, and took his sword under his arm, and so in his mantle that noble knight put himself in great jeopardy; and so he passed till he came to the queen's chamber, and then Sir Lancelot was lightly [quickly] put into the chamber.

And then, as the French book saith, the queen and Lancelot were together. And whether they were abed or at other manner of disports, me list [I wish] not hereof make no mention, for love that time was not as is nowadays. But thus as they were together, there came Sir Agravain and Sir Mordred, with twelve knights with them of the Round Table, and they said with crying voice: "Traitor knight, Sir Lancelot du Lake, now art thou taken." And thus they cried with a loud voice, that all the court might hear it; and they all fourteen were armed at all points, as they should fight in a battle.

"Alas," said Queen Guinevere, "now are we mischieved both." "Madam," said Sir Lancelot, "is there here any armour within your chamber, that I might cover my poor body withal? And if there be any, give it me, and I shall soon stint their malice, by the grace of God." "Truly," said the queen, "I have none armour, shield, sword, nor spear; wherefore I dread me sore our long love is come to a mischievous end, for I hear by their noise there be many noble knights, and well I wot they be surely armed; against them ye may make no resistance. Wherefore ye are likely to be slain, and then shall I be brent [burnt]. For an ye might escape them," said the queen, "I would not doubt but that ye would rescue me in what danger that ever I stood in." "Alas," said Sir Lancelot, "in all my life thus was I never bestad [beset] that I should be thus shamefully slain for lack of mine armour."

But ever in one Sir Agravain and Sir Mordred cried: "Traitor knight, come out of the queen's chamber, for wit thou well, thou art so beset that thou shalt not escape." "O Jesu mercy," said Sir Lancelot, "this shameful cry and noise I may not suffer, for better were death at once than thus to endure this pain."

Then he took the queen in his arms and kissed her, and said: "Most noble Christian queen, I beseech you as ye have been ever my special good lady, and I at all times your true poor knight unto my power, and as I never failed you in right nor in wrong sithen the first day King Arthur made me knight, that ye will pray for my soul if that I here be slain. For well I am assured that Sir Bors, my nephew, and all the remnant of my kin, with Sir Lavain and Sir Urry, that they will not fail you to rescue you from the fire; and therefore, mine own lady, recomfort yourself, whatsoever come of me, that ye go with Sir Bors, my nephew, and Sir Urry, and they all will do you all the pleasure that they can or may, that ye shall live like a queen upon my lands."

"Nay, Lancelot," said the queen, "wit thou well, I will never live after thy days, but an thou be slain, I will take my death as meekly for Jesu Christ's sake as ever did any Christian queen."

"Well, madam," said Lancelot, "sith it is so that the day is come that our love must depart, wit you well: I shall sell my life as dear as I may; and a thousandfold," said Sir Lancelot, "I am more heavier for you than for myself. And now I had liefer than to be lord of all Christendom, that I had sure armour upon me, that men might speak of my deeds or [ere] ever I were slain."

"Truly," said the queen, "I would it might please God that they would take me and slay me, and suffer you to escape."

"That shall never be," said Sir Lancelot. "God defend me from such a shame, but Jesu be thou my shield and mine armour!"

And therewith Sir Lancelot wrapped his mantle about his arm well and surely; and by then they had gotten a great form [bench] out of the hall, and therewithal they rushed at the door. "Fair lords," said Sir Lancelot, "leave your noise and your rushing, and I shall set open this door, and then may ye do with me what it liketh you."

"Come off, then," said they all, "and do it, for it availeth thee not to strive against us all; and therefore let us into this chamber, and we shall save thy life until thou come to King Arthur."

Then Lancelot unbarred the door, and with his left hand he held it open a little, so that but one man might come in at once; and so there came striding a good knight, a much man and large, and his name was Colgrevance of Gore, and he with a sword struck at Sir Lancelot mightily. And he [Lancelot] put aside the stroke and gave him such a buffet upon the helmet that he fell grovelling dead within the chamber door. And then Sir Lancelot with great might drew that dead knight within the chamber door. And Sir Lancelot with help of the queen and her ladies was lightly armed in Sir Colgrevance's armour.

And ever stood Sir Agravain and Sir Mordred crying: "Traitor knight, come out of the queen's chamber."

"Leave your noise," said Sir Lancelot unto Sir Agravain, "for wit you well, Sir Agravain, ye shall not prison me this night; and therefore an ye do by my counsel, go ye all from this chamber door, and make not such crying and such manner of slander as ye do. For I promise you by my knighthood, an ye will depart and make no more noise, I shall as to-morn appear afore you all before the king, and then let it be seen which of you all, outher [or] else ye all, that will accuse me of treason; and there I shall answer you as a knight should, that hither I came to the queen for no manner of mal engine [evil intent], and that will I prove and make it good upon you with my hands."

"Fie on thee, traitor," said Sir Agravain and Sir Mordred. "We will have thee maugre [despite] thy head, and slay thee if we list; for we let thee wit we have the choice of King Arthur to save thee or to slay thee."

"Ah sirs," said Sir Lancelot, "is there none other grace with you? Then keep yourself."

So then Sir Lancelot set all open the chamber door, and mightily and knightly he strode amongst them, and anon at the first buffet he slew Sir Agravain. And twelve of his fellows after, within a little while after, he laid them cold to the earth, for there was none of the twelve that might stand Sir Lancelot one buffet. Also Sir Lancelot wounded Sir Mordred, and he fled with all his might.

And then Sir Lancelot returned again unto the queen, and said: "Madam, now wit you well all our true love is brought to an end, for now will King Arthur ever be my foe; and therefore, madam, an it like you that I may have you with me, I shall save you from all manner adventures dangerous."

"That is not best," said the queen. "Meseemeth now ye have done so much harm, it will be best ye hold you still with this. And if ye see that as to-morn they will put me unto the death, then may ye rescue me as ye think best."

"I will well," said Sir Lancelot, "for have ye no doubt: while I am living I shall rescue you." And then he kissed her, and either gave other a ring; and so there he left the queen, and went until his lodging.

When Sir Bors saw Sir Lancelot, he was never so glad of his homecoming as he was then. "Jesu mercy," said Sir Lancelot, "why be ye all armed? What meaneth this?" "Sir," said Sir Bors, "after ye were departed from us, we all that be of your blood and your well-willers were so dretched [troubled] that some of us leapt out of our beds naked, and some in their dreams caught naked swords in their hands. Therefore," said Sir Bors, "we deem there is some great strife at hand; and then we all deemed that ye were betrapped with some treason, and therefore we made us thus ready, what need that ever ye were in."

"My fair nephew," said Sir Lancelot unto Sir Bors, "now shall ye wit all: that this night I was more harder bestad [beset] than ever I was in my life, and yet I escaped." And so he told them all how and in what manner, as ye have heard tofore. "And therefore, my fellows," said Sir Lancelot, "I pray you all that ye will be of good heart in what need soever I stand, for now is war come to us all."

"Sir," said Bors, "all is welcome that God sendeth us, and we have had much weal [happiness] with you and much worship, and therefore we will take the woe with you as we have taken the weal."

"And therefore," they said all (there were many good knights), "look ye take no discomfort, for there is no bands of knights under heaven but we shall be able to grieve them as much as they may us. And therefore discomfort not yourself by no manner, and we shall gather together that we love, and that loveth us, and what that ye will have done shall be done. And therefore, Sir Lancelot," said they, "we will take the woe with the weal."

"Grant mercy," said Sir Lancelot, "of your good comfort, for in my great distress, my fair nephew, ye comfort me greatly, and much I am beholding unto you. But this, my fair nephew, I would that ye did in all haste that ye may, or it be forth days [before long], that ye will look in their lodging that be lodged here nigh about the king which will hold with me and which will not, for now I would know which were my friends from my foes."

"Sir," said Sir Bors, "I shall do my pain [effort], and or it be seven of the clock I shall wit of such as ye have said before, who will hold with you."

Then Sir Bors called unto him Sir Lionel, Sir Ector de Maris, Sir Blamore de Ganis, Sir Bleoberis de Ganis, Sir Gahalantine, Sir Galihodin, Sir Galihud, Sir Menaduke, Sir Villiers the Valiant, Sir Hebes le Renoumes, Sir Lavain, Sir Urry of Hungary, Sir Neroveous, Sir Plenorius. These two [last] knights Sir Lancelot made, and the one he won upon a bridge, and therefore they would never be against him. And Harry le Fitz du Lake, and Sir Selises of the Dolorous Tower, and Sir Melias de Lille, and Sir Bellengere le Beuse, that was Sir Alexander's son Le Orphelin, because [of] his mother, Alice la Belle Pellerine, and she was kin unto Sir Lancelot, and he held with him. So there came Sir Palomides and Sir Safir, his brother, to hold with Sir Lancelot, and Sir Clegis, Sir Sadok, and Sir Dinas, Sir Clarrus of Cleremont.

So these two-and-twenty knights drew them together, and by then they were armed on horseback, and promised Sir Lancelot to do what he would. Then there fell to them, what of North Wales and of Cornwall, for Sir

Lamorak's sake and for Sir Tristram's sake, to the number of a four-score knights.

"My lords," said Sir Lancelot, "wit you well: I have been ever since I came into this country well-willed unto my lord, King Arthur, and unto my lady, Queen Guinevere, unto my power. And this night because my lady the queen sent for me to speak with her, I suppose it was made by treason, howbeit I dare largely excuse her person, notwithstanding I was there by a forecast [plot] near slain; but as Jesu provided me, I escaped all their malice and treason." And then that noble knight Sir Lancelot told them all how he was hard bestad in the queen's chamber, and how and in what manner he escaped from them. "And therefore," said Sir Lancelot, "wit you well, my fair lords, I am sure there is but war unto me and mine. And for because I have slain this night these knights, I wot well, as Sir Agravain, Sir Gawain's brother, and at the least twelve of his fellows, for this cause now I am sure of mortal war, for these knights were sent and ordained by King Arthur to betray me. And therefore the king will in this heat and malice judge the queen to the fire, and that may I not suffer, that she should be brent for my sake. For an I may be heard and suffered and so taken, I will fight for the queen, that she is a true lady unto her lord. But the king in his heat, I dread me, will not take me as I ought to be taken."

"My lord, Sir Lancelot," said Sir Bors, "by mine advice ye shall take the woe with the weal, and take it in patience, and thank God of it. And sithen it is fallen as it is, I counsel you keep yourself, for an ye will [guard] yourself, there is no fellowship of knights christened that shall do you wrong. Also I will counsel you, my lord Sir Lancelot, that an my lady, Queen Guinevere, be in distress, insomuch as she is in pain for your sake, that ye knightly rescue her; an ye did otherwise, all the world will speak of you shame to the world's end. Insomuch as ye were taken with her, whether ye did right or wrong, it is now your part to hold with the queen, that she be not slain and put to a mischievous death, for an she so die, the shame shall be yours."

"Jesu defend me from shame," said Sir Lancelot, "and keep and save my lady the queen from villainy and shameful death, and that she never be destroyed in my default. Wherefore, my fair lords, my kin, and my friends," said Sir Lancelot, "what will ye do?"

Then they said all: "We will do as ye will do."

"I put this to you," said Sir Lancelot: "that if my lord Arthur by evil counsel will to-morn in his heat put my lady the queen to the fire there to be brent, now I pray you counsel me what is best to do."

Then they said all at once with one voice: "Sir, us thinketh best that ye knightly rescue the queen; insomuch as she shall be brent, it is for your sake; and it is to suppose, an ye might be handled [captured], ye should have the same death, or a more shamefuller death. And sir, we say all, that ye have many times rescued her from death for other men's quarrels, [and so] us seemeth it is more your worship that ye rescue the queen from this peril, insomuch she hath it for your sake."

Then Sir Lancelot stood still and said: "My fair lords, wit you well I would be loath to do that thing that should dishonour you or my blood, and wit you well I would be loath that my lady, the queen, should die a shameful death; but an it be so that ye will counsel me to rescue her, I must do much harm or I rescue her; and peradventure I shall destroy some of my best friends; that should much repent me; and peradventure there be some, an they could well bring it about or disobey my lord King Arthur, they would soon come to me, the which I were loath to hurt. And if so be that I rescue her, where shall I keep her?"

"That shall be the least care of us all," said Sir Bors. "How did the noble knight Sir Tristram, by your good will? Kept not he with him La Belle Isolde near three year in Joyous Gard? The which was done by your althers [unanimous] device, and that same place is your own; and in likewise may ye do an ye list, and take the queen lightly away, if it so be the king will judge her to be brent; and in Joyous Gard ye may keep her long enough until the heat of the king be past. And then shall ye bring again the queen to the king with great worship; and then peradventure ye shall have thanks for her bringing home, and love and thank whether others shall have maugre [spite]."

"That is too hard to do," said Sir Lancelot, "for by Sir Tristram I may have a warning: for when by means of treaties, Sir Tristram brought again La Belle Isolde unto King Mark from Joyous Gard, look what befell on the end: how shamefully that false traitor King Mark slew him as he sat harping afore his lady La Belle Isolde; with a grounden glaive [sword], he thrust him in behind to the heart. It grieveth me," said Sir Lancelot, "to speak of his death, for all the world may not find such a knight."

"All this is truth," said Sir Bors, "but there is one thing shall [en]courage you and us all: ye know well King Arthur and King Mark were never [a]like of conditions, for there was never yet man could prove King Arthur untrue to his promise."

So to make short tale, they were all consented that, for better outher for worse, if so were that the queen were on that morn brought to the fire, shortly they all would rescue her. And so by the advice of Sir Lancelot, they put them all in an embushment [ambush] in a wood, as nigh Carlisle as they might, and there they abode still, to wit what the king would do.

Now turn we again unto Sir Mordred, that when he was escaped from the noble knight, Sir Lancelot, he anon got his horse and mounted upon him, and rode unto King Arthur, sore wounded and smitten, and all forbled. And there he told the king all how it was, and how they were all slain save himself all only.

"Jesu mercy, how may this be?" said the king. "Took ye him in the queen's chamber?"

"Yea, so God me help," said Sir Mordred. "There we found him unarmed, and there he slew Colgrevance, and armed him in his armour." And all this he told the king from the beginning to the ending.

"Jesu mercy," said the king, "he is a marvellous knight of prowess. Alas, me sore repenteth," said the king, "that ever Sir Lancelot should be against me. Now I am sure the noble fellowship of the Round Table is broken forever, for with him will many a noble knight hold; and now it is fallen so," said the king, "that I may [continue] not with my worship, but the queen must suffer the death."

So then there was made great ordinance in this heat, that the queen must be judged to the death. And the law was such in those days that whatsoever they were, of what estate or degree, if they were found guilty of treason, there should be none other remedy but death; and either the men or the taking with the deed [in the act] should be causer of their hasty [quick] judgment. And right so was it ordained for Queen Guinevere because Sir Mordred was escaped sore wounded, and the death of thirteen knights of the Round Table. These proofs and experiences caused King Arthur to command the queen to the fire, there to be brent.

Then spake Sir Gawain, and said: "My lord Arthur, I would counsel you not to be overhasty, but that ye would put it in respite, this judgment of my lady the queen, for many causes. One it is: though it were so that Sir Lancelot were found in the queen's chamber, yet it might be so that he came thither for none evil; for ye know my lord," said Sir Gawain, "that the queen is much beholden unto Sir Lancelot, more than unto any other knight, for ofttimes he hath saved her life, and done battle for her when all the court refused the queen. And peradventure she sent for him for goodness and for none evil, to reward him for his good deeds that he had done to her in times past. And peradventure my lady, the queen, sent for him to that intent that Sir Lancelot should come to her good grace privily and secretly, weening to her that it was best so to do, in eschewing and dreading of slander; for ofttimes we do many things that we ween it be for the best, and yet peradventure it turneth to the worst. For I dare say," said Sir Gawain, "my lady, your queen, is to you both good and true; and as for Sir Lancelot," said Sir Gawain, "I dare say he will make it good upon any knight living that will put upon himself villainy or shame, and in like wise he will make good for my lady, Dame Guinevere."

"That I believe well," said King Arthur, "but I will not [act] that way with Sir Lancelot, for he trusteth so much upon his hands and his might that he doubteth no man; and therefore for my queen he shall never fight more, for she shall have the law. And if I may get Sir Lancelot, wit you well he shall have a shameful death."

"Jesu defend," said Sir Gawain, "that I may never see it."

"Why say ye so?" said King Arthur. "Forsooth ye have no cause to love Sir Lancelot, for this night last past he slew your brother, Sir Agravain, a full good knight, and almost he had slain your other brother, Sir Mordred, and also there he slew thirteen noble knights; and also, Sir Gawain, remember ye he slew two sons of yours, Sir Florence and Sir Lovel."

"My lord," said Sir Gawain, "of all this I have knowledge, of whose deaths I repent me sore; but insomuch I gave them warning, and told my brethren and my sons aforehand what would fall in the end, insomuch they would not do by my counsel, I will not meddle me thereof, nor revenge me nothing of their deaths; for I told them it was no boot [good] to strive with Sir Lancelot. Howbeit I am sorry of the death of my brethren and of my sons, for they are the causers of their own death; for ofttimes I warned my brother Sir Agravain, and I told him the perils the which be now fallen."

Then said the noble King Arthur to Sir Gawain: "Dear nephew, I pray you make you ready in your best armour with your brethren, Sir Gaheris and Sir Gareth, to bring my queen to the fire, there to have her judgment and receive the death."

"Nay, my most noble lord," said Sir Gawain; "that will I never do; for wit you well I will never be in that place where so noble a queen as is my lady, Dame Guinevere, shall take a shameful end. For wit you well," said Sir

Gawain, "my heart will never serve me to see her die; and it shall never be said that ever I was of your counsel of her death."

Then said the king to Sir Gawain: "Suffer your brothers Sir Gaheris and Sir Gareth to be there."

"My lord," said Sir Gawain, "wit you well they will be loath to be there present, because of many adventures the which be like there to fall, but they are young and full unable to say you nay."

Then spake Sir Gaheris and the good knight Sir Gareth unto Sir Arthur: "Sir, ye may well command us to be there, but wit you well it shall be sore against our will; but an we be there by your straight commandment, ye shall plainly hold us there excused. We will be there in peaceable wise, and bear none harness of war upon us."

"In the name of God," said the king, "then make you ready, for she shall soon have her judgment anon."

"Alas," said Sir Gawain, "that ever I should endure to see this woeful day." So Sir Gawain turned him and wept heartily, and so he went into his chamber.

And then the queen was led forth without Carlisle, and there she was despoiled into her smock; and so then her ghostly [spiritual] father was brought to her, to be shriven of her misdeeds. Then was there weeping and wailing and wringing of hands, of many lords and ladies, but there were but few in comparison that would bear any armour for to strength [support] the death of the queen. Then was there one that Sir Lancelot had sent unto that place for to espy what time the queen should go unto her death; and anon as he saw the queen despoiled into her smock, and so shriven, then he gave Sir Lancelot warning.

Then was there but spurring and plucking up of horses, and right so they came to the fire. And who that stood against them, there were they slain; there might none withstand Sir Lancelot, so all that bore arms and withstood them, there were they slain, full many a noble knight. For there was slain Sir Belliance le Orgulous, Sir Segwarides, Sir Griflet, Sir Brandiles, Sir Aglovale, Sir Tor, Sir Gauter, Sir Gillimer, Sir Reynolds' three brethren, Sir Damas, Sir Priamus, Sir Kay the Stranger, Sir Driant, Sir Lambegus, Sir Herminde, Sir Pertilope, Sir Perimones, two brethren that were called the Green Knight and the Red Knight. And so in this rushing and hurtling, as Sir Lancelot thrang [dashed] here and there, it mishapped him to slay Gaheris and Sir Gareth, the noble knight, for they were unarmed and unware. For as the French book saith, Sir Lancelot smote Sir Gareth and Sir Gaheris upon the brainpans, wherethrough they were slain in the field. Howbeit in very truth Sir Lancelot saw them not, and so were they found dead among the thickest of the press.

Then when Sir Lancelot had thus done, and slain and put to flight all that would withstand him, then he rode straight unto Dame Guinevere and made a kirtle and a gown to be cast upon her; and then he made her to be set behind him, and prayed her to be of good cheer. Wit you well, the queen was glad that she was escaped from the death. And then she thanked God and Sir Lancelot; and so he rode his way with the queen, as the French book saith, unto Joyous Gard, and there he kept her as a noble knight should do. And many great lords and some kings sent Sir Lancelot many good knights, and many noble knights drew unto Sir Lancelot. When this was known openly, that King Arthur and Sir Lancelot were at debate, many knights were glad of their debate, and many were full heavy of their debate.

So turn we again unto King Arthur, that when it was told him how and in what manner of wise the queen was taken away from the fire, and when he heard of the death of his noble knights, and in especial of Sir Gaheris and Sir Gareth's death, then the king swooned for pure sorrow. And when he awoke of his swoon, then he said: "Alas, that ever I bore crown upon my head! For now have I lost the fairest fellowship of noble knights that ever held Christian king together. Alas, my good knights be slain away from me. Now within these two days I have lost forty knights, and also the noble fellowship of Sir Lancelot and his blood, for now I may never hold them together no more with my worship. Alas that ever this war began. Now fair fellows," said the king, "I charge you that no man tell Sir Gawain of the death of his two brethren, for I am sure," said the king, "when Sir Gawain heareth tell that Sir Gareth is dead, he will go nigh out of his mind. Mercy Jesu," said the king, "why slew he Sir Gareth and Sir Gaheris, for I dare say, as for Sir Gareth, he loved Sir Lancelot above all men earthly."

"That is truth," said some knights, "but they were slain in the hurtling as Sir Lancelot thrang in the thick of the press; and as they were unarmed, he smote them and wist not whom that he smote, and so unhappily they were slain."

"The death of them," said Arthur, "will cause the greatest mortal war that ever was; I am sure, wist Sir Gawain that Sir Gareth were slain, I should never have rest of him till I had destroyed Sir Lancelot's kin and himself both, outher [or] else he to destroy me. And therefore," said the king, "wit you well my heart was never so heavy as it is now, and much more I am sorrier for my good knights' loss than for the loss of my fair queen; for queens I might have enow, but such a fellowship of good knights shall never be together in no company. And now I dare say," said King Arthur, "there was never Christian king held such a fellowship together; and alas that ever Sir Lancelot and I should be at debate. Ah Agravain, Agravain," said the king, "Jesu forgive it thy soul, for thine evil will that thou and thy brother Sir Mordred hadst unto Sir Lancelot hath caused all this sorrow." And ever among these complaints the king wept and swooned.

Then there came one unto Sir Gawain, and told him how the queen was led away with Sir Lancelot, and nigh a twenty-four knights slain. "O Jesu defend my brethren," said Sir Gawain, "for full well wist I that Sir Lancelot would rescue her, outher else he would die in that field; and to say the truth, he had not been a man of worship had he not rescued the queen that day, insomuch she should have been brent for his sake. And as in that," said Sir Gawain, "he hath done but knightly, and as I would have done myself, an I had stood in like case. But where are my brethren?" said Sir Gawain, "I marvel I hear not of them."

"Truly," said that man, "Sir Gareth and Sir Gaheris be slain."

"Jesu defend," said Sir Gawain, "for all the world I would not that they were slain, and in especial my good brother, Sir Gareth."

"Sir," said the man, "he is slain, and that is great pity."

"Who slew him?" said Sir Gawain.

"Sir," said the man, "Lancelot slew them both."

"That may I not believe," said Sir Gawain, "that ever he slew my brother Sir Gareth; for I dare say my brother Gareth loved him better than me, and all his brethren, and the king both. Also I dare say, an Sir Lancelot had desired my brother Sir Gareth with him, he would have been with him against the king and us all, and therefore I may never believe that Sir Lancelot slew my brother."

"Sir," said this man, "it is noised that he slew him."

"Alas," said Sir Gawain, "now is my joy gone!" And then he fell down and swooned, and long he lay there as [if] he had been dead. And then, when he arose of his swoon, he cried out sorrowfully, and said: "Alas!" And right so Sir Gawain ran to the king, crying and weeping: "O King Arthur, mine uncle, my good brother Sir Gareth is slain, and so is my brother Sir Gaheris, the which were two noble knights." Then the king wept, and he both; and so they fell on swooning. And when they were revived, then spake Sir Gawain: "Sir, I will go see my brother, Sir Gareth."

"Ye may not see him," said the king, "for I caused him to be interred, and Sir Gaheris both; for I well understood that ye would make over-much sorrow, and the sight of Sir Gareth should have caused your double sorrow."

"Alas, my lord," said Sir Gawain, "how slew he my brother Sir Gareth? Mine own good lord, I pray you tell me."

"Truly," said the king, "I shall tell you how it is told me: Sir Lancelot slew him and Sir Gaheris both."

"Alas," said Sir Gawain, "they bare none arms against him, neither of them both."

"I wot not how it was," said the king, "but as it is said, Sir Lancelot slew them both in the thickest of the press and knew them not; and therefore let us shape a remedy for to revenge their deaths."

"My king, my lord, and mine uncle," said Sir Gawain, "wit you well now, I shall make you a promise that I shall hold by my knighthood: that from this day, I shall never fail Sir Lancelot until the one of us have slain the other. And therefore I require you, my lord and king, dress you to the war, for wit you well: I will be revenged upon Sir Lancelot; and therefore, as ye will have my service and my love, now haste you thereto, and assay [assemble] your friends. For I promise unto God," said Sir Gawain, "for the death of my brother Sir Gareth, I shall seek Sir Lancelot throughout seven kings' realms, but I shall slay him or else he shall slay me."

"Ye shall not need to seek him so far," said the king, "for as I hear say, Sir Lancelot will abide me and you in the Joyous Gard; and much people draweth unto him, as I hear say."

"That may I believe," said Sir Gawain; "but my lord," he said, "assay your friends, and I will assay mine."

"It shall be done," said the king, "and as I suppose, I shall be big enough to draw him out of the biggest tower of his castle." So then the king sent letters and writs throughout all England, both in the length and the breadth, for to summon all his knights. And so unto Arthur drew many knights, dukes, and earls, so that he had a great host. And when they were assembled, the king informed them how Sir Lancelot had bereft him his queen. Then the king and all his host made them ready to lay siege about Sir Lancelot, where he lay within Joyous Gard. Thereof heard Sir Lancelot, and purveyed him of many good knights, for with him held many knights; and some for his own sake, and some for the queen's sake. Thus they were on both parties well furnished and garnished of all manner of thing that longed to the war. But King Arthur's host was so big that Sir Lancelot would not abide him in the field, for he was full loath to do battle against the king. But Sir Lancelot drew him to his strong castle with all manner of victual, and as many noble men as he might suffice within the town and the castle. Then came King Arthur with Sir Gawain with an huge host and laid a siege all about Joyous Gard, both at the town and at the castle, and there they made strong war on both parties. But in no wise Sir Lancelot would ride out, nor go out of his castle, of long time; neither he would [allow] none of his good knights to issue out, neither none of the town nor of the castle, until fifteen weeks were past.

Then it befell upon a day in harvest time, Sir Lancelot looked over the walls, and spake on high unto King Arthur and Sir Gawain: "My lords both, wit ye well: all is in vain that ye make at this siege, for here win ye no worship but maugre [ill will] and dishonour; for an it list me to come myself out and my good knights, I should full soon make an end of this war." "Come forth," said Arthur unto Lancelot, "an thou durst, and I promise thee I shall meet thee in midst of the field." "God defend me," said Sir Lancelot, "that ever I should encounter with the most noble king that made me knight." "Fie upon thy fair language," said the king, "for wit you well and trust it: I am thy mortal foe, and ever will to my death day; for thou hast slain my good knights, and full noble men of my blood, that I shall never recover again. Also thou hast lain by my queen, and holden her many winters, and sithen like a traitor taken her from me by force."

"My most noble lord and king," said Sir Lancelot, "ye may say what ye will, for ye wot well: with yourself will I not strive. But thereas ye say I have slain your good knights, I wot well that I have done so, and that me sore repenteth; but I was enforced to do battle with them in saving of my life, or else I must have suffered them to have slain me. And as for my lady, Queen Guinevere, except your person of your highness, and my lord Sir Gawain, there is no knight under heaven that dare make it good upon me, that ever I was traitor unto your person. And where it please you to say that I have holden my lady your queen years and winters, unto that I shall ever make a large answer, and prove it upon any knight that beareth the life, except your person and Sir Gawain, that my lady, Queen Guinevere, is a true lady unto your person as any is living unto her lord, and that will I make good with my hands. Howbeit it hath liked her good grace to have me in charity, and to cherish me more than any other knight; and unto my power I again have deserved her love, for ofttimes, my lord, ye have consented that she should be brent and destroyed, in your heat, and then it fortuned me to do battle for her; and or I departed from her adversary, they confessed their untruth, and she full worshipfully excused. And at such times, my lord Arthur," said Sir Lancelot, "ye loved me and thanked me when I saved your queen from the fire; and then ye promised me forever to be my good lord; and now methinketh ye reward me full ill for my good service. And, my good lord, meseemeth I had lost a great part of my worship in my knighthood an I had suffered [let] my lady, your queen, to have been brent, and insomuch she should have been brent for my sake. For sithen I have done battles for your queen in other quarrels than in mine own, meseemeth now I had more right to do battle for her in right quarrel. And therefore my good and gracious lord," said Sir Lancelot, "take your queen unto your good grace, for she is both fair, true, and good."

"Fie on thee, false recreant knight," said Sir Gawain. "I let thee wit my lord, mine uncle, King Arthur, shall have his queen and thee, maugre [despite] thy visage, and slay you both whether it please him."

"It may well be," said Sir Lancelot, "but wit you well, my lord Sir Gawain: an me list to come out of this castle, ye should win me and the queen more harder than ever ye won a strong battle."

"Fie on thy proud words," said Sir Gawain. "As for my lady, the queen, I will never say of her shame. But thou, false and recreant knight," said Sir Gawain, "what cause hadst thou to slay my good brother Sir Gareth, that loved thee more than all my kin? Alas, thou madest him knight with thine own hands; why slew thou him that loved thee so well?"

"For to excuse me," said Sir Lancelot, "it helpeth me not, but by Jesu and by the faith that I owe to the high order of knighthood, I should with as good will have slain my nephew, Sir Bors de Ganis, at that time. But alas that ever I was so unhappy," said Lancelot, "that I had not seen Sir Gareth and Sir Gaheris."

"Thou liest, recreant knight," said Sir Gawain, "thou slewest him in despite of me; and therefore, wit thou well: I shall make war to thee, and all the while that I may live."

"That me repenteth," said Sir Lancelot, "for well I understand it helpeth not to seek none accordment while ye, Sir Gawain, are so mischievously set. And if ye were not, I would not doubt to have the good grace of my lord Arthur."

"I believe it well, false recreant knight," said Sir Gawain, "for thou hast many long days overlaid [oppressed] me and us all, and destroyed many of our good knights."

"Ye say as it pleaseth you," said Sir Lancelot, "and yet may it never be said on me and openly proved, that ever I by forecast of treason slew no good knight, as my lord, Sir Gawain, ye have done; and so did I never, but in my defense that I was driven thereto, in saving of my life."

"Ah, false knight," said Sir Gawain, "that thou meanest by Sir Lamorak; wit thou well I slew him."

"Ye slew him not yourself," said Sir Lancelot. "It had been overmuch on hand for you to have slain him, for he was one of the best knights christened of his age, and it was great pity of his death."

"Well, well," said Sir Gawain to Lancelot, "sithen thou upbraidest me of Sir Lamorak, wit thou well I shall never leave thee till I have thee at such avail that thou shalt not escape my hands."

"I trust you well enough," said Sir Lancelot, "an ye may get me, I get but little mercy."

But as the French book saith, the noble King Arthur would have taken his queen again, and have been accorded with Sir Lancelot, but Sir Gawain would not suffer him by no manner of mean. And then Sir Gawain made many men to blow upon [defame] Sir Lancelot; and all at once they called him false recreant knight. Then when Sir Bors de Ganis, Sir Ector de Maris, and Sir Lionel heard this outcry, they called to them Sir Palomides, Sir Safir's brother, and Sir Lavain, with many more of their blood. And all they went unto Sir Lancelot, and said thus: "My lord Sir Lancelot, wit ye well we have great scorn of the great rebukes that we heard Gawain say to you. Wherefore we pray you, and charge you as ye will have our service, keep us no longer within these walls. For wit you well plainly, we will ride into the field and do battle with them; for ye fare as a man that were afeared, and for all your fair speech, it will not avail you. For wit you well, Sir Gawain will not suffer you to be accorded with King Arthur, and therefore fight for your life and your right, an ye dare."

"Alas," said Sir Lancelot, "for to ride out of this castle and to do battle, I am full loath." Then Sir Lancelot spake on high unto Sir Arthur and Sir Gawain: "My lords, I require you and beseech you, sithen that I am thus required and conjured to ride into the field, that neither you, my lord King Arthur, nor you Sir Gawain, come not into the field."

"What shall we do then?" said Sir Gawain. "Is this the king's quarrel with thee to fight? And it is my quarrel to fight with thee, Sir Lancelot, because of the death of my brother Sir Gareth."

"Then must I needs unto battle," said Sir Lancelot. "Now wit you well, my lord Arthur and Sir Gawain, ye will repent it whensoever I do battle with you."

And so then they departed either from other; and then either party made them ready on the morn for to do battle, and great purveyance was made on both sides; and Sir Gawain let purvey many knights for to wait upon Sir Lancelot, for to overset him and to slay him. And on the morn at undorne [nine o'clock] Sir Arthur was ready in the field with three great hosts. And then Sir Lancelot's fellowship came out at three gates, in a full good array; and Sir Lionel came in the foremost battle, and Sir Lancelot came in the middle, and Sir Bors came out at the third gate. Thus they came in order and rule, as full noble knights; and always Sir Lancelot charged all his knights in any wise to save King Arthur and Sir Gawain.

Then came forth Sir Gawain from the king's host, and he came before and proffered to joust. And Sir Lionel was a fierce knight, and lightly he encountered with Sir Gawain; and there Sir Gawain smote Sir Lionel throughout the body, that he dashed to the earth like as he had been dead; and then Sir Ector de Maris and other more bare him into the castle.

Then there began a great stour [battle], and much people was slain; and ever Sir Lancelot did what he might to save the people on King Arthur's party, for Sir Palomides and Sir Bors and Sir Safir overthrew many knights, for they were deadly knights. And Sir Blamore de Ganis, and Sir Bleoberis de Ganis, with Sir Bellengere le Beuse, these six knights did much harm; and ever King Arthur was nigh about Sir Lancelot to have slain him, and Sir Lancelot suffered him, and would not strike again. So Sir Bors encountered with King Arthur, and there with a spear Sir Bors smote him down; and so he alit and drew his sword, and said to Sir Lancelot: "Shall I make an end of this war?" And that he meant to have slain King Arthur.

"Not so hardy [violent]," said Sir Lancelot, "upon pain of thy head, that thou touch him no more, for I will never see that most noble king that made me knight neither slain nor shamed."

And therewithal Sir Lancelot alit off his horse and took up the king and horsed him again, and said thus: "My lord Arthur, for God's love, stint this strife, for ye get here no worship, and I would do mine utterance [utmost], but always I forbear [spare] you, and ye nor none of yours forbeareth me; my lord, remember what I have done in many places, and now I am evil rewarded."

Then when King Arthur was on horseback, he looked upon Sir Lancelot, and then the tears brast [burst] out of his eyen, thinking on the great courtesy that was in Sir Lancelot more than in any other man. And therewith the king rode his way, and might no longer behold him, and said: "Alas, that ever this war began!"

And then either parties of the battles withdrew them to repose them, and buried the dead, and to the wounded men they laid soft salves; and thus they endured that night till on the morn. And on the morn by undorne they made them ready to do battle. And then Sir Bors led the forward. So upon the morn there came Sir Gawain as brym [fierce] as any boar, with a great spear in his hand. And when Sir Bors saw him, he thought to revenge his brother Sir Lionel of the despite that Sir Gawain did him the other day. And so they that knew either other feutred [fixed] their spears, and with all their mights of their horses and themselves, they met together so feloniously that either bare other through, and so they fell both to the earth; and then the battles joined, and there was much slaughter on both parties. Then Sir Lancelot rescued Sir Bors, and sent him into the castle; but neither Sir Gawain nor Sir Bors died not of their wounds, for they were all holpen.

Then Sir Lavain and Sir Urry prayed Sir Lancelot to do his pain, and fight as they had done. "For we see ye forbear and spare, and that doth much harm. Therefore we pray you spare not your enemies no more than they do you."

"Alas," said Sir Lancelot, "I have no heart to fight against my lord Arthur, for ever meseemeth I do not as I ought to do."

"My lord," said Sir Palomides, "though ye spare them all this day, they will never conne you thank [be grateful]; and if they may get you at avail [disadvantage] ye are but dead." So then Sir Lancelot understood that they said him truth; and then he strained himself more than he did aforehand, and because his nephew Sir Bors was sore wounded.

And then within a little while, by evensong [sunset] time, Sir Lancelot and his party better stood, for their horses went in blood past the fetlocks, there was so much people slain. And then for pity Sir Lancelot withheld his knights and suffered King Arthur's party for to withdraw them inside. And then Sir Lancelot's party withdrew them into his castle, and either parties buried the dead, and put salve unto the wounded men. So when Sir Gawain was hurt, they on King Arthur's party were not so orgulous [eager] as they were toforehand to do battle.

Of this war was noised through all Christendom, and at the last it was noised afore the Pope; and he, considering the great goodness of King Arthur and of Sir Lancelot, that was called the most noblest knights of the world, wherefore the Pope called unto him a noble clerk that at that time was there present. The French book saith it was the Bishop of Rochester; and the Pope gave him bulls under lead unto King Arthur of England, charging him upon pain of interdicting of all England that he take his queen Dame Guinevere unto him again, and accord with Sir Lancelot.

So when this Bishop was come to Carlisle, he showed the king these bulls. And when the king understood these bulls he nyst [knew not] what to do:

full fain he would have been accorded with Sir Lancelot, but Sir Gawain would not suffer him; but as for to have the queen, thereto he agreed. But in no wise Sir Gawain would not suffer the king to accord with Sir Lancelot; but as for the queen, he consented. And then the Bishop had of the king his great seal, and his assurance, as he was a true anointed king, that Sir Lancelot should come safe and go safe, and that the queen should not be spoken unto of the king, nor of none other, for no thing done aforetime past; and of all these appointments the Bishop brought with him sure assurance and writing, to show Sir Lancelot.

So when the Bishop was come to Joyous Gard, there he showed Sir Lancelot how the Pope had written to Arthur and unto him, and there he told him the perils if he withheld the queen from the king. "It was never in my thought," said Lancelot, "to withhold the queen from my lord Arthur; but, insomuch she should have been dead for my sake, meseemeth it was my part to save her life, and put her from that danger, till better recover might come. And now I thank God," said Sir Lancelot, "that the Pope hath made her peace; for God knoweth," said Sir Lancelot, "I will be a thousandfold more gladder to bring her again, than ever I was of her taking away; with this, I may be sure to come safe and go safe, and that the queen shall have her liberty as she had before; and never for no thing that hath been surmised afore this time, she never from this day stand in no peril. For else," said Sir Lancelot, "I dare adventure me to keep her from an harder shower [battle] than ever I kept her."

"It shall not need you," said the Bishop, "to dread so much. For wit you well, the Pope must be obeyed, and it were not the Pope's worship nor my poor honesty to wit you distressed, neither the queen, neither in peril, nor shamed." And then he showed Sir Lancelot all his writing, both from the Pope and from King Arthur.

"This is sure enough," said Sir Lancelot, "for full well I dare trust my lord's own writing and his seal, for he was never shamed of his promise. Therefore," said Sir Lancelot unto the Bishop, "ye shall ride unto the king afore, and recommend me unto his good grace, and let him have knowledging that this same day eight days [from now] by the grace of God I myself shall bring my lady, Queen Guinevere, unto him. And then say ye unto my most redoubted [noble] king, that I will say largely for [defend] the queen, that I shall none except for [spare] dread nor fear but the king himself and my lord Sir Gawain; and that is more for the king's love than for himself." So the Bishop departed and came to the king at Carlisle, and told him all how Sir Lancelot answered him; and then the tears brast out of the king's eyen.

Then Sir Lancelot purveyed him an hundred knights, and all were clothed in green velvet, and their horses trapped to their heels; and every knight held a branch of olive in his hand, in tokening of peace. And the queen had four-and-twenty gentlewomen following her in the same wise; and Sir Lancelot had twelve coursers following him, and on every courser sat a young gentleman, and all they were arrayed in green velvet, with sarpys [bands] of gold about their quarters, and the horse trapped in the same wise down to the heels, with many ouches [ornaments] set with stones and pearls in gold, to the number of a thousand. And she and Sir Lancelot were clothed in white cloth of gold tissue; and right so as ye have heard, as the French book maketh mention, he rode with the queen from Joyous Gard to Carlisle. And so Sir Lancelot rode throughout Carlisle, and so in the castle, that all men might behold; and wit you well, there was many a weeping eye.

And then Sir Lancelot himself alit and voided his horse, and took the queen, and so led her where King Arthur was in his seat; and Sir Gawain sat afore him, and many other great lords. So when Sir Lancelot saw the king and Sir Gawain, then he led the queen by the arm, and then he kneeled down, and the queen both. Wit you well, then was there many bold knight there with King Arthur that wept as tenderly as though they had seen all their kin [dead] afore them. So the king sat still, and said no word.

And when Sir Lancelot saw his countenance, he arose and pulled up the queen with him, and thus he spake full knightly: "My most redoubted king, ye shall understand, by the Pope's commandment and yours, I have brought to you my lady the queen, as right requireth; and if there be any knight, of whatsoever degree that he be, except your person, that will say or dare say but that she is true and clean to you, I here myself, Sir Lancelot du Lake, will make it good upon his body, that she is a true lady unto you; but liars ye have listened, and that hath caused debate betwixt you and me. For time hath been, my lord Arthur, that ye have been greatly pleased with me when I did battle for my lady, your queen; and full well ye know, my most noble king, that she hath been put to great wrong or this time; and sithen it pleased you at many times that I should fight for her, meseemeth, my good lord, I had more cause to rescue her from the fire, insomuch she should have been brent for my sake. For they that told you those tales were liars, and so it fell upon them; for by likelihood had not the might of God been with me, I might never have endured fourteen knights, and they armed and afore-purposed, and I unarmed and not purposed. For I was sent for unto my lady your queen, I wot not for what cause; but I was not so soon within the chamber door, but anon Sir Agravain and Sir Mordred called me traitor and recreant knight."

"They called thee right," said Sir Gawain.

"My lord Sir Gawain," said Sir Lancelot, "in their quarrel they proved themselves not in the right."

"Well, well, Sir Lancelot," said the king, "I have given thee no cause to do to me as thou hast done, for I have worshipped thee and thine more than any of all my knights."

"My good lord," said Sir Lancelot, "so ye be not displeased, ye shall understand I and mine have done you oft better service than any other knights have done, in many diverse places; and where ye have been full hard bestad diverse times, I have myself rescued you from many dangers. And ever unto my power I was glad to please you, and my lord Sir Gawain, both in jousts, and tournaments, and in battles set. Both on horseback and on foot, I have often rescued you and my lord Sir Gawain and many more of your knights in many diverse places."

"For now I will make a vaunt," said Sir Lancelot. "I will that ye all wit that yet I found never no manner of knight but that I was overhard for him, an I had done my utterance [utmost], thanked be God; howbeit I have been matched with good knights, as Sir Tristram and Sir Lamorak, but ever I had a favour unto them and a deeming what they were. And I take God to record," said Sir Lancelot, "I never was wroth nor greatly heavy with no good knight, an I saw him busy about to win worship; and glad I was ever when I found any knight that might endure me on horseback and on foot. Howbeit Sir Carados of the Dolorous Tower was a full noble knight and a passing strong man, and that wot ye, my lord Sir Gawain; for he might well be called a noble knight when he by fine force pulled you out of your saddle, and bound you overthwart [crosswise] afore him to his saddle bow; and there, my lord Sir Gawain, I rescued you, and slew him afore your sight. Also I found his brother, Sir Tarquin, in like wise leading Sir Gaheris, your brother, bound afore him; and there I rescued your brother and slew that Tarquin, and delivered threescore and four of my lord Arthur's knights out of his prison. And now I dare say," said Sir Lancelot, "I met never with so strong knights, nor so well fighting, as was Sir Carados and Sir Tarquin, for I fought with them to the uttermost. And therefore," said Sir Lancelot unto Sir Gawain, "meseemeth ye ought of right to remember this; for, an I might have your good will, I would trust to God to have my lord Arthur's good grace."

"The king may do as he will," said Sir Gawain, "but wit thou well, Sir Lancelot, thou and I shall never be accorded while we live, for thou hast slain three of my brethren; and two of them ye slew traitorly and piteously, for they bare none harness against thee, nor none would bear."

"God would they had been armed," said Sir Lancelot, "for then had they been on life. And wit ye well, Sir Gawain, as for Sir Gareth, I love none of my kinsmen so much as I did him. And ever while I live," said Sir Lancelot, "I will bewail Sir Gareth's death, not all only for the great fear I have of you, but many causes cause me to be sorrowful. One is, for I made him knight; another is, I wot well he loved me above all other knights; and the third is, he was passing noble, true, courteous, and gentle, and well conditioned; the fourth is, I wist well, anon as I heard that Sir Gareth was dead, I should never after have your love, but everlasting war betwixt us; and also I wist well that ye would cause my noble lord Arthur forever to be my mortal foe. And as Jesu be my help," said Sir Lancelot, "I slew never Sir Gareth nor Sir Gaheris by my will, but alas that ever they were unarmed that unhappy day. But thus much I shall offer me," said Sir Lancelot, "if it may please the king's good grace and you, my lord Sir Gawain: I shall first begin at Sandwich, and there I shall go in my shirt, barefoot; and at every ten miles' end I will found and gar make [cause built] an house of religion, of what order that ye will assign me, with an whole convent, to sing and read, day and night, in especial for Sir Gareth's sake and Sir Gaheris. And this shall I perform from Sandwich unto Carlisle; and every house shall have sufficient livelihood. And this shall I perform while I have any livelihood in Christendom; and there is none of all these religious places, but they shall be performed, furnished and garnished in all things as an holy place ought to be, I promise you faithfully. And this, Sir Gawain, methinketh were more fairer, holier, and more better to their souls, than [for] ye, my most noble king, and you, Sir Gawain, to war upon me, for thereby shall ye get none avail."

Then all knights and ladies that were there wept as they were mad, and the tears fell on King Arthur's cheeks. "Sir Lancelot," said Sir Gawain, "I have right well heard thy speech, and thy great proffers, but wit thou well:

let the king do as it pleaseth him; I will never forgive my brothers' death, and in especial the death of my brother Sir Gareth. And if mine uncle, King Arthur, will accord with thee, he shall lose my service, for wit thou well, thou art both false to the king and to me."

"Sir," said Lancelot, "he beareth not the life that may make that good; and if ye, Sir Gawain, will charge me with so high a thing, ye must pardon me, for then needs must I answer you."

"Nay," said Sir Gawain, "we are past that at this time, and that caused the Pope, for he hath charged mine uncle, the king, that he shall take his queen again, and to accord with thee, Sir Lancelot, as for this season, and therefore thou shalt go safe as thou camest. But in this land thou shalt not abide past fifteen days, such summons I give thee; so the king and we were consented and accorded or thou camest. And else," said Sir Gawain, "wit thou well thou shouldst not have come here, but if it were maugre thy head. And if it were not for the Pope's commandment," said Sir Gawain, "I should do battle with mine own body against thy body, and prove it upon thee, that thou hast been both false unto mine uncle King Arthur, and to me both; and that shall I prove upon thy body, when thou art departed from hence, wheresoever I find thee."

Then Sir Lancelot sighed, and therewith the tears fell on his cheeks, and then he said thus: "Alas, most noble Christian realm, whom I have loved above all other realms, and in thee I have gotten a great part of my worship, and now I shall depart in this wise. Truly me repenteth that ever I came in this realm, that should be thus shamefully banished undeserved and causeless; but fortune is so variant, and the wheel so movable, there is none constant abiding, and that may be proved by many old chronicles, of noble Hector and Troilus and Alexander the mighty Conqueror, and many more others; when they were most in their royalty, they alit lowest. And so fareth it by me," said Sir Lancelot, "for in this realm I had worship, and by me and mine all the whole Round Table hath been increased more in worship by me and mine blood than by any other. And therefore wit thou well, Sir Gawain, I may live upon my lands as well as any knight that here is. And if ye, most redoubted king, will come upon my lands with Sir Gawain to war upon me, I must endure you as well as I may. But as to you, Sir Gawain, if that ye come there, I pray you charge me not with treason nor felony, for an ye do, I must answer you."

"Do thou thy best," said Sir Gawain. "Therefore hie thee fast that thou were gone, and wit thou well we shall soon come after, and break the strongest castle that thou hast upon thy head." "That shall not need," said Sir Lancelot, "for an I were as orgulous set as ye are, wit you well I should meet you in the midst of the field."

"Make thou no more language," said Sir Gawain, "but deliver the queen from thee, and pick thee lightly out of this court."

"Well," said Sir Lancelot, "an I had wist of this shortcoming, I would have advised me twice or that I had come hither; for an the queen had been so dear to me as ye noise her, I durst have kept her from the fellowship of the best knights under heaven."

And then Sir Lancelot said unto Guinevere, in hearing of the king and them all: "Madam, now I must depart from you and this noble fellowship forever; and sithen it is so, I beseech you to pray for me, and say me well;

and if ye be hard bestad by any false tongues, lightly my lady send me word, and if any knight's hands may deliver you by battle, I shall deliver you." And therewithal Sir Lancelot kissed the queen. And then he said all openly: "Now let see what he be in this place that dare say the queen is not true unto my lord Arthur; let see who will speak an he dare speak."

And therewith he brought the queen to the king, and then Sir Lancelot took his leave and departed; and there was neither king, duke, nor earl, baron nor knight, lady nor gentlewoman, but all they wept as people out of their mind, except Sir Gawain. And when the noble Sir Lancelot took his horse to ride out of Carlisle, there was sobbing and weeping for pure dole of his departing; and so he took his way unto Joyous Gard. And then ever after he called it the Dolorous Gard. And thus departed Sir Lancelot from the court forever.

And so when he came to Joyous Gard, he called his fellowship unto him, and asked them what they would do. Then they answered all wholly together with one voice, they would [do] as he would do. "My fair fellows," said Sir Lancelot, "I must depart out of this most noble realm, and now I shall depart, it grieveth me sore, for I shall depart with no worship, for a flemed [banished] man departed never out of a realm with no worship; and that is my heaviness. Forever I fear after my days that men shall chronicle upon me that I was flemed out of this land; and else, my fair lords, be ye sure, an I had not dread shame, my lady, Queen Guinevere, and I should never have departed."

Then spake many noble knights, as Sir Palomides, Sir Safir his brother, and Sir Bellengere le Beuse, and Sir Urry, with Sir Lavain, with many others: "Sir, an ye be so disposed to abide in this land, we will never fail you; and if ye list not to abide in this land, there is none of the good knights that here be will fail you, for many causes. One is: all we that be not of your blood shall never be welcome to the court. And sithen it liked us to take part with you in your distress and heaviness in this realm, wit you well it shall like us as well to go in other countries with you, and there to take such part as ye do."

"My fair lords," said Sir Lancelot, "I well understand you, and as I can, thank you: and ye shall understand, such livelihood as I am born unto, I shall depart [share] with you in this manner of wise; that is for to say, I shall depart all my livelihood and all my lands freely among you, and I myself will have as little as any of you; for have I sufficient that may [be]long to my person; I will ask none other rich array; and I trust to God to maintain you on my lands as well as ever were maintained any knights."

Then spake all the knights at once: "He [should] have shame that will leave you; for we all understand: in this realm will be now no quiet, but ever strife and debate, now the fellowship of the Round Table is broken; for by the noble fellowship of the Round Table was King Arthur upborne, and by their noblesse, the king and all his realm was in quiet and rest, and a great part they said all was because of your noblesse."

"Truly," said Sir Lancelot, "I thank you all of your good saying. Howbeit, I wot well, in me was not all the stability of this realm, but in that I might, I did my devoir; and well I am sure I knew many rebellions in my days that by me were peaced, and I trow [believe] we all shall hear of them in short space, and that me sore repenteth. For ever I dread me," said Sir Lancelot, "that Sir Mordred will make trouble, for he is passing envious and applieth him to trouble."

So they were accorded to go with Sir Lancelot to his lands; and to make short tale, they trussed [equipped] and paid all that would ask them. And wholly an hundred knights departed with Sir Lancelot at once, and made their avows they would never leave him for weal nor for woe. And so they shipped at Cardiff, and sailed unto Benwick. Some men call it Bayonne, and some men call it Beaune, where the wine of Beaune is. But to say the sooth, Sir Lancelot and his nephews were lords of all France, and of all the lands that [be]longed unto France; he and his kindred rejoiced [possessed] it all, through Sir Lancelot's noble prowess. And then Sir Lancelot stuffed and furnished and garnished all his noble towns and castles. Then all the people of those lands came to Sir Lancelot on foot and hands.

And so when he had stablished all these countries, he shortly called a parliament; and there he crowned Sir Lionel King of France; and Sir Bors crowned him king of all King Claudas' lands; and Sir Ector de Maris, that was Sir Lancelot's youngest brother, he crowned him King of Benwick, and king of all Guienne, that was Sir Lancelot's own land. And he made Sir Ector prince of them all, and thus he departed.

Then Sir Lancelot advanced all his noble knights, and first he advanced them of his blood: that was, Sir Blamore, he made him Duke of Limousin in Guienne; and Sir Bleoberis, he made him Duke of Poitiers; and Sir Gahalantine, he made him Duke of Auvergne; and Sir Galihodin, he made him Duke of Santonge; and Sir Galihud, he made him Earl of Perigord; and Sir Menaduke, he made him Earl of Rouerge; and Sir Villiars the Valiant, he made him Earl of Béarn; and Sir Hebes le Renoumes, he made him Earl of Comminges; and Sir Lavain, he made him Earl of Armagnac; and Sir Urry, he made him Earl of Estrake; and Sir Neroveous he made him Earl of Pardiak; and Sir Plenorius he made Earl of Foix; and Sir Selises of the Dolorous Tower, he made him Earl of Marsan; and Sir Melias de Lille, he made him Earl of Tursar, and Sir Bellengere le Beuse, he made Earl of the Landes; and Sir Palomides, he made him Duke of the Provence; and Sir Safir, he made him Duke of Languedoc; and Sir Clegis he gave him the Earldom of Agen; and Sir Sadok, he gave him the Earldom of Sarlat; and Sir Dinas le Seneschal, he made him Duke of Anjou; and Sir Clarrus, he made him Duke of Normandy. Thus Sir Lancelot rewarded his noble knights and many more, that meseemeth it were too long to rehearse.

So leave we Sir Lancelot in his lands, and his noble knights with him, and return we again unto King Arthur and to Sir Gawain, that made a great host ready, to the number of threescore thousand; and all thing was made ready for their shipping to pass over the sea, and so they shipped at Cardiff. And there King Arthur made Sir Mordred chief ruler of all England, and also he put Queen Guinevere under his governance; because Sir Mordred was King Arthur's son, he gave him the rule of his land and of his wife. And so the king passed the sea and landed upon Sir Lancelot's lands, and there he brent and wasted, through the vengeance of Sir Gawain, all that they might overrun.

When this word came to Sir Lancelot, that King Arthur and Sir Gawain were landed upon his lands, and made a full great destruction and waste, then spake Sir Bors, and said: "My lord Sir Lancelot, it is shame that we suffer them thus to ride over our lands, for wit you well, suffer ye them as long as ye will, they will do you no favour an they may handle you." Then said Sir Lionel, that was wary and wise: "My lord Sir Lancelot, I will give this counsel, let us keep our strong walled towns until they have hunger and cold, and blow on their nails; and then let us freshly set upon them, and shred them down as sheep in a field, that aliens may take example forever how they land upon our lands."

Then spake King Bagdemagus to Sir Lancelot: "Sir, your courtesy will shende [destroy] us all, and thy courtesy hath waked all this sorrow; for an they thus over our lands ride, they shall by process bring us all to nought whilst we thus in holes us hide."

Then said Sir Galihud unto Sir Lancelot: "Sir, here be knights come of kings' blood, that will not long droop [cower], and they are within these walls; therefore give us leave, like as we be knights, to meet them in the field, and we shall slay them, that they shall curse the time that ever they came into this country."

Then spake seven brethren of North Wales, and they were seven noble knights; a man might seek in seven kings' lands or [before] he might find such seven knights. Then they all said at once: "Sir Lancelot, for Christ's sake, let us out ride with Sir Galihud, for we be never wont to cower in castles nor in noble towns."

Then spake Sir Lancelot, that was master and governor of them all: "My fair lords, wit you well I am full loath to ride out with my knights for shedding of Christian blood; and yet my lands I understand be full bare for to sustain any host awhile, for the mighty wars that whilom [previously] made King Claudas upon this country, upon my father King Ban, and on mine uncle King Bors; howbeit we will as at this time keep our strong walls, and I shall send a messenger unto my lord Arthur, a treaty for to take; for better is peace than always war."

So Sir Lancelot sent forth a damosel and a dwarf with her, requiring King Arthur to leave his warring upon his lands; and so she start upon a palfrey, and the dwarf ran by her side. And when she came to the pavilion of King Arthur, there she alit; and there met her a gentle knight, Sir Lucan the Butler, and said: "Fair damosel, come ye from Sir Lancelot du Lake?" "Yea sir," she said; "therefore I come hither to speak with my lord the king." "Alas," said Sir Lucan, "my lord Arthur would love Lancelot, but Sir Gawain will not suffer him." And then he said: "I pray to God, damosel, ye may speed well, for all we that be about the king would Sir Lancelot did best of any knight living." And so with this, Lucan led the damosel unto the king, where he sat with Sir Gawain, for to hear what she would say.

So when she had told her tale, the water ran out of the king's eyen, and all the lords were full glad for to advise the king as to be accorded with Sir Lancelot, save all only Sir Gawain. And he said: "My lord mine uncle, what will ye do? Will ye now turn again, now ye are passed thus far upon this journey? All the world will speak of your villainy."

"Nay," said Arthur, "wit thou well, Sir Gawain, I will do as ye will advise me. And yet meseemeth," said Arthur, "his fair proffers were not good to be refused; but sithen I am come so far upon this journey, I will that ye give the damosel her answer, for I may not speak to her for pity, for her proffers be so large."

Then Sir Gawain said to the damosel thus: "Damosel, say ye to Sir Lancelot that it is waste labour now to sue to mine uncle; for tell him, an he would have made any labour for peace, he should have made it or this time, for tell him now it is too late. And say that I, Sir Gawain, so send him word, that I promise him by the faith I owe unto God and to knighthood, I shall never leave him till he hath slain me or I him."

So the damosel wept and departed, and there were many weeping eyen; and so Sir Lucan brought the damosel to her palfrey, and so she came to Sir Lancelot where he was among all his knights. And when Sir Lancelot had heard this answer, then the tears ran down by his cheeks. And then his noble knights strode about him and said: "Sir Lancelot, wherefore make ye such cheer? Think what ye are, and what men we are, and let us noble knights match them in midst of the field."

"That may be lightly done," said Sir Lancelot, "but I was never so loath to do battle, and therefore I pray you, fair sirs, as ye love me, be ruled as I will have you, for I will always flee that noble king that made me knight. And when I may no further, I must needs defend me, and that will be more worship for me and us all than to compare with that noble king whom we have all served."

Then they held their language, and as that night [came], they took their rest. And upon the morn early, in the dawning of the day, as knights looked out, they saw the city of Benwick besieged round about; and fast they began to set up ladders, and then they defied them out of the town, and beat them from the walls mightily.

Then came forth Sir Gawain well armed upon a stiff steed, and he came before the chief gate, with his spear in his hand, crying: "Sir Lancelot, where art thou? Is there none of you proud knights dare break a spear with me?"

Then Sir Bors made him ready, and came forth out of the town, and there Sir Gawain encountered with Sir Bors. And at that time he smote Sir Bors down from his horse, and almost he had slain him; and so Sir Bors was rescued and borne into the town. Then came forth Sir Lionel, brother to Sir Bors, and thought to revenge him; and either feutred [fixed] their spears, and ran together; and there they met spitefully, but Sir Gawain had such grace that he smote Sir Lionel down, and wounded him there passing sore; and then Sir Lionel was rescued and borne into the town.

And this Sir Gawain came every day, and he failed not but that he smote down one knight or other. So thus they endured half a year, and much slaughter was of people on both parties. Then it befell upon a day, Sir Gawain came afore the gates armed at all pieces on a noble horse, with a great spear in his hand; and then he cried with a loud voice: "Where art thou now, thou false traitor, Sir Lancelot? Why hidest thou thyself within holes and walls like a coward? Look out now, thou false traitor knight, and here I shall revenge upon thy body the death of my three brethren."

All this language heard Sir Lancelot [in] every deal; and his kin and his knights drew about him, and all they said at once to Sir Lancelot: "Sir Lancelot, now must ye defend you like a knight, or else ye be shamed forever; for now ye be called upon [accused of] treason, it is time for you to stir, for ye have slept overlong and suffered overmuch."

"So God me help," said Sir Lancelot, "I am right heavy of Sir Gawain's words, for now he charged me with a great charge; and therefore I wot it as well as ye, that I must defend me, or else to be recreant."

Then Sir Lancelot bade saddle his strongest horse, and bade let fetch his arms, and bring all unto the gate of the tower; and then Sir Lancelot spake on high unto King Arthur, and said: "My lord Arthur, and noble king that made me knight, wit you well I am right heavy for your sake, that ye thus sue upon me; and always I forbare you, for would I have been vengeable, I might have met you in midst of the field, and there to have made your boldest knights full tame. And now I have forborne half a year, and suffered you and Sir Gawain to do what ye would do. And now may I endure it no longer, for now must I needs defend myself, insomuch Sir Gawain hath appelled [accused] me of treason, the which is greatly against my will that ever I should fight against any of your blood, but now I may not forsake it; I am driven thereto as a beast till a bay."

Then Sir Gawain said: "Sir Lancelot, an thou durst do battle, leave thy babbling and come off, and let us ease our hearts." Then Sir Lancelot armed him lightly, and mounted upon his horse, and either of the knights gat great spears in their hands, and the host without stood still all apart, and the noble knights came out of the city by a great number, insomuch that when Arthur saw the number of men and knights, he marvelled, and said to himself: "Alas, that ever Sir Lancelot was against me, for now I see he hath forborne me." And so the covenant was made, there should no man [draw] nigh them, nor deal with them, till the one were dead or yielded.

Then Sir Gawain and Sir Lancelot departed a great way asunder, and then they came together with all their horses' might as they might run, and either smote other in midst of their shields. But the knights were so strong, and their spears so big, that their horses might not endure their buffets, and so their horses fell to the earth; and then they voided their horses, and dressed their shields before them. Then they stood together and gave many sad strokes on diverse places of their bodies, that the blood brast out on many sides and places.

Then had Sir Gawain such a grace and gift that an holy man had given to him, that every day in the year, from underne [nine o'clock] till high noon, his might increased those three hours as much as thrice his strength, and that caused Sir Gawain to win great honour. And for his sake King Arthur made an ordinance that all manner of battles for any quarrels that should be done afore King Arthur should begin at underne; and all was done for Sir Gawain's love, that by likelihood, if Sir Gawain were on the one part, he should have the better in battle while his strength endureth three hours. But there were but few knights that time living that knew this advantage that Sir Gawain had, but King Arthur only.

Thus Sir Lancelot fought with Sir Gawain, and when Sir Lancelot felt his might evermore increase, Sir Lancelot wondered and dread him sore to be shamed. For as the French book saith, Sir Lancelot weened, when he felt Sir Gawain double his strength, that he had been a fiend and none earthly man; wherefore Sir Lancelot traced and traversed, and covered himself with his shield, and kept his might and his breath during three hours. And that while Sir Gawain gave him many sad brunts, and many sad strokes, that all the knights that beheld Sir Lancelot marvelled how that he might endure him; but full little understood they that travail that Sir Lancelot had for to endure him.

And then when it was past noon, Sir Gawain had no more but his own might. When Sir Lancelot felt him so come down, then he stretched him up and stood near Sir Gawain, and said thus: "My lord Sir Gawain, now I feel ye have done; now my lord Sir Gawain, I must do my part, for many great and grievous strokes I have endured you this day with great pain." Then Sir Lancelot doubled his strokes and gave Sir Gawain such a buffet on the helmet that he fell down on his side, and Sir Lancelot withdrew him from him.

"Why withdrawest thou thee?" said Sir Gawain. "Now turn again, false traitor knight, and slay me, for an thou leave me thus, when I am whole I shall do battle with thee again."

"I shall endure you, sir, by God's grace, but wit thou well, Sir Gawain, I will never smite a felled knight." And so Sir Lancelot went into the city, and Sir Gawain was borne into King Arthur's pavilion, and leeches were brought to him, and [he was] searched and salved with soft ointments. And then Sir Lancelot said: "Now have good day, my lord the king, for wit you well ye win no worship at these walls; and if I would my knights outbring, there should many a man die. Therefore, my lord Arthur, remember you of old kindness; and however I fare, Jesu be your guide in all places."

"Alas," said the king, "that ever this unhappy war was begun; for ever Sir Lancelot forbeareth me in all places, and in like wise my kin, and that is seen well this day by my nephew Sir Gawain." Then King Arthur fell sick for sorrow of Sir Gawain, that he was so sore hurt, and because of the war betwixt him and Sir Lancelot. So then they on King Arthur's part kept the siege with little war without, and they within kept their walls, and defended them when need was. Thus Sir Gawain lay sick three weeks in his tents, with all manner of leechcraft that might be had.

And as soon as Sir Gawain might go and ride, he armed him at all points, and started upon a courser, and gat a spear in his hand, and so he came riding afore the chief gate of Benwick; and there he cried on high: "Where art thou, Sir Lancelot? Come forth, thou false traitor knight and recreant, for I am here, Sir Gawain, [and] will prove this that I say on thee."

All this language Sir Lancelot heard, and then he said thus: "Sir Gawain, me repents of your foul saying, that ye will not cease of your language. For you wot well, Sir Gawain, I know your might and all that ye may do; and well ye wot, Sir Gawain, ye may not greatly hurt me."

"Come down, traitor knight," said he, "and make it good the contrary with thy hands, for it mishapped me the last battle to be hurt of thy hands; therefore wit thou well, I am come this day to make amends, for I ween this day to lay thee as low as thou laidest me."

"Jesu defend me," said Sir Lancelot, "that ever I be so far in your danger as ye have been in mine, for then my days were done. But Sir Gawain," said Sir Lancelot, "ye shall not think that I tarry long, but sithen that ye so unknightly call me of treason, ye shall have both your hands full of me." And then Sir Lancelot armed him at all points, and mounted upon his horse, and gat a great spear in his hand, and rode out at the gate. And both the hosts were assembled, of them without and of them within, and stood in array full manly. And both parties were charged to hold them still, to see and behold the battle of these two noble knights. And then they laid their spears in their rests, and they came together as thunder, and Sir Gawain brake his spear upon Sir Lancelot in an hundred pieces unto his hand; and Sir Lancelot smote him with a greater might, that Sir Gawain's horse's feet raised, and so the horse and he fell to the earth.

Then Sir Gawain deliverly [quickly] voided his horse, and put his shield afore him, and eagerly drew his sword, and bade Sir Lancelot: "Alight, traitor knight, for if this mare's son hath failed me, wit thou well a king's son and a queen's son shall not fail thee." Then Sir Lancelot voided his horse, and dressed his shield afore him, and drew his sword; and so stood they together and gave many sad strokes, that all men on both parties had thereof passing great wonder. But when Sir Lancelot felt Sir Gawain's might so marvellously increase, he then withheld his courage and his wind, and kept himself wonder[fully] covert of his might; and under his shield he traced and traversed here and there, to break Sir Gawain's strokes and his courage; and Sir Gawain enforced himself with all his might and power to destroy Sir Lancelot. For as the French book saith, ever as Sir Gawain's might increased, right so increased his wind and his evil will. Thus Sir Gawain did great pain unto Sir Lancelot three hours, that he had right great pain for to defend him.

And when the three hours were passed, that Sir Lancelot felt that Sir Gawain was come to his own proper strength, then Sir Lancelot said unto Sir Gawain: "Now have I proved you twice that ye are a full dangerous knight, and a wonderful man of your might; and many wonderful deeds have you done in your days, for by your might increasing you have deceived many a full noble and valiant knight; and now I feel that ye have done your mighty deeds; now wit you well, I must do my deeds." And then Sir Lancelot stood near Sir Gawain, and then Sir Lancelot doubled his strokes. And Sir Gawain defended him mightily, but nevertheless Sir Lancelot smote such a stroke upon Sir Gawain's helm and upon the old wound that Sir Gawain sinked down upon his one side in a swoon.

And anon as he did awake, he waved and foined [thrust] at Sir Lancelot as he lay, and said: "Traitor knight, wit thou well, I am not yet slain; come thou near me and perform this battle unto the uttermost."

"I will no more do than I have done," said Sir Lancelot, "for when I see you on foot, I will do battle upon you all the while I see you stand on your feet; but for to smite a wounded man that may not stand, God defend me from such a shame."

And then he turned him and went his way toward the city. And Sir Gawain evermore calling him traitor knight, and said: "Wit thou well, Sir Lancelot, when I am whole I shall do battle with thee again, for I shall never leave thee till that one of us be slain."

Thus as this siege endured and as Sir Gawain lay sick near a month, and when he was well recovered and ready within three days to do battle again with Sir Lancelot, right so came tidings unto Arthur from England that made King Arthur and all his host to remove.

XXI. The Last Departing of Arthur and Lancelot's Revenge

As Sir Mordred was ruler of all England, he did do make letters as though that they came from beyond the sea, and the letters specified that King Arthur was slain in battle with Sir Lancelot. Wherefore Sir Mordred made a parliament and called the lords together, and there he made them to choose him king; and so was he crowned at Canterbury, and held a feast there fifteen days. And afterward he drew him unto Winchester, and there he took the Queen Guinevere, and said plainly that he would wed her, which was his uncle's wife and his father's wife. And so he made ready for the feast, and a day prefixed that they should be wedded; wherefore Queen Guinevere was passing heavy. But she durst not discover her heart, but spake fair, and agreed to Sir Mordred's will. Then she desired of Sir Mordred for to go to London, to buy all manner of things that longed unto the wedding. And by cause of her fair speech Sir Mordred trusted her well enough, and gave her leave to go.

And so when she came to London, she took the Tower of London and suddenly in all haste possible she stuffed it with all manner of victual, and well garnished it with men, and so kept it. Then when Sir Mordred wist and understood how he was beguiled, he was passing wroth out of measure. And a short tale for to make, he went and laid a mighty siege about the Tower of London, and made many great assaults thereat, and threw many great engines unto them, and shot great guns. But all might not prevail Sir Mordred, for Queen Guinevere would never for fair speech nor for foul, would never trust to come in his hands again.

Then came the Bishop of Canterbury, the which was a noble clerk and an holy man, and thus he said to Sir Mordred: "Sir, what will ye do? Will ye first displease God and sithen shame yourself, and all knighthood? Is not King Arthur your uncle, no farther but your mother's brother, and on her himself King Arthur begat you upon his own sister; therefore how may you wed your father's wife? Sir," said the noble clerk, "leave this opinion or I shall curse you with book and bell and candle."

"Do thou thy worst," said Sir Mordred; "wit thou well I shall defy thee."

"Sir," said the Bishop, "and wit you well I shall not fear me to do that me ought to do. Also, where ye noise where my lord Arthur is slain, and that is not so, and therefore ye will make a foul work in this land."

"Peace, thou false priest," said Sir Mordred, "for an thou chafe me any more, I shall make strike off thy head." So the Bishop departed and did the cursing in the most orgulist [proudest] wise that might be done. And then Sir Mordred sought the Bishop of Canterbury, for to have slain him. Then the Bishop fled, and took part of his goods with him, and went nigh unto Glastonbury; and there he was as priest hermit in a chapel, and lived in poverty and in holy prayers, for well he understood that mischievous war was at hand.

Then Sir Mordred sought on Queen Guinevere by letters and sondes [messages], and by fair means and foul means, for to have her to come out of the Tower of London. But all this availed not, for she answered him shortly, openly and privily, that she had liefer slay herself than to be married with him.

Then came word to Sir Mordred that King Arthur had raised the siege for Sir Lancelot, and he was coming homeward with a great host, to be avenged upon Sir Mordred; wherefore Sir Mordred made write writs to all the barony of this land, and much people drew to him. For then was the common voice among them that with Arthur was none other life but war and strife, and with Sir Mordred was great joy and bliss. Thus was Sir Arthur depraved [defamed] and evil said of. And many there were that King Arthur had made up of nought, and given them lands, might not then say him a good word.

Lo, ye all Englishmen, see ye not what a mischief here was! For he that was the most king and knight of the world, and most loved the fellowship of noble knights, and by him they were all upholden, now might not these Englishmen hold them content with him. Lo, thus was the old custom and usage of this land; and also men say that we of this land have not yet lost nor forgotten that custom and usage. Alas, this is a great default of us Englishmen, for there may no thing please us no term! And so fared the people at that time: they were better pleased with Sir Mordred than they were with King Arthur; and much people drew unto Sir Mordred, and said they would abide with him for better and for worse. And so Sir Mordred drew with a great host to Dover, for there he heard say that Sir Arthur would arrive, and so he thought to beat his own father from his lands; and the most part of all England held with Sir Mordred; the people were so new-fangled.

And so as Sir Mordred was at Dover with his host, there came King Arthur with a great navy of ships, and galleys and carracks. And there was Sir Mordred ready awaiting upon his landing, to let [prevent] his own father to land upon the land that he was king over. Then there was launching of great boats and small, and full of noble men of arms; and there was much slaughter of gentle knights, and many a full bold baron was laid full low, on both parties. But King Arthur was so courageous that there might no manner of knights let him to land, and his knights fiercely followed him; and so they landed maugre [despite] Sir Mordred and all his power, and put Sir Mordred aback, that he fled and all his people.

So when this battle was done, King Arthur let bury his people that were dead. And then was noble Sir Gawain found in a great boat, lying more than half-dead. When Sir Arthur wist that Sir Gawain was laid so low, he went unto him; and there the king made sorrow out of measure, and took Sir Gawain in his arms, and thrice he there swooned. And then when he awaked, he said: "Alas, Sir Gawain, my sister's son, here now thou liest, the man in the world that I loved most. And now is my joy gone, for now, my nephew Sir Gawain, I will discover me unto [disclose] your person: in Sir Lancelot and you, I most had my joy, and mine affiance [trust], and now have I lost my joy of you both. Wherefore all mine earthly joy is gone from me."

"Mine uncle King Arthur," said Sir Gawain, "wit you well my death-day is come, and all is through mine own hastiness and willfulness; for I am smitten upon the old wound the which Sir Lancelot gave me, on the which I feel well I must die. And had Sir Lancelot been with you as he was, this unhappy war had never begun; and of all this am I causer, for Sir Lancelot and his blood, through their prowess, held all your cankered enemies in subjection and daunger. And now," said Sir Gawain, "ye shall miss Sir Lancelot. But alas, I would not accord with him, and therefore," said Sir Gawain, "I pray you, fair uncle, that I may have paper, pen, and ink, that I may write to Sir Lancelot a cedle [letter] with mine own hands."

And then when paper and ink was brought, then Gawain was set up weakly by King Arthur, for he was shriven a little tofore. And then he wrote thus, as the French book maketh mention: "Unto Sir Lancelot, flower of all noble knights that ever I heard of or saw by my days, I, Sir Gawain, King Lot's son of Orkney, sister's son unto the noble King Arthur, send thee greeting, and let thee have knowledge that the tenth day of May I was smitten upon the old wound that thou gavest me afore the city of Benwick, and through the same wound that thou gavest me I am come to my death-day. And I will that all the world wit, that I, Sir Gawain, knight of the Table Round, sought my death, and not through thy deserving, but it was mine own seeking; wherefore I beseech thee, Sir Lancelot, to return again unto this realm, and see my tomb, and pray some prayer more or less for my soul. And this same day that I wrote this cedle, I was hurt to the death in the same wound, the which I had of thy hand, Sir Lancelot, for of a more nobler man might I not be slain. Also Sir Lancelot, for all the love that ever was betwixt us, make no tarrying, but come over the sea in all haste, that thou mayst with thy noble knights rescue that noble king that made thee knight, that is my lord Arthur. For he is full straitly bestad [harshly beset] with a false traitor, that is my half-brother, Sir Mordred; and he hath let crown him king, and would have wedded my lady Queen Guinevere; and so had he done, had she not put herself in the Tower of London. And so the tenth day of May last past, my lord Arthur and we all landed upon them at Dover; and there we put that false traitor, Sir Mordred, to flight, and there it misfortuned me to be stricken upon thy stroke. And at the date of this letter was written, but two hours and a half afore my death, written with mine own hand, and so subscribed with part of my heart's blood. And I require thee, most famous knight of the world, that thou wilt see my tomb."

And then Sir Gawain wept, and King Arthur wept; and then they swooned both. And when they awaked both, the king made Sir Gawain to receive his Saviour. And then Sir Gawain prayed the king for to send for Sir Lancelot, and to cherish him above all other knights. And so at the hour of noon Sir Gawain yielded up the spirit; and then the king let inter him in a chapel within Dover Castle. And there yet all men may see the skull of him, and the same wound is seen that Sir Lancelot gave him in battle.

Then was it told the king that Sir Mordred had pyghte [pitched] a new field upon Barham Down. And upon the morn, the king rode thither to him, and there was a great battle betwixt them, and much people was slain on both parties; but at the last Sir Arthur's party stood best, and Sir Mordred and his party fled unto Canterbury.

And then the king let search all the towns for his knights that were slain, and interred them; and salved them with soft salves that so sore were wounded. Then much people drew unto King Arthur. And then they said that Sir Mordred warred upon King Arthur with wrong. And then King Arthur drew him with his host down by the seaside westward toward Salisbury; and there was a day assigned betwixt King Arthur and Sir Mordred, that they should meet upon a down beside Salisbury, and not far from the seaside. And this day was assigned on a Monday after Trinity Sunday, whereof King Arthur was passing glad, that he might be avenged upon Sir Mordred.

Then Sir Mordred raised much people about London, for they of Kent, Sussex, and Surrey, Essex, and of Suffolk, and of Norfolk held the most part with Sir Mordred; and many a full noble knight drew unto Sir Mordred and to the king. But they [who] loved Sir Lancelot drew unto Sir Mordred.

So upon Trinity Sunday at night, King Arthur dreamed a wonderful dream, and that was this: that him seemed he sat upon a chaflet [platform] in a chair, and the chair was fast to a wheel, and thereupon sat King Arthur in the richest cloth of gold that might be made; and the king thought there was under him, far from him, an hideous deep black water, and therein were all manner of serpents and worms and wild beasts, foul and horrible; and suddenly the king thought the wheel turned up-so-down, and he fell among the serpents, and every beast took him by a limb; and then the king cried as he lay in his bed and slept: "Help!"

And then knights, squires, and yeomen awaked the king; and then he was so amazed that he wist not where he was; and then he fell on slumbering again, not sleeping nor thoroughly waking. So the king seemed verily that there came Sir Gawain unto him with a number of fair ladies with him. And when King Arthur saw him, then he said: "Welcome, my sister's son; I weened thou hadst been dead, and now I see thee on life, much am I beholden unto almighty Jesu. O fair nephew and my sister's son, what be these ladies that hither be come with you?"

"Sir," said Sir Gawain, "all these be ladies for whom I have foughten when I was man living, and all these are those that I did battle for in righteous quarrel; and God hath given them that grace at their great prayer, because I did battle for them, that they should bring me hither unto you. Thus much hath God given me leave, for to warn you of your death; for an ye fight as to-morn with Sir Mordred, as ye both have assigned, doubt ye not ye must be slain, and the most part of your people on both parties. And for the great grace and goodness that almighty Jesu hath unto you, and for pity of you, and many more other good men there shall be slain, God hath sent me to you of his special grace, to give you warning that in no wise ye do battle as to-morn, but that ye take a treaty for a month day; and proffer you largely, so as to-morn to be put in a delay. For within a month shall come Sir Lancelot with all his noble knights, and rescue you worshipfully, and slay Sir Mordred, and all that ever will hold with him." Then Sir Gawain and all the ladies vanished.

And anon the king called upon his knights, squires, and yeomen, and charged them wightly [quickly] to fetch his noble lords and wise bishops unto him. And when they were come, the king told them his avision, what Sir Gawain had told him, and warned him that if he fought on the morn he should be slain. Then the king commanded Sir Lucan the Butler and his brother Sir Bedivere, with two bishops with them, and charged them in any wise, an they might: "Take a treaty for a month day with Sir Mordred, and spare not; proffer him lands and goods as much as ye think best."

So then they departed, and came to Sir Mordred, where he had a grim host of an hundred thousand men. And there they entreated Sir Mordred long time; and at the last Sir Mordred was agreed for to have Cornwall and Kent, by Arthur's days; after[ward], all England, after the days of King Arthur.

Then were they condescended [consented] that King Arthur and Sir Mordred should meet betwixt both their hosts, and every each of them should bring fourteen persons; and they came with this word unto Arthur. Then said he: "I am glad that this is done." And so he went into the field. And when Arthur should depart, he warned all his host that, an they see any sword drawn: "Look ye come on fiercely, and slay that traitor Sir Mordred, for I in no wise trust him."

In like wise Sir Mordred warned his host that: "An ye see any sword drawn, look that ye come on fiercely, and so slay all that ever before you standeth; for in no wise I will not trust for this treaty, for I know well my father will be avenged on me."

And so they met as their appointment was, and so they were agreed and accorded thoroughly; and wine was fetched, and they drank. Right soon came an adder out of a little heath bush, and it stung a knight on the foot. And when the knight felt him stung, he looked down and saw the adder, and then he drew his sword to slay the adder, and thought of none other harm. And when the host on both parties saw that sword drawn, then they blew beams [small horns], trumpets, and horns, and shouted grimly. And so both hosts dressed them together.

And King Arthur took his horse and said: "Alas, this unhappy day!" and so rode to his party. And Sir Mordred in like wise. And never was there seen a more dolefuller battle in no Christian land, for there was but rushing and riding, foining and striking, and many a grim word was there spoken either to other, and many a deadly stroke. But ever King Arthur rode throughout the battle of Sir Mordred many times, and did full nobly as a noble king should, and at all times he fainted never; and Sir Mordred that day put him in devoir [need] and in great peril. And thus they fought all the long day, and never stinted till the noble knights were laid to the cold earth; and ever they fought still till it was near night, and by that time was there an hundred thousand laid dead upon the down. Then was Arthur wood wroth [madly angry] out of measure, when he saw his people so slain from him.

Then the king looked about him, and then was he ware [that] of all his host and of all his good knights were left no more on life but two knights: that one was Sir Lucan the Butler, and his brother Sir Bedivere, and they were full sore wounded. "Jesu mercy," said the king, "where are all my noble knights become? Alas, that ever I should see this doleful day, for now," said Arthur, "I am come to mine end. But would to God that I wist where were that traitor Sir Mordred, that hath caused all this mischief!"

Then was King Arthur ware where Sir Mordred leaned upon his sword among a great heap of dead men. "Now give me my spear," said Arthur unto Sir Lucan, "for yonder I have espied the traitor that all this woe hath wrought."

"Sir, let him be," said Sir Lucan, "for he is unhappy [brings misfortune]. And if ye pass this unhappy day ye shall be right well revenged upon him. Good lord, remember ye of your night's dream, and what the spirit of Sir Gawain told you this night, yet God of his great goodness hath preserved you hitherto. Therefore, for God's sake, my lord, leave off by this, for blessed be God ye have won the field, for here we be three on life, and with Sir Mordred is none on life; and if ye leave off now, this wicked day of destiny is past."

"Tide me death, betide me life," saith the king. "Now I see him yonder alone, he shall never escape mine hands, for at a better avail shall I never have him."

"God speed you well," said Sir Bedivere.

Then the king gat his spear in both his hands and ran toward Sir Mordred, crying: "Traitor, now is thy death day come!" And when Sir Mordred heard Sir Arthur, he ran until him with his sword drawn in his hand. And there King Arthur smote Sir Mordred under the shield, with a foin of his spear, throughout the body, more than a fathom. And when Sir Mordred felt that he had his death-wound, he thrust himself with the might that he had up to the bur [hand-guard] of King Arthur's spear. And right so he smote his father Arthur, with his sword holden in both his hands, on the side of the head, that the sword pierced the helmet and the brain-pan, and therewithal Sir Mordred fell stark dead to the earth; and the noble Arthur fell in a swoon to the earth, and there he swooned ofttimes.

And Sir Lucan the Butler and Sir Bedivere ofttimes heaved him up. And so weakly they led him betwixt them both, to a little chapel not far from the seaside. And when the king was there, he thought him well eased. Then heard they people cry in the field. "Now go thou, Sir Lucan," said the king, "and do me to wit what betokens that noise in the field."

So Sir Lucan departed, for he was grievously wounded in many places. And so as he yede [went], he saw and harkened by the moonlight how that pillers [pillagers] and robbers were come into the field, to pill and to rob many a full noble knight of brooches and beads, of many a good ring, and of many a rich jewel; and [those] who that were not dead all out, there they slew them for their harness and their riches. When Sir Lucan understood this work, he came to the king as soon as he might, and told him all what he had heard and seen. "Therefore by my rede [advice]," said Sir Lucan, "it is best that we bring you to some town."

"I would it were so," said the king. "But I may not stand, mine head works [hurts] so. Ah, Sir Lancelot," said King Arthur, "this day have I sore missed thee. Alas, that ever I was against thee, for now have I my death, whereof Sir Gawain me warned in my dream."

Then Sir Lucan took up the king the one part, and Sir Bedivere the other part, and in the lifting, the king swooned; and Sir Lucan fell in a swoon with the lift, that the part of his guts fell out of his body, and therewith the noble knight's heart brast. And when the king awoke, he beheld Sir Lucan, how he lay foaming at the mouth, and part of his guts lay at his feet. "Alas," said the king, "this is to me a full heavy sight, to see this noble duke so die for my sake, for he would have holpen me, that had more need of help than I. Alas, he would not complain him, his heart was so set to help me: now Jesu have mercy upon his soul!" Then Sir Bedivere wept for the death of his brother.

"Leave this mourning and weeping," said the king, "for all this will not avail me; for wit thou well: an I might live myself, the death of Sir Lucan would grieve me evermore; but my time hieth fast," said the king. "Therefore," said Arthur unto Sir Bedivere, "take thou Excalibur, my good sword, and go with it to yonder waterside, and when thou comest there, I charge thee: throw my sword in that water, and come again and tell me what thou there seest." "My lord," said Bedivere, "your commandment shall be done, and lightly bring you word again."

So Sir Bedivere departed, and by the way he beheld that noble sword, that the pommel and the haft was all of precious stones; and then he said to himself: "If I throw this rich sword in the water, thereof shall never come good, but harm and loss." And then Sir Bedivere hid Excalibur under a tree. And so, as soon as he might, he came again unto the king, and said he had been at the water, and had thrown the sword in the water. "What saw thou there?" said the king. "Sir," he said, "I saw nothing but waves and winds." "That is untruly said of thee," said the king; "therefore go thou lightly again, and do my commandment; as thou art to me lief and dear, spare not, but throw it in."

Then Sir Bedivere returned again, and took the sword in his hand; and then him thought sin and shame to throw away that noble sword, and so eft [again] he hid the sword, and returned again, and told to the king that he had been at the water and done his commandment. "What saw thou there?" said the king. "Sir," he said, "I saw nothing but the waters wappe [lap] and waves wan." "Ah, traitor untrue," said King Arthur, "now hast thou betrayed me twice. Who would have weened that—thou that hast been to me so lief and dear? And thou art named a noble knight, and would betray me for the richness of the sword. But now go again lightly, for thy long tarrying putteth me in great jeopardy of my life, for I have taken cold. And but if thou do now as I bid thee, if ever I may see thee, I shall slay thee with mine own hands; for thou wouldst for my rich sword see me dead."

Then Sir Bedivere departed and went to the sword, and lightly took it up, and went to the waterside; and there he bound the girdle about the hilts, and then he threw the sword as far into the water as he might; and there came an arm and an hand above the water and met it, and caught it, and so shook it thrice and brandished, and then vanished away the hand with the sword in the water. So Sir Bedivere came again to the king, and told him what he saw. "Alas," said the king, "help me hence, for I dread me I have tarried over long."

Then Sir Bedivere took the king upon his back, and so went with him to that waterside. And when they were at the waterside, even fast by the bank hoved a little barge with many fair ladies in it, and among them all was a queen, and all they had black hoods, and all they wept and shrieked when they saw King Arthur. "Now put me into the barge," said the king. And so he did softly; and there received him three queens with great mourning; and so they set them down, and in one of their laps King Arthur laid his head. And then that queen said: "Ah, dear brother, why have ye tarried so long from me? Alas, this wound on your head hath caught overmuch cold."

And so then they rowed from the land, and Sir Bedivere beheld all those ladies go from him. Then Sir Bedivere cried: "Ah my lord Arthur, what shall become of me, now ye go from me and leave me here alone among mine enemies?" "Comfort thyself," said the king, "and do as well as thou mayest, for in me is no trust for to trust in; for I will into the vale of Avalon to heal me of my grievous wound. And if thou hear nevermore of me, pray for my soul." But ever the queens and ladies wept and shrieked, that it was pity to hear.

And as soon as Sir Bedivere had lost the sight of the barge, he wept and wailed, and so took [to] the forest; and so he went all that night, and in the morning he was ware betwixt two holts hoar, of a chapel and an hermitage. Then was Sir Bedivere glad, and thither he went; and when he came into the chapel, he saw where lay an hermit grovelling on all four, there fast by a tomb was new graven. When the hermit saw Sir Bedivere, he knew him well, for he was but little tofore Bishop of Canterbury, that Sir Mordred flemed [banished]. "Sir," said Bedivere, "what man is there interred that ye pray so fast for?" "Fair son," said the hermit, "I wot not verily, but by deeming [guessing]. But this night, at midnight, here came a number of ladies, and brought hither a dead corpse, and prayed me to bury him; and here they offered an hundred tapers, and they gave me an hundred besants." "Alas," said Sir Bedivere, "that was my lord King Arthur, that here lieth buried in this chapel."

Then Sir Bedivere swooned, and when he awoke, he prayed the hermit he might abide with him still there, to live with fasting and prayers. "For from hence will I never go," said Sir Bedivere, "by my will, but all the days of my life here to pray for my lord Arthur."

"Ye are welcome to me," said the hermit, "for I know ye better than ye ween that I do. Ye are the bold Bedivere, and the full noble duke Sir Lucan the Butler was your brother." Then Sir Bedivere told the hermit all, as ye have heard tofore. So there bode Sir Bedivere with the hermit that was tofore Bishop of Canterbury, and there Sir Bedivere put upon him poor clothes, and served the hermit full lowly in fasting and in prayers.

Thus of Arthur I find nevermore written in books that be authorized, nor more of the very certainty of his death heard I never read, but thus was he led away in a ship wherein were three queens: that one was King Arthur's sister, Queen Morgan le Fay, the other was the Queen of Northgalis, the third was the Queen of the Waste Lands. Also there was Ninive, the chief lady of the lake, that had wedded Pelleas the good knight; and this lady had done much for King Arthur, for she would never suffer Sir Pelleas to be in no place where he should be in danger of his life; and so he lived to the uttermost of his days with her in great rest. More of the death of King Arthur could I never find, but that ladies brought him to his burials; and such one was buried there, that the hermit bare witness that sometime was Bishop of Canterbury, but yet the hermit knew not in certain that he was verily the body of King Arthur. For this tale Sir Bedivere, knight of the Table Round, made it to be written.

Yet some men say in many parts of England that King Arthur is not dead, but had by the will of our Lord Jesu into another place; and men say that he shall come again, and he shall win the holy cross. I will not say it shall be so, but rather I will say, here in this world he changed his life. But many men say that there is written upon his tomb this verse: HIC JACET ARTHURUS REX, QUONDAM REXQUE FUTURUS [Here lies King Arthur, former King and future].

Thus leave I here Sir Bedivere with the hermit, that dwelled that time in a chapel beside Glastonbury, and there was his hermitage. And so they lived in their prayers and fastings and great abstinence. And when Queen Guinevere understood that King Arthur was slain, and all the noble knights, Sir Mordred and all the remnant, then the queen stole away, and five ladies with her, and so she went to Amesbury. And there she let make herself a nun, and wore white clothes and black, and great penance she took, as ever did sinful lady in this land, and never creature could make her merry; but lived in fasting, prayers, and alms-deeds, that all manner of people marvelled how virtuously she was changed.

Now leave we Queen Guinevere in Amesbury, a nun in white clothes and black, and there she was abbess and ruler, as reason would; and turn we from her, and speak we of Sir Lancelot du Lake.

And when he heard in his country that Sir Mordred was crowned king in England, and made war against King Arthur, his own father, and would let [forbid] him to land in his own land—also it was told Sir Lancelot how that Sir Mordred had laid siege about the Tower of London, because the queen would not wed him—then was Sir Lancelot wroth out of measure and said to his kinsmen: "Alas, that double traitor Sir Mordred! Now me repenteth that ever he escaped my hands, for much shame hath he done unto my lord Arthur; for all I feel by the doleful letter that my lord Sir Gawain sent me, on whose soul Jesu have mercy, that my lord Arthur is full hard bestad. Alas," said Sir Lancelot, "that ever I should live to hear that most noble king that made me knight thus to be overset with his subject in his own realm! And this doleful letter that my lord Sir Gawain hath sent me afore his death, praying me to see his tomb, wit you well: his doleful words shall never go from mine heart, for he was a full noble knight as ever was born. And in an unhappy hour was I born that ever I should have that unhap to slay first Sir Gawain, Sir Gaheris the good knight, and mine own friend Sir Gareth, that full noble knight. Alas, I may say I am unhappy," said Sir Lancelot, "that ever I should do thus unhappily; and, alas, yet might I never have hap to slay that traitor, Sir Mordred."

"Leave your complaints," said Sir Bors, "and first revenge you of the death of Sir Gawain; and it will be well done that ye see Sir Gawain's tomb, and secondly that ye revenge my lord Arthur and my lady Queen Guinevere."

"I thank you," said Sir Lancelot, "for ever ye will my worship." Then they made them ready in all the haste that might be, with ships and galleys, with Sir Lancelot and his host to pass into England. And so he passed over the sea till he came to Dover, and there he landed with seven kings, and the number was hideous to behold. Then Sir Lancelot spered [inquired] of men of Dover where was King Arthur become. Then the people told him how that he was slain, and Sir Mordred and an hundred thousand died on a day; and how Sir Mordred gave King Arthur there the first battle at his landing, and there was good Sir Gawain slain; and on the morn Sir Mordred fought with the king upon Barham Down, and there the king put Sir Mordred to the worse.

"Alas," said Sir Lancelot, "this is the heaviest tidings that ever came to me! Now, fair sirs," said Sir Lancelot, "show me the tomb of Sir Gawain." And then certain people of the town brought him into the Castle of Dover, and showed him the tomb. Then Sir Lancelot kneeled down and wept and prayed heartily for his soul. And that night he made a dole [wake], and all they that would come had as much flesh, fish, wine, and ale, and every man and woman had twelve-pence, come who would. Thus with his own hand dealt he this money, in a mourning gown. And ever he wept, and prayed them to pray for the soul of Sir Gawain.

And on the morn all the priests and clerks that might be gotten in the country were there, and sang mass of requiem. And there offered first Sir Lancelot, and he offered an hundred pound; and then the seven kings offered forty pound apiece; and also there was a thousand knights, and each of them offered a pound; and the offering [en]dured from morn till night, and Sir Lancelot lay two nights on his tomb in prayers and weeping.

Then on the third day Sir Lancelot called the kings, dukes, earls, barons, and knights, and said thus: "My fair lords, I thank you all of your coming into this country with me, but we came too late, and that shall repent me while I live; but against death may no man rebel. But sithen it is so," said Sir Lancelot, "I will myself ride and seek my lady, Queen Guinevere, for as I hear say, she hath had great pain and much disease [sorrow] and I heard say that she is fled into the west. Therefore, ye all shall abide me here, and but if [unless] I come again within fifteen days, then take your ships and your fellowship, and depart into your country, for I will do as I say to you."

Then came Sir Bors de Ganis, and said: "My lord Sir Lancelot, what think ye for to do, now to ride in this realm? Wit ye well: ye shall find few friends."

"Be as be may," said Sir Lancelot, "keep you still here, for I will forth on my journey, and no man nor child [squire] shall go with me." So it was no boot [use] to strive, but he departed and rode westerly, and there he sought a seven or eight days.

And at the last he came to a nunnery, and then was Queen Guinevere ware of Sir Lancelot as he walked in the cloister. And when she saw him there, she swooned thrice, that all the ladies and gentlewomen had work enough to hold the queen up. So when she might speak, she called ladies and gentlewomen to her, and said: "Ye marvel, fair ladies, why I make this fare. Truly," she said, "it is for the sight of yonder knight that yonder standeth; wherefore, I pray you all, call him to me."

When Sir Lancelot was brought to her, then she said to all the ladies: "Through this man and me hath all this war been wrought, and the death of the most noblest knights of the world; for through our love that we have loved together is my most noble lord slain. Therefore, Sir Lancelot, wit thou well: I am set in such a plight to get my soul heal. And yet I trust through God's grace that after my death to have a sight of the blessed face of Christ, and at Doomsday to sit on His right side, for as sinful as ever I was are saints in heaven. Therefore, Sir Lancelot, I require thee and beseech thee heartily, for all the love that ever was betwixt us, that thou never see me more in the visage; and I command thee, on God's behalf, that thou forsake my company and to thy kingdom thou turn again, and keep well thy realm from war and wrake [ruin]; for as well as I have loved thee, mine heart will not serve me to see thee, for through thee and me is the flower of kings and knights destroyed. Therefore, Sir Lancelot, go to thy realm, and there take thee a wife, and live with her with joy and bliss; and I pray thee heartily: pray for me to our Lord that I may amend my misliving."

"Now, sweet madam," said Sir Lancelot, "would ye that I should now return again unto my country, and there to wed a lady? Nay, madam, wit you well: *that* shall I never do, for I shall never be so false to you of that I have promised. But the same destiny that ye have taken you to, I will take me unto for to please Jesu, and ever for you I cast me specially to pray."

"If thou wilt do so," said the queen, "hold thy promise, but I may never believe but that thou wilt turn to the world again."

"Well, madam," said he, "ye say as pleaseth you, yet wist you me never false of my promise, and God defend but I should forsake the world as ye have done. For in the quest of the Sangrail I had forsaken the vanities of the world, had not your lord been. And if I had done so at that time with my heart, will, and thought, I had passed all the knights that were in the Sangrail except Sir Galahad, my son. And therefore, lady, sithen ye have taken you to perfection, I must needs take me to perfection, of right. For I take record of God: in you I have had mine earthly joy; and if I had found you now so disposed, I had cast [resolved] to have had you into mine own realm. But sithen I find you thus disposed, I ensure you faithfully: I will ever take me to penance, and pray while my life lasteth, if I may find any hermit either gray or white that will receive me. Wherefore, madam, I pray you kiss me, and never no more."

"Nay," said the queen, "that shall I never do, but abstain you from such works." And they departed. But there was never so hard-an-hearted man but he would have wept to see the dolour that they made; for there was lamentation as [if] they had been stung with spears; and many times they swooned, and the ladies bare the queen to her chamber.

And Sir Lancelot awoke, and went and took his horse, and rode all that day and all night in a forest, weeping. And at the last he was ware of an hermitage and a chapel [that] stood betwixt two cliffs; and then he heard a little bell ring to mass, and thither he rode and alit, and tied his horse to the gate, and heard mass. And he that sang mass was the Bishop of Canterbury. Both the Bishop and Sir Bedivere knew Sir Lancelot, and they spake together after mass. But when Sir Bedivere had told his tale all whole, Sir Lancelot's heart almost brast for sorrow, and Sir Lancelot threw his arms abroad, and said: "Alas, who may trust this world?" And then he kneeled down on his knee and prayed the Bishop to shrive him and assoil [absolve] him. And then he besought the Bishop that he might be his brother. Then the Bishop said: "I will gladly!" And there he put an habit upon Sir Lancelot, and there he served God day and night with prayers and fastings.

Thus the great host abode at Dover. And then Sir Lionel took fifteen lords with him, and rode to London to seek Sir Lancelot; and there Sir Lionel was slain and many of his lords. Then Sir Bors de Ganis made the great host for to go home again. And Sir Bors, Sir Ector de Maris, Sir Blamore, Sir Bleoberis, with more other of Sir Lancelot's kin, took on them to ride all England overthwart and endlong, to seek Sir Lancelot. So Sir Bors by fortune rode so long till he came to the same chapel where Sir Lancelot was; and so Sir Bors heard a little bell knell that rang to mass; and there he alit and heard mass. And when mass was done, the Bishop, Sir Lancelot, and Sir Bedivere came to Sir Bors. And when Sir Bors saw Sir Lancelot in that manner clothing, then he prayed the Bishop that he might be in the same suit. And so there was an habit put upon him, and there he lived in prayers and fasting.

And within half a year, there was come Sir Galihud, Sir Galihodin, Sir Blamore, Sir Bleoberis, Sir Villiars, Sir Clarrus, and Sir Gahalantine. So all these seven noble knights there abode still. And when they saw Sir Lancelot had taken him to such perfection, they had no list to depart, but took such an habit as he had. Thus they endured in great penance six year; and then Sir Lancelot took the habit of priesthood of the Bishop, and a twelvemonth he sang mass. And there was none of these other knights but they read in books, and holp for to sing mass, and rang bells, and did bodily all manner of service. And so their horses went where they would, for they took no regard of no worldly riches. For when they saw Sir Lancelot endure such penance, in prayers and fastings, they took no force [care] what pain they endured, for to see the noblest knight of the world take such abstinence that he waxed full lean.

And thus upon a night, there came a vision to Sir Lancelot, and charged him, in remission of his sins, to haste him unto Amesbury: "And by then thou come there, thou shalt find Queen Guinevere dead. And therefore take thy fellows with thee, and purvey them of an horse bier, and fetch thou the corpse of her, and bury her by her husband, the noble King Arthur." So this vision came to Sir Lancelot thrice in one night.

Then Sir Lancelot rose up or day, and told the hermit. "It were well done," said the hermit, "that ye made you ready and that you disobey not the vision." Then Sir Lancelot took his seven fellows with him, and on foot they yede from Glastonbury to Amesbury, the which is little more than thirty mile. And thither they came within two days, for they were weak and feeble to go. And when Sir Lancelot was come to Amesbury within the nunnery, Queen Guinevere died but half an hour afore. And the ladies told Sir Lancelot that Queen Guinevere told them all, or she passed, that Sir Lancelot had been priest near a twelvemonth: "And hither he cometh as fast as he may to fetch my corpse, and beside my lord, King Arthur, he shall bury me." Wherefore the queen said in hearing of them all: "I beseech Almighty God that I may never have power to see Sir Lancelot with my worldly eyen." "And thus," said all the ladies, "was ever her prayer these two days, till she was dead."

Then Sir Lancelot saw her visage, but he wept not greatly, but sighed. And so he did all the observance of the service himself, both the dirge at night, and on the morn he sang mass. And there was ordained an horse bier; and so with an hundred torches ever burning about the corpse of the queen, and ever Sir Lancelot with his seven fellows went about the horse bier, singing and reading many an holy orison, and frankincense upon the corpse incensed. Thus Sir Lancelot and his seven fellows went on foot from Amesbury unto Glastonbury.

And when they were come to the chapel and the hermitage, there she had a dirge with great devotion. And on the morn the hermit that sometime was Bishop of Canterbury sang the mass of requiem with great devotion. And Sir Lancelot was the first that offered, and then also his seven fellows. And then she was wrapped in cered [waxed] cloth of Raines [Rennes] from the top to the toe in thirtyfold; and after she was put in a web of lead, and then in a coffin of marble.

And when she was put in the earth, Sir Lancelot swooned, and lay long still, while the hermit came and awaked him and said: "Ye be to blame, for ye displease God with such manner of sorrow making." "Truly," said Sir Lancelot, "I trust I do not displease God, for He knoweth mine intent. For my sorrow was not, nor is not, for any rejoicing of sin, but my sorrow may never have end. For when I remember of her beauty, and of her noblesse, that was both with her king and with her, so when I saw his corpse and her corpse so lie together, truly mine heart would not serve to sustain my careful [care-filled] body. Also when I remember me how by my default, mine orgule [arrogance] and my pride, that they were both laid full low that were peerless that ever was living of Christian people, wit you well," said Sir Lancelot: "this remembered—of their kindness and mine unkindness—sank so to mine heart that I might not sustain myself." So the French book maketh mention.

Then Sir Lancelot never after ate but little meat or drank till he was dead. For then he sickened more and more, and dried, and dwined [wasted] away. For the Bishop nor none of his fellows might not make him to eat, and little he drank, [so] that he was waxen by a cubit shorter than he was, that the people could not know him. For evermore, day and night, he prayed, but sometime he slumbered a broken sleep. Ever he was lying grovelling on the tomb of King Arthur and Queen Guinevere. And there was no comfort that the Bishop nor Sir Bors, nor none of his fellows could make him; it availed not.

So within six weeks after, Sir Lancelot fell sick, and lay in his bed; and then he sent for the Bishop that there was hermit, and all his true fellows. Then Sir Lancelot said with dreary steven [voice]: "Sir Bishop, I pray you give to me all my rites that longeth to a Christian man." "It shall not need you," said the hermit and all his fellows, "it is but heaviness of your blood; ye shall be well mended by the grace of God to-morn." "My fair lords," said Sir Lancelot, "wit you well: my careful body will into the earth. I have warning more than now I will say; therefore give me my rites." So when he was houseled [given the Eucharist] and enelid [received extreme unction], and had all that a Christian man ought to have, he prayed the Bishop that his fellows might bear his body to Joyous Gard. Some men say it was Alnwick, and some men say it was Bamborough.

"Howbeit," said Sir Lancelot, "me repenteth sore, but I made mine avow sometime, that in Joyous Gard I would be buried. And because of breaking of mine avow, I pray you all, lead me thither."

Then there was weeping and wringing of hands among his fellows. So at a season of the night they all went to their beds, for they all lay in one chamber. And so after midnight, against day, the Bishop that was hermit, as he lay in his bed asleep, he fell upon a great laughter. And therewithal the fellowship awoke, and came to the Bishop, and asked him what he ailed. "Ah Jesu mercy," said the Bishop, "why did ye awake me? I was never in all my life so merry and so well at ease." "Wherefore?" said Sir Bors. "Truly," said the Bishop, "here was Sir Lancelot with me with more angels than ever I saw men in one day. And I saw the angels heave up Sir Lancelot unto heaven, and the gates of heaven opened against him." "It is but dretching [confusion] of swevens [dreams]," said Sir Bors, "for I doubt not Sir Lancelot aileth nothing but good." "It may well be," said the Bishop. "Go ye to his bed, and then shall ye prove the sooth."

So when Sir Bors and his fellows came to his bed, they found him stark dead, and he lay as he had smiled, and the sweetest savour about him that ever they felt. Then was there weeping and wringing of hands, and the greatest dole they made that ever made men. And on the morn the Bishop did his mass of requiem; and after the Bishop and all the nine knights put Sir Lancelot in the same horse bier that Queen Guinevere was laid in tofore that she was buried. And so the Bishop and they all together went with the body of Sir Lancelot daily, till they came to Joyous Gard; and ever they had an hundred torches burning about him.

And so within fifteen days they came to Joyous Gard. And there they laid his corpse in the body of the quire, and sang and read many psalters and prayers over him and about him. And ever his visage was laid open and naked, that all folks might behold him. For such was the custom in those days, that all men of worship should so lie with open visage till that they were buried. And right thus as they were at their service, there came Sir Ector de Maris, that had seven years sought all England, Scotland, and Wales, seeking his brother, Sir Lancelot.

And when Sir Ector heard such noise and light in the quire of Joyous Gard, he alit and put his horse from him, and came into the quire, and there he saw men sing and weep. And all they knew Sir Ector, but he knew not them. Then went Sir Bors unto Sir Ector, and told him how there lay his brother, Sir Lancelot, dead; and then Sir Ector threw his shield, sword, and helm from him. And when he beheld Sir Lancelot's visage, he fell down in a swoon. And when he waked, it were hard any tongue to tell the doleful complaints that he made for his brother.

"Ah Lancelot," he said, "thou were head of all Christian knights, and now I dare say," said Sir Ector, "thou Sir Lancelot, there thou liest, that thou were never matched of earthly knight's hand. And thou were the courteoust knight that ever bare shield. And thou were the truest friend to thy lover that ever bestrad horse. And thou were the truest lover of a sinful man that ever loved woman. And thou were the kindest man that ever struck with sword. And thou were the goodliest person that ever came among press of knights. And thou were the meekest man and the gentlest that ever ate in hall among ladies. And thou were the sternest knight to thy mortal foe that ever put spear in the rest."

Then there was weeping and dolour out of measure. Thus they kept Sir Lancelot's corpse on loft [display] fifteen days, and then they buried it with great devotion. And then at leisure they went all with the Bishop of Canterbury to his hermitage, and there they were together more than a month.

Then Sir Constantine, that was Sir Cador's son of Cornwall, was chosen king of England. And he was a full noble knight, and worshipfully he ruled this realm. And then this King Constantine sent for the Bishop of Canterbury, for he heard say where he was. And so he was restored unto his Bishopric, and left that hermitage. And Sir Bedivere was there ever, still hermit to his life's end. Then Sir Bors de Ganis, Sir Ector de Maris, Sir Gahalantine, Sir Galihud, Sir Galihodin, Sir Blamore, Sir Bleoberis, Sir Villiars le Valiant, Sir Clarrus of Clermont—all these knights drew them to their countries. Howbeit King Constantine would have had them with him, but they would not abide in this realm. And there they all lived in their countries as holy men.

And some English books make mention that they went never out of England after the death of Sir Lancelot, but that was but favour [whim] of makers. For the French book maketh mention, and is authorized, that Sir Bors, Sir Ector, Sir Blamore, and Sir Bleoberis went into the Holy Land thereas Jesu Christ was quick and dead, and anon as they had stablished their lands. For the book saith, so Sir Lancelot commanded them for to do, or ever he passed out of this world. And these four knights did many battles upon the miscreants or Turks. And there they died upon a Good Friday for God's sake.

Here is the end of the book of King Arthur, and of his noble knights of the Round Table, that when they were whole together, there was ever an hundred and forty. And here is the end of the death of Arthur. I pray you all, gentlemen and gentlewomen that readeth this book of Arthur and his knights, from the beginning to the ending, pray for me while I am on life, that God send me good deliverance, and when I am dead, I pray you all pray for my soul. For this book was ended the ninth year of the reign of King Edward the Fourth [1469], by Sir Thomas Maleore, knight, as Jesu help him for his great might, as he is the servant of Jesu both day and night.

SOME GENERAL BOOKS IN ENGLISH FOR FURTHER READING

[*Readers should also refer to the bibliographic notes ending each chapter. Asterisked items below contain full bibliographies.*]

Alcock, Leslie. *Arthur's Britain*. Penguin, 1971.

Ashe, Geoffrey. *A Guidebook to Arthurian Britain*. Longman, 1980; rev. Aquarian, 1983.

———. *Kings and Queens of Early Britain*. Methuen, 1982.

———, ed. *The Quest for Arthur's Britain*. Praeger, 1968; rev. Paladin, 1982.

Barber, Richard W. *Arthur of Albion*. Barnes and Noble, 1971 (extensively revised as *King Arthur in Legend and History*, Cardinal, 1973).

———, ed. *Arthurian Literature*. 2 vols. Rowman and Littlefield, 1981–82.

Bruce, J. D. *The Evolution of Arthurian Romance*. 2 vols. Johns Hopkins University, 1923; rpt. Peter Smith, 1958.

*Chambers, E. K. *Arthur of Britain*. Sidgwick & Jackson, 1927; rpt. Barnes and Noble, 1964.

Darrah, John. *The Real Camelot*. Thames and Hudson, 1981.

Duxbury, Brenda, and William Michael. *King Arthur Country in Cornwall*; bound with: Wilson, Colin. *The Search for the Real Arthur*. Bossiney Books, 1979.

Hanning, Robert W. *The Vision of History in Early Britain*. Columbia University, 1966.

Jenkins, Elizabeth. *The Mystery of King Arthur*. Coward, McCann & Geoghegan, 1975.

Loomis, Roger Sherman. *The Development of Arthurian Romance*. Harper & Row, 1964.

———, ed. *Arthurian Literature in the Middle Ages*. Oxford, 1959.

———, and Laura Hibbard Loomis. *Arthurian Legends in Medieval Art*. Oxford, 1938.

Luttrell, Claude. *The Creation of the First Arthurian Romance*. Northwestern University, 1974.

Moorman, Charles. *The Book of Kyng Arthur*. University of Kentucky, 1965.

———, and Ruth Moorman. *An Arthurian Dictionary*. University of Mississippi, 1979.

Morris, John. *The Age of Arthur*. Scribner, 1973.

Morris, Rosemary. *The Character of King Arthur in Medieval Literature*. Brewer, 1982.

Owen, D. D. R., ed. *Arthurian Romance: Seven Essays*. Barnes and Noble, 1971.

* Pickford, C. E., and R. W. Last, eds. *The Arthurian Bibliography: I. Author Listing; II. Index*. Brewer, 1981.

*Reiss, Edmund, Louise Horner Reiss, and Beverly Taylor. *Arthurian Legend and Literature: An Annotated Bibliography*. 2 vols. Garland, 1984.

Tatlock, J. S. P. *The Legendary History of Britain*. University of California, 1950.

Treharne, R. F. *The Glastonbury Legends*. Cresset, 1967; rpt. Sphere, 1971.

Varty, Kenneth, ed. *An Arthurian Tapestry*. University of Glasgow, 1981.

Vinaver, Eugène. *The Rise of Romance*. Oxford, 1971.

Weston, Jessie L. *From Ritual to Romance*. Cambridge University, 1920; rpt. Anchor, 1957.

Wilson, Anne. *Traditional Romance and Tale: How Stories Mean*. Brewer, 1976.

INDEX

The Garland Library
of Medieval Literature